An Introduction to Modern
Political Theory

By the same author

Hayek's Social and Economic Philosophy
On Classical Liberalism and Libertarianism
The New Right
Welfare
Classical Liberalism in the Age of Postcommunism
Business Ethics
The Morality of Business Enterprise

An Introduction to Modern Political Theory

Fourth Edition

Norman Barry

palgrave

First edition 1981
Reprinted 1982, 1983, 1984, 1985, 1987
Second edition 1989
Reprinted 1990, 1992, 1994
Third edition 1995
Fourth edition 2000

Published 2000 by
PALGRAVE
Houndmills, Basingstoke, Hampshire RG21 6XS and
175 Fifth Avenue, New York, N.Y. 10010
Companies and representatives throughout the world

PALGRAVE is the new global academic imprint of
St. Martin's Press LLC Scholarly and Reference Division and
Palgrave Publishers Ltd (formerly Macmillan Press Ltd).

Outside North America
ISBN 0–333–91288–8 hardcover
ISBN 0–333–91289–6 paperback

Inside North America
ISBN 0–312–23516–X

This book is printed on paper suitable for recycling and
made from fully managed and sustained forest sources.

A catalogue record for this book is available
from the British Library.

Cataloging-in-Publication data is available from the Library of Congress

10   9   8   7   6   5   4   3   2
10   09 08 07 06 05 04 03 02

Copy-edited and typeset by Povey-Edmondson
Tavistock and Rochdale

Printed and bound in Great Britain by
Creative Print & Design (Wales), Ebbw Vale

Contents

Preface to the Fourth Edition

It is now nearly 20 years since the first edition of this book was published and there have been very many dramatic changes in the political world, and also in the academic study of theorising about politics. Although political theory was beginning to flourish in the 1970s, after a period of stagnation produced by Logical Positivism and analytic philosophy, the atmosphere now is remarkably different. There has been a real flood of books and papers on the traditional subjects of political philosophy: the state, jurisprudence, power and authority, democracy and the staple topics in moral and political theory: freedom, equality, rights and the common good. The study of the various theories of justice has almost become a subject in its own right.

Also, more directly 'ideological' approaches, such as Marxism – though its influence has now waned – and feminism and communitarianism, have established strong positions in the discipline. The collapse of communism has encouraged a re-evaluation of classical liberalism and conservative political philosophy and political economy. Certainly the free market has earned a kind of worldwide, if not yet academic, respectability

There is now a lot more in the book about communitarianism and feminism but they are treated not so much as separate doctrines but as distinctive contributions to the standard issues of political theory. I have retained the analytical style which I consider the most suitable method of studying political theory. However, changing academic fashions mean that certain topics have been excluded. There is now very little on Logical Positivism and Marxism is mentioned much less. The liberal individualist approach which has been a feature of all editions has been retained and indeed the world of the start of the 21st century is politically, and even academically, more receptive to that approach than when the book was first written.

In this edition I have added a completely new chapter on the theory of welfare and the welfare state. I have also included a section on animals in the chapter on rights. Also, I have made minor modifications to much of the material. I am grateful for many friends and colleagues who have enlightened me over the years. At Buckingham I am indebted to my assistant, Rasangi Prematilaka, for her help with the preparation of the text. I should also like to thank my publisher Steven Kennedy for his very helpful advice over the years, especially for this edition.

Buckingham   NORMAN BARRY

Glossary

Below are listed the meanings of various terms used in the text. It should be made clear at the outset that no attempt is being made to give *exact* definitions of these terms. All that is being conveyed is an indication of the way the words are used in the political analysis and argument that appear in the book.

Anthropomorphism. The attribution of human properties to inanimate things. 'Society' is frequently treated anthropomorphically, as if it were capable of being praised or blamed in the way that humans are. A crude example is the phrase 'it is all society's fault'.

Autonomy. In moral philosophy, the capacity in individuals for making judgements uninfluenced by any considerations other than principle. Almost always opposed to external authority. In social philosophy it requires redistribution of resources so that people's decisions are not the result of adverse economic circumstances.

Behaviouralism. A form of social explanation in which observed behaviour is stressed rather than the simple description of institutions. In behavioural political science formal political institutions are dissolved into 'systems' and 'processes'. It is distinct from *behaviourism* in that it is not a psychological theory about individual behaviour but involves sociological statements about collectivities.

Behaviourism. The psychological doctrine which holds that the only basis for the study of human behaviour is *observable* behaviour. Therefore all statements about mental phenomena, such as motives and intentions, are irrelevant because they depend upon introspective knowledge which cannot be verified by experimental methods.

Civil Society. That complex of intermediary associations that stand between the individual and the state. They include ethnic, religious and other voluntary bodies.

Collectivism. The methodological doctrine that collective terms such as 'state', 'society' and 'class' stand for entities which have a real

x

existence over and above that of individuals. Collectivists argue that theories of social phenomena cast solely in terms of individual action fail to capture the significance of general social factors in the determination of events.

Communitarianism. Doctrine that presupposes that the identity of individuals can only be established by reference to pre-existing social forms. Objective moral standards are determined by an exploration of the meanings of these forms. Opposed to abstract individualism.

Deduction. The form of reasoning in which the conclusion of an argument *necessarily* follows from the premises. The validity of a deductive argument is established if it is impossible to assert the premises and deny the conclusion without self-contradiction. In the social sciences only economic theory makes extensive use of the deductive method.

Deontology. The ethical theory that holds that certain moral duties are absolutely binding irrespective of consequences. Normally it emphasises the importance of strict compliance with moral rules to the exclusion of a consideration of the benefits which adherence to the rules may or may not bring about.

Emotivism. The doctrine that claims that ethical statements do not convey information. They are designed to excite the emotions and produce favourable or unfavourable responses.

Empiricism. The epistemological doctrine that the only foundation for knowledge, apart from mathematical and logical relationships, is experience. It is contrasted with the various forms of *rationalism*, all of which maintain that the mind is already equipped with the conceptual apparatus which enables us to understand the external world. In the social sciences empiricists reject *a priori* reasoning about man and society in favour of factual and statistical enquiries. See also *behaviourism* and *positivism*.

Epistemology. The theory of knowledge. The major questions of epistemology concern the nature of our knowledge of the external world, the source of knowledge and how claims to knowledge can be substantiated.

Essentialism. The doctrine that the key to the understanding of social phenomena lies in discerning the true nature or essence of things which lies behind their external manifestations. In Plato's theory of the state, for example, it is argued that existing state organisations are pale reflections of an underlying essence or *form* of the state, knowledge of which is acquired by philosophical reflection.

Historical Materialism. The Marxist doctrine that the factors determining historical development are ultimately economic. Changes in the 'superstructure' of society – that is, the state organisation, law, religion and morality – are a function of changes in the substructure – that is, the economic mode of production. The doctrine is especially directed at those theories that emphasise the independent influence of ideas in the determination of historical change.

Historicism. The doctrine, mainly but by no means exclusively associated with Marxism, which maintains that the study of history reveals trends or patterns, of a law-like kind, from which it is possible to predict *future* economic and social structures and historical events. Historicist 'laws' are of a quasi-empirical kind in that they are based on supposedly observable regularities and are therefore different from the laws of conventional economics which are ahistorical deductions from axioms of human nature.

Individualism. The methodological doctrine, associated with Popper and Hayek, that collective words such as 'state' or 'society' do not stand for real entities. The behaviour of collectivities can only be understood in terms of individual motivations and volitions.

Induction. The method of reasoning by which general statements are derived from the observation of particular facts. Therefore inductive arguments are always *probabilistic*, in contrast to deductive arguments. Induction was thought to characterise physical science in that laws were established by the constant confirmation of observed regularities. However, since no amount of observations can establish a general law (the most firmly established regularity may be refuted in the future), the generalities established by science seemed to rest on insecure, if not irrational, foundations. Popper argued that while theories cannot logically be established by repeated confirmations they may be falsified.

Logical Positivism. The philosophical doctrine which holds that the only meaningful statements are the tautologies of mathematics or synthetic statements of empirical science. All others, including those of ethics and religion, are, strictly speaking, nonsense.

Metaphysical. A metaphysical proposition is one which cannot be tested by normal empirical methods. Logical Positivists thought that a statement which was neither tautological nor empirically verifiable was metaphysical and hence meaningless. Metaphysical statements are not normally thought to be meaningless by contemporary philosophers.

Natural Law. Legal doctrine that assesses the validity of claims to law by reference to a universal morality.

Negative Income Tax. The welfare policy that aids the poor by cash payments. It precludes the compulsory and collective delivery of welfare goods.

Nominalism. The theory of language that accounts for the meaning of general words *not* in terms of some universal entity they represent, but as *labels* to attach to things that share a common property. Nominalism is the approach to language adopted by the empirical sciences.

Nomothetic. A nomothetic law is a statement of regularity which holds universally irrespective of time or circumstance. It is a statement of causality from which predictions about future events can be derived. In the social sciences only economic theory can claim to have produced nomothetic laws.

Normative. Normative statements set standards and prescribe forms of conduct; they do not describe facts or events. While they are frequently used in connection with moral standards, this is not always the case. Legal rules are technically normative in that they make certain forms of conduct obligatory, but they are not necessarily moral. Normative statements typically involve the use of words such as 'ought', 'should' and 'must'.

Persuasive Definition. A definition of a word which is designed not to explicate its meaning but to excite favourable (or unfavourable) attitudes. Persuasive definitions of the state, for example, do not convey information about existing states but aim at provoking approval (or disapproval) of it.

Positive Law.   The legal doctrine that determines validity of claims to law not by its content, or any moral standard, but by reference to observable phenomena such as a sovereign parliament or a constitution. There are many types of positive law.

Positivism.   This has two meanings. First, a positivist believes in the clear separation of fact and value and argues that theoretical and descriptive accounts of man and society can be made which do not involve evaluative judgements. For example, in jurisprudence a positive lawyer maintains that law must be separated from morals so that a rule is assessed for legal validity not by reference to its content but to certain objective, non-moral criteria. In the second and more extreme sense, it is the theory that only phenomena which are in principle capable of being observed are of any significance for social science. See also *empiricism* and *behaviourism*.

Realism.   Legal theory that emphasises the importance of the courts in the creation of law. Dominant in the US and influential in social policy.

Republicanism.   The doctrine that values participatory political activity by citizens. It is opposed to excessive privacy and individualism.

Social Market Economy.   A system that accepts the free market but modifies its rigour by welfare policy and restrictions on market transactions that lead to monopoly or other types of market power.

Sociology of Knowledge.   The attempt to explain the social origins of beliefs that people hold. It is also used by some Marxists to mean that all knowledge in the social sciences is *relative* to the particular class position of those who profess it, so that there cannot be *objective* knowledge of society.

Teleology.   A doctrine that explains the nature of things in terms of the ends of purposes they are supposed to bring about. In teleological ethics, moral action is evaluated in accordance with how far it brings about a desirable state of affairs. For example, utilitarian ethics evaluates actions in terms of their contribution to the general happiness.

1
Political Philosophy and Political Thought

1 The current state of political theory

The major difficulty in introducing the subject of political theory to the student is the fact that there is so little agreement amongst the practitioners as to what the subject is about. While it is true of all social science subjects that they involve from the outset highly contentious methodological questions, so much so that the concepts in social science have been called 'essentially contested' concepts (see below), the difficulty seems to be greater in political theory than in, say, economic theory. While economists do engage in fierce methodological disputes, especially in macroeconomics, there is nevertheless some considerable agreement about the contents of an introductory course book for students. At least such books are not likely to handle radically different material and, within the limits of the Western world, are not likely to differ all that much from place to place.

But in political theory this state of affairs is only true of courses in the history of political thought. Books in this area consist largely of *descriptions* of particular political philosophies plus an historical account of the subject's development, usually from Plato to the present day. While such enquiries involve considerable sophistication, the subject as a whole is not thought to be a genuinely theoretical discipline in the sense that other social science subjects might claim to be. It has been argued that in the great works of political philosophy there are generalisations of a sociological kind, usually to do with the requisite conditions for political stability, but these works are more often studied for a rather different reason. It is that they contain *normative* statements about the desirability of certain types of laws and institutions and such recommendations are supported by rational argument. The 'classics' of political philosophy are thought to contain

1

truths and insights which are of permanent relevance for anyone who thinks philosophically about man and society.

There has developed, however, a broadly philosophical subject called political theory which is analytical in style and concerned with methodology, the clarification of concepts and, in contrast with earlier positivism, the logic of political appraisal. Much of this book is written in this vein. Indeed, it is important to note that it is a much richer vein than that which existed 40 years ago, when there was very little interesting work in analytical political theory of this type. For the early part of the postwar period, only in the philosophy of law did the new, analytical techniques appear to yield interesting results for the student of society. However, in the last three decades the writings of, amongst others, Rawls (1972), Nozick (1974), Dworkin (1977), Walzer (1983), MacIntyre (1981) and Raz (1986) (and the uses made of some fairly elementary principles of political economy) have breathed new life into the discipline so that to say that political philosophy is dead, as was once said so confidently, would be a gross exaggeration. Of particular significance is the revival of that traditional method in political philosophy – contractarianism. Furthermore, the excessive individualism of some of these approaches has led to a spirited response from thinkers who stress the intrinsic social nature of man – he cannot be detached from his social moorings and made an abstract chooser of rules via a hypothetical contract. This is the foundation of communitarianism. From these observations it should be apparent that political theory is an eclectic subject that draws upon a variety of disciplines. There is no body of knowledge or method of analysis which can be classified as belonging exclusively to political theory. In the rest of this book we shall be concerned with exploring the connection between politics and a number of differing subject areas and methodological approaches. Hence the book will be as much about philosophy, law, ethics and political economy as it is about politics.

2 Language

Political theorists are now more self-conscious about language than they were in the past. But this emphasis on language can be overstated. Whatever may have been considered the case in formal philosophy, especially in Britain under the influence of Logical Positivism, it was never true that the problems of political philosophy were exhausted by

the clarification of concepts. This is partly because political philosophers are concerned with the rather larger questions of justice, rights,
liberty, the limitations on the state and so on, and clarification is only
a preliminary to these enquiries. Also, political philosophers are
concerned with genuinely explanatory, even predictive, theories in
the social sciences. Indeed Sir Karl Popper, one of the most distinguished philosophers of science of this century, who has also written
extensively on the philosophy of politics, has explicitly stated important objections to linguistic philosophy (Popper, 1976, pp. 22–4). In
his view it is *theories*, and whether they are true or false, that are
important, and not the *meanings* of words. Nevertheless, we shall
maintain that the clarification of concepts is important in political
analysis. It may not be the case that political arguments turn upon the
use of words, but it is certainly true that conceptual clarification is
required even to know what the arguments are about. A moment's
reflection on the use of the concept of liberty in contemporary
arguments about the relationship between the individual and the state
should confirm this.

Furthermore, Popper has himself contributed much to the kind of
analysis that is important in political philosophy. His attack on
essentialism (Popper, 1962, I, pp. 31–4), the idea that words like 'state'
and 'society' stand for necessary entities which it is the duty of the
philosopher to discern by the use of a special intellectual intuition,
which he has detected in political philosophy from Plato through to
Marx, would be applauded by all contemporary linguistic philosophers. It is largely because of his work that political theorists are less
likely to ask such essentialist questions as 'what is the state?' or 'what
is law?'

It is true, though, that Popper goes no further on language than this
but adopts the methodological nominalist's position that words are no
more than labels of convenience used to describe phenomena in the
generation of explanatory social theories. However, we shall have to
say a little more about conceptual questions in this book. For one
thing, in social philosophy we cannot find explanatory theories as
powerful as those found in the natural sciences. It is the case that in
the economic theory of democracy we shall adopt a broadly nominalist approach precisely because that is a social theory that has some
predictive power. Questions of meaning here are less important than
the truth or falsehood of the theory. But this is certainly not true of the
theory of law, where questions of, for example, *validity* in a legal
system or the problem of whether a legal order can be satisfactorily

understood in terms of primary and secondary rules, or as the commands of a sovereign, do involve crucial conceptual issues.

Unfortunately, what distinguishes the words typically used in discourse about politics, society and law is that they do not have precise definitions. Not only do the words seem to have no secure and stable meanings, but their very ambiguity has provoked perennial disputes which have led to the construction of political and legal theories which seriously distort the phenomena they are designed to explain. Exact definition may be appropriate in scientific classification where there is no dispute about the nature of the phenomena but this is not true of social phenomena (Hart, 1961, pp. 14–15). The main reason for the disappointing results of the search for meaning in terms of exact definition was that single words such as law, state, sovereignty and rights were taken out of the context of their typical usage and defined as separate entities. For example, it was assumed that the word 'state' represented some factual counterpart in the empirical world which could be clearly and indisputably identified. The task of analysis was therefore to reduce complicated verbal expressions to observable phenomena. In the command theory of law, it was traditionally maintained that *all* law was a species of command, emanating from a determinate sovereign backed up by sanctions. But this simple and appealing theory seriously distorts the very *different* types of phenomena which expressions containing the word law typically describe.

The problem is especially difficult in social and political philosophy where so many of the words in use appear to refer to collective entities; words such as 'state', 'society' and 'class'. It is impossible to identify such collective entities in the empirical world, yet it is clear that these words do have meanings and are an indispensable part of any discourse in politics. The problem is further compounded in political philosophy by the fact that many of the key words are often given 'persuasive definitions' by social theorists, that is, definitions designed to provoke some favourable or unfavourable response from the reader. In the history of political thought the concept of the state has been a frequent victim of this approach, being defined sometimes in highly favourable and at others in highly derogatory terms.

Linguistic philosophy is not concerned with definitions but with the meanings that concepts have in typical usages. Since common usage itself is the benchmark of meaningfulness there is a great variety of linguistic formulations in law and politics. The emphasis moved away from the problem of defining words to the complex task of elucidating the use that key concepts have in typical sentences. Linguistic analysis consists, then, in unravelling some of the puzzling features that characterise common utterances about politics, taking ordinary language as the canon of meaningfulness (see Miller, 1983). Of course, on substantive questions such as 'what are the grounds of political obligation?' or 'what are the criteria for a just distribution of income?' the school of ordinary language was insistent that philosophy on its own could not determine their resolution. However, it would at least concede that such questions are meaningful.

However, an exclusive concern with language is a declining feature of contemporary political theory. There are a number of reasons for this. The two most important are interrelated: one involves the denial that linguistic philosophy can be a disinterested, neutral enquiry into concepts but must involve a commitment to the *status quo*, the other challenges its whole intellectual programme by maintaining that the complexity of the language of politics precludes the kind of precision at which analytical philosophers aim.

This stress on the significance of language has been renewed with the rise of feminist political thought for, as we shall see, a part of the objection here to a male-dominated, patriarchal society is derived from an analysis of political concepts which sees them as inherently masculine: in their analysis, the words power, authority, responsibility, rights and so on relate exclusively to the public, political and masculine world. However, feminists are anxious to point out that these words are also descriptive of the private world of marriage, the family and sexual relationships; areas in which male power and influence had hitherto been unnoticed by primarily male political theorists.

An implicit, and often explicit, position in the modern critic of linguistic philosophy is addressed to its ahistorical nature. Linguistic philosophy (following its commitment to the analytic–synthetic distinction[1]) prides itself on being a second-order discipline which does not convey any empirical knowledge about the social world: this is a matter for political science, history and economics.[2] Again, this reticence, it is claimed, had the unfortunate effect of disqualifying the political philosopher from a proper understanding of the economic and social structures of the contemporary world and an appreciation of the economic circumstances in which, say, *power* is exercised. Apart from its alleged endorsement of the world as it is, analytical political philosophy is condemnable because of its deliberate eschewal of the pursuit of 'truth'.

However, it is not at all clear how linguistic analysis itself commits the philosopher to support the political and economic *status quo*. It may be thought to be a trivial exercise in comparison to the exercises in 'grand theory' carried out by traditional political philosophers, but that is quite another point. To say that 'clarification is not enough' is not to say that it is inherently ideological. Again, the heuristic role that the analytical philosopher plays in exposing the conceptual confusion that often lies at the heart of some overtly prescriptive political theories does not entail that he therefore has to reject their substantive content. A linguistic philosopher would no doubt argue that many of the traditional arguments for 'natural law' are meaningless, but this would not entail that he accepted the argument that positive laws could not be morally appraised. Furthermore, since many of the political concepts used in ordinary language are radical, 'social justice' being an obvious example, it is hard to see that an analysis of them is somehow 'necessarily' conservative. It is, of course, true that it is difficult to maintain in practice a distinction between the explication of the meaning of a political principle and the construction of a substantive political argument but this does not logically make the enterprise itself value-laden. Value positions of political theorists can be made independent of the role of linguistic analysis itself. It is also worth pointing out that analytical philosophers are on the whole moderately collectivist in their political leanings, though they would deny that it had anything to do with their professional philosophical interests (see Barry, N., 1987, pp. 4–5).

However, there has been in recent years a subtly different objection to the aims of analytical political philosophy. The argument here relates to the alleged impossibility of elucidating a perfectly 'neutral' set of political concepts – that is, constructing meanings of key words which betray no particular general philosophical or ethical view of the world. The idea of a neutral political vocabulary is common to both positivists and linguistic philosophers, no matter how much they may differ as to how it is to be constructed. A sanitised political language, cleansed of impurities and ambiguities, is thought by some theorists to be an essential prelude to enquiry of a substantive ethical or, perhaps more importantly, scientific enquiry (Oppenheim, 1981, Ch. 9). If there are to be falsifiable theories say, about democracy, there must be, it is claimed, little or no dispute about the phenomenon itself, otherwise the predictions of those theories would be worthless. Although the complexity of political language may appear to make this a difficult task, at least in comparison to the physical sciences whose 'objective' subject matter makes an uncomplicated methodological nominalism more appropriate, it must be attempted if a science of politics is to be at all possible.

Against this quest for neutrality, it is maintained that the 'essential contestability' of political concepts (Gallie, 1964; Gray, 1978 and 1983;[3] Connolly, 1983) makes this impossible. Notice here that the claim is not merely that people will differ about values but the more disturbing argument that there is no core of settled meaning in the concepts employed in political argument. Again, essentially contested concepts do not display a confusion about usage which can be resolved by appropriate analytical methods but reflect radical and intractable disputes about ways of life. John Gray (1978, p. 394) writes: 'A concept moves into an area of essential contestability when any use of it involves taking up a partisan, non-neutral standpoint with respect to rival forms of life and their associated patterns of thought.' It appears to be impossible to define the necessary and sufficient conditions for the application of an essentially contested concept. Political philosophy is not condemnable for its abandonment of the pursuit of truth: it is rather that it is a delusion to suppose that there is any such thing which can be described conceptually.

Some examples, to be discussed in detail in later chapters, may illustrate the matter. The concept of justice would appear to be characterised by at least two rival interpretations: one understands it in terms of those simple rules of fairness that govern the relationships between *individuals*, the other, more properly called 'social' justice, maintains that it is applicable to an economy or a society as an *entity*. While both are about distribution, their concerns with this are radically different. Furthermore, both refer to competing ways of life: the one to a form of individualistic order in which justice relates to personal entitlement, the other to a more communitarian form of arrangement in which wealth is distributed according to social criteria. Is there any way to adjudicate between these two competing definitional claims?

The concepts of freedom, power, democracy and so on seem to display similar features. Can freedom be understood merely as the absence of (alterable) restraints on individual action, irrespective of the range of opportunities that are available to the person? Do any criteria of rationality have to be laid down before an action can legitimately be said to be free? Is it possible to construct a theory of power entirely in *causal* terms? Is the account of democracy exhausted by a description of 'representative democracy' in which parties compete for the votes of a more or less passive electorate, or is the notion of active participation by citizens under conditions of some social and economic equality more faithful to an 'exemplar' (Gallie's term used to describe an original notion of the concept to which contestants appeal[4]). It might appear to be odd that there could be any room for such an original exemplar in a world of apparently irresolvable differences but the idea makes sense if political (ideological?) argument is actually a battle to recapture or recover this original meaning. The very essence of ideological debate is the attempt to close off or 'decontest' whole areas of debate about language. In this sense, the theory of the essential contestability of political concepts is quite consistent with the ideal of a liberal, open society – that is, one which permits the arguments to go on. Indeed, within each overt political position there must be some features of the concept which are subject to less dispute – for example, whatever contested meanings liberalism may have it must surely contain some commitment to individualism and constraints on government (though the constraints may vary, see below).

A number of features of essentially contested concepts can be elucidated: they are appraisive, internally complex, open-textured, and there are no fixed criteria for their application (they are 'cluster' concepts, see Connolly, 1983, p. 14). What is particularly relevant to the problem of language in the social sciences is the rejection of the analytic–synthetic distinction by the essential contestability school. In politics it is maintained that no words can be given precise, analytical definitions (in comparison to words such as 'bachelor') and that they do not have exact empirical counterparts. This, of course, makes it virtually impossible for there to be a nomothetic political science.

It is, of course, true that many of the concepts in political discourse are used to appraise laws, politics and institutions and that disputes in politics are both conceptual and substantive. But it is not at all clear that exercises in political theory are irredeemably vitiated by the theorist's *own* values: or that his values cannot be disentangled from the conceptual analysis.

The complexity and open-textured nature of some political concepts are undoubtedly problems. Normally, political theorists argue that at the outer edges of a concept there is considerable and perhaps intractable dispute, even though there may be some agreement at the core. For example, although there is clearly disagreement amongst legal theorists, even of a positivist persuasion, as to whether Nazi law was really 'law' properly understood, it is still maintained that the notion of law used to describe ongoing legal systems has some settled meaning, despite the variety of legal phenomena. It is only in the overtly value-laden arguments that essential contestability comes into its own and surely some concepts in political theory can be understood in the context of a separation between analysis and appraisal. It may be difficult, but if it were an impossible enterprise political theory would surely be impoverished. The search for a completely neutral political vocabulary, one that conveys no policy prescription, may be difficult given the richness of political thought but there is always the opposite danger – the collapse into relativism.

A similar problem occurs with the range of human and social activities over which concepts apply. The most notable example here is 'politics' itself, for it is often claimed that it is arbitrary to limit the applicability of the word to the familiar areas of voting, law-making, pressure group activity and 'governing' in the conventional sense. We now have the politics of the family, of sex, of industrial organisations and other phenomena outside the formal apparatus of the state. This has had at least two deleterious effects on political studies. First, the term 'politics' becomes devoid of descriptive meaning if it can be legitimately expanded in this way. Secondly, this extension, intentionally or not, smuggles in a serious misdescription: for it implies that many areas of social life which could accurately be described as 'co-operative' become discordant and conflictual if they are described as 'political'. We shall show in later chapters that the emphasis by feminists on the family as a source of political conflict is an example of this promiscuous use of the word. If this is permitted by the 'essential contestability' thesis then an unnecessary confusion of language is created.

The most significant effect of the whole argument about essential contestability lies in the doubt that it casts on the possibility of a genuine science of politics. This is especially important in relation to power; for if there is genuine doubt about the phenomena that this concept describes, then the quantification which accompanies sociological theories of power is pointless. But in other branches of political science the thesis may not be so compelling. For example, the economic theory of democracy, which analyses competitive party democracies with the traditional tools of microeconomic analysis (see below, Chapter 11) has made considerable progress despite the alleged contestability of the concept of democracy.

Thus while there is a concern for language throughout this book it must be stressed that this is *not* the only interest of the political philosopher. Of particular importance is the general discussion of *collective* words in the next two chapters, and that of the difference between 'emotive' and 'descriptive' meaning in our normative enquiries. But these and other examples of linguistic analysis are presented as aids in the investigation of the traditional problems of political theory rather than as ends in themselves It is also important to note that the most impressive single work in analytical social philosophy, H. L. A. Hart's *The Concept of Law*, can hardly be described as merely clarificatory. In this book the reader is presented with much more than an account of the verbal perplexities associated with the word 'law'. Furthermore, in those subjects which have a claim to be scientific, such as economics and the application of economic theory to political and social phenomena, questions of meaning are of much less relevance than the truth and predictive power of the particular theories. These considerations, plus the recent appearance of important books on the substantive questions of justice, freedom, rights and democracy, suggest that the unrivalled dominance of the purely linguistic approach to political philosophy is at an end.

A convenient, albeit necessarily crude, way of approaching some of the problems of political theory is through particular frameworks of analysis: of a methodological rather than an overtly political kind. In the next two sections distinctive types of liberalism (liberal individualism and political liberalism) and the varieties of communitarian thought are analysed. In these areas problems of language, meaning, the explanation of social order and substantive normative justification appear together and the activity of political theorising consists very much in elucidating these aspects. The general philosophy of liberalism is considered in a little more detail not only because it is a crucially important mode of western political thought (even though liberals differ remarkably in their substantive commitments) but also because some of the most important contributions to contemporary analytical political philosophy are written in that mode. As Michael Freeden (1996, p. 27) cogently argues: '... political philosophy is not in a mutually exclusive relationship with ideology'. However, the ideologies implicitly and explicitly considered are somewhat muted, even modest, in comparison to those of the past; redolent of different intellectual approaches to some common problems rather than aggressive and proselytising schemes for radical social reform (such as Marxism once was and nationalism still is).

3 Liberal individualism⁵

Liberal individualism, sometimes known as classical liberalism or liberal rationalism (I shall use these terms interchangeably), embraces both *explanation* and *evaluation*. Its explanatory concern is accounting for that order of events which we call a *social order*; and this includes economic, legal and political phenomena. Its interest in evaluation consists largely in showing how, from the standpoint of a particularly individualistic conception of liberty, existing social orders may be improved. However, liberals maintain that these two aspects are separate and that their contributions to the scientific study of society are valuable in their own right irrespective of the individualistic bias of their evaluative and prescriptive writings. In fact, most of the early chapters of this book are concerned mainly but not exclusively with the liberal contribution to the scientific understanding of society – such as its explanation of familiar institutions such as law and state.

Liberals maintain that the regularities that undoubtedly characterise social life can be given a scientific explanation but their views on this differ considerably from others who also believe in a scientific study of society. It is instructive to consider first the views of their rivals in scientific explanation briefly. Those who have traditionally believed in the 'unity of scientific method' based their argument on the claim that there were regularities in the social world analogous to regularities in the physical world which could in principle be given a mechanical explanation not dissimilar to that found in physics. It was thought that there were *regularities* in the social world which enabled *generalisations* to be made about behaviour. They could be established by direct observation and predictions of future events derived from them. In this *inductive* approach, 'scientific laws' of society are *trends*, statements of probability or statistical generalisations which are based on observations of past events.

The more extreme exponents of this methodology asserted that it was the business of social science to discover certain 'historical' laws which explained social development and from which could be derived prophecies about the future course of history. The most famous example of this is Marxism which, in at least one interpretation, supposes that social structures change in accordance with changes in the mode of production so that the modern industrial world can be understood in terms of a series of 'revolutions'; bourgeois capitalism emerged necessarily from feudalism and capitalism would itself give way to socialism and, ultimately, communism. The future course of events could be predicted then from the knowledge of historical laws which operated independently of man's will.

In fact, there are less spectacular examples than this of the purely observational, inductive approach and it would be true to say that most adherents of this methodology are not historicists. Nevertheless, there are many social scientists who believe that a genuine social science must be based on empirical observation. A good example, from earlier in this century, was the attempt to explain and predict booms and slumps in the capitalist market economy by extrapolating trends from extensive inductive enquiries into the course of the business cycle. In political sociology, those who try to explain power in society by repeated observations of decision-making in the political system reveal a similar commitment to empiricism. In psychology, the 'behaviourist' school rejects any explanation of human action in terms of 'intentions' and 'motives' precisely because such mental phenomena cannot be observed and measured by the external enquirer. Whatever their other differences, these approaches may be called positivist in that they restrict knowledge in the social sciences to that which is empirically verifiable. This identification of science with the inductive bias was one of the unfortunate legacies of Logical Positivism.

Now liberal-rationalists claim that they are 'positivist' in the sense that they eliminate values from formal social science, but emphatically reject the central tenet of the positivist epistemology which claims that the purpose of social science is to discover empirical regularities in the social world (Popper, 1957, pp. 105–19). Laws are not derived inductively but are *deduced* from a small number of simple propositions about human nature. The regularities revealed by social science are not historical or social 'facts' but are properties of human nature which can be assumed to be unchanging. It is, of course, classical liberal economics which has produced the most systematic body of *theoretical* knowledge, and indeed a large part of economic theory consists of highly sophisticated deductions from simple axioms based on human nature. The 'laws of economics' are said to be universal because they are derived from an unchanging concept of man (Hayek, 1952, pp. 74–6).

Microeconomics provides the best examples of theoretical knowledge of this kind. If we want to understand the role of the price mechanism in the allocation of resources in a market economy, we have to use certain generalisations about consumer behaviour. Decreasing marginal utility theory tells us that an individual will consume units of a good until the marginal utility of the last unit of the good equals its cost, in terms of other goods she must forego in order to consume it. From this fundamental generalisation we can predict that if the price of a good falls, the demand will go up. But it is to be noted that while generalisations of this type are not historical trends based on observation, nevertheless they do generate theories with some predictive power. For example, the laws of consumer behaviour can be used to predict that if the government subsidises the rent of council housing the demand for such housing will go up and queues will develop; this is a theoretical inference of what must happen if certain generalisations are true and if certain initial conditions are met. While such 'laws' are not derived from 'facts' most liberal-rationalists maintain that the general predictions derived from their theories can be tested empirically. Indeed, it is possible to deduce the complex structure of the order of a self-correcting market from a small number of axioms (Hayek, 1952, ch. 4; and 1967, ch. 1). Many policies of the welfare state have been criticised using this 'scientific' method (see Barry, N., 1999a).

This methodology has been applied to political systems as well as economic systems and in the final chapter of this book we shall consider the economic theory of democracy, but at this point the other features of liberal-rationalism must be sketched. A crucial point is that explanation is couched entirely in individualistic terms. Social processes are understandable only as reconstructions out of individual actions. Collective words such as 'class', 'state' or 'society' do not describe observable entities, and statements containing them only have meaning when translated into statements about individual action. For example, we do not say a 'class' or 'society' saves or invests, since saving and investment are functions of individuals; and actions of the 'state' must be interpreted as the actions of individual officials operating under certain rules. Furthermore, and this point has been consistently opposed by collectivist social theorists, the individual under consideration is *abstracted* from historical and social circumstances. The concept of man that underlies the methodological individualist's model is based on a few very simple propositions about human nature: that men act so as to put themselves in a preferred position (though this does not have to be understood in purely monetary terms); that they prefer present to future satisfactions; and that they can have only a limited knowledge of the world around them. This information about persons is available to us all by what is called the method of 'introspection'. It is assumed that people are pretty much the same throughout the world and that by examining ourselves we can have knowledge of how others will act; for example, introspective knowledge of human nature will tell us that the imposition of very high marginal rates of taxation is likely to have some effect on people's work patterns and/or lead to widespread attempts at tax evasion.

A further aspect of the liberal-rationalist explanation of social regularities is the emphasis on *rules* and *rule-following*. This is not the simple point that a market exchange system requires a *particular* set of rules – i.e. those which respect personal and property rights – but the more complex argument that *all* social order, continuity and permanence are explicable only in terms of the notion of rule-following. The major rival scientific explanation of social order comes from the positivist theory of society and a description of this would be helpful in understanding liberal-rationalism. In the positivist explanation of social order, rules and rule-following are not considered to be adequate for a scientific explanation of that order because their effects are not susceptible to direct empirical observation. Positivists tend to look for so-called observable phenomena, like class or power.

Liberal social science completely rejects the idea that conformity and social order are products of class relationships, or any form of social 'conditioning', and maintains that such regularity as there is is a consequence of individuals following and internalising rules (Winch, 1958; Hart, 1961). This presupposes that individuals can understand that rules set appropriate standards of behaviour to which they ought to conform. In the simple case of regularised behaviour on the road we say that this is a function of traffic rules setting standards of motoring rather than an example of road-users being conditioned to do the correct thing by the appropriate reinforcing agencies. For example, we would say that the lights changing to red *means* stop, rather than that it *causes* drivers to stop. All rules operate as aids which make life reasonably predictable for the participants in a social process by indicating the range of permitted actions.

Some general features of rules may now be delineated. First, all rules, whether they are legal, moral, religious or political, are normative or prescriptive. So far we have been using the word normative in a moral sense only – in distinguishing moral or evaluative statements from scientific statements. But not all normative arguments are moral, and not all uses of the word 'ought' are moral uses. Thus a simple legal rule which makes driving on the left obligatory sets standards which *ought* to be followed just as much as our moral rules do. Furthermore, although general rules indicate the right thing to do, this does not mean that it is right in a moral sense. Indeed, many simple, primitive societies have customary rules which would be regarded as objectionable from the point of view of a critical Western morality. Rule-governed action is often contrasted with habitual or automatic behaviour on the ground that it involves the idea of 'internalisation'. A rule is internalised when it is understood by participants in a social practice as indicating a right and wrong way of doing things (Hart, 1961, pp. 55–6). Furthermore, rules entail the idea of choice, for unlike well-trained animals, humans may disobey rules. Sanctions are, of course, needed to cope with the minority of rule-breakers but this does not mean that sanctions can replace internalisation as the guarantor of regularised behaviour. It should be obvious that a social system which relied solely on sanctions to secure conformity would be highly insecure. For one thing, it would require a very large police force to impose the sanctions. But in that event, how could obedience by the police be ensured?

Rules must be carefully distinguished from predictions. Some empirically minded social theorists have argued that a rule is a disguised prediction that if a forbidden course of action is undertaken a court will impose a sanction; or if it is a moral rule that is broken the community will express its displeasure in some less precise manner. But this is false. That a rule has been breached constitutes a *reason* or *justification* for the imposition of the sanction. It is because the internal obligatory nature of a rule cannot be verified by external observation that some extreme empiricists have tried to translate them into predictions; in their analysis rules appear as 'ghostly entities' and the only relevant features of a social system are those that are observable.

Moral and legal rules are devices for regulating personal conduct while political rules govern the allocation of power and authority in a society. An example of a moral rule might be the rule that says one ought to look after one's aged parents; a legal rule is one that makes driving on the left obligatory; and a political rule is one that requires the Prime Minister to resign if he/she fails to secure a majority in the House of Commons. Although these rules are clearly distinct – they emanate from different sources, and breaches are met with different sanctions – they exhibit the same logic. They are normative statements, as distinct from factual statements. The most important feature is that they put limitations on individual conduct by making the performance of some actions in some sense obligatory.

It is clear that systems of rules do not have to be 'created' or emanate from a particular source; indeed, classical liberals argued persuasively that the most reliable systems were those that had evolved spontaneously, such as the common law. While conceding that political and constitutional rules were essential, they denied that all social order was a product of political will. In fact, the complete breakdown of a social order is much rarer than is sometimes supposed even though many countries experience frequent constitutional change and upheaval. It is because of the relative instability of political rules that contemporary liberal-rationalists wish to limit the area of social life occupied by *public* rules, and this assumes that social order, brought about by rule-following, can survive with little political direction. What is of particular interest to the liberal individualist social theorist is the existence of general systems such as legal and economic orders which, although not designed or intended by any one single individual or group, serve human purposes more effectively than deliberately contrived or planned institutions (Hayek, 1967, ch. 6; Barry, N., 1988a).

Liberal social theory, however, finds it difficult to explain certain sorts of institutions which appear not to emerge spontaneously: the 'public goods' of defence, law and order and the state itself are the obvious examples. Thus although it is quite plausible to trace out the development of legal rules in British law as a product of quasi-natural processes – for example, the law of contract is not derived from statute but from judicial decision-making – it is not so easy to explain the whole *system of law-enforcement* and other conventional aspects of the state in a similar way. This is because, although such institutions are in the interests of each person as a member of the community, the members of a community have no incentive to produce them in their private capacities. Thus each person would not pay for state activities unless others are willing to pay: and in the *absence* of compulsion there is no guarantee that they will do so.

The familiar problems of 'Prisoners' Dilemmas' and public good traps will be considered later (see below, Chapter 3) but it is worth pointing out at this stage the weakness in liberal rationalist political theory which they illustrate. It is that the account of the liberal self in individualistic utility-maximising terms seems, superficially, to preclude these features of man which make social life possible. It is indeed true that much of liberal individualist social theory is underpinned by a 'fragmented' view of the person: a view that works well enough in relation to the explanation of the regularities of the market but is less satisfactory elsewhere. This fragmentation of the person involves the detachment of agents from their social settings and treats them as rational choosers or utility-maximisers.

This disability in liberal-rationalism, its difficulty in explaining collective institutions, derives mainly from its reluctance to concede the political significance of common purposes. The assumption is that the diversity of human values and purposes precludes the existence of sufficient agreement about social ends which would validate an extensive role for the state. Its claim is that a stable order is consistent with a variety of individually chosen plans of life. In a phrase that has become indissolubly associated with almost all forms of liberalism, the state should be 'neutral about the good', in other words, its role should not be to impose any one conception of value on communities characterised by a diversity of moral ends. The significant achievement of a liberal society is its ability to preserve order and continuity in the absence of an overriding social and moral purpose.

Liberalism is, however, a many-sided political doctrine. The features just outlined represent a particular *explanatory* aspect of it; that concerned with an account of those institutional arrangements which, since at least David Hume, have been identified with the conditions of social order. The elementary principles of justice, which constitute a framework of predictability within which individuals can pursue their self-chosen goals, constitute the best examples of the rules of a liberal social order. The range of collective institutions is limited to those that are essential for the peaceful and harmonious satisfaction of necessarily subjective desires. This is obviously exemplified in market arrangements which, it is claimed, spontaneously emerge as decentralised procedures for the co-ordination of private activities. Public institutions, such as law and the state, have no intrinsic value and are therefore entitled to no loyalty apart from that generated by their success in the harmonisation of potentially disparate human actions.[6]

From this perspective, the rules and institutions that govern a society have a claim to universality; they constitute a kind of generic moral code which all societies should aspire to, whatever other differences they display. There is a tradition in classical liberal thought that understands the basic rules of justice, such as respect for property and the inviolability of contract, as artificial in the sense of being the constructs of human endeavour, in contradistinction to the purely natural affections, yet they are somehow natural precisely because they meet with universal needs. In Hume's memorable phrase: 'though the rules of justice be artificial, they are not arbitrary. Nor is the expression improper to call them laws of nature, if by natural we understand what is common to any species' (Hume, 1972, p. 216).

4 Political liberalism

Contemporary political liberalism is more ambitious than this for it is now concerned as much with distributive questions as it is with rules of order.[7] It is also more a feature of American political thought; in Europe, liberalism tends to be much closer to the classical variant. American liberals would regard those doctrines as too redolent of conservatism to constitute a self-contained ideology. Still, both versions of liberalism are rationalistic in that they tend to justify their position by reference to an abstract reason, which is very unconservative. A clear distinction can be drawn between two competing versions of contemporary liberalism on the issue of redistribution. The classical, or economic, liberals preclude the state from any role in the redistribution of income and wealth, either because of the effect that this would have on efficiency or because of a commitment to the non-violation of a natural right to ownership.

However, most contemporary liberals are more egalitarian. They do not regard the institutions of a liberal society as mere protective devices to provide security for individuals to pursue self-determined plans, or to enable subjective desires to be co-ordinated. To limit their role in these ways would, in fact, compromise liberal neutrality for it would arbitrarily privilege some purposes over others and provide a spurious legitimacy to an initially random distribution of resources. While both sorts of liberalism might share some concepts, such as freedom, equality, individuality, personal autonomy and a more or less non-intrusive role for the state in the private world, their differing conceptions of these desiderata generate radically differing policy agendas. In the aftermath of the collapse of communism, political argument has to some extent been dominated by these rivalrous versions of liberalism; although classical or economic liberalism has probably been more significant in public policy debate (and more attractive to former communist regimes) than in academic political philosophy.

But the two liberalisms have much in common, especially at the foundational level. They highlight the priority of the right over the good. By this it is meant the belief that what each person values as contributory to the good life is a personal decision for which no help ought to be sought from communal values or any kind of collectivism. In this they have been accused of adopting that emotivism in ethics cited earlier. Although political liberals insist that procedural rules can be demonstrated by some version of reason, and may even be considered objective, they try to remain broadly 'neutral' about life-styles and no one should have priority over others, and certainly no special protection from the law. Political liberals therefore tend to be politically active over such things as freedom of speech, separation of church and state and abortion rights. In this they are specifically anti-majoritarian and are in the vanguard of a view of rights that normally demands more than those granted by the positive law.

However, an indifference to the outcomes of a social process does not extend to the results of free exchange. Although it would be quite wrong to suggest that political liberals are hostile to the free market, they are often very critical of the results, the distribution of income and wealth, that system generates. Hence, although they agree with classical liberals about the necessity for procedural rules, their norma-tive description of them extends way beyond the mere enforcement of criminal law, property and contract. And they certainly do not endorse the given distribution of wealth from which free exchange begins. As we shall see in Chapters 6 and 7, that critical attitude towards the existing spread of assets even extends beyond the inheri-tance of wealth and property to the allocation of natural gifts and talents, which earn a high income. These are frequently claimed to be a product of nature to which the lucky recipient has no entitlement. A truly liberal society would correct these 'injustices' of an arbitrary nature. What this means is that although both versions of liberalism share a belief in the importance of procedural rules (and a hostility to the imposition of outcomes) they differ very much on what these rules should be.

5 The decline of Marxism and the rise of communitarianism[8]

The collapse of Marxist regimes since 1990 has produced some disarray in collectivist circles. The apologetic cry that what was practised in the Soviet Union and Eastern Europe was not really Marxist was a poor excuse: there have been so many different claims for the true Marx that it is hard to imagine that the above-mentioned regimes did not fit the demands of one of them. More important, the manifest failure of any form of socialism to match the productivity of capitalism, or remotely to approach the record of liberal capitalist regimes in the protection of civil liberties, has forced followers of socialist economics and ethics into some dramatic rethinking. As we shall see, anti-capitalist and anti-individualist thought have flourished in the post-collectivist world but the inspiration for this has not been traditional Marxist economics. Collectivist thought has continued in a rather scholastic way, with unceasing enquiries into the true meaning of Marxism, but its influence on public policy, and perhaps public philosophy, has been much less than earlier in the century.

The major dispute within Marxist thought for a long time was whether the doctrine should be interpreted as an objective, value free social science or as a moral, or at least critical, doctrine which had as much to do with an ethical evaluation of typical capitalist institutions as it has with scientifically predicting their downfall. Perhaps the 'scientific' version of Marxism failed as an explanatory theory of society because it was structured around a somewhat perverted notion of positivism and a completely mistaken notion of 'laws' in the social sciences. In traditional or orthodox Marxism a scientific law was a prophecy of the future course of events which was derived from extensive historical enquiries (Marx, 1977). The structure of social change was based upon economics, and economic history and social class systems would change in accordance with changes in the mode of production: thus feudalism would give way to capitalism and this would be replaced by socialism. The last phase would give rise, ultimately, to communism which would dispense with the familiar institutions of Western society; all law was thought to be coercive and states were understood in terms of repression based on class relations. Private property and the division of labour would not be required in a world in which the supposedly universal features of scarcity and self-interest have been replaced by abundance and a new spirit of communalism. In the Marxist utopia change of self would correlate with change of circumstance.

But this is a very different sort of positivism from that which has always characterised liberal economics. As we have already noted, social laws here are understood as inferences or deductions from certain features of the human condition that are assumed to be universal. People will always value things at the margin, human desires are unlimited, scarcity is a permanent feature of the human condition and not a contingent fact of capitalism; furthermore, a by no means necessarily harmful self-interest characterises human nature in whatever situation people find themselves. The universal (and non-historical) features of this explanation derive from the modest predictions (not prophecies of future events) that are made from it: inflation always follows an increase in the money supply when unaccompanied by an increase in production, rental control has persistently created housing shortages and excessive welfare produces defection from work and dysfunctional social behaviour. Marxist prophecies might be more glamorous but they lack the precision and accuracy of the predictions of their more modest rivals.

Associated with the fallacious economic and social theories of Marxism is the lacuna in its explanation of how a future socialist society might function in terms of efficiency. As is well-known, Marx laid down no blueprint for a future communist economy; and this reticence is quite consistent with his utopian world-view. Capitalism would have solved the initial problems of production and left a world of abundance. But the societies in which we have always lived require that these questions of efficiency and resource allocation be answered. Planned economies could never solve the problem of the co-ordination of knowledge: how can the actions of dispersed individuals in a large society be so arranged that an output of goods and services is produced which meets with people's desires? Under capitalism the signalling mechanism of the market attracts the factors of production to activities consonant with efficiency and an array of goods and services is generated which satisfies people's desires. Even if central planners had the right moral motivations there is no way they could cope with the informational problems of a world without markets.

But even if these problems were soluble, and decades of experience of centrally planned economies in which permanent shortages were a universal feature indicates they are not, Marxist social theory comes up against a problem analysed at great length by liberal social science: the public good dilemma. If the oppressed in an advanced industrial society are dispersed and motivated by self-interest, how can they co-operate to produce a desirable outcome, for example, redistribution from the capitalist class to the deprived, when the difference one person's actions makes to social affairs is minutely small (see Buchanan, A. 1986)? How can an individual be expected rationally to work for common class ends when he cannot be sure that others will be so public spirited? The dubious promise of future socialist abundance has not been a sufficient motivation to generate such co-operation and, indeed, even moderate socialist practice has resulted in squabbling between rival interest groups rather class co-operation. It is no good saying that the arrival of socialism will produce a less egoistic person when that clearly has not happened under any form of collectivism. The failure to solve the above problems might well explain the coercive rule of one unified elite, the communist party, that has been such a feature of centrally-planned economies.

It might be thought that the capitalist class must surely be subject to the same problem since the logic of Marxist theory implies that any one capitalist producer can only succeed by extracting more surplus value from the worker; yet this will only impoverish the proletariat and bring about revolution. Thus rational action by individual capitalists would theoretically bring down the whole system. However, classical liberalism has solved this problem by increasing wealth and by ensuring that labour gets a return in accordance with its marginal productivity. Perhaps also the capitalists have acquiesced in the introduction of the welfare state; or at least tolerated those democratic reforms that made it possible. The workers clearly have not been impoverished under capitalism.

The dismal performance of Marxism as a social science has undoubtedly led to a different emphasis: on its moral or critical claims rather than its achievement as science. And here the influence of Marx's early writings, where communism seems to be reached via a moral critique of capitalism, has become important (Marx, 1971). Typical capitalist practices, such as an advanced division of labour and an exclusively money economy, are condemnable for their dehumanising effects. This approach is specifically non-positivist and directs the believers to take a critical attitude to society rather than wait for the laws of historical development to unfold. Still, even orthodox Marxism consisted of a curious amalgam of scientism and revolutionary activism evinced in a famous Marxist aphorism: 'Philosophers have only interpreted the world ... the point, however, is to change it' (Marx and Engels, 1968, p. 30).

In modern Marxist theory, capitalism is deficient from the standpoint of a critical reason: the market's production of power and money distorts an almost Kantian ideal of a society of autonomous, rational individuals who would otherwise take a critical attitude towards social relationships. But capitalism, because of its capacity for wealth creation, has created a passive population that is supine in the face of its own oppression (Marcuse, 1964, 1969). The most regrettable feature of market society is its corroding of the public sphere. Here, contemporary critical Marxists are provoked by the concept of instrumentalist reason which permeates liberal capitalism. It is a notion that restricts our critical, rational faculties to the organisation of means to ends and forbids exploration of the ends themselves.

The individualistic assumptions of the market apparently pose a constant threat to shared values on which a rational society depends. But a more communicable, and superficially more potent, critique of individualism is that of contemporary communitarianism: a doctrine unencumbered by heady Marxist metaphysics or its anachronistic political economy.

Although most of the prominent communitarians owe little to Marxism, the doctrines they espouse share something of that hostility to abstract individualism that Marxism has often displayed. The apparent practical success of market economies has not resulted in any kind of triumph of the philosophy that underlies that economic system, which is specifically criticised for being too universalistic and too detached from those social forms that shape and condition (if not determine) the kinds of individuals that participate in them. The claim is not merely that market systems must have a social dimension (Barry, N., 1993a) if they are to satisfy conventional ethical standards (and the most prominent of these is social justice) but also that institutional arrangements that give meaning to individuals' lives are not reducible to the choice calculus of liberal economics.

In other words, people invariably are situated in social contexts which are not explicable in terms of their preferences: we do not choose the rules under which we live but in fact *receive* certain norms and roles which make social life possible. Notions of loyalty, friendship and communal affiliations are required to explain continuity and solidarity and these are not captured by a philosophy that abstracts individuals from the social nexus and makes their actions comprehensible only in terms of the familiar economic constraints of scarcity and cost. A person concerned merely with her own satisfactions cannot be a full citizen because citizenship itself involves social roles which are defined independently of choice. Indeed, it is claimed that some of the most successful market economies (the best example is perhaps Japan's[9]) thrive precisely because the market operates in a social system whose norms require considerable subordination of individual gratification to communal ends. Even the most determined liberal economists have some difficulty in explaining how public goods are generated from individual choice (see below, Chapter 3), or why people bother to vote and to follow voluntarily conventions and practices. Communal societies flourish without that *formal* rule-following which seems to be such a feature of Western orders.

It is true that economic liberalism is particularly vulnerable to communitarianism precisely because its conception of the person is specifically rooted in utility-maximising terms, and it is also highly critical of any egalitarianism that might attenuate the efficiency of the market. But those political liberals who stress an activist role for the state in the creation of equal liberties are said to be equally deficient to the extent that they couch their recommendations in the form of an abstract universalism that occludes the nuances of social forms. The idea of the community as a source of those values that exist independently of individual desires fills the gap left by all forms of liberalism; a philosophical doctrine which apparently makes the freely-floating individual, unconstrained by anything other than socially necessary rules, the only focus of morality.

The current emphasis on community (see Mulhall and Swift, 1992) is not merely a party political doctrine that recommends a softening of the rigours of a harsh market system that might be objected to because it generates socially unacceptable inequalities or that liberal capitalism is often destructive of established communities because of the ceaseless change that it tends to generate. The issue is deeper than this. That it is philosophical rather than political is revealed by the fact of communitarians coming from both left and right of the political spectrum. Indeed, the most succinct summary and critique of abstract individualism was made by the conservative philosopher Roger Scruton, who described liberalism as 'the principal enemy of conservatism with all its attendant" trappings of individual autonomy and the "natural rights of man"' (Scruton, 1981, p. 16). Furthermore, some liberals (Rawls, 1972; Dworkin, 1986) are emphatically egalitarian in economic matters. The dispute between liberals and communitarians is not just about public policy but concerns the nature of political judgement, the theory of the self and the understanding of society.

In important ways communitarianism arises out of its objection to subjectivism, the belief that moral utterances were private expressions of feelings, which until very recently was such a feature of moral and political philosophy. Alasdair MacIntyre (1981) bases his communitarianism on a critique of the kind of moral nihilism that subjectivism is said to have produced: the rejection of objective standards of good and bad, right and wrong and so on has meant, he claims, that Western societies have abandoned genuine ethics for the satisfaction of preferences. Of course, some versions of liberalism do proclaim a belief in objective values but this is normally limited to the rules of a social practice, about which some agreement is possible. It is not thought that social 'ends' of practices have any virtue since such a presupposition would imply that a form of value is possible which transcends individual choice. Free market liberalism and egalitarian liberalism are fundamentally similar in their dismissal of the over-riding *moral* claims of an ongoing community. MacIntyre traces the origin of this disorder to Hume and the founders of liberal theory. They had (MacIntyre, 1981, pp. 214–17) mistakenly taken the con-tingent features of the person associated with the burgeoning liberal-individualist orders of the late eighteenth century to be universal properties of man. Thus, liberal society's essential anonymity and almost deliberate purposelessness was proclaimed to be an appropriate general form of social life when at most it is a *particularity*, a form of living associated with a particular class within that society. Again, when modern liberalism assumes an individual rights-based style of politics, it is particularly corrosive of morality precisely because this quasi-legalistic mode of reasoning separates persons from their com-munities.

The major concern of communitarianism is to establish the identity of the self and this cannot be satisfactorily achieved through an individualism, either of a rights-claiming or a utility-maximising type; it is detached from given social forms. Knowledge of the self is discovered through an understanding of the whole congeries of communal bonds which determines character, and this in turn depends on an appreciation of the 'narrative' of social life: 'personal identity is just that identity presupposed by the unity of character which the unity of narrative requires' (MacIntyre, 1981, p. 140). In other words, that objective value structure, which is rejected by liberalism, is to be found in given social forms that provide shared meanings; phenomena that are entirely absent from the artificial world created by liberal theorists. To take a concrete example, justice; this is not a set of abstract rules for anonymous agents to live by, but consists of distributive practices, sanctioned by a tradition of behaviour, within which identifiable agents can achieve some kind of unity with a social whole that exists apart from their choices. Thus desert and deserving-ness are inextricably bound up with shared meanings. Of course, most communitarians would not deny that there is a liberal tradition which is revealed by a communal narrative history but they would insist that it is not a universal form decreed by reason (even the much attenuated notion of reason used by some liberals), but the outgrowth of a particular form of life.

From this perspective, familiar social institutions such as the state and the law can never be neutral between competing ways of life but must preserve the form of life in which individuals are ineluctably embedded. The individual is not prior to social arrangements but constituted by them. This approach clearly undermines that purported universalism that characterises much of liberal theory, at least in its normative mode, and would seem to limit social criticism to an exploration of the meanings of forms of life. A person's autonomy is not established by a kind of release from social constraints, so that the unencumbered self can realise individually determined ends, but is realised through full participation in the civic order. We shall see in later chapters whether this entails a kind of relativism about values, but superficially the confinement of evaluation to the context of given social forms does seem to preclude those cross-cultural comparisons that political theorists often make.

This dispute between liberalism and communitarianism features in both the institutional and the normative aspects of political theory. For the liberal, law and state appear to be necessary conveniences for individuals who, either in a Hobbesian sense are fearful for their own security, or in the more optimistic modern view have legitimate moral claims against authority, need a generic moral and legal code. Such a code will undoubtedly vary significantly from society to society but it will meet with supposedly universal human motivations. To the communitarian such purported necessities are in fact trivial, the key to understanding a social order is an appreciation of those features that differentiate social and political forms and which provide a focus for individual identity and loyalty. Institutions therefore must have some intrinsic value. Indeed, one of the most distressing features of liberal society for the communitarian is the legalism that it tends to inspire, a tendency that is expressed in the current emphasis on individual rights *against* the state and society: a process which inevitably undermines intrinsic value and corrupts civic virtue.

A real clash between liberalism and communitarians has occurred through the addition of 'multiculturalism' to the agenda of the latter (see Taylor, C., 1992). For communitarians would like to soften and modify the sometimes rigid application of liberal constitutional principles; the rigorous enforcement of equality before the law can lead to a kind of imposed liberalism. The example of Quebec shows the tension between communitarianism and liberalism, for many Quebeckers fear that since the adoption of a liberal constitution in 1982 the French way of life is threatened by the rise of the English language (and American values). Hence a law was passed which forbade the use of English in shop signs and compelled the children of French speakers and immigrants to be educated in French-language schools. All sorts of complex intellectual manoeuvres have been used by liberals (see Barry, N., 1998a) to make the abstract legalism of liberalism consistent with multiculturalism but the enterprise would appear to be doomed at the foundational level.

What really worries communitarians is the inexorable progress of the market throughout the world since the collapse of communism and the decline of appeal of even mild versions of socialism. Since the market is apparently a venue inhabited by abstract, utility-maximising agents who follow the more or less universal rules of the property, tort and contract system it must constitute a threat to those intermediary institutions (the family and the local community being the best examples) of civil society. If the only goal is profit, many of them would not survive and the logic of the market would preclude state activity from aiding those institutions that could not survive in a free economy. MacIntyre clearly resents this process: in his distinction between *internal* and *external* goods (1981, pp. 187–91) he maintains that the liberal market economy can only produce consumer goods, goods that are not defined in any communal sense. What it cannot provide is those goods that are necessary for the survival of a *practice*, a form of organisation which is defined in non-economic terms. It is a way of life, a set of shared values which is integral to the life of the community

What concerns communitarians is not so much the market, in fact they would admire it to the extent that it promoted shared values, but 'soulless' big business. Sandel (1984, pp. 15–17) worries about '... the concentration of power in the corporate economy and the erosion of intermediate forms of community'. Apparently, the large corporation is unaccountable and unreceptive to anything except shareholder value and obviously shareholders will not have the community in mind when they make, or withdraw, their investments. Indeed, they are the same dispersed, abstract agents who have no loyalty to anything but the accumulation of external goods. In fact, this critique of capitalist, liberal market systems is grossly misleading since it should be obvious to the communitarians that the most vibrant communities, those most anxious to preserve a received (not chosen) way of life, are the market economies of Japan and East Asia. They have even managed to resist the corporate raider who might break up smaller companies and threaten established ways of life. The efficiency properties of liberal economies are consistent with a variety of ways of life, of which the Anglo-American model is only one (Barry, 1998b, ch. 7).

6 Feminism

We have already seen the effect that feminism has had on the language of political thought and it is now important to examine some of its basic ideological features, features that have had an impact on contemporary political argument. Again, feminism should not be associated with ideology in the party sense or in the familiar indivi-dualist-collectivist dichotomy. Although the doctrine tends toward political radicalism, there are, not surprisingly, Marxist versions of feminism, at the analytical level it is capable of being embraced by a variety of normative frameworks. There are even free market feminists (Taylor J., 1992) who argue that continued state intervention in the economy actually worsens the position of women: not because it is the institutional embodiment of male power but because they believe that the exchange system, conducted under equal opportunity and the rule of law, increases female opportunities, their independence and autonomy.

Historically feminism can be seen as an offshoot of liberal ideology, feminists wanted its main features extended to women. Early writings, such as Mary Wollstonecraft's *A Vindication of the Rights of Women*, were demands to incorporate women's concerns into the conventional structure of liberal political thought. John Stuart Mill's *On the Subjection of Women* is a further example of this identification of female political aspirations with the male liberal political order. The liberties and equalities of the embryonic democracies of the nineteenth and early twentieth centuries were not available to women in impor-tant areas until quite late. Women in France did not get the vote until 1946 and in some cantons of Switzerland it was granted even later. But even when these procedural deficiencies were rectified, discrimination continued unabated in the economy. However, the claim was made that no new concepts were needed to describe the political problems. All that was required was the extension and reinforcement of tradi-tional liberal values. Still, the application of abstract rules which are supposed to be blind to irrelevant differences, based on race or sex, may not do very much for women whose social roles, perhaps arbitrarily determined, put them in an inferior position. The traditional rules, no matter how liberal, took no account of sociological and other factors which assigned women to particular social functions. The feminist argument became that women's opportunities are fewer to the extent that men predominate in the making of the rules.

Hence the 'second wave' of feminism (Pateman, 1983; Mackinnon, 1989), which is a much more radical attack on the structure of what became known as 'patriarchy': a repressive social arrangement based on a male domination which derives from the role of the father in the family. Important here is the distinction made between 'public' and 'private' (or domestic). The argument is that traditional political theory has been almost exclusively about the public world of law and state (Pateman, 1983). It is a world of rights and duties defined in terms entirely favourable to men. The 'social contract', by which these are sometimes validated in liberal political theory, did not include women, their consent was not required for law and public policy. The private world of family, domestic and personal relationships, to which women are often arbitrarily confined, is supposed to be controlled by a kind of 'natural' morality; it is not formalised but flows spontaneously from human predispositions.

In traditional liberal political theory there had always been a distinction between private and public, or civil society and the state. Civil society, which necessarily includes the private economy, has always been venerated because it is characterised by voluntariness. The state had been resisted, especially in personal and moral matters, precisely because it was a threat to individual self-development and a cause of a stultifying conformity. However, to a feminist this is an inadequate distinction because civil society itself is governed by rules and practices that perpetuate male domination. Civil society, or the private world, is not an arena of voluntariness for women. It is not enough, however, to correct discrimination in civil society, for this still leaves women at the mercy of men in the domestic sphere. For although women writers are very much concerned with the family, their understanding of it could not be more different from that of conservatives. The family is almost a political institution where power, in the context of biased law, predominates rather than morality: there is no freedom or equality, only patriarchy.

2
Law and Social Control

1 Law and social philosophy

Political philosophers have always been very much concerned with questions of jurisprudence, or the philosophy of law, and there has been a great variety of these questions. Dominating them all is the essentialist question of 'what is law?' The assumption behind this question is that there is a set of necessary and sufficient conditions for the truth of statements about the word law. Essentialist definitions depend upon there being a set of properties which the word law uniquely describes. The difficulty is, however, that all the proposed definitions have, in their endeavour to capture in a phrase or sentence the essential properties of law, misrepresented the familiar features of legal systems, or arbitrarily restricted the range of application of the word law. The most obvious example is the command theory of law, which defined law solely in terms of the orders of a determinate sovereign and therefore excluded many familiar forms of law (such as international law, constitutional law and tribal law) from the category of 'proper' law. Another example is the attempt to assimilate the notion of legal rules to moral rules, which results in a concealment of the different features of law and morality and a misrepresentation of the different ways in which they regulate social behaviour.

While it is probably true now to say that the search for an exclusive definition of law has been called off, the familiar questions in jurisprudence remain. These centre on the problem of the necessary conditions for the existence of a legal system; criteria of validity of legal rules; the role of sanctions; and the relationship between law and morality. Is it necessary, for example, that a legal system should have courts and organised sanctions? Is it possible to locate a definitive test for the validity of a purported rule of law in a legal system? Is a sanction a necessary condition for the existence of a legal rule? And does the *content* of any particular law have to meet with supposed universal standards of morality for the law to be a genuine law?

30

Perhaps the most elementary distinction to be made in jurisprudence is that between natural law and positive law: for although there are many types of positive law they are all united in a fundamental opposition to natural law (Hart, 1958). The distinction turns upon questions of the meaning of law and the validity of purported claims to law. Natural law (see Finnis, 1980), which has a long and honourable tradition that dates back to ancient Greece, holds that not only must we evaluate law in accordance with universal moral standards, but that for a rule to be accorded the dignity and status of the word 'law' it must satisfy these standards. Questions about validity turn necessarily upon the *content* of the rules in a legal system. Thus a particular rule would not be entitled to be called valid law if in substance it breached a moral principle – even if it emanated from an authoritative source and was legitimate in a formal sense.

Positivists, however, insist upon a logical separation between law and morality and maintain that the content of a law (that is, the ends or purposes which it is designed to bring about) has no relevance to its status as a law; although, as we shall see in the next section, not all legal theorists who call themselves positivists maintain quite this indifference to the content of law. This doctrine does not in any way imply a lack of interest in moral questions on the part of positivist legal theorists – on the contrary, many legal positivists have been rigorous critics of existing legal systems – but it does mean that if intellectual clarity is to be achieved and some element of certainty in the law guaranteed, questions of validity have to be separated from questions of moral worth. One of the objections made by an eminent legal positivist to the use of natural law criteria in postwar West German courts, in consideration of the difficult questions as to whether Nazi statutes were really law, turned precisely on the claim that the admission of such criteria would make for potential confusion and uncertainty in the law (Hart, 1961, pp. 205–7).

2 Natural law

The history of jurisprudence reveals a great variety of theories of natural law and perhaps the only common factor in the conflicting doctrines is an aversion to legal positivism. For convenience they may be divided into two categories: highly abstract and 'rationalistic' theories which rest upon the assumption that the human mind is capable of determining a set of moral principles of universal validity which should govern all social, political and personal relationships; and more modest doctrines which maintain that societies spontaneously develop systems of rules which protect personal and property rights (the English common law is an example of such a system), and that statute or 'created' law should be strictly limited to making piecemeal improvements on 'natural' systems.

As we remarked earlier in this chapter, what characterises the 'rationalist' models of natural law is that they maintain that law must have some specific content if it is to be valid. St Thomas Aquinas's jurisprudence, which still underlies contemporary Catholic teaching on politics, law and morals, illustrates this point. From the simple proposition that 'good is to be done and pursued and evil avoided' he hoped to deduce the whole body of natural law concerning life and death, marriage, the family and economic and political relationships. Any laws at variance with natural law were not proper laws.

The difficulty with all natural law theories of the absolutist kind is that of securing agreement on the ends which people ought to pursue. Natural lawyers often write as if their prescriptions were as necessary as the laws that govern the physical world but clearly this is not so. Natural law relates to human conduct and has therefore quite a different logic from scientific law; it is normative, not predictive or descriptive. What is controversial about traditional natural law theories is their supposition that reason can determine a unique set of moral principles which should determine the content of law. But people's needs and desires change and actions which were regarded as immoral by one generation may be acceptable to another. Even the absolutist nature of Thomist natural law is qualified by the admission that the subsidiary rules of natural law may alter. In fact, social and economic consequences have seen a number of changes in Catholic natural law, most notably the lifting of the prohibition on usury in the Middle Ages (O'Connor, 1967, pp. 78–9). Natural lawyers do try to maintain the absolute nature of their prescriptions by making them highly general in form. This, however, makes them difficult to apply in particular cases. The natural law against the arbitrary taking of life may be superficially uncontroversial but men sincerely differ over cases in which the taking of life is or is not justified.[1]

It is doubtful whether any contemporary natural law theorist supposes that the *legality* or validity of a municipal legal system can be determined by rationalistic criteria, independently of more formal or procedural considerations. Indeed, if the whole concept of law is not to be reduced to an irresolvable contestability, some features of a legal order must be delineated independently of the substantive ends and purposes which may be pursued by political authorities. The subjectivist influence on modern ethics and politics has effectively prevented a definition of law in terms of substantive values, about which there appears to be little agreement. However, it should be pointed out that to account for the meaning of law in terms of formal criteria (as legal positivism does) does not necessarily commit the legal philosopher to that other tenet of positivism, *non-cognitivism* – the ethical doctrine that value judgements have no foundation in reason but are merely the expression of the arbitrary opinions of the speaker. On the contrary, it is the case that many legal positivists, including Bentham, were rationalist in ethics. The point is that they argued that a proper moral evaluation of law is only possible when the logical separation of the two phenomena is affirmed (Hart, 1958, pp. 462–70). Indeed, it could well be argued that if law is defined exclusively in terms of morality this might actually weaken the case for resistance to rules perceived to be unjust since this conceptual link gives the law a kind of extra dignity and status.

A modern version of natural law, for example the work of Lon Fuller (1969), tries to show that an acceptable account of law necessitates the use of certain basic moral concepts, about which there can be some agreement, but that this is consistent with the recognition of value differences at other levels. Jurisprudence can locate the basic core meaning of law but must be silent at the more substantive aims which legal systems should pursue. Fuller distinguishes between the morality of 'duty' and the morality of 'aspiration' to make the point that whatever else law may aim at, it is properly law only if it satisfies certain procedural requirements of justice. Law is defined as 'the centrepiece of subjecting human conduct to the governance of rules' (Fuller, 1969, p. 53). In this approach, the limits of natural law seem to be defined by the criteria of the 'rule of law'. Although this is not definitionally associated with liberal capitalism, it is difficult to make communist regimes comply with it.

Fuller delineates eight key features of law: characteristics which express the 'inner morality' of law. They are the requirements of generality, promulgation, non-retroactivity, clarity, non-contradiction, possibility of compliance, some degree of permanence, and congruence between official action and declared rule. Not all these requirements have to be met for a rule to be a genuine legal rule (some retroactivity may be unavoidable – for example, in relation to tax law and in the workings of the common law) but although they look formal and procedural they are supposed to express the minimum purposes that law *ought* to serve if it is to be considered as law.

The difficulty with theories of this type is that in the desire to make the basic elements of law non-contestable, or at least not dependent on any substantive morality, their authors admit into the category of law those very orders the theories are designed to exclude. For example, it is not at all clear that South Africa's apartheid law would have been disqualified by Fuller's procedural requirements. Although the racial classifications were arbitrary and led to absurdities as well as obvious injustices, it is not clear that they were 'illegal' in Fuller's sense. They were certainly promulgated in advance, more or less non-retroactive and reasonably clear. Not only that but certain reverse discrimination laws that favour racial minorities in democratic societies exhibit the same *logic* and few have questioned their legality (see Harris, 1980, p. 132). As with other rule of law criteria, Fuller's 'inner morality' of law makes dictatorship *difficult* to square with law but not impossible. What is perhaps more surprising is that Fuller's criteria do not include conventional criteria of legality such as an independent judiciary and limitations on legislatures. One wonders quite what the advantage is in *not* making a straightforward distinction between law and morality: the natural lawyer's refusal to do this makes it that much more difficult to locate a settled meaning to the concept of law. Furthermore, an obvious difference between law and morality is that the former is often about unimportant matters (it is not important which side of the road we drive on as long as there is a rule) while the latter normally relates to significant aspects of human conduct. Yet we still require criteria for determining what law actually is.

All that can be said of natural law is the negative point that it is a rare positivist who states that law can have any content, that its validity is a function entirely of formal criteria with no reference at all to human nature or to man's ends and purposes. Even such an avowed positivist as H.L.A. Hart concedes that there is a core of basic truth in natural law and he constructs a tentative theory of 'natural law with minimum content' (Hart, 1961, pp. 189–95). This content consists in no more than those basic features of the human condition which any legal order must recognise if it is to be at all viable: such features do not constitute immutable standards of morality but rather the recognition of necessity. The approach derives from Hume (1972) who argued that such unalterable 'facts' as scarcity and limited benevolence led to the development of certain conventions and 'artificial' rules which all societies need: such rules of justice might just as well be called 'natural laws' despite their conventional origins.

Similarly Hart argues that certain 'truisms', contingent but not logically necessary truths of human nature and society, mean that there have to be some rules limiting the use of violence, rules of property, elementary forms of government and the authorisation of sanctions. They do not, however, dictate any supposed 'rational' form of legal order: the unalterable fact of scarcity means that there must be rules of property but it does not prescribe that they be either public or private forms of ownership or any particular mixture of the two. Again, under Hart's theory many oppressive laws would count as legal, and legal orders that did not fully extend legal protection to minorities could pass his technical text of validity. In fact, Hart's rules are so minimal as to make this aspect of his jurisprudence unacceptable to conventional natural law theorists.

3 Law as command

The command theory is really a rather simple theory in that it hopes to encapsulate the essence of legal phenomena in a precise definition. Austin first of all distinguished law from morality.[2] While not denying that there was an historical connection between law and morality, or that in English law one could find examples of the law expressing moral principles, he nevertheless emphatically asserted that a rule which broke a moral principle was still a rule if it emanated from a determinate sovereign, and that the moral desirability of a rule was not sufficient to make it a genuine law.

Austin defined a law as: 'a rule laid down for the guidance of an intelligent being by an intelligent being have power over him' (1954, p. 14). There are four essential elements in the structure of a municipal legal system: command, sanction, duty and sovereignty. Before looking at these properties in detail it would be wise to comment briefly on the nature of this definition, for it immediately seems to exclude some familiar types of legal phenomena – notably, customary law, international law and constitutional law. Austin called these 'laws by analogy' only; in his view the rules of international law were merely rules of positive morality since there was no sovereign with sanctions to enforce obedience to them. It has often been pointed out that Austin, by concentrating exclusively on the penal statute of the municipal legal system, systematically distorted the familiar features of legal systems.

If Austin's account of law is intended as a *definition* of law then, in a sense, it cannot be falsified, so that attempts to refute it by pointing to examples of legal systems without sovereigns are beside the point (the rules in such a system would not be 'laws'); but such a restricted stipulative definition would be of little help in understanding the wide range of legal phenomena in the world.

What distinguishes, for Austin, a command from other significations of desire is that 'the party to whom it is directed is liable to evil ... in case he comply not with desire'. What characterises the commands in a legal system is that they are backed by sanctions; they are orders backed by threats. Duty is defined then in terms of the fear of sanctions. A person is under a duty when a command is issued and it is backed by a sanction: any other explanation of duty, perhaps one deriving from morality, would be dismissed as metaphysical and irrelevant to the science of law.

The notion of sovereignty is vital to the understanding of Austin's jurisprudence. The sovereign, the author of law, is defined as that determinate person, or body of persons, to whom the bulk of the population owes habitual obedience, while he, the sovereign, owes obedience to no other person or body. A sovereign is said to be logically necessary for the existence of a legal system and must be illimitable (that is, he [it] cannot be restrained by any fundamental law) and indivisible (that is, sovereign power cannot be divided up into two or more bodies without destroying the unity of that sovereign power). It is to be noted that Austin's theory of law is a combination of two distinct elements: these are command and habitual obedience to an all-powerful sovereign. The first element (command) refers to the logical form in which laws must be cast if they are to qualify as laws, the second to a certain factual or sociological requirement for a legal system to exist, which is the fact of habitual obedience to the sovereign.

While logically all laws must emanate from the sovereign to be proper laws, Austin was obviously aware of the existence of the common law, the law created by judicial interpretation of rules from case to case. In the command theory it is recognised that the sovereign cannot be in complete control of the legal system and therefore courts appear as agents of the sovereign which, although they may create new rules in discharging their duties, nevertheless owe their existence to the will of the sovereign. Furthermore, common law is emphatically subordinate to statute law and, although its content might appear to emanate from a source other than the sovereign, the command theorists argue that it is implicitly a product of the sovereign's will since it only survives with his consent. The sovereign could repeal the whole of the common law overnight.

Many critics of the command system have argued that just because the sovereign can, as a matter of fact, repeal the whole of the common law, this does not make him its author (Hayek, 1973, pp. 45–6). The content of the common law is the product of hundreds of years of judicial reasoning, and that, according to critics of the command theory, is its virtue. For many command theorists the judiciary is responsible for the needless technicalities, illogicalities and conservative elements in the law. Bentham was especially critical of what he called 'Judge and Co.' and looked forward to a legal utopia in which judges would be deprived of discretion and reduced to the role of clerks administering a comprehensive system of law based on statute.

The common criticism levelled against Austin's command theory is that it tries to reduce all law to one type – the duty-imposing type. The criminal statute does seem to some extent to resemble this type since it lays duties upon individuals to perform, or refrain from performing, certain actions under fear of penalty. Also, the law of torts, since it involves damages for wrongful actions, could be made to fit the command model. Yet the legal system of a modern state is characterised not just by duty-imposing laws but by what are called power-conferring rules (Hart, 1961, pp. 27–33). Power-conferring laws are legal devices to enable people to do certain things such as marry, leave wills, convey property and so on. Obviously, there is no legal duty to do any of these things, but a framework of rules is required for their performance. The whole structure of civil law, which largely consists of power-conferring rules, seems not to be explicable in the command theory's terms.

A crucial error in the simple command model is its failure to account for the complex structure of legislative authority that exists in modern states. It is perfectly possible for subordinate bodies to be granted legislative power, but the constitutional rules which regulate such grants of power cannot be understood as duty-imposing laws (Hart, 1961, pp. 30–3). These rules indicate the range of activities on which the subordinate body has power to legislate. If that body should go beyond this then its legislation merely fails to take effect; it is not genuine law. Rules that determine the lawfulness of the acts of subordinate authorities do not impose duties on them in the sense defined by the command model. The rules simply impose disabilities on inferior legislative bodies. The Government of Ireland Act, passed by the Westminster Parliament in 1920, empowered the subordinate Parliament in Northern Ireland to make laws for the province subject to the conditions laid down in the 1920 Act. It would be incorrect to interpret such legal limitations as a species of command or instruction; the rules that govern subordinate legislative bodies are power-conferring rules. The granting of a devolved government to Scotland in 1998 involved precisely this.

Another major attack on the command model has centred on its central tenet that in any legal system there must be a sovereign, as the author of all law, to whom the bulk of the population owe habitual obedience, and who in turn owes obedience to no one. Early critics of the doctrine were quick to point out that it failed to explain law in federal systems where there appeared to be no one illimitable and indivisible sovereign. Also, it was pointed out that primitive societies had some form of social control through law but no sovereigns or organised sanctions; and indeed the history of medieval Europe seemed to be characterised by despotic rulers who, although they might in some sense fit the Austinian model, were not regarded as authorised to make 'law'. While these empirical refutations might appear to vitiate Austin's theory, they cannot really do so if the theory is regarded as *a definition*: in the federal example, Austinians maintain that there is a sovereign somewhere, and in other deviant cases, such as primitive society, it might be maintained that law, properly understood, does not exist.

A more effective attack on the necessity of sovereignty thesis is to explore the inner logic of the thesis to see whether it explains certain crucial features of a legal system in the context most favourable to the theory, that of the municipal legal system familiar to Western writers on jurisprudence. One of the major criticisms of the command model is that it fails to explain the element of continuity in a legal system. Austin's own experience was of a political/legal order with very few artificial 'breaks' (or revolutions) and it is this that distinguishes a system of law from the casual commands of the leader of an organised gang. Can the concept of sovereignty provide that element of persistence which clearly characterises legal orders?

As long as sovereignty is defined solely in terms of *power*, which itself, according to the command theory, generates legitimacy, it is clear that it cannot do the job assigned to it. Hobbes, the originator of the command theory, was aware of the difficulty of transmitting sovereign power from one person (or body) to another. He says that, in the question of succession, the sovereign indicates or *points to* his successor and the authority of the new sovereign is a consequence of the power of the incumbent (Hobbes, 1968, pp. 247–9). But, in the sovereign power model, the obligation of the citizens is owed to the person who indicates the successor, not the successor himself. Once the sovereign dies the authority of his commands dies with him. In fact the sovereignty model which identifies authority by reference to *persons* rather than rules or procedures, entails a legal hiatus every time a sovereign dies or is replaced.

There are further problems in the sovereignty thesis, which are of relevance not only to Austin's jurisprudence but to political theory in general. There is the confusion between *de jure* sovereignty, the formalised legal claim to supreme legislative power, and *de facto* sovereignty, the actual exercise of power. As Dicey and other later theorists of sovereignty recognised, the two may not always be in the same hands; Parliament might be the supreme legislative power but it might be, as a matter of fact, dictated to by some outside body. Austin, by defining sovereignty in terms of habitual obedience, cannot properly explain the situation in which a supreme legislative power habitually obeys some other powerful body, yet the commands of the latter are not, properly speaking, law and it is not therefore a *de jure* sovereign. Austin was not much interested in sociological questions about the factual basis of sovereignty even though his theory of validity partly turns on this.

The theory of illimitable sovereignty breaks down because it cannot admit constitutions into the explanation of law. According to Austin, a sovereign cannot be limited by positive law since he is the author of all law, therefore constitutional law is not really law. This must follow because in Austin's theory the existence of a legal limitation implies the existence of a duty, and no sovereign can be under a duty. But even an extreme sovereignty theorist must admit some *procedural* considerations into the understanding of a legal system, since what counts as a sovereign is an important question. There must be some minimal rules to determine who the sovereign is. The question 'what is Parliament?' has turned out to be a very real one in the past 40 years in legal systems which are nominally of the sovereignty type. Also, it makes perfect sense to speak of the procedural rules that govern sovereignty while accepting that there are no formal limitations on the substantive content of the acts of the sovereign. Since Austin rejected constitutional law on *a priori* grounds there is no way of distinguishing between the *public* and *private* acts of the sovereign in his system (Raz, 1970, p. 38).

In fact, it is perfectly in order to speak of legal limitations on sovereign authority, as the existence of constitutional government has amply demonstrated: general rules may limit supreme legislatures or divide up legislative authority between a number of bodies, as in a federal system. The existence of legislative *supremacy* does not logically imply the existence of a sovereign because this exclusive law-making power can still be subject to rules. But since Austin saw laws only as the duty-imposing type he thought there must be some *ultimate* sovereign behind all complex rule structures.

In the United States, for example, he thought that there must be a sovereign somehow 'behind' the Constitution and he located it in the peculiar, 'aggregate body' that amends the Constitution – two-thirds of Congress and three-quarters of the states' legislatures. But it is surely eccentric to attribute sovereignty to a body that exercises legislative power so rarely. Furthermore, there is one clause in the American Constitution that cannot be amended.[3] Even the British system, which superficially resembles the Austinian model, is, as the author of the command theory had to admit, difficult to represent accurately in terms of the sovereign power model. Since the composition of Parliament is partly the product of the electoral process, Austin claimed that the real sovereign in Britain is the electorate. It is, however, extremely difficult to conceive of the electorate as a 'sovereign' in the original sense of the term (Hart, 1961, p. 76), that is as one determinate body issuing orders to the general population – owing a duty to it. It is true that Bentham's version of the theory (Bentham, 1970b) is more sophisticated than Austin's but it does not substantially change the logic of that jurisprudence.

The problem with the command theory is that it is not only positivist in that it separates law from morality; it is also positivist in the sense that it explains the existence of a legal system in terms of observable sanctions. It cannot explain legal systems in the language of rules since rules which authorise and validate claims to authority are not strictly observable in the way that commands backed up by sanctions may be said to be. The problem goes back to Hobbes, the originator of the theory, who regarded rules as ghostly or metaphysical entities that could not possibly create legal obligations in the way that the command of a sovereign with sanctions could. Yet, as we have seen, the idea of rules, the obligatory nature of which cannot be explained in terms of sanctions, is logically necessary for the explanation of the transmission of legal authority.

There are other positivist theories of law which, in their different ways, misunderstand the nature and purposes of rules in the explanation of a legal order. One of the most interesting for the political theorist is American realism. This is because the advocates of the theory not only attempted to give a 'scientific' explanation of law but were also eager to show how law could be used as a method of social control.

4 Legal realism

Realism began at the turn of the century as a reaction against the formalism of all types of European jurisprudence which saw the judicial decision as a logical deduction from a general rule. In contrast, American realism focused attention on the independent role that the courts have in law creation, the sociological factors that determine the judicial decision and the use to which the law can be put for social control if the right sort of empirical knowledge of society is available.

It was not surprising that scepticism about the binding nature of rules should emerge in the United States since that country's federal system gives a much greater opportunity for judicial legislation than does a country like Britain, which is characterised by parliamentary sovereignty and a limited role for judicial review. Since the Supreme Court can declare that a Congressional statute, or one from a state legislature, is unconstitutional and therefore invalid, it has considerable influence in determining the shape of a government's law and policy. Because of what Hart has called the 'open texture' of law (Hart, 1961, pp. 121 7), the fact that particular legal rules are at points indeterminate so that disputes inevitably arise as to what they mean and where they should apply, the formal model of the judicial decision as an axiomatic deduction from a general rule is clearly inadequate. It was, in effect, the 'open texture' of law that provided what intellectual justification there was for Justice Holmes's (1897, p. 461) famous statement that 'the prophecies of what the courts will do in fact, and nothing more pretentious, are what I mean by the law'. Holmes also called this the 'bad man's' view of law, meaning that people are interested in the likely decision of a particular court and that this fact is a much more significant determinant of behaviour than understanding a rule.

There are really two major aspects of American realism: an intellectual approach to the study of jurisprudence, and a sociologically-based use of law as an instrument of social control. The intellectual approach, from Holmes, was that rules were only useful as aids to the prediction of court decisions. The important point, however, is that most realists stressed that court decisions were less predictable if the observer were to rely *only* on the rules of law. The attempt was made therefore to find uniformities or regularities in actual judicial behaviour. It is this that constituted the 'brute empiricism' or positivism of some realists in that laws lost their normative character in setting standards and prescribing conduct and were treated as observable 'facts' for the purpose of scientific investigation.

The other feature of realism, which is about the use of law in social engineering, also in a sense derives from Holmes. It would appear to be the realists' view that the law should be concerned with social policy, that it must be appropriate for the needs of a developing and changing society: the lawyer, therefore, must be equipped with the relevant empirical knowledge. A classic instance of Holmes's general approach is his dissenting opinion in *Lochner* v. *New York* (1905), a case in which the Supreme Court declared a statute limiting the number of hours a person may work in a bakery unconstitutional (see Lloyd, 1972, pp. 432–3). Holmes argued that 'The Fourteenth Amendment does not enact Mr. Herbert Spencer's *Social Statics*': and to the suggestion that the statute violated liberty, Holmes said that the court was constantly interfering with personal liberty and would continue to do so in the light of social needs and purposes. Holmes's views represented not just a rejection of the mechanistic jurisprudence provided by a strict rules model of law, but also the *individualism* that the traditional common law embodies. Holmes was, in fact, a utilitarian who recognised the social functions of law. But this does not mean that he thought that rules should be lightly cast aside. A utilitarian can recognise some consequentialist value in rule-following, at least to guarantee some predictability, even though she would not treat rules with the same respect as formalists do. However, many have associated the rise of legal realism in the United States with the transition from an extremely individualistic society to a more collectivist society with considerable central authority in the economy and in welfare, health and housing (see Siegan, 1980).[4]

The lasting contribution that American realism made to jurisprudence was its stress on that lacuna or gap between the description of the rules, statutes, cases and so on that are relevant to the judicial decision and the decision itself. In formalistic jurisprudence that gap is relatively small, the legal decision is an inference from a general rule to a particular case: and it was this that (allegedly) provided 'certainty' and predictability in the law. The sociologists of law attempted to provide a surrogate for this in empirical, behavioural investigations of judicial decision-making. The effect of this, however, is to eliminate the autonomy of law and to make order in society something other than the product of the 'governance of rules'. Other legal theorists, desirous of retaining the autonomy of law, have endeavoured to fill the gap by the invocation of certain principles of interpretation which extend the notion of legality beyond the description of rules. Either way, such theorising tends to cast doubt on the possibility of law having a settled meaning.

5 Legal systems as systems of rules

The dominant theory of law in Western democracies has probably been that which understands a legal system as, in some sense or other, a *system of rules*. The clearest exposition of this view is in H.L.A. Hart's *The Concept of Law* (1961). Of course, it is *not* a truism to say that a legal system consists of a system of rules, since we have already seen two important theories that deny this – the command theory and the realist theory. In fact Hart's theory of law emerges from a criticism of these two theories since both were deficient in that they ignored the *internal* aspect of rules (see Chapter 1). It would follow that the rules theory is not merely a doctrine of jurisprudence but an attempt to describe the general features of a legal system in the context of a general theory of society. Thus Hart is not concerned with 'real definition', the delineation of the necessary and sufficient conditions for the use of the word 'law', but with reproducing the main features of a municipal legal system. It is for this reason that Hart, although he is a legal positivist in the sense of separating law from morality, insists that law must have some purpose. Certain enduring features of man and society make some sorts of rules essential.

Arising out of the criticism of the command theory of law came a distinction between duty-imposing and power-conferring rules. As we have seen, this is the distinction between rules that prescribe certain courses of conduct as obligatory (as, for example, the criminal law does) and those that *enable* individuals, or public authorities, to pursue certain courses of action. Hart makes a further distinction between primary and secondary rules and uses this to explain the foundations of a legal system. However, certain critics have suggested that there is some inconsistency in his analysis in that it is not clear whether power-conferring rules are primary or secondary rules (Sartorius, 1971, pp. 136–8).

The 'key' to jurisprudence is described as the 'union of primary and secondary rules'. The primary rules, such as systems of criminal and civil law, set standards and regulate behaviour and therefore provide the 'content' of a legal system, while secondary rules, such as rules that govern legislatures and courts, are concerned with the primary rules themselves (Hart, 1961, pp. 77–9). While it is true that a society could maintain itself by a system of primary rules alone, and many have done so, such a system has three major disadvantages: uncertainty, which means that there is no mechanism for determining disputed rules; the fact that in a system consisting of primary rules alone change is slow; and the fact that such a system lacks an agency for determining conclusively the case of a breach of the rules (Hart, 1961, p. 92). To remedy these deficiencies, Hart says that a mature legal system will develop secondary rules of adjudication and change, and rules for the determination of transgressions of the primary rules. Thus there will be a rule of *recognition*, an ultimate constitutional rule which will determine the validity of primary rules, rules governing the operation of legislatures or other institutions empowered to introduce new primary rules, and rules authorising courts to make decisions concerning breaches of rules (Hart, 1961, pp. 92–3).

Hart (1961, ch. 6) maintains that the step from a primitive society governed by only primary rules to a more complex system that includes secondary rules is as important a step for mankind as the invention of the wheel. A more helpful analogy for the social theorist might be the invention of money. Just as the use of a common medium of exchange frees people from inconveniences and inefficiencies of a barter economy, so the discovery of secondary rules removes the uncertainties, insecurities and wasteful expenditure in decentralised systems of rule enforcement, which characterise systems consisting only of primary rules. Furthermore, the theorist does not have to observe primitive societies because she can mentally reconstruct what a society would look like without secondary rules or money in order to appreciate their importance.

The most important single feature of Hart's doctrine is the rule of recognition, which functions as a replacement of the Austinian concept of a sovereign to settle the question of validity in a legal system. In a mature legal system there must be some ultimate rule by which the validity of subordinate rules can be tested. The rule of parliamentary sovereignty, where the final authority of law is located in the will of parliament, is an example of a simple rule of recognition, the American Constitution is an example of an extremely complex one. It is to be noted that the rule of recognition is not itself a rule of law, like the law of contract, but is a rule by which the validity of subordinate rules can be established. It is a rule which has to be internalised by the courts, so that their interpretation of its meaning is the key to validity. Although it is a secondary rule it imposes a duty on judicial personnel; in the sense that it must be applied by them so that disputes about what is or is not law may be authoritatively resolved. In a mature legal system the bulk of the population obeys the rules more or less unthinkingly (in the manner described by Austin) but a crucial role is played by the judiciary. It is its interpretive activity which provides continuity in a legal system; in the crude sovereignty model power has to exist before there can be legality, yet in an ongoing legal order legal authority obtains in the absence of power. Of course, this is not to deny that legal systems may break down, that the rules, although formally valid, are no longer internalised. In such circumstances, the sovereign power model comes into its own. But this is a feature of temporary 'moments' in judicial history rather than a description of an ongoing legal *order* which is dependent on authority rather than power.

Thus, although the notion of parliamentary sovereignty looks as if it fits the Austinian system this is not so. For the validity of the statement that 'whatever parliament wills is law' depends on the prior acceptance of that rule. Parliament cannot create that rule by command because we could then ask – what makes that valid? Parliament's commands are the highest form of law, superior to common law, because the courts since the eighteenth century accepted (and, indeed, developed) a rule of recognition that authorised sovereignty. The rule of recognition cannot itself be tested for validity since it is used by the courts as a test of all claims to law.

There is, however, something of a problem for Hart's theory of validity since the courts both use the rule of recognition as a touchstone for legality and to some extent determine its evolution. The rule of recognition may change over time through judicial activity and the continuity of a legal system may depend on whether the population 'obeys' various judicial innovations. An intriguing, and politically important, example of a change in the rule (or rules) of recognition has occurred as a consequence of Britain's entry into the European Community (now Union). It is apparent that the original notion of parliamentary sovereignty no longer properly describes the structure of law in this country (see Barry, N., 1994a). In certain areas, European law now takes precedence over domestic law as a result of the signing of the Treaty of Rome, and subsequent European agreements. It is true that all of this has been embodied in parliamentary statutes, the most important of these is the European Communities Act (1972), so that the original rule of recognition was complied with, but later developments have brought about significant constitutional changes. The most important of these is the fact that the distinctive property of the rule of parliamentary sovereignty, that no one parliament can bind another, no longer holds. Whereas in the past a later statute implicitly repealed an earlier statute if there were a conflict between the two, this is no longer so: European legal rights which are embodied in the 1972 Act cannot be abrogated by a later statute. This was illustrated in the *Factortame* case in which a 1988 British statute denied foreign European citizens' rights guaranteed under European law. In a later case, the House of Lords reaffirmed the change in the rule of recognition when it disallowed an employment statute because it was held to be inconsistent with certain equality provisions of European law.[5] From these judicial rulings, it is clear that the British Parliament no longer displays the kind of sovereignty described by Dicey.

It is impossible to predict constitutional developments in Britain. Political disquiet at the increasing encroachment of European legislation on the domestic legal system may well increase so that the original rule of recognition, which entailed more or less full parliamentary sovereignty, is restored. Still, none of these developments can be explained in terms of the crude sovereign 'power' model; legal phenomena can be understood only in terms of the rules that govern political change and since these rules may often be fuzzy or indeterminate at the edges there will be inevitably an important role for the judiciary. As the significance of sovereignty diminishes in the British legal system it is likely to become more controversial because the determination of what is law has become more politicised as a result of Britain's European involvement. Still, none of this affects the positivist's claim that formal criteria alone are sufficient to determine validity, it just makes the task of the courts more complex.

6 Principles, rules and the law

The major contemporary rival to Hart's theory of law, that of Ronald Dworkin (1977, 1986), explicitly puts the judiciary at the forefront of the legal process and assigns to it a more directly political role. In a sustained attack on legal positivism Dworkin maintains that: 'Law is deeply ... and thoroughly political. Lawyers and judges cannot avoid politics in the broad sense of political theory' (1986, p. 146). It is not meant that judges should take an ideological or party political stance but that in their interpretative activity they must necessarily invoke broadly shared moral and political principles. He denies that validity is determined by an appeal to an hierarchy of rules, headed by a rule of recognition, and argues that legality is a matter of determining the principles that underlie, and give meaning to, the formal statements of the rules. This is not an old-fashioned natural law theory, which would make validity turn upon the supposed dictates of a universal morality, but rather a claim to the effect that legal systems cannot be properly understood without the invocations of moral values which are embedded in a social order.

This is so, it is claimed, because of 'hard cases', – that is, those cases where either no rule at all applies or the rules are simply unclear. In such circumstances, positivists say that the judiciary simply invents new rules and makes innovative decisions which are not initially sanctioned by the legislature or by precedent. Positivists argue that judges should base their decisions on the kind of principles that would secure general social agreement, and perhaps they ought to anticipate what the legislature would have done but, nevertheless, they insist that there are gaps in the legal system which are filled by a certain kind of creativity. It is, of course, true that the common law develops in this way and it inevitably involves a certain amount of retroactivity since litigants cannot know in advance what the law is. However, hard cases constitute a minute portion of the law so it still consists broadly of a predictable structure of rules.

However, Dworkin's argument is that, although a legal system is complex, there are no cases for which there is not a right answer; it is autonomous in the sense that its integrity does not depend on the invocation of extra-legal criteria. Although legal systems consist of rules and principles and although principles are logically a part of the legal order, there are distinctions between the two phenomena which are vital, he claims, for a proper understanding of law. Rules are precise and it is possible to enumerate the applications of a rule, while principles are necessarily imprecise and must be 'weighed'. Further-more, principles do not merely dictate a particular decision but suggest reasons or justifications for a decision. A legal principle, unlike a rule, may not apply in all cases. An example of a principle he gives is: 'no man may profit from his own wrongs' (Dworkin, 1977, ch. 2). Dworkin then shows that it may or may not apply in particular cases, and this will be a matter of judicial interpretation. Judges are necessarily indulging in political theory in making their decisions, in that they will weigh principles and balance one against another. However, their interpretive power does not mean they have complete freedom, for the principles, which reflect prevailing constitutional standards, do control what they do, and judges' decisions are always subject to criticism. Dworkin claims that the complexity of a legal system cannot be described by the model of rules and that the idea of a master rule, the rule of recognition, as a determinant of validity, cannot possibly be applied to principles (Dworkin, 1977, pp. 39–45). Principles do not form a hierarchy, with one superior principle determining the validity of subordinate ones, but they are necessary if law is to be properly autonomous.

Dworkin, however, distorts the function of rules in society by suggesting that the distinction between rules and principles turns upon the fact that all the applications of a rule can be specified. But this is not so. All rules may to some extent reveal indeterminacies but the virtue of a legal system in which the judiciary, in interpreting parti-cular rules, is nevertheless controlled by more general rules and procedures lies in the fact that this makes life more predictable for citizens.[6] By admitting necessarily vague and imprecise principles into law, and arguing that decision-making in law can only take place by reference to a general political theory so that legal rules become a species of moral rules, Dworkin's approach comes close to destroying the distinction between politics and law. This becomes apparent when his set of principles turns out to be a radical conception of liberal rights which are often invoked against positive legislation. Yet Dwor-kin insists that judges do not reach out for extra-legal criteria in hard cases but make decisions, according to principles, which can be assessed as right or wrong. The only area in which judges do not have wide interpretative powers is in public policy because here he assumes that no fundamental constitutional rights or principles are at stake.

Dworkin's jurisprudence appears to derive from the political liberal-ism outlined in Chapter 1. His adherence to the idea that law is an arena in which individuals claim rights, which 'trump' considerations of utility or majoritarianism, seems to differentiate him clearly from communitarians who would be highly sceptical of the value of this kind of heavy legalism. Writers from the communitarian left are especially critical of the pre-eminent role ascribed to judges in the determination of complex problems and the lack of consideration that Dworkin gives to the sociology of the judiciary. However, he ultimately *founds* rights and principles on the idea of community. He claims that 'collective agencies, such as courts, take actions which are identified and individuated as those of the community as a whole, rather than of members of the community as individuals' (Dworkin, 1986, p. 146). In fact, he has to do this, otherwise the judiciary would have more or less complete discretion in the determination of hard cases.

It may be doubted, however, whether the community can be uncontroversially invoked as a source of rights. Dworkin's examples are mainly drawn from America, whose written Constitution (and Bill of Rights) is in parts so ambiguously worded that competing claims to rights regularly arise. In the famous *Roe* v. *Wade* (1973) case which created the constitutional right to abortion (deriving from a controversial 'right to privacy'), it is not easy to argue that this was an expression of the law, as opposed to a piece of judicial creativity. Indeed, a convinced communitarian might plausibly argue that under the American federal system the component states had, prior to *Roe*, expressed their views on this intractable issue; some had very liberal abortion laws, others were extremely restrictive. Perhaps the reason why the issue became so intractable was that both sides conducted the argument in terms of rights, which have such compelling force. Both the 'right to life' and the 'right to choose' protagonists could appeal to the Fourteenth Amendment to the Constitution (which forbids the states abrogating the right to life, liberty and property without due process of law).

Dworkin's jurisprudence no doubt has considerable plausibility in the American context, where judicial interpretation is likely to be very much influenced by conceptions of rights: though even there positivists might well question an approach that grants to judges an authority which often seems to compete with that of legislatures. In other jurisdictions, especially those which do not have such a potent institution of judicial review, it is less convincing. In these jurisdictions the distinction between law and policy, on which Dworkin's jurisprudence ultimately depends, is much harder to sustain. One modest

normative implication of the positivist's approach is that the predictability and certainty of a legal order are more likely to be preserved
(though, of course, these properties can never be absolutely guaranteed) if morality is not used to influence the determination of what the
law is. The positivist does not underestimate the importance of judicial
interpretation but she would deny that this has to be made in more or
less overriding moral terms. We have already noted judicial activity in
the development of the rule of recognition but this has little to do with
ethics. It has, however, everything to do with validity and the distinction between legal and other types of social control.

7 The rule of law

The recent interest in the rule of law is not entirely a result of the
collapse of legality in the communist world, for the believers in the
doctrine also say that much milder policies of welfare and planning
may bring about totalitarian results not intended by the authors of the
schemes. It is argued that the substantial increase in state activity in
Western countries in the last 40 years has not only had economic
consequences but also has subtly changed the nature of the kind of
legal systems operating in these societies. Instead of a society's legal
system being characterised by a set of general rules which enables
individuals to pursue their private plans with reasonable security and
predictability, it is said that the collectivised delivery of welfare
services (health, education, pensions and so on) brings about a vast
increase in *public* law, the law that authorises officials to carry out
public plans. Such law invests these officials with great discretionary
power over individuals (Hayek, 1960, ch. 17).

The rule of law doctrine then appears to be not unlike the natural
law doctrine in that it provides for the critical evaluation of existing
laws. But unlike traditional natural law doctrines it does not so much
base this evaluation on a set of external moral norms, held to be
objectively true, as on a consideration of the *procedural* requirements
that a purported law must satisfy if it is to be law. Thus the positivist's
rule of recognition in the legal system could be assessed by the criteria
contained in the rule of law doctrine. Indeed, the rule of parliamentary
sovereignty has been specifically criticised as being incompatible with
the rule of law since it invests more or less unlimited authority in one
institution. Implicit in the rule of law doctrine is a distinction between
law and the state. The argument is that legal systems develop

spontaneously those rules required for the protection of free exchanges between individuals and do not require the coercive power of the state to validate them. The common law tradition is perhaps the best example of this and it contrasts strongly with the command theory which specifically locates validity in the will of the sovereign.

The aim of the rule of law doctrine is that citizens should know how laws will affect them. The main elements of the doctrine can be briefly summarised (Hayek, 1960, pp. 153–61; Lucas, 1966, pp. 106–17; Raz, 1977). Laws should be perfectly *general* in form so that no individual or group is specifically picked out for preferential treatment; they should treat people equally; they should not be retrospective in application; and all laws should bind everyone, including government. This last point links the idea of the rule of law to the idea of *constitutionalism* and may be exemplified by systems of government that have a rigorous separation of powers, written constitutions and other devices to limit the actions of officials by general rules. It should be clear that the doctrine is, in principle, in conflict with the notion of sovereignty as traditionally understood since in a sovereignty system, although the unlimited power of parliament is authorised by the rule of recognition, the legislative body is permitted to do things which are in conflict with the rule of law. The demands for a written constitution in Britain are essentially demands to put the legislature under the rule of law. The sovereignty of parliament provides for technical validity only: it is quite compatible with laws that violate conventional moral standards.

It is, however, extremely difficult to formulate a set of criteria of the rule of law which would entirely eliminate arbitrary legislation. It has often been pointed out that it is possible to formulate perfectly general laws in such a way that they do pick out individuals for special treatment; in a mainly Protestant country a law forbidding Sunday sport may be perfectly general, yet it discriminates against Roman Catholics, who normally play sport on a Sunday. Furthermore, as noted above, there is an unavoidable element of retroactivity in common law systems since the inevitable uncertainty in them means that not all rules can be known in advance. A more traditional natural lawyer (such as Fuller) might claim that it is not enough merely to look at the *form* in which a law is cast – one must also examine its *content* in order to adjudicate on its 'legality'.

In addition to this problem, collectivist critics would argue that, so far from being a 'neutral' criterion of legality, the rule of law doctrine, as described by writers like F. A. Hayek (1960, ch. x), is necessarily linked to the capitalist market economy with its associated system of private property rights. The point here is that many legal theorists see the rule of law as exemplified best in the common law and are distrustful of the extensive intrusion of public and statutory law into the legal world that has occurred throughout the twentieth century (see Barry, N., 1988b). The common law in principle is a set of rules that has emerged largely through case law (contract, torts and much of the criminal law) to settle, primarily, disputes between *individuals*: it is, in fact, what lawyers tend to mean by the 'law'. But since perfectly acceptable legal orders can exist without some, or even all of these properties, it would be wrong to associate legality with this notion of the rule of law. The latter could be said to be a complete social philosophy, covering economics, property and rights, rather than a description of lawfulness. From this perspective, the rule of law represents a particular normative idea which competes with other social purposes (which are equally capable of being achieved lawfully).

Still there are interesting claims to be made on behalf of this concept of the rule of law. It is often thought to be efficient in the economist's sense (see Posner, 1990, ch. 12). Thus, the law of contract enables individuals to make agreements with some security and predictability. The law of torts, by imposing damages for wrongful actions, has the effect of both encouraging individual responsibility for action and restoring harmed individuals to the position they were in before the wrongful action took place. Whether the common law adjudication processes are more 'efficient' than public law and regulation is not perhaps a question of jurisprudence but more of economics. For it is obvious that efficiency is not the sole aim of a legal system. Indeed, Dworkin's conception of the rule of law expands the notion of mere legality by adding a strong conception of rights, some of which – such as those to do with equal opportunities and affirmative action – have little to do with efficiency. The rule of law, then, turns out not to be a neutral concept at all but is highly contestable.

The justification of the intrusion of public law into the realm of private actions inevitably involves the question of the role of the state in modern society. The remedy for the deficiencies of the common law/private rights system – its failure to provide genuine public services and its apparent protection of purely private activities – has always been found in the state. Although it is conceptually possible to distinguish between law and state, in that theoretically legal rules do not have to emanate from political authorities (and historically they have developed autonomously on many occasions), in the modern world 'state' and 'law' have become intertwined. Again the analysis of state and law is unavoidably normative, perhaps ideological, for it is the case that those who make the conceptual distinction between the two phenomena do so for a political reason, i.e. it is maintained that the modern tendency for public law, emanating from often capricious legislatures, to replace private law, especially in the realms of welfare and planning, attenuates the predictability and stability that are thought to be features of common law systems. But the implication of the preceding analysis is that the question of the role of the state has to be discussed on substantive economic and moral grounds. It is not answered by conceptual analysis of law alone (as Hayek seemed to imply).

8 Radical legal doctrines and the rule of law

The ideal of the rule of law has been compromised in recent years not just by communism and welfarism but by doctrines in the West that seem to strike at the very heart of what we conventionally understand by legality and its role in maintaining a free and predictable social order. I refer in particular to Critical Legal Studies and feminism (see Posner, 1990, ch. 13). Both of these legal philosophies reject the idea that conventional legality can guarantee fairness and impartiality; they maintain that legal rules do little more than preserve some hegemonic power system. In Critical Legal Studies it is the prevailing property and class system that a bogus 'legality' protects while in feminist legal theory it is male dominance that is subtly masked by judicial forms.

   Although Critical Legal Studies looks, superficially, as if it is another version of Marxism, its roots are in fact in American jurisprudence, specifically the realist doctrine which was considered earlier. It will be recalled that in realism it is maintained that law is not a system of rules that are mechanically applied but it is actually created by an active judiciary in hard cases. Because of the gap between the rule and the decision the judge was authorised to use sociological and other material to reach a verdict, and hence create a new rule. Critical Legal Studies goes a lot further and claims that the radical uncertainty, subjectivism and indeterminism of legal processes means that legal decisions are not the product of objective reasoning; they will inevitably reflect the class interests of the judges, and those of the ruling class. Even when they clearly do not, especially in civil cases where the rise of tort law in America has adversely affected business interests, the aberrant cases are explained away as part of the subtle process of deception by that class; a mere veneer of legality is preserved by judges occasionally finding against their class interest. Indeed, many Critical Legal Studies writers (Boyle, 1985) argue that legal reasoning can support either side in a dispute; the law dictates no incontrovertible solution. There is something of the postmodernist[7] in these theories – they argue that because hard cases exist, for which no easy solution is possible, the whole of law must be a mass of uncertainty, and the discretion that the common law gives to the judiciary promotes and reinforces an inevitable subjectivism. It is interesting to note here that a main target of the Critical Legal Studies is Dworkin: although his radical reading of legal materials has angered conservatives at least he stresses the integrity and autonomy of law. But as Kennedy (1982, p. 47) claims: 'There is never a "correct legal solution" that is other than the correct ethical and political solution to that legal problem.' All law is politics.

If there is any persuasiveness about this movement it derives entirely from the fact, which had been noted by conventional philosophers of law, that there can be no mechanical legal process, all legal decisions of any significance involve a certain 'creativity'. Indeed, at the foundational level there is some similarity between Critical Legal Studies and legal economics. For, although they come up with diametrically opposed positions with regard to policy, both depend on the invocation of extra-legal principles in their understanding of law. For example, the economists interpret the process in efficiency terms and think that hard cases should be decided in accordance with the maximisation of aggregate utility with no reference to social justice. But if legal processes are characterised by radical uncertainty and if conventional rules can do no more than affirm the prevailing distribution of property, what other doctrine is to provide the intellectual material for the settlement of disputes, which will occur in any society? Followers of Critical Legal Studies make occasional reference to the community as the solvent for the familiar legal conundrums. But such is the variety, and sometimes spectacular indeterminacy, of communitarian thought that it is difficult to imagine that it could play a constructive role in law. Indeed, Critical Legal Studies has had very little direct influence on the American judicial process.

In feminism, we find a similar rejection of conventional law but here the doubt about legality is not quite so pronounced. It is not that feminists deny the applicability of law and legal principles to the human predicament, it is that they offer a different – and competing – selection of them. It is not that feminist legal theory concentrates on exclusively women's issues, such as childbirth, the law of rape and so on, since it also focuses attention on more general themes. The emphasis here is on legal language and the masculine bias of the legal process. This masculine approach to law, which perhaps derives from legal positivism (Posner, 1990, pp. 404–5), is almost exclusively concerned with abstractions such as rights, duties, responsibilities, liabilities and so on. And, furthermore, male legalism (*pace* Critical Legal Studies) deals with determinate solutions to legal problems by the invocation of a general rule. Such universal rules are applied irrespective of the nuances of the case. Feminist ethical theory is very much concerned with particularities, special facts about an issue which are not captured, or appreciated by a general rule. Conventionally law, for example in a tort case, deals with only who has the right to recover and does not deal with facts which might make a moral difference. Of course, the special difficulties that women face have a special resonance for this view of law. Feminist law tends to derive from feminist ethics so that its legal theorists adopt the ethics of care, favoured by Carol Gilligan (1982). Robin West (1988) recommends an empathic approach, by which the legal agents would familiarise themselves with, and understand from an internal point of view, the issues at stake and the personalities involved in a legal case.

In fact, this approach is not exclusively feminist for many men, both theorists and practitioners, have favoured a less universalist style of legal reasoning. As a doctrine, utilitarianism is specifically concerned with the calculation of aggregate happiness and the promotion of this demands that formal legal rights should give way to this maximand if the occasion demands. And, in practice, the potential rigour of contract has been ameliorated by the invocation of special conditions that have to be satisfied if an agreement is to be validated. But the problem with the particularist approach to law is that if it were taken as a serious guide to judicial decision-making there are limits to the range of people who are to be subject to our feelings of empathy – they tend to extend not much beyond family and close friends. And law has to operate by general rules if it is to be a consistent and predictable system. A certain formality is the unavoidable price that we have to pay for the preservation of the rule of law. This indispensable condition of civility is vulnerable to the potential depredations of Critical Legal Studies and feminist law. Of particular importance here is the belief that both schools seem to have – that human nature can somehow be changed.[8] But the great achievement of conventional legal orders is that they have developed appropriate responses and institutional protection from the sometimes malign effects of a more or less unchanging human nature.

What is crucially important for law is the role played by rules in the reduction of uncertainty. All human interaction is conducted in a context of doubt about future events, about the consequences of human, especially political, action and about the changes that are likely to occur in the technology that confronts agents. If there is an established rule to guide conduct we know that there is some security – that contracts will be kept and that damages will be awarded for harms caused. They provide an essential incentive structure for normally self-interested agents.

Of course, it might be the case that some greater social advantage might be achieved by the relaxation of rules, as Critical Legal Studies and feminist jurisprudence might suggest, but there is considerable risk attached to such an abandonment of the modest utility provided by a commitment to established practices. Women ought to be especially aware of the social advantages of a rule-governed society, for they have most to lose from any relaxation of strict standards of impartiality, legal phenomena which took so long to achieve.

3
The State

1 The state in political philosophy

Despite the emphasis on the state in the history of political philosophy, the twentieth century has been characterised by a remarkable lack of philosophical reflection on the concept. Until recently analytical philosophy had eschewed those evaluative arguments about political obligation and the limits of state authority that were typical of political theory in the past in favour of the explication of the meaning of the concept. However, even here the results have been disappointing. Empiricists' attempts to locate some unique phenomenon which the word state described proved unsuccessful, and indeed led to the odd conclusion that there was nothing about the state that distinguished it from some other social institutions. For example, its coercive power was said to be not unique: in some circumstances, trade unions and churches exercised similar power over their members. Ordinary language philosophers were far more interested in the complexities that surround words such as law, authority and power than in the state. In all this there was perhaps the fear that to concentrate attention on the *state* was implicitly to give credence to the discredited doctrine that it stood for some metaphysical entity; propositions about which could not be translated into propositions about the actions of *individuals*, and which represented higher values than those of ordinary human agents.

In all this, political philosophy was in an unconscious alliance with empirical political science: a discipline which has been obsessively anxious to dissolve political phenomena into readily observable 'facts' about groups, parties and other agencies whose behaviour was thought to be explicable, in principle, by testable theories. Yet to do so is surely to drain modern politics of its most salient features, since our understanding of it is not exhausted by a mere description of the actions of particular authorities. For authorities, governments and officials act under rules of an association, the state, which are quite

57

different from other associations and hence there is a task for political philosophy to unravel the meaning of such rules. Thus although in the notorious Clive Ponting case (Peele, 1986) the court ruled that, in the context of the Official Secrets Act, government actions should be treated as the actions of the state, this was merely a legal convenience. It prevented the defence arguing that a betrayal of government secret information was not an action against the state, but it did not, of course, tell us anything about the state.

Despite the absence of any philosophical guidance, we do in normal speech, and in political argument especially, refer to the state as if it were an institution, or perhaps complex of institutions, qualitatively different from others in society. The existence of a state is not self-justifying, as is perhaps the case with a system of law. Although one can obviously protest at *particular* laws on the ground that they are not consonant with certain moral principles, it would be odd to suggest that we could do without a system of rules of some kind. The briefest reflections on the human condition suggest the necessity for some form of regulation: indeed, the concept of society implies a distinction between rule-governed, and hence more or less predictable action, and haphazard, unco-ordinated and *asocial* behaviour. The unalterable 'facts' of scarcity, ignorance, vulnerability and so on dictate the necessity for some rules, whatever their substantive content. But do those 'facts' dictate the necessity of a *state*?

Thus the most casual observation of the features of the modern state, such as determinate boundaries, centralised authority, the claim (not always successful) to a monopoly of coercion, and the assumption of the power of law creation (or sovereignty) suggests an *artifice* or contrivance which stands in need of some external justification (from ethics and perhaps political economy) rather than something intrinsic to the nature of man. The very fact that most states are a product of force, as Hume argued, suggests this. Indeed, historically in Western Europe the state is a comparative latecomer, not really emerging until the sixteenth and seventeenth centuries. Prior to that, social relationships were regulated by customary law, the remnants of Roman Law and Christian natural law. The idea that law could be deliberately created by a centralised agency was alien to the medieval mind; as indeed was the notion even of a 'country'. Again, anthropologists have vividly described 'stateless' societies (Krader, 1968): communities regulated by law, and even characterised by rudimentary forms of 'government', yet lacking those specific features of statehood I have just adumbrated.

For what is so characteristic of empirical states is political *inequality*; the existence of a public set of rules that authorise some individuals to perform actions not permitted to others, the authority to tax, conscript individuals into an army and, perhaps more significantly, to make law. The philosophical anarchist R. P. Wolff (1976) argues that the state must be illegitimate since its existence implies the authority to give commands and orders simply because it is the state. Yet obedience to such orders cannot be a moral action (although it is presumably prudential) because it would necessarily be an attenuation of personal autonomy; to submit to authority merely because it is the state's is to eliminate moral freedom in the Kantian sense.[1]

However, the above reflections on the problems of the state may be said to be seriously deficient in that they illicitly pose the question of legitimacy in terms favourable to an individualistic methodology – that is, the state appears as an alien entity, the justification for which depends on it being consonant with traditional liberal values of choice and freedom. Thus, so far from an account of the modern state in terms of the public nature of its rules, determinate nature of its boundaries, sovereignty and so on, being a 'neutral' definition, which leaves us free to evaluate its actions by reference to other principles, such as economic efficiency or human rights, it is actually already loaded with contentious assumptions about the nature of man, law and morality. There are surely other equally plausible accounts of its meaning.

If the state is a contested concept about which there are rival and incompatible theories, a proposition on which I shall cast some doubt later, at least two such rivals may be distinguished. The distinction turns upon the notion of the self and individuality and it is a recurring *motif* in all the major philosophical theories of the state. In liberal individualism the self is conceived as an abstraction, divorced from pre-existing social and political forms, and appropriate or legitimate state-like institutions are a function of individual, abstract choice. The state appears then to be an artifice or agency for maximising satisfactions. This methodology finds its purest expression in the economic theory of the state. In communitarian or organic theories, the state is said to be an *objective* order which exists independently of the rational choices of individuals: it is not a mere mechanism for transmitting individual preferences for necessary public services but is a necessary precondition for the exercise of any individual choice at all.

These two approaches do not necessarily generate different policy prescriptions, though the liberal view has historically tended to be associated with a limited state. The organic theory has been blamed for the rise of the absolute state in the twentieth century but the connection is not a logical one.[2] The point about such theories is that they would determine the limits of state action from history and tradition rather than by abstract choice theory.

In the organic theory the state has a naturalistic foundation: it is a product of the natural historical evolution rather than the choices of individuals abstracted from society. Since in organic theories it is specifically denied that morality can be derived from choice, political and legal institutions themselves embody those values of permanence and stability which atomised individuals cannot generate themselves. This is a well-known feature of Hegel's political philosophy (1942, pp. 160–223). Here, the state is conceived as an objective order of law standing over and above, and regulating, the conflict between atomised individuals of 'civil society'.[3] In the absence of a neutral arbiter, the state, civil society would be chaotic. The point that Hegel is making here is that if individuals are as liberal political economy describes them, mere maximisers of subjective utility, then they could not generate a neutral, impartial body from their subjective choices. The state is, therefore, for organic theorists, located in history and tradition and thence cannot be limited by individualistic principles, such as 'utility' or 'rights'.[4]

While the organic theories of the state appear to grant that institution, by definition, almost unlimited powers which, from a liberal point of view, would mean the abolition of individuality, a rival theory, by a similar verbal sleight of hand, necessarily reduces the state to a minimal role. In this, classical liberal theory, the state is defined exclusively in terms of coercion and therefore is restricted to the role of law enforcement through its monopoly of coercive power. The state is strongly contrasted with society on the ground of its involuntary character.

There are many versions of this theory. It is often associated with some versions of the social contract idea, most notably that of Locke, which envisage, either hypothetically or actually, individuals unanimously agreeing to set up certain central institutions with limited powers of protection and law enforcement. The state has no purpose beyond the purposes of the individuals who create it; the state is bound by natural law, and citizens always retain a right of resistance against it. The most well-known version of this limited state theory is probably the 'night watchman' philosophy of the state found in nineteenth-century *laissez-faire* economic theories. As we shall show, this type of theory is undergoing something of a revival at the moment and some extremely sophisticated theories, which entail a severely limited role for the state, have been produced by economists in the last 20 years (see Barry, N., 1986).

The common objection to those sorts of theories was that by defining the state solely in terms of coercion, and society in terms of voluntary action, they excluded two possibilities. First, that the state may not simply act coercively, that is maintain law and order, but may act in a non-coercive manner. The state's delivery of *welfare* services is given as a typical example of this. Secondly, a definition of the state solely in terms of its monopoly of coercive power ignores the fact that other institutions in society may be as coercive towards individuals. Of course, many theorists would argue that the 'welfare state' is a coercive state, because it can only finance its services by taxation, and also that many institutions in society that appear to be as involuntary as the state such as churches and trade unions, are only so because of special privileges conferred upon them by the state.

In fact the liberal theory of the state did spotlight one key element in its account – its coercive aspect – but it was deficient in a number of ways. The account of the state as a purely coercive institution is peculiarly sketchy in that it does not tell us much about the relationship between law and state, the nature of the state's rule or how states emerge. It tells us very little, in fact, about existing states. Furthermore, it really was a prescriptive account of the state, which recommended that states ought to be limited to the law and order function, disguised as a definition. There may be a sound case for a limited state, but this has to be established by theoretical argument – it ought not to be asserted as part of the definition of the state.

This brief discussion of the way the word state is used in political philosophy seems to confirm the original contention that the state is a complex, heavily normative concept that has no settled meaning, even at the inner core. It would appear to be impossible to provide a neutral definition of the state separate from a consideration of its ends or purposes. However, it may be feasible to isolate some features of the modern state which, although not completely uncontroversial, sum to an entity whose contours are familiar to political scientists and political philosophers. Arguments about the state between individuals and collectivists may not always be inconclusive at the conceptual level. The rivalrous ideologies, concerned with the role of the state, may turn then on competing conceptions of the state, rather than the concept itself.

2 Analysis of the state

We can understand some of the properties of the state by trying to imagine what social life would be like without it. The first thing to note is that the absence of the state would not mean the absence of rules, though Hobbes thought otherwise. In the absence of a state the breach of a rule would not mean that the interests of the 'public' had been adversely affected but only that a person had been harmed. That person would be entitled to take appropriate action under the rules to seek compensation for the harm done. In tribal societies which have not developed specialised state institutions there need not necessarily be a 'police power' to protect the public generally against rule-breakers. There may be a variety of methods by which a person may seek restitution for a wrong suffered and in a tribal society such methods are likely to be *decentralised* to individuals and kin groups. Therefore the rules that operate in stateless societies are basically private rules governing the relationships between people who are bound together by common ties of kinship. There are no public rules that authorise officials to enforce sanctions or which permit a centralised court system to make authoritative decisions on disputed questions of the rules (Gluckman, 1965, ch. 3). While it would be wrong to overemphasise the presence of vendettas, feuds and persistent acts of vengeance in stateless societies, it is not difficult to understand that those things will occur in a society without a centralised police function.

In a modern, complex society with a state organisation, acts of robbery, violence, murder and so on are not regarded only as harms against individuals but also as acts against society or the public. It is the responsibility of the state to take appropriate action against those who commit these rule-breaches, and, while that function may be delegated to subordinate bodies under public rules, it cannot be decentralised to private individuals or organisations.

Of course, the liberal theorists of limited government would restrict the role of the state to enforcing those basic rules which prohibit acts of violence and other sorts of unfair and fraudulent actions against individuals. There would be little need for the state to create new laws in this field since the liberal believes that a legal system will spontaneously develop a common framework of general rules to govern individual relationships independently of the state. While the state will enforce these basic compulsory rules, which forbid certain courses of action, it will leave the bulk of social and economic relationships to be governed by non-compulsory rules of civil law where its only role is to provide a unified court system to settle disputes.

One measure of the extent of the state's authority is indeed the volume of 'compulsory' law. It is logically possible, even in modern complex societies, to envisage the complete removal of the state. If, for example, two individuals were involved in a motor accident in an imaginary stateless modern society, the dispute would centre entirely on the question of liability for damage, which is a private matter between the individuals. There would be no question of the state being involved by way, for example, of prosecution for dangerous driving. The same logic could apply to more obvious cases of crime such as violence and robbery, protection against which could be secured through private arrangements, with insurance companies perhaps, without the need for the state's monopoly. However, the development of the state has meant that a range of actions, which in stateless societies are purely private in character, are now thought to have a public dimension. Whether this can provide an adequate justification for the state is, however, another matter.

The first two features of the state which we can identify then are the public nature of its rules and the fact of the centralisation of its authority. The fact that the state acts publicly does not, of course, imply that the state acts in the public interest: it could certainly be argued that the state generally acts in the interests of particular classes or groups. The above features merely imply that certain sorts of action have a public aspect and therefore cannot be settled by private negotiation between individuals. Also, the fact that the state is a centralised institution does not imply that particular states do not vary considerably in the extent of their centralisation: compare the former East Germany with the United States.

There are other features of the state, the most important being the fact that the state possesses determinate geographical boundaries. This means that once a particular territory has been marked out by boundaries as a 'state' then the nature of the rules that govern social relationships changes. In a tribal society without a formal state apparatus the rules apply only to the members of the tribe or social grouping. The range of application of the rules is a function of the social ties that bind individuals together and not a function of geographical area. But the laws of a modern state apply to whoever happens to be within the boundaries of the geographical area and not merely to the indigenous population.

It is often suggested that sovereignty is a necessary feature of the state: indeed the modern history of Western Europe is often written as the history of the rise of the sovereign state. The United Nations Organisation is said to be composed of sovereign states. However, it is not easy to see the significance of the concept of sovereignty for the political theorist. States cannot be uniquely identified in terms of sovereignty, if that is defined in terms of unlimited legal authority, since this is a most misleading way of looking at legal-political systems. With regard to their relationship with individuals, states vary a great deal. In federal systems, such as the United States, sovereignty is deliberately divided between the component states and the federal organs, and the use of the word sovereignty there seems to have little or no descriptive value. In all states where the actions of officials of the state are subject to established rules and bills of rights, the traditional notion of sovereignty seems to be irrelevant.

Even in the international sphere the phrase 'sovereign state' may be equally unilluminating. To call a state sovereign does not imply that it cannot incur obligations under international law. On entering the European Economic Community in 1973, the United Kingdom to some extent accepted the superiority of law which emanates from international institutions over domestic legislation. The subsequent development of that organisation (now called the European Union) has led to a gradual erosion of 'sovereignty' so that the country is now, in some areas, regulated by law not directly of its own making. Of course, the United Kingdom, by an exercise of sovereignty in a political sense, could leave that organisation, but this does not affect the fact that up to that point the state is under a kind of international rule of law.

It is logically possible, therefore, that international law in Europe might develop in such a way as seriously to undermine the structure of independent 'sovereign' states. Some liberals may very well envisage Europe as a kind of utopia characterised by very general rules of conduct which guarantee all the traditional economic and civil liberties, and which would virtually end the monopoly power that individual states have over their citizens. State borders may become merely honorific rather than indicative of any kind of legal integrity. A modern secular version of the medieval Christian commonwealth may very well emerge. However, it is just as likely that the rules that emanate from European institutions may not be general, and may be as coercive as those of present nation-states. In which case the features of existing states will have merely reappeared on a much larger scale.

Although even if this did happen it would be odd to describe the emerging entity as a sovereign state.

It should be clear that those features of the state that we have singled out for consideration, namely geographical integrity, public nature of the rules, centralisation and the monopoly of coercive power, do not constitute the elements of an essentialist definition of the state. As has often been pointed out, the claim to possess a monopoly of coercive power may not be realised in practice, as, for example, the British have found out in Northern Ireland. It is also said that other organisations in society may be as compulsory and coercive as the state itself. Perhaps the only necessary conditions for the existence of a state seem to be geographical integrity and the machinery for the making of some public rules. But states can continue for long periods either with their boundaries in dispute, or with less than universal acceptance of their rules, or both.

It is most important that an analysis of the distinctive features of the state should not mislead us into thinking that it is an entity with a 'will' of its own which is superior to that of its citizens. There is indeed a tradition of state-worship in the history of political thought which we have already discussed. The acts of the state, however, are always the acts of officials authorised by the rules of the state and the ends of the state are always the ends of the individuals and groups that use its machinery. Our account of the state is neutral, at least in the sense that it does not identify the institution with any special purpose. The state is no more than a set of rules, and while it is perfectly legitimate to criticise those rules on moral or other grounds, the danger of anthropomorphic accounts of the state must be avoided.

We normally make a distinction between state and government on the ground that the word state in certain propositions cannot be replaced by the word government without some considerable loss in meaning. The institutions of the state are clearly not the same as the 'government'. We speak of the state when we wish to describe a set of rules which *authorise* particular groups to act (normally in a coercive manner). However, when we speak in the economic sphere of the extent of state control we can just as well speak of the role of government since in both cases we are normally talking about the relative merits of *public* or *private* control of economic matters. In such disputes the argument must be conducted in terms of principles which are not themselves contained in the definition of the word state. Nothing, in other words, follows about what the state ought to do, from the account of the meaning of the word state. It is conceptions of the state that normally contain evaluative principles that determine the proper range of its activity.

In fact, the ambit of state activities has developed significantly in this century in Western democracies with little contribution from political philosophers in the way of *theory* which might justify such an extension of the public sphere. There has certainly been no systematic analysis of the question as to whether the collective (state) delivery of certain goods and services is superior to their private production and even less of the question of whether the state as a collective institution can properly be said to express individual preferences. Too often in the history of political thought the state has been presented as a special kind of entity and the relationship between the ends of the state and those of the individuals never fully explained.

It was certainly assumed that the actions of the state must necessarily be for the common good in contrast to private, economic transactions which were thought to be purely self-regarding. It was not realised that the state can only act through its officials and that there can be no guarantee that such officials, either elected or appointed, will not be governed by the same motives as private individuals: if they are so governed then it does not at all follow that the state will represent the 'common good'.

3 The economic theory of the state

The economic theory, or conception, of the state is in principle individualist in a methodological sense. This means that it deals only with individual values and ends and denies that a collective entity can have a purpose apart from individual purposes. The economic theory presupposes that the state is a device (or agency) for the production of public goods which is to be used only when market transactions fail to deliver what individuals want. Of course, the tradition of liberal economics contains a number of different theories of state activity but they would all claim to be based on this individualistic premise (Baumol, 1965; Whynes and Bowles, 1981). In this theory individuals are identified as anonymous utility-maximisers rather than as members of pre-existing social organisations that determine their goals and values.

The economic theory assumes that in a free market exchanges between individuals will lead to an efficient or optimal allocation of resources. The decentralised market system enables individuals to maximise their utilities and is the method by which production reflects the desires of consumers. In a free market, utility-maximising individuals will make gains from trade so that a market is efficient to the extent that all possibilities of exchange are exhausted. Political interference with the process causes inefficiency to the extent that it directs production away from that pattern of goods and services which would occur from the uncoerced exchanges of individuals. Stark examples of this can be seen in state-directed economies where queues, shortages and, of course, black markets occur when production is directed towards the ends of the state managers rather than those of individuals.

The efficiency criterion of a market economy is called the Pareto-optimality criterion, after the Italian economist and sociologist, Vilfredo Pareto. A situation is Pareto-optimal if no improvement can be made in the positions of individuals without making someone worse off (see Ng, 1979, ch. 2). If further improvements would not make anyone worse off, then the position is sub-optimal and gains from trade are possible. The Pareto criterion assumes only that an efficient allocation will occur through free exchange between individuals: it says nothing about the *initial* distribution of wealth amongst individuals. Since a Pareto-optimal outcome is possible from any given distribution of wealth, it has nothing logically to do with ethical principles of equality or social justice. A socialist could recommend that, on some moral ground, the state should equalise wealth and still adhere to the Pareto criterion from that point onwards. The argument of the liberal economist is that, given a particular distribution, and free individual choice, the state, as a matter of scientific demonstration, can only improve on the market in special circumstances. And it is here that the economic theory of the state emerges. It is based entirely on the argument that the state should give effect only to the subjective preferences of its members.

Economists, following A. Pigou (1920), said there are special cases where the market is inefficient in that it does not adequately reflect what people want: state action may therefore produce a Pareto-efficient outcome. This is in the fields of externalities and public goods. Actually both of these concepts are logically similar but it is convenient to separate them. An externality occurs when there is a difference between marginal private costs and marginal social costs in some activity. Thus, in the familiar example, a producer using the least-cost method of production may impose costs on the community at large by polluting the air and these costs do not appear in his profit-maximising calculus. But not all externalities are 'bads': some external effects of individual activity are positive, that is, they benefit the community at large without the producer of them being fully rewarded.

Public goods are really extreme cases of externality. A public good is normally defined as a good the consumption of which by one person does not reduce the amount available for others – it is non-rival in consumption. Obvious examples are defence, clean air and a system of law. A second property is non-excludability. The point here is that once such goods are made available for one person they are made available for all. This means that it is impossible to prohibit someone from consuming the good who has not paid for it. In these circumstances, individuals have no incentive to reveal their preferences so that in a market system it can never be known what the true demand is for a public good. This is what is known as the 'free rider' problem, and its existence means that in a free market inhabited only by utility-maximisers outcomes will be generated which are counter to the interests of those same self-interested individuals.

Notice there that education and health are not public goods, although they are provided at zero prices in welfare states, since they are not non-rival in consumption and it would be easy to eliminate free riders. However, some welfare economists have suggested that because they give positive 'externalities' to the community at large, in addition to the benefits they give to individuals, they would be underproduced in a free market and this justifies state intervention. However, the problem here is that once the market mechanism is removed from their production it is difficult to know what is the optimal supply of these goods and services. The state, even in a democracy, is recognised to be an inferior mechanism for the registering of preferences. It is just as likely either to oversupply or to undersupply them. In any case, their delivery would to an extent be paternalistic.

The presence of externalities and public goods, then, provided the justification for state intervention for welfare economists of the 'Pigovian' school – a form of intervention which was justified not because of some external moral principle but because it was required to 'correct' and improve upon the market so as to approach more closely a Pareto-optimal allocation. The state, precisely because of the universality of its rules and its monopoly of coercion, could produce things which, although generally desired, would not be produced privately. An additional argument for state involvement derives from the problem of knowledge. Some theorists of the market claim that it can only work efficiently when each participant is fully-informed of all possible options (though not all market advocates agree, some argue that the accumulation and circulation of knowledge actually depends on the market process, however technically inefficient it may be, see Barry, N., 1990) so that there is a justification for the state where the possession of unequal knowledge may give some transactors power over others. The justification for the control, or the socialisation, of health care rests partially on these grounds. The kinds of intervention favoured by this school are subsidies (to prevent underproduction), taxes on producers (to prevent external bads) and perhaps outright nationalisation. A further impetus to the justification of a greater role for the state comes from the recent concern that free markets will exhaust certain natural resources at a quicker rate than would be desired by individuals. With regard to the environment, too, it is often maintained that external bads will be generated by unrestrained market exchanges. However, although this implies a role for the state it could actually mean a diminution of its internal authority. This is because pollution often crosses boundaries. The state may then have to submit to international rules if the original aim is to be satisfied.

For the economic liberal the theory of the state so described is normative: it tells us what the state *ought* to do, that is provide public goods in the presence of market failure, but it does not explain its emergence or, indeed, existence. It is a kind of exogenous 'given' to be invoked in various emergencies. What is particularly disturbing is that it suggests that the concept of self-interest, so useful a notion in the explanation of conventional market behaviour, is inadequate for the explanation of political and social phenomena (law and state). The existence of law and state depends on a form of social co-operation which seems to be precluded by the presuppositions of individualistic liberal theory.

This problem of providing public goods and services from the premises of an unsullied individualism is simply an application of the familiar 'Prisoners' Dilemma' of modern game theory (see Pettit, 1984). In this 'game' two suspects, Smith and Jones, are questioned separately by the District Attorney about a robbery they have committed. If they both remain silent they will face a less serious charge carrying a short prison sentence of three years; if they both confess to the serious offence they will get ten years each; if one, e.g. Smith, confesses and implicates Jones (who remains silent) in the serious offence, Smith will get off scot free but Jones will receive a punitive sentence of twelve years. The best co-operative outcome – that is, the outcome which involves the minimum combined prison sentence (a total of six years) – would require both prisoners to remain silent. However, since they cannot trust one another, rationality dictates that they confess, hoping to implicate the other in order to get the reduced sentence. The interrogator has so arranged the 'pay-offs' that whatever strategy is selected by Jones it is better for Smith to confess and vice versa. Confession is the 'dominant' strategy for both. The problem is shown in the table below, which illustrates all possible outcomes. Even if the prisoners could communicate, each could not be sure the other would co-operate.

It is easy to show that the familiar public good problems, such as pollution, despoliation of the natural environment, the rapid depletion of scarce resources in the absence of enforceable property rights and voluntary 'social' contracts between trade unions and governments to keep wages down during inflationary periods, are all exemplifications of the Dilemma. It also undermines the distinction between law and state that is carefully made by classical liberals, for all those rules of crime, property, tort and contract seem to require a public system of creation and enforcement which no rational individual has an incentive to produce or sustain. The problem was, of course, first diagnosed by Hobbes, whose solution was a unanimous agreement to the creation of absolute sovereignty (in which law and state are not conceptually distinct).

The modern economic theory of the state proceeds on not-dissimilar lines: the state is seen as an agency, authorised by an hypothetical 'contract' or by general utilitarian considerations, to generate those goods and services which are not produced by free exchange. Yet the justification for state action along these lines is not without its difficulties. For, if the only rationale for the state is its ability to meet the *subjective* desires of its citizens, how can we know what these are in the absence of a market exchange system? The key feature in 'Prisoners' Dilemmas' is that rational self-interested individuals have every reason to conceal their true preferences for public goods. The economic theory of the state requires then a voting procedure for transmitting individual preferences for public goods. However, no system has been devised which is entirely satisfactory (see below, Chapter 11). Anything short of unanimity means that some voters can impose their choices on others, while unanimity is such a stringent requirement that hardly anything would get done at all. Small

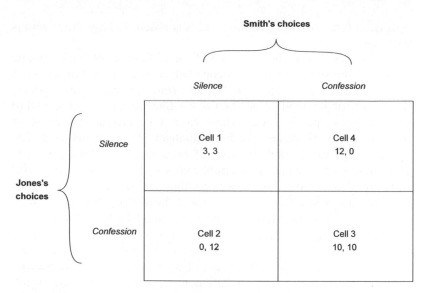

Figure 3.1   The Prisoner's Dilemma

minorities could hold out for a very high price for their agreement to co-operate in the supply of a public good.

Those liberal economists who fear that the argument from 'Prisoners' Dilemmas' may be used to smuggle in public policies that have only a remote connection with subjective choice have used a variety of arguments to show how co-ordination can take place without the state (see Sugden, 1986). It is now agreed that in repeated plays of the Prisoners' Dilemma' (the 'supergame') individuals will by a learning process see the benefits of co-operation (Axelrod, R., 1984). This is a likely occurrence as long as small numbers of people are involved and the social game is repeated (in the first example in this chapter it was a 'one-shot' dilemma): these factors mean that those who do not co-operate and try to take a free ride can be punished.[5] However, where large numbers of people are involved, so that the supply of the public good does not depend on the participation of each individual, the probability of mass defection is high: thus the good will not be supplied and the state will have to step in, validated perhaps by a social contract, to fill the gap. It is to be stressed that in the sophisticated and ingenious solutions to the Prisoners' Dilemma that have been proposed their success depends upon the contribution each person makes to the supply of the public good. That is why co-operation turns out to be rational. This is absent in large, anonymous societies.

It was suggested earlier that one of the difficulties of the economic theory of the state was that it depended upon a distinction between law and state: that is, individuals could transact under general rules, thus generating individual satisfactions, while the state is authorised to generate those public goods which cannot be produced because of market failure. However, the individualism of the theory is undermined to the extent that the general rules (contract, tort, property, crime and so on) are themselves public goods which require a powerful state for their production as well as their enforcement. It was this consideration which led Hobbes to assert the identity of law and state. In his view only instantaneous contracts could be valid without the state because any transactions over even a short period of time require an element of 'trust' that is, the belief that the terms of the agreement will be honoured without the threat of coercion. In his view, because the slightest suspicion of non-fulfilment nullified a contract, an all-powerful sovereign state was necessary for commercial society to be viable.

It is not clear, though, that the Hobbesian solution is unavoidable. After all, law did precede the development of the modern state in European history. In many cases statutes simply codified those rules and practices that had emerged spontaneously. There is indeed a quite plausible theoretical explanation for this. People will realise the advantages that accrue from the keeping of promises and, although, from a purely self-interested perspective, each person may think that he or she will gain even more from the unilateral breach of an agreement, that tactic is sure to prove counterproductive over a series of projects: people will not deal with those who regularly show unreliability. It is in this way that the necessary element of trust is built up over time. Evolution can therefore be used to explain how such things as commercial law developed without the aid of the state (see Trakman, 1983). This does not, of course, negate the necessity for the state. The anonymity of large modern societies makes it unlikely that defectors from agreements can be detected and punished. But it does go some way towards the explanation of the emergence of the common law and it also casts doubt on the modern claim that the state is required to solve every co-ordination problem. At least it preserves the conceptual distinction between law and state.

The economic theory of the state has shifted in emphasis in recent years. In its original formulation the role of government was to provide some optimal allocation of resources in the face of market failure. The state was 'legitimate' to the extent that it satisfied the demand for public goods. However, since, for reasons considered above, this demand can never be known, state action is quite likely to be arbitrary. The Public Choice-Property Rights school of political economy (see Buchanan, 1975; Cheung, 1978; de Jasay, 1985) stresses at least two things that are relevant to the argument. First, public officials should be treated as utility-maximisers (driven as much by self-interest as ordinary market traders) so that government failure is as prevalent as market failure. Second, in view of this point, it is maintained that there may be more possibilities for overcoming public good problems than was hitherto thought if people are allowed to trade in property rights.

It is maintained that externalities such as pollution could be 'internalised' if there were an appropriate legal-political framework in which the parties could continue to transact until all gains from trade were realised. That is to say, questions of smoky chimneys could be settled by legal claims in which persons whose property was damaged would receive compensation. The need for state action in the form of taxes and subsidies to produce an optimal outcome would therefore be removed if individuals were able to conduct voluntary negotiations within the context of a known legal framework. The trouble with government action is that it is likely itself to be inefficient – since government officials do not have the same incentive to be as informed as private individuals and it is also likely to 'attenuate' property rights, that is, through restrictive laws it will reduce the opportunities for individuals to trade in property rights.

The major objection to the use of the state to solve the public good problem of pollution is that such 'command and control' methods reduce the opportunities for people to trade their way out of the difficulty. Almost any industrial activity generates some adverse effects so that the real question is: how can damage be compensated without at the same time eliminating the efficiency advantages that accrue from the market's allocation of resources? If property rights are adequately specified it would be (theoretically) possible for the potential harm-generator to buy out the rights of the person likely to be damaged. Of course, she will pay just that amount which is sufficient to make the productive activity worthwhile. In fact, Ronald Coase (1960), one of the pioneers in this field, argued that if transaction costs are zero and income effects are not relevant (that is, if different income levels do not affect the pattern of demand), then an efficient allocation of resources is possible whatever the distribution of property rights.[6] Thus under these conditions, which allow individuals through negotiation to make gains from trade in the presence of externalities, many externalities can be internalised without state intervention. Though the problems appear to be intractable when pollution takes on an international aspect.

In this model the state would be limited to the authoritative specification of property rights (although many of these will have emerged spontaneously, there will obviously be some doubts about ownership). If such schemes sound a little fanciful it should be remembered that the very worst pollution problems occurred in those social systems (former communist regimes) where there were few private property rights and in which the state was the sole determinant of industrial production and environmental protection (Bernstram, 1991). The problems were fundamentally generated by the complete fusion of law and state and the absence of incentives for state officials to care about the environment.

It is true, however, that transaction costs are unlikely to be zero, especially when large numbers are involved. It is very difficult for people who are affected by pollution of the atmosphere to combine to take the appropriate action against factory owners. Furthermore, the distribution of property rights may be said to have an effect on the outcome of an economic process in that the wealth (and perhaps social power) of minorities may enable them to persist in imposing externalities on others which may only be removable by political action. Some members of the Public Choice-Property Rights School do seem to regard the present distribution of property rights as inviolable (Furniss, 1978, pp. 402–3).

Some of the problems are clearly not susceptible of easy solutions within the economic theory of the state. The reason for this, claim its critics, is that it is misleading to attribute legitimacy to the state exclusively in terms of its satisfying the subjective (and transient) wants of citizens. This is perhaps a typical case of the economist abstracting the 'self' from an appropriate social and institutional setting in the attempt to construct some 'calculus' of legitimacy. For rival conceptions, however, the notion of an abstract individual, fragmented into public and private roles, is meaningless: we can only understand persons as members of given, *objective* social and political orders (political 'forms of life' that exist independently of abstract choice).

4 The organic theory of the state

The organic conception of the state seeks to establish legitimacy by reference to authority rather than individual choice. The primary argument here is that the whole notion of authority must be rooted in specific historical experience and in traditional structures of rules: and these must precede the notion of individuality (Barry, N., 1991). What is specifically excluded is a criterion of legitimacy that has a pretence to a *universal* validity; whether such a purported validity is parasitic upon man as a utility-maximiser or the bearer of natural rights is immaterial. Rather than individuals delegating authority to the state to do certain things, the state is a conduit for the transmission of private desires for public goods, the authority of the state is said to exist prior to the actions of its officials. An obvious implication of this is that the social contract, the device often recommended as a solution to the public good problem, cannot be a grounding for legitimacy since it attempts to derive authority from a moral vacuum. The organic theory trades heavily on the obvious fact that the description of a continuing political order (or any public institution) will be in terms of concepts not readily translatable into those describing individual volitions and intentions. To suppose, then, that the legitimacy of a social institution is deliberately chosen or intended is a peculiar form of individualistic rationalism. The nature of political institutions is that they are essentially *public*, and the validity of them is not a function of subjective choice.

If the conditions and circumstances that determine the legitimacy of the state are neither chosen nor intended, how then are they understood? In Roger Scruton's political theory, people's obligations are defined by particular facts rather than any purportedly universal features of the human condition. Individuals cannot be abstracted from their history and tradition and treated merely as abstract choosers. He writes that:

> Their very existence is burdened with a debt of love and gratitude, and it is in responding to that burden that they begin to recognise the power of 'ought'. This is not the abstract universal 'ought' of liberal theory ... but the concrete, immediate 'ought' of family attachments. It is the 'ought' of piety, which recognizes local transitory and historically conditioned social bonds. (Scruton, 1980, pp. 201–2)

The origins of these thoughts lie, of course, in Hegel's idea of the 'ethical state': a form of political organisation which unites the subjective self of whim and inclination with the objective self subject to concretised obligations. Obedience to this form of organisation does not diminish freedom because the freedom of liberal theory is illusory: it is a notion of liberty that is realised only in the satisfaction of momentary, ephemeral desires. It is these ephemeral desires that caused the problems of public goods. Indeed, before contracts can be valid, the idea of a promise has to be socially validated.

It should be noted that the view of political authority here is not necessarily conservative in a *substantive sense*. In fact, it can easily be made consistent with the features of a classical liberal order, private property, market exchange, the rule of law and so on, but the moral value of these phenomena is a function of a continuing tradition of authority rather than some notion of indefeasible individualistic claims. It is also the case that not dissimilar anti-individualistic theoretical views are espoused by left-wing thinkers. They argue that the penetration of social life by the commercial ethic undermines those communal obligations which are essential for order. This, in effect, means that the 'abstract' individual is not only unintelligible but radically subversive of society.

On all of those views, political philosophy should be concerned with the investigation of forms of life and the *meanings* of rules, institutions and practices integral to them, of which politics is simply one aspect. One implication of such an investigation would be that the distinction between law and state (which is germane to the liberal theory) is fallacious precisely because it fragments the self into private and public capacities when, it is claimed, in contrast, all political and social life is necessarily public. Put more prosaically, this means that there never was a set of private rules which existed independently of some public authorization and, more precisely, enforcement. Thus, although it might look as if the common law preceded what we now think of as the state, this is only because we tend to think of the state in modernistic (that is, liberal) terms as a mere agency.

It does not follow necessarily from the organic theory that a critical attitude towards politics is excluded. The exploration of the meanings inherent in a form of life will itself reveal principles and values relevant to the evaluation of political action. In a familiar example, the imposition of a *laissez-faire* economy on an ongoing form of political life may very well be condemnable. This would be so if it failed to inculcate a sense of community, by, for example, excluding sections of the population from political life because of their inability to survive in the market. A free market society which rejected any bonds other than those associated with the cash nexus would simply reproduce that alienation which the state exists to overcome. What is excluded is the limitation of the state's authority by abstract principles. We cannot stand outside a given, objective political order (and its history) and evaluate it by values external to it.

However persuasive this account of political order may be, it is vulnerable to a crucially important criticism from the economic theory. It is that by refusing to separate out the various aspects of 'governing' into legal and political modes the organic theory disables itself from a sustained critical analysis of the actions of the officials of the state. For while it may make sense to describe the state in terms of an objective structure of rules, it is also the case that it is manned by individuals whose behaviour can be analysed (and indeed interpreted in predictive terms) with the utility-maximising theory of liberal-individualist political economy. Decisions made by officials of the state, although they are authorised by pre-existing rules, are nevertheless, subjective decisions. States do not act. It is claimed, of course, by organic theorists that governments can be criticised if they do not reproduce the ends inherent in a political form of life, but what are those ends if they are not the subjective choices of individuals? Since no real distinction is made between state and law, there can be no theoretical limits on state action in the organic theory. Thus this theory turns out to be merely an account of what the state *is*, rather than a normative theory of the legitimacy of its actions. Just because the state's actions are 'right', since they proceed from an objective authority, it does not follow that they are immune from criticism, or that the structure of authority is itself the sole depository of rationality

Indeed, the seemingly inexorable increase in the size of the state in all Western democracies from at least the beginning of the century can only be satisfactorily explained in terms of the economic theory. The state is clearly not limited to the supply of genuine public goods, although there is some controversy as to their permissible range, but it now produces what are technically private goods – goods that could be produced by the market since they do not have the properties of non-rivalness and non-excludability. The modern state has been depicted as a battleground in which rival groups use its machinery to press for sectional advantages at the cost of that (limited) public interest which they do share. In other words, Prisoners' Dilemmas occur in the state just as much as in the market. Modern politics has been depicted as a Hobbesian 'war of all against all', in group rather than individualistic form, in which the benign notion of community has been transformed from collective endeavour to group egoism.

5   Anarchism

As has been suggested earlier, philosophical or ethical anarchism poses the question: why should a person be expected to obey the authority of the state, *for that reason alone*, if he is himself prepared to follow the dictates of a morality that recognises the integrity of other persons? It is a question that is difficult to answer without recourse to merely prudential justifications for the existence of a centralised body with a monopoly of power. However, within the broad tradition of the social sciences and political philosophy (see Miller, 1984) there have been anarchist theories which have tried to demonstrate that a stateless society is not only philosophically justifiable but also viable. Anarchism emanates from both left and right of the political spectrum. However, one would logically expect extreme, individualist *laissez-faire* economic philosophies to be more consistent with the demands of a stateless society than collectivist ones. The real difference between individualist and collectivist theories is that the latter depend very much on a change in human nature if a stateless society without private property and monetary exchange is to be at all feasible: individualists claim, perhaps implausibly, that their prescriptions do not require such a transformation.

Although Marxist theory might ultimately be anarchistic, communist states in practice have been totalitarian, the transformation in human nature that the theory requires has never occurred and communist states have been among the most coercive in history. Marx puts the state analytically in the context of class conflict: it is there to protect the economic interests of the ruling class and cannot be an objective, neutral body. It is part of the *epiphenomena* of society along with law, morality and religion, and changes its form as society progresses through revolutionary moments. Ultimately, with the abolition of property, money and the division of labour, the state must 'wither away' as there will be no need for its coercive functions. There is no conceptual distinction between law and state, for the new 'self' that is to emerge once class relationships have been transcended will not require coercive law but only routine administration.

There is, however, another theory of the state (described in Marx's *Eighteenth Brumaire of Louis Napoleon*) in Marxism which is more plausible and does not define the institution on terms of class relationships but as functional necessity in certain societies (Marx, 1971). It is required to maintain order between conflicting groups. But as Marx and later Marxists noticed, there is a tendency for it to become an independent class in its own right and not defined in economic or 'ownership' terms: it lives off the productive activities of others. There is some similarity between this and *laissez-faire* political economy. Given this point and the fact that communist societies operate entirely through the coercive state (their rulers behave in the exploitative manner described in Marx's later account of the institution) it is hard to see what is left of the original vision of the disappearance of the coercive state under collectivism.

Although individualistic theories of anarchy are often identified with *laissez-faire* capitalism (anarcho-capitalism) the connection is not a logical one (see Barry, N.P., 1986, ch. 9). Rather, it is the case that capitalist relationships tend to emerge from the withdrawal of the monopoly state: there is, however, no necessity for this and, indeed, if property rules turned out to be communitarian this would be perfectly legitimate. The individualist anarchist (Rothbard, 1970) rejects the state on grounds of efficiency (the private market, it is claimed, can deliver public services effectively according to price) and morality (the state claims by its authority to do things that are not permitted to ordinary individuals). This is the source of the essential inequality of political relationships.

One of the most philosophically interesting of those arguments emerged from the publication of Robert Nozick's *Anarchy, State and Utopia* (1974). For although a large part of that book consisted of a refutation of anarchy (of the individualistic, property rights variety), Nozick tried to show that the existence of a minimal state was consistent with the anarchist's fundamental proposition: that no political authority may legitimately possess more rights than private individuals, although this is, of course, a somewhat ambitious enterprise.[7]

Nozick claims that one can imagine the emergence of a state by a kind of 'Invisible Hand' process from a Lockean state of nature, in which each individual has fundamental rights. An 'Invisible Hand' process is one which produces a beneficial outcome for individuals in society, such as the efficient allocation of resources in a market economy, even though it is not the specific intention of any one individual (Nozick, 1974, pp. 18–22; Ullman-Margalit, 1979; Barry, N. P., 1988a). In Nozick's scheme the state, with a monopoly of coercive power, emerges from the state of nature through stages. In the first instance a number of agencies compete for the delivery of the protection good, but because of the nature of the good – a kind of natural monopoly – one dominant protective agency will emerge. The *ultraminimal* state emerges when the dominant protective agency excludes other defence agencies from operating within its area. However, it provides protection at this stage only to those who have paid for it and becomes a *minimal* state when it provides protection for those who would not pay for the service themselves (Nozick, 1974, pp. 26–8). This process takes place, it is maintained, without the violation of anybody's rights. The minimal state is justified in prohibiting 'risky' activities, that is the actions of rival defence agencies, because it *compensates* those who would undertake risky activities by providing protection at zero price (Nozick, 1974, ch. 4).

The major criticism of *this* aspect of Nozick's thought has come from libertarians (anarcho-capitalists) who deny that the minimal state is the product of an 'Invisible Hand' that violates no one's rights (see Barry, N. P. 1986, ch. 8). It can only exist through the forceful imposition of its will on individuals. Since in Nozick's scheme the essential feature is the *monopoly* of coercion possessed by the state, anarcho-capitalists claim that there is no limit to the transition from a minimal to a maximal state. It is true that Nozick's state contains none of the traditional apparatus of limited government, separation of powers and so on, and though Nozick claims that it is *illegitimate* for the state to go beyond protection, anarcho-capitalists would argue that his system cannot prevent this (Rothbard, 1977). In fact, this might well occur from the logic of Nozick's own theory: for individuals would have a rational incentive to become 'independents', that is, not members of the Dominant Protection Agency. They would get protection without paying for it. The agency would then either disintegrate or be forced to use coercion, namely taxation, to finance its actions.

The libertarian's description of a stateless society (see Rothbard, 1973; Friedman, D., 1973; Barry, N. P., 1986, ch. 9) may be very remote from political reality but it is interesting for the light it sheds on our understanding of the state. In a stateless society there would be a code of law, based on the fundamental premise that personal and property rights are inviolable. Firms would provide protection in the market, and it is claimed that, as in every other market, competition would reduce risk. In fact, the anarcho-capitalist claims that risks are increased enormously when the individual is at the mercy of the monopolistic state. The crucial feature of the stateless society is that it is entirely individualistic: there are no collective (state) goods or services.

Such theories, despite their admitted ingenuity, would be dismissed as idle speculations, both by socialists who demand a more active role for the state in the economy and in welfare, and by conservative organic philosophers of the state (Scruton, 1981). The latter view holds that anarcho-capitalism is the logical (and bizarre) outcome of that political philosophy which takes as its starting point the fragmented self of individualistic theory: a self abstracted from natural society where the only political loyalties are those determined by contracts and agreements. That is, it is maintained, too fragile a notion on which to found a stable social order.

6 The contemporary debate about the state

In current political discussion there is a curious contradictoriness about the role of the state. People are clearly unhappy about the vast increase in its size that has occurred in the twentieth century but are reluctant to recommend radical measures which would diminish its scope. Political liberals are naturally concerned that its intrusiveness is potentially a threat to civil liberties but rarely concede the point that historically the greatest threat to personal freedom has come from the state. They are too anxious to maintain its welfare role to condemn the institution outright. Again feminists (Mackinnon, 1989) are adept at pointing to the state as the major source of male power, and its exclusion of women from any serious political role, but are normally as hostile to the market, despite its historic function as an anti-state institution.[8] All too often these critical theorists are under the illusion that the state would be acceptable if it were somehow moralised and are confident that its coercive features would be acceptable if they were in the right hands. Nationalism, which wants to delimit the legal aspects of state sovereignty and to make its coercive features accord with 'romantic' ideals of culture and language, shows no desire whatever to promote individualistic, anti-collectivist values. At least public choice, with its stress on the more or less universal features of human behaviour, maintains a rigorous consistency: the state is needed to provide public goods but its potentiality for predatory, rent-seeking activity is always a threat to individual liberty.

All too often the argument about the role of the state is disabled by a misleading dichotomy between the market and the state or individualism versus collectivism. In reality, there is a myriad of intermediary institutions between these antagonistic value positions. Churches, voluntary associations and even local governments make up the structure of what we now call civil society and all of these stand in between the free-floating, potentially alienated and anonymous individual and the uniform and coercive state. One of the dire legacies of the communist state was its destruction of civil society and its elevation of the state (despite Marxist theory) to a completely dominant, hegemonic position in social life.

It is here that one would expect some significant contributions from communitarianism since, in principle, it looks to intermediary institutions to provide that solidarity which individuals apparently cannot find from either the market the state. But communitarians are so concerned about the market/state dichotomy, and so obsessed with the dehumanising role of the free exchange system that they overlook the fact that these secondary social institutions spring from exactly the same source as the market – freedom under the rule of law. As we shall see, many of the welfare arrangements that are now automatically handled by the state, were originally the responsibility of the institutions of civil society, the members of which had a knowledge of local affairs that made them peculiarly competent at managing the typical welfare, education and health problems. Charles Taylor (1992) has highlighted the demands for cultural recognition by minority groups but has condemned the market, and in effect, all voluntary non-state associations in the provision of welfare. He does not consider the possibility that cultural groups should have the right of 'exit' from the monopoly state. That would be too redolent of choice in the market. In effect the community has been 'nationalised' by communitarians (Grasso, 1998, pp. 20–2) so that certain activities must be protected from infection by the market. The superficial allure of the public discussion of political affairs (see below, Chapter 11) seems to preclude choice, be it in the market or in the local community.

4
Authority and Power

1 Authority, power and coercion

A major difficulty with the analysis of authority and power is that
while they appear to describe different phenomena, they can often be
used interchangeably in ways that mask the differences. Normally
people want to describe authority relationships in terms of 'legitimacy'
and 'rightfulness', and power relationships in terms of the causal
factors that enable one person, or group of persons, to determine
the actions of others. But also we speak of, say, police or governmental authority when 'power' would do just as well. When social
scientists research into 'community power structures', they are engaged in trying to determine power in the causal sense, but they are
clearly not studying the kind of power exercised by the Mafia. It is this
permissive aspect of ordinary language which has led to the frequent
identification of power with authority so that they both appear as
types of causal influence, albeit operating rather differently, and seem
to be a threat to rationality and liberty.

It is important, though, to keep the conceptual distinction clearly in
mind not only for analytical rigour but also in order to appreciate the
differing explanatory concepts in social science. To elucidate the
distinction between authority and power it might be helpful to suggest
that the former is a philosophical concept while the latter is sociological. To ask questions about somebody in authority is, in essence,
to ask a normative question about the right of that person to give
orders, or to make pronouncements or decisions under a set or rules,
although it may be possible to speak of instances of authority not
grounded upon specific rules. Notice that the language used to
describe authority is entirely prescriptive. As J. R. Lucas (1966, p. 16)
says, 'a man has authority if it follows from his saying 'let x happen',
that x ought to happen'. It is true that if authority is to be effective,

83

and if authoritative laws are to be obeyed, then certain sociological conditions will have to be met, but to establish a claim to authority is to meet certain criteria of legitimacy, not to satisfy criteria of efficacy. Whether someone is in authority or not cannot be established by mere observation of his success in getting his way. But we shall see that authority is not always used philosophically and that some theorists treat it in a more sociological way so that it differs from power only in degrees.

However, questions about power in society are superficially more clearly sociological questions in which observation is, of course, highly relevant. To speak of a power relationship is implicitly to give a prediction of future behaviour derived from a purported causal explanation. Therefore the validity of a statement about power turns not upon the question of rules but on the adequacy of the causal theory which attempts to predict what person, or group, will prevail in social decision-making. It is the purpose of social scientists who are engaged in empirical studies of political decision-making to find out who wields power in society. The phrases used in the empirical studies bring home the full force of this distinctive feature of power, even though there has been little agreement amongst the investigators on what a correct theory of power would be like. When sociologists talk of a 'power elite' in a political community they must mean, at least implicitly, that over a given range of issues a particular group – which can be identified by some set of observable, empirical characteristics – will dominate. The question of whether the group's decisions are right or 'authoritative' is not relevant to the question of whether the group is able to get its way.

The trouble with treating power as a purely sociological concept is that there is no real agreement among its users as to what it denotes. Indeed, many writers (for example, Connolly, 1983; Lukes, 1974) argue that it is necessarily an essentially contested concept. If there are to be satisfactory predictive theories of power, they will depend on uncontroversial applications of the concept; yet it is precisely those which are lacking in empirical political science. Compared to the physical sciences, where methodological nominalism is entirely appropriate, the social sciences seem to be condemned to disputes over definitions. For this reason the results of empirical investigations into the phenomenon are bound to be unconvincing to those who do not agree on what it is that is to be measured. Power elite theories tend to become irrefutable. Thus if evidence of a particular elite's success is not readily available it is often claimed that power is still exercised but in a form not susceptible to conventional empirical observation. Hence the claim that power is present in non-decisions.

To distinguish the notion of power by reference to causality and prediction, and to contrast this with the prescriptive use of the word authority, is not to deny that the exercise of power may be perfectly legitimate. While the ordinary citizen is likely to respond to the authority of the policeman, a criminal may very well only be restrained by the policeman's power. When we speak of the 'power' of the Prime Minister, the Cabinet or Parliament, we may say that it is too great, perhaps in the sense that the actions of political leaders and public officials limit too severely the private choices of individuals, but such power, although it is causal, is certainly legitimate in the way that the power of a bank-robber is not. But it is true that the political official and the bank-robber are able to cause people to act in desired ways because they have coercion at their disposal. It is because of this that despite the differences between power and authority the two concepts do seem to occupy the same ground in some familiar social and political situations. As we shall see below, an *authoritarian* state is one in which the free choices of individuals are severely limited by the commands of the authorities – commands which affect the individual in an almost entirely causal way.

There are, nevertheless, pejorative overtones which can be detected in the use of the word power. It is presented as the currency of politics and in political studies the focus of attention on power relationships is thought to indicate a suitable 'realistic' approach. The idea that power is to politics what money is to economics has a superficial appeal but it is not all that helpful. Money is clearly measurable in the way that power is not. Indeed, the meaning of money, and its use in exchange, is a product of agreement between transactors but there is little evidence of such a consensus about power. Furthermore, power, unlike money, varies in different contexts: it has a variety in scope and domain (some social relationships are not governed by power) which money does not possess (Baldwin, 1989, pp. 28–30). Anyway, the use of money is governed by rules whereas the sociological approach to power wants to detach it (perhaps inaccurately) from this notion.

The idea that the behaviour of political actors cannot be limited by rules derives, in modern times, from Machiavelli's *The Prince*, which is perhaps the most famous essay on the mechanics of power. It can be read as a specific refutation of the medieval notion that the Christian Commonwealth is ordered by a body of natural law which underlies the authority of the rulers, and which prescribes moral limitations on the actions of everybody. The modern realists who see politics as the pursuit of power and social order entirely as a product of threats may be considered, not inaccurately, as the heirs of the Machiavellian tradition.[1]

From this perspective, contemporary critics of power demand some *moral* justification for its use. They do so precisely because the exercise of power, the *ability* to get things done, often involves the overriding of some people's *interests* by others. Steven Lukes argues that all interpretations are exemplifications 'of one and the same underlying concept of power, according to which *A* exercises power over *B* when *A* affects *B* in a manner contrary to *B*'s interests' (1974, p. 27: see also Connolly, 1983, p. 88). It is, of course, true that it is not at all easy to establish what a person's 'interests' are uncontroversially: the concept maybe as intractable as power itself. However, what is implicit in the critique of power is the fact that the infringement of freedom of choice that its exercise entails is *prima facie* undesirable.

Closely related to this is the idea that a proper account of power must include the notion that responsibility can be attributed to those who exercise power: 'there is a particularly intimate connection between alleging that A has power over B and concluding that A is properly held responsible to some degree for B's conduct or situation' (Connolly, 1983, p. 95). In such approaches power is almost always interpreted in the sense of 'power *over*' (where one person or group has the ability to determine the actions of others) rather than in the sense of 'power *to*' (which refers to power as the ability to get things done for the benefit of, say, the community). This sense of power obviously has a little more respectability for it is true that in some circumstances people acting in a collective way can get more things done than if they were behaving in a purely individualistic manner. But this concept comes up against the familiar public good problems described in the last chapter (see Dowding, 1996). How can people co-operate to their own advantage when there is every incentive for them to break a putative agreement and take a free ride? Yet to prevent such behaviour might well require an enforcement agency which will wield to a morally unacceptable extent threat and coercion – power over.

Of course, the sense of 'power over' is not restricted to overt acts but can include *omissions*, where one person or group has the ability to act in the interests of others but deliberately refuses to do so. The omission is thought to indicate the illegitimate overriding of an interest. One difficulty in the attribution of responsibility to agents in the account of power is the question of social power: can we legitimately speak of power being exercised by social structures and institutions where it is difficult if not impossible to identify responsible agents? Radical theorists of power wish to say that certain social institutions and 'power structures' do result in the interests of others being adversely affected but maintain, nevertheless, that power and responsibility can be attributed to persons or groups acting or failing to act within those structures. It is their control of these structures that gives them power.

These critical views of power have a strong normative input in that their aim is to construct a model of society in which power is reduced to a minimum, if not eliminated. It is assumed that in a rightly ordered society there can be no real conflicts of interests and therefore no necessity that some people's actions be determined by others. The difference in political ideology will be a function of the differences in the sources of power that the various writers detect. Thus for a classical liberal the state interfering with (voluntary) exchanges between individuals is the paradigm case of power. For the socialist, the unequal distribution of property itself is a source of power – the means by which some can manipulate or threaten others. Furthermore, the differing interpretations of 'interests' are relevant: for the individualist they are normally seen as a 'given',[2] for the socialist, interests themselves may be products of manipulative forces.

The above interpretation of power, however, is by no means the only way in which the concept may be understood. Not all writers view it in pejorative terms and they deny that the notion of responsibility can be easily attached to it. It may be that power, as a certain kind of ability, is neutral and that we can only use praise or blame in respect of the uses to which it is put. Certainly, the theory that there can be a society without power is scarcely conceivable. The diversity of people's interests, and certain ineradicable features of the human condition, imply that the prospect of 'common purposes' on which the elimination, or indeed, reduction, in power depends is illusory. From this perspective, power is not merely exercised when threats or sanctions are its base but is also present when inducements are offered to get people to do things they would not otherwise do. Power politics is not only inevitable but invaluable. This conception of power is to an extent parasitic on rules and legitimacy. Indeed, power can be legitimated by reference to legal rules, its consistency with shared beliefs and its validation through a form of consent (Beetham, 1991).

Nevertheless, it is quite clear that the explanation of the continuity and cohesion of society cannot be explained entirely by reference to power alone. What characterises continuity in social relations is surely some minimal agreement about social values and rules so that there are 'right ways of doing things' and authoritative procedures. It is true, of course, that the need for someone in authority to make binding decisions arises because we cannot agree on all things, but nevertheless, the acceptance of this presupposes some minimal agreement on social procedures, if not social ends. In revolutionary situations, the power or *ability* to bring about desired actions in others may properly describe the behaviour of the ruler, but this can only be temporary. If the social order is to survive then power must become authority, or, at least, legitimate, if only to economise on the resources that have to be expended on the army, police and so on. But even when order does depend upon threats there must be some semblance of legitimacy, if only to guarantee the loyalty of the army. This is what Hume meant when he said that governors depend upon *opinion* since force is always on the side of the masses.

> The soldan of Egypt or the Emperor of Rome might drive his harmless subjects like brute beasts against their sentiments and inclination. But he must, at least, have led his mamelukes or praetorian bands, like men, by their opinion. (Aiken, 1948, p. 307).

One of the indications that authority has broken down in society is evidence of an increase in the use of power that has been made in order to get people to obey. It is part of the philosophical conception of a social science to show that a greater understanding of social regularities can be derived from the explanation of authority, which describes the internal aspects of behaviour, than from the study of power, which merely reveals the *external*, observable aspects of society, such as decision-making in political and economic affairs.

Another way of bringing out the particular significance of power is to contrast it with exchange. By exchange we simply mean a voluntary act between two or more people that, because it is free and uncoerced, puts them in a preferred position to not making the exchange. The economist in explaining how resources are allocated in a free exchange economy has no use for the concept of power precisely because in his model actions are product of choices, not of threats of sanctions. Exchange is said to depend on co-operation while power is characterised by conflict. When he explains the effect of a price change on the pattern of demand, he is deducing what will happen, given certain elementary assumptions about human nature, and not making observations in the manner of a political sociologist. Theories of exchange are therefore highly general, and their truth does not depend upon observations in particular societies, while theories of power are particular, and rooted in specific, historical and social circumstances. This is only another way of saying that theories of power belong to the positivist – empiricist branch of social science, even though they do not have to be, and in most cases are not, historicist.

There is, however, a possible objection to this distinction between exchange and power. This treats the power relationship itself as explicable in exchange terms (Barry, B. 1976, pp. 67–101). Thus, if *A* has power over *B* in the sense of being able to determine his actions by threats, it might still be maintained that the relationship is one of exchange since *B* could, technically, have acted otherwise. Since somebody who obeys through fear of sanctions is making a choice it is logically possible to treat these types of power relationships with the same 'logic of choice' apparatus that is used in formal economics. But from the political theorist's point of view this masks some important distinctions. Somebody whose freedom of choice is limited by the threat of sanctions has to that extent had his will determined by another, whereas someone who exchanges with another without such threats exercises his will autonomously. It is of the essence of power relationships that they involve the diminution of liberty, but this is not normally a characteristic of exchange. To the extent that exchange takes place within a context of authoritative rules, freedom and authority may not be incompatible. However, while this form of authority may be compatible with liberty, it is quite likely that other types of authority relationships are not. As we shall see below, we have the notion of the 'authoritarian' state to describe that situation where legitimately constituted authorities make severe inroads into individual liberty.

We have not considered the relationship between power, coercion and force, but clearly these are analytically distinct concepts even though they are frequently used together. Authority and power are different ways of securing obedience, getting things done and so on, and while it is true that the *threat* of force is one of the most important bases of power, coercion itself is not the same as power. The exercise of superior force, signifies the absence of power and the failure of threats to put *B* in the power of *A*. While in most cases the threat of force will be sufficient to secure obedience this is not necessarily so, as can be seen in the cases of people with strong religious or moral beliefs refusing to submit to overwhelming force. Coercive power might be described as that type of power which is a function of a successful threat: a threat which no rational person could be expected to resist.

Thomas Hobbes was acutely aware of the distinction between power and force, even though his major work in political theory, *Leviathan*, is often taken, erroneously, to be a justification of a 'might is right' doctrine. Hobbes distinguished between political power and physical power (or power over things). The former indicates a genuine social relationship such that A is able to secure obedience from B: even though such obedience may be obtained because of the threat of overwhelming sanctions, it nevertheless rests upon a form of consent. It is not therefore the mere existence of coercion that creates power but the fact that people are sufficiently motivated, albeit through fear, to obey 'voluntarily'. For this reason, Hobbes is able to say that 'sovereignty by acquisition' – that is, by conquest – has exactly the same consequences as sovereignty by contract – that is, by agreement between individuals. Hobbes put the point thus:

> It is not therefore the victory, that giveth the right of dominion over the vanquished, but his own covenant. Nor is he obliged because he is conquered ... but because he cometh in and submitteth to the victor. (1968, pp. 255–6)

Political power is a circular, or relational, concept and its existence presupposes some interaction between the parties in conflict.

In contrast, physical power is the exercise of force when there is no submission. A person who shoots another does not have power over that person, although the fact that he does this may be sufficient to give him power over *others*. Of course, the exercise of force may enable someone to get what he wants. The highwayman may kill his victim and make off with the money but it would be extremely odd to say that this has anything to do with power. It is for this reason that Hobbes had little interest in 'physical power' for, unlike political power, this concept has little explanatory value.

It follows from this analysis that it is false to say that power increases positively with an increase in the amount of force. The Americans in Vietnam were able to deliver massive force but this obviously did not give them power. In fact, the involvement of the US in Vietnam was characterised by the absence of power despite their possession of the instruments of force. It could not secure obedience. If power is a relational concept, it does not necessarily follow that relationships of command and obedience follow on from possession of physical things.

A modern analysis, however, would depart significantly from that of Hobbes on one crucial point. Hobbes is saying that since all power rests ultimately on consent it must be the same as authority. If a person through fear consents to obey then he is the *author* of all the acts of the sovereign (Hobbes, 1968, p. 232), and consent through fear is for Hobbes just as voluntary as an uncoerced promise or agreement. All the acts of a sovereign are authorised by his subjects. The phrase 'abuse of power' is therefore meaningless since all power is legitimate. Of course, Hobbes had good reasons for saying this. He thought that continuity and social cohesion were products of political power and could not conceive of the 'natural' evolution of laws and institutions providing stability without there being an observable sovereign.

Modern political theory distinguishes between power and authority by reference to the way obedience is secured. The existence of a person, or body of persons, in authority suggests that obedience is secured by other means than threats and implies that the exercise of authority is a product of rules. Furthermore, it is maintained that continuity and stability cannot be guaranteed by power alone, although this will characterise temporary moments in a society's development such as revolutions and *coups d'état*. In fact Hobbes himself had great difficulty in explaining the transmission of political power without reference to rules which exist independently of the sovereign.

2 The nature of authority

Some theorists interpret all cases of authority as in some sense dependent upon rules and on the notion of 'rightfulness'. It is a concept that refers to *internal* relationships. This is to say that authority relationships cannot simply be matters of command and obedience but must involve ideas of rationality and criticism. Others, however, suggest that authority must involve the suspension of rationality, and indeed freedom, such that obedience to authority cannot be consistent with rational criticism.

The modern discussion of authority begins with the German sociologist Max Weber's classification of the types of authority (1947, pp. 324–9). Weber distinguished between rational-legal authority, traditional authority and charismatic authority. Rational-legal authority is characteristic of the modern, industrial, bureaucratic state in which those entitled to make orders and pronouncements do so because of impersonal rules, the existence of which can be justified on more or less rational grounds. In traditional authority, unwritten but internally binding rules, the explanation of which is historical rather than rational, entitle individuals to obedience. The authority of the tribal chief is an instance of this. Charismatic authority, however, appears to be unrelated to rules, but is explained in terms of some *personal* quality that an individual may have which entitles him to obedience. The standard examples of charismatic authority are Jesus and Napoleon; more recent examples might be Hitler or de Gaulle. Weber presented these types of authority as 'ideal' types, essential for social analysis rather than exact descriptions of reality. Most societies will in fact exhibit elements of all three types, although one is likely to be predominant.

It might be the case that Weber's types of authority are reducible to a variety of rule-governed notions of authority. This, of course, would entail the elimination of charismatic authority as a special type of authority. Some writers have indeed maintained that the idea of charisma is meaningless outside a set of rules that in some sense authorises an individual, and as a necessary consequence limits what she can do in the way of making orders. Such rules would then provide grounds for the rational criticism of her actions. It would indeed be difficult to maintain that an individual could exercise authority solely because of some kind of personal magnetism. It has been pointed out that all the suggested examples of charismatic authority were successful in so far as their actions were in some way related to an ongoing set of traditional rules – even if their actions may have in some sense involved departures from the rules (Winch, 1967, pp. 107–8). It may be possible to explain cases of charismatic authority by the application of 'tests' and these tests will reflect standards of appropriate behaviour which are independent of the qualities of the suggested charismatic leader.

Weber was more interested in sociological investigations into types of authority than in a philosophical analysis of the concept. Much of this analysis of authority itself turns upon a proposed distinction between *de facto* and *de jure* authority. Authority *de jure* means that someone is entitled to obedience because of a rule – although it is to be noted that *de jure* authority may not always be effective. Authority *de facto* exists where someone is able to get her way without either a ground or entitlement and yet without recourse to threats. While it is true that authority can be exercised in this way, the notion of *de facto* authority is difficult to grasp without the notion of a ground or entitlement creeping in, though this does not have to be a legal ground or entitlement. Peters's example (1967, p. 84) of *de facto* authority, the man in the cinema fire who directs people out of the building without having any right to do so, hardly seems good enough.[3]

If the *de facto* concept of authority is to be any use in social theory it must surely describe situations of a more or less permanent kind rather than temporary crises. A more likely candidate would be the position of the gang-leader who is able to exercise continuing authority over his followers and whose survival largely depends upon their agreement. Yet this seems to be at some remove from pure *de facto* authority in that the more successful the gang-leader is the more he will become entitled to be obeyed by his followers. While it is suggested that there is a use for the concept of authority outside the framework of rules, that concept seems peculiarly difficult to pin down and seems to contribute little to our understanding of the role that authority plays in explaining the unity and cohesion of a society. Nevertheless, there does seem to be some use for *de facto* authority in the explanation of people's obedience to the whole structure of rules. They are indeed accepted as a matter of fact, since there can be no higher rule that validates that acceptance. The concept of *de jure* authority then underwrites the particular roles that various individuals – judges, policemen, political leaders and so on – play in the system.

The easiest cases of people being in authority are provided by the rules of a legal system which authorise certain individuals to make decisions. The kind of authority here is that exercised by policemen, officials of the legal system, ministers and so on. Such individuals are in authority by rules but it is, of course, legitimate to ask what makes these rules authoritative. As we have seen in the theory of law, in any legal system, beyond the very simple type, there will be secondary rules that authorise people to adjudicate on and alter rules. The authority to make new laws even in a system of parliamentary sovereignty depends ultimately on a secondary rule which cannot logically be a product of parliament itself. We cannot, in legal contexts, make sense of someone being in authority without the concept of secondary rules. But cases of being in authority are not exhausted by the legal system and it is quite permissible to speak of someone being in authority where the authority is not a product of legal rules but is a function of moral or religious rules, for example, in the case of a parent or a priest.

While most (but not all) writers argue for the necessity of authority, and some would argue that it is not automatically inconsistent with liberty and reason, its very existence nevertheless poses at least a threat to certain values, especially autonomy (Wolff, 1976). While obedience brought about by authority is not the same as that induced by threat it does seem to involve a surrender of judgement. It may be right to follow its dictates because the rules of an institution or practice say so but it may not be justifiable by the tenets of a *critical* morality that transcends orderly procedures. It may be essential for the exercise of liberty that rules guaranteeing some predictability should be enforced but their existence implies at least the possibility, if not probability, that freedom will be threatened. When one acts autonomously one acts according to reasons, and one's actions are uninfluenced by the demands of an external authority, or even by the thought of favourable consequences. These phenomena seriously dilute the sense of rightness that should solely determine individual judgement. When we obey authority we seem to obey for no easily discernible reason: the commander ought to be obeyed simply by virtue of his or her office. It is the right to command that is crucial, not the reason for the right.

It is true, of course, that we do sometimes speak of authority where reference to some sort of qualification (beyond a position in a hierarchy) is relevant to obedience. When we defer to scientific authority, for example, it is the possession of specialised knowledge that justifies the deference. This is precisely the meaning of the expression 'an authority' (on something) in contrast to the phrase 'in authority' (by reference to a rule). Someone in a scientific community is an authority not because of her rank but because of her achievement in advancing knowledge according to rational tests. Furthermore, the utterances of an authority are always open to challenge, based on more or less objective standards, whereas those of someone in authority are not (except to the extent that the commands may exceed legitimacy, authority does not have to be absolute in order to be decisive).

It would be extremely odd to describe typical authorities, such as politicians, officials and judges, as being entitled to obedience because they possess superior knowledge that explains why they are entitled to obedience (as in the case of an authority). It is simply the rules that give them authority. Even when they make mistakes, that does not itself disqualify them (though repeated mistakes will, presumably, gradually undermine the efficacy of authority). The point here is that authoritative utterances are 'content-independent' (Hart, 1982, p. 254;

Green, L., 1988, pp. 49–51). By this it is meant that individual assessments of the qualities of a particular command are set aside or pre-empted (Raz, 1990, p. 123) by authority. To some extent, obedience to authority is therefore non-rational.

The convinced anarchist, if she recognises the need for some rules but rejects authority because of its elimination of autonomy, is in something of a quandary. The only legitimate rules would appear to be self-imposed restraints, and the demand for these might be met by voluntary associations (or perhaps the unanimity rule for public decision-making). But even these, by imposing constraints over time, undermine autonomy. Does not a truly autonomous person change her mind? Even the notion of a promise is not strictly binding on a truly autonomous agent because altered circumstances might undermine the authoritative nature of prior agreements (Green, L., 1988, p. 32). Also, extreme utilitarians cannot accept authority since its existence implies that rules will potentially prevent the production of public goods. Though, of course, moderate, or rule-utilitarians, may justify authoritative procedures on the ground that their existence has long-term social value even though their occasional relaxation might actually be productive of the good.

Other writers deny that the existence of authority implies a loss of reason and maintain that authority is never simply a matter of issuing commands but always involves an action for which *reasons* can be given. C. J. Friedrich argues that authority involves reasoning and says that this is not the reasoning of mathematics and logic but 'the reasoning which relates actions to opinions and beliefs, and opinions and beliefs to values, however defined' (1973, p. 172). He argues that any social system involves the communication of values and beliefs, and these values and beliefs constitute the basis of authority. Thus the actions of authority can be said to be subject to rational appraisal although, of course, this rationality will not be of an absolute kind. He says that those who sever the link between authority and reason confuse authority with totalitarianism.

But not only is acting for a reason in authority relationships unlike the reasoning involved in logic or mathematics, it is also unlike the reasoning that pertains to morality. For the rightfulness that attaches to the decisions of authority is not necessarily moral, it is a product of enough people recognising, and internalising a set of rules. Thus, although authority does imply legitimacy that may not be moral legitimacy. Indeed, few people would concede that authoritative rules always bind individuals. Problems with authority occur not only when the formalised rules and practices do not reflect the underlying *mores* of a community (they fail to become internalised so that authority loses its efficacy) but also when individuals come up against a conflict between their consciences and authoritative rules.

Thus, despite the apparent disjuncture between authority and reason, the former can be given a rational justification, though this is not the justification that we find in, for example, substantive moral argument. Authority arises out of, and is validated by, the needs of society, especially large-scale, more or less anonymous societies in which individuals are ignorant of everything but their immediate circumstances. This is perhaps why recourse to *legal* authority in them is more frequent than in smaller, more intimate communities. In the former, where individualism has replaced communal attachments, co-ordination problems are particularly acute. It is here that the justice of authoritative procedures becomes important, even if on occasions they produce judgements that do not conform to more abstract conceptions of justice. But some social conformity is necessary. We have already seen (in Chapter 3) that Prisoners' Dilemmas generate the necessity for the state and authoritative rules since reliance on individual judgement is destructive of the long-term interests of individuals themselves. Authority is then validated by practical reason rather than by the reason that justifies ultimate truths. Indeed, when authority is embedded in established customs and practices it will contain (implicitly) more knowledge than that which is available to individuals, equipped only with an 'abstract' reason. Viewed in this light, the damage that authority does to autonomy is not as great as the critics suppose: the existence of authoritative rules, which guarantee some predictability, enable more projects to be undertaken and plans to be pursued than would otherwise be the case. The freedom that is lost through submission to authoritative rules is merely a special form of 'rational freedom'. A more prosaic notion of freedom depends on there being authoritative rules for there to be some predictability in society. Still, the contentless nature of authority means there is always the possibility of a conflict between conscience and firmly established rules.

It is probably the case that those who tie authority and rationality closely together are confusing political authority with authority in general. It seems to be in the nature of the modern state that its actions, although they may be supportable in principle by rational argument, affect people rather differently from other sorts of authority. It is the case that the state, or rather its officials, have the *right*, at least in the positive sense of right, to tax, conscript and coerce in other ways, but this is not the same sense of right action as that suggested by Friedrich. The distinguishing feature of the state's authority is, of course, its use of sanctions and this is very different from the authority of, say, a priest. Furthermore, obedience to direct commands is not very much like the recognition of traditional, enabling rules.

It is undoubtedly the strength of the modern state, and its mode of operation, that has given rise to a view amongst some political theorists that there has been a 'loss' of authority in the modern world. It is not always clear what this means but it might be exemplified by the decline of the moral authority that used to be exercised by churches, parents and others, so that individuals are in a sense thrown back on their own resources without the guidance of traditional standards. More importantly, the fact that on many occasions in the twentieth century political rulers have acted tyrannically, and have in many cases done so with mass approval, supports the view that societies are no longer held together by authority. Hannah Arendt (1961) was of the opinion that this was indeed so and that the collapse of authority in the modern world preceded totalitarianism. In her view genuine authority cannot conflict with liberty and liberals are therefore wrong in thinking that a loss of authority leads to a gain in liberty. Authoritarianism ought not to have the pejorative overtones that it undoubtedly has and many governments classified as authoritarian she would call totalitarian. In fact, traditional liberals would say only that a fall in *political* authority increases liberty; they would not deny the dependence of liberty on general, authoritative rules of conduct.

In this view, authoritarian government severely limits the range of choices open to the individual without at the same time postulating any ends for society at large. Thus in this 'law and order' model, characteristic of military regimes, an individual may have to conform only outwardly to certain dictates; he is not required to display any ideological support for the authorities. In fact, regimes of this type may have no grand design or overall purposes for society beyond the maintenance of stability. Such authoritarian regimes may be compatible with a considerable degree of individual liberty in certain specified areas provided that such free action does not pose a threat to what the authorities regard as law, order and social stability.[4]

By contrast, totalitarian regimes do not merely demand observance of the dictates of authority but require also a positive commitment to the ends and purposes of society. The difference between authoritarianism and totalitarianism then is not one of degree, in that the latter limits personal freedom more than the former, but rather that the two sorts of social order have different ends in view. A totalitarian regime is not simply concerned with stability but with the realisation of an ideology and with the inculcation of a new personality. Such a social order may, in theory at least, be compatible with a significant degree of participation, and certainly with positive displays of enthusiasm for its purposes.

These two sorts of social order may be contrasted by reference to the way that dissidents are treated in each. In an authoritarian society a dissident will simply be locked up, and the penalty, although it is likely to be harsh, may be fixed and known in advance. Under totalitarianism, however, a political law-breaker is often regarded as in some way mentally deranged in not appreciating the true purposes of society. He therefore requires 'treatment' rather than formal punishment. The consequences of dissidence may in fact be less harsh than in authoritarian societies and may be limited, in some cases, to public degradation and humiliation.

In practice, however, this theoretical distinction may not amount to much. Totalitarian democracies notoriously fail in their aims of creating a new 'man' and often are reduced to maintaining stability by harsh, repressive measures so that the ultimate ideological purposes of creating a new society are neglected. The histories of Marxist 'totalitarian democracies' seem to confirm this in that early ideological fervour eventually gives way to routinised *authoritarian practice*. Nevertheless, the distinction is worth retaining because it does point to some differences between the various forms of non-liberal rule and does indicate the logical possibility of the maintenance of a limited freedom of choice in purely authoritarian regimes.

3 Some problems with power

Modern, empirically minded political scientists have been interested in power precisely because it appears, in principle, that statements about power are eminently suited to observation and quantification – unlike statements about authority. Some theorists of power go even further and suggest that societies are somehow held together by the exercise of power, as if there has to be in every society some unique and determinate source of power. It would not be too inaccurate to interpret those theories as modern versions of that traditional doctrine in jurisprudence which holds that in every legal system 'sovereign power', or the ability to determine other men's actions, must reside somewhere. Contemporary 'power elite' theories are saying that whatever the formal structure of authority, the constitution and the system of rules, there is always a group of people who can actually get their way on a given range of issues. It is assumed to be the business of the social scientist to unravel the complexities of power in modern society[5].

On the normative side of political theory, power has been, in the main, interpreted either neutrally or considered to be in principle undesirable. A neutral interpretation of power maintains that power in itself cannot be evaluated as good or evil but that such evaluation applies only to the uses to which it is put. The exercise of power to achieve desirable goals in society is not thought to be of itself reprehensible. Of course, the persuasiveness of this view depends upon a considerable amount of agreement on the proposed ends of society.

It is at this point that the normative critic of power would object. He would say that if there is this agreement about ends then power would not be needed at all to implement them, they would come about non-coercively. In other words, power can never be neutral; every exercise of power involves the imposition of someone's values upon another. For this reason, liberal critics of power recommend strict limits on the exercise of power whatever its source, including the 'uncorrupted people'. Doctrines such as the 'separation of powers' and constitutionalism in general are precisely concerned with the problem of curbing power. This is regarded as an impossibility by the 'sovereign power' theorists, whether they are old-fashioned legal positivists or modern, quantitatively minded sociologists.

We know that power relationships are a type of causal relationship in which one person, or a group of persons, can bring about certain actions in others and that, unlike in authority relationships, the determinants of these actions are such things as threats, sanctions, propaganda and psychological pressure. But it may be difficult to distinguish this phenomenon from, say, 'influence'. In fact, influence may be legitimately regarded as a type of power in that a person who is influenced to act in a certain way may be said to be caused so to act, even though an overt threat of sanctions will not be the motivating force. However, if influence is a type of power it is difficult to see how it can be assimilated to most models of power since the person influenced, or caused to act, will not normally be aware of this.

In a famous definition Bertrand Russell said that power was the 'production of intended effects' (1938, p. 25) and while this clearly indicates an important aspect of power, it misses a crucial feature of the concept. This is that the exercise of power in society always reduces the area of choice left open to individuals while not all cases of power as the production of intended effects involve this. Sometimes we do speak of someone having the power to produce certain effects which may not involve the loss of freedom to others – for example, the power of the scientist. The peculiarly *social* significance of the exercise of power is that it limits the range of choices open to individuals. Power may also be intimately linked to the production of unintended effects. Some people may be said to have power over others, in the sense of determining their actions, without deliberately intending to do so, as perhaps a pop star may determine the dress and lifestyles of his followers without specifically meaning to: although, it could be said that this is an example of influence rather than power. Some sociological theories of political power have, however, suggested that a group may exercise political power, perhaps because it has a *reputation* of power, without this being visible in a direct, intended way.

A more fruitful approach to the conceptual problem of power than the search for a watertight definition would be to consider some of the proposed explanations of the phenomenon. We know that it is not misleading to consider the exercise of power as being, in some sense, about the capacity of someone to determine another's actions and so to reduce the other's range of choice that his behaviour conforms to the will of the person who exercises the power, but the interesting question concerns just those factors that produce this. In other words, what are the social bases of power? In the final section of this chapter we shall consider some sociological *theories* of power, but at this stage some general comments must be made on the kinds of social phenomena that generate power. There have been many suggested bases of power but three – the coercive, the psychological and the economic – are particularly important.

We have already considered some aspects of coercion when discussing Hobbes on power and undeniably this is the most important source of power. When we talk of military power we mean precisely that the ability to dispose of sanctions enables some to move others in desired directions. The power of the state similarly consists of the fact that it can induce obedience by threats, even though it may be denied that the state always acts in this way. As we said earlier, the important point to remember about coercion is that the power that emanates from this is still dependent ultimately on a kind of choice: since not all people choose to obey threats backed by sanctions, the possession of coercion does not automatically guarantee power. Power relationships that arise out of coercion are circular; there is no such thing as a 'lump' of power in the form of weaponry.

We should also include positive sanctions (rewards) the existence of which can move or cause people to act in ways different from those in which they would act in the absence of the rewards. The inclusion of positive sanctions draws attention to the relational aspects of power. Some offers may be quite irresistible. Furthermore, an offer in certain circumstances may involve something essential to life that its withdrawal would be equivalent to a negative sanction (or threat). The offer of water to a person in the desert (Oppenheim, 1981, p. 41) clearly involves power since its withdrawal puts the victim in a much worse situation, even though no actual coercion is threatened.

When we come to psychological power the circular aspects of power seem to diminish. We can undoubtedly speak of power in the sense of a person being psychologically caused to act in certain ways without having the very limited choice that exists in power by coercion. The clear cases of such psychological persuasion are brainwashing and other forms of indoctrination. Here one person is made the tool of another without there being overt sanctions. It would not be correct to use the word 'influence' here as it is not strong enough to bring out the crucial element of overwhelming pressure.

The difficulty with the psychological concept of power is that it can so easily be used to describe situations which fall well short of the clear case of brainwashing. It has been suggested that the 'persuasive powers' exercised by advertisers are significant enough to eliminate, or severely reduce, the freedom of consumers. Newspaper editors and proprietors are said to exercise power over their readers in a not dissimilar way, in that they can manipulate opinions and use propaganda so as to influence significantly the course of political and economic events. We speak frequently of the 'power of the press' in exactly this sense.

It is quite likely that the powers of these 'persuaders' have been greatly exaggerated. It would be extremely odd to liken advertising to brainwashing, because in the latter literally no freedom of choice is involved. Some advertising campaigns have been notoriously unsuccessful. In fact, the technique of the advertiser is to find out what people want and then to advertise the appropriate product rather than to attempt to manipulate wants. It is, of course, extremely difficult to get convincing evidence of the ability of advertisers to exercise power in the manner that has been suggested. This applies equally to the power of the press. It could be said that newspaper 'propaganda' is simply an aspect of the continual process of persuasion that characterises an open society. All political leaders are involved in exactly the same activity, this being an essential part of liberal-democractic politics. Arguments about the power of the press to mould opinion are more convincing the nearer a *monopoly* is approached. Still, it would be foolish to deny that the press can influence behaviour, and influence is a sub-category of power.

A further area of social life where power may be said to be exercised without the explicit threat of sanctions is the economy. The philosophical defenders of the free market economy maintain that this system is characterised by exchange, which is assumed to be voluntary; each party to an exchange puts herself in a preferred position by making the transaction. The particular virtues of an exchange process are that it allocates goods and services efficiently, in the sense of satisfying the desires of individuals as expressed by their preferences, and produces a social order that minimises power and maximises liberty. The plausibility of this argument derives from the claim that power is asymmetrical, i.e. the more power A possesses the less B can have. Exchange, in contrast, benefits both parties. But if we specify the terms of an exchange, which may produce vastly disproportionate benefits, and take account of positive sanctions that may have to be delivered to secure power, the contrast between the two types of social relationship may not be as great as some have suggested.

The collectivist argument – that the exchange process does not reduce power – is difficult to formulate precisely. It could mean that the *conditions* under which exchange takes place, that is, the prevailing system of property rights, are so unequal that they generate a system of *market power* which enables owners virtually to enslave non-owners. Or it could mean that there is something about exchange itself, under whatever conditions it takes place, that creates social and economic power.

The former argument is more plausible; it is possible to conceive of, and indeed demonstrate empirically, conditions under which market power exists. Inequality of wealth through inheritance, the concentration of industry and the exploitation of workers by monopoly, may well give people little genuine choice in nominally free societies, especially in times of economic recession. An employer who is able to dictate onerous terms to an employee can exercise power over her and therefore an employee suffers a loss of liberty when she has little alternative but to accept those terms. While there are cases when this is so, and someone who is able to withhold a vital service from another constitutes a similar example of economic power, their incidence has probably been much exaggerated[6].

Still, some of the most sophisticated market theorists this century, the German Ordo liberals, sometimes called social market theorists (see Barry, N., 1993a), were acutely aware of the tendency of unaided markets to generate market power quite spontaneously in the form of monopolies and cartels. The unlimited freedom to contract could, over a period of time, undermine contractual liberty by reducing the range of choice available to individuals. This can happen without threats. Therefore, it was recommended that political power should be used to promote liberty as autonomy, rather than a specific type of welfare, utility or equality. In effect, the attempt was made in postwar Germany to reproduce by political methods the absence of power that characterises the perfectly competitive market economy. This is, then, a benign use of power. It could be describable in terms of power over, in that the policy involved some compulsion, but it would be directed towards power to, i.e. increasing people's power to make their own projects and plans in a way that would not have been possible if economic society were left to purely spontaneous processes. Whether or not such policies lead to an overall increase in powers is perhaps an empirical question. But such is the multifaceted nature of power that it is doubtful as to whether a definitive answer will ever be found.

At the heart of the second objection to the exchange model (that markets by nature are coercive) is the metaphysical contention that its vision of man as a purely self-interested maximiser is a deficient concept of human nature. It is held that people do not realise their true powers through exchange since that process is entirely self-regarding. Instead of man realising his true potential as a social being, in that what he creates through co-operative activity becomes peculiarly his own, he becomes, under a market system, the prisoner of his ephemeral desires. This is what Marx probably meant by 'alienation'. The demise of Marxism has not meant that this anti-market philosophy has lost its appeal. Communitarianism (in some of its versions) depends on the view that the market involves a peculiar kind of power – a power that drives people towards individual self-fulfillment and away from their social attachments. The more goods and services that are subject to market methods of production the less opportunities there are for social production and consumption. If this is an example of power it is clearly not the power of one individual (or group of individuals) over others because the notion of responsibility for the resulting outcome is impossible to attribute to identifiable agents. It is an impersonal system that is said to produce a certain kind of power and a consequent loss of liberty.

4   Social theories of power

It was suggested at the beginning of this chapter that power purports to be a sociological concept: statements about power are thought to be, in principle, statements that are testable. The definitions used by political scientists and sociologists in their studies of power are said to be operationally significant in that they point to phenomena which are observable, and which can be explained by the traditional methods of empirical social science. It is to be noted that, in this respect, such studies of power as have been produced are of the extreme positivist kind. This means that the science of power consists almost entirely of empirical work based on particular case studies. There are no general theories of power or universally true generalisations about the phenomenon which have the logical coherence and explanatory significance of the theorems of economics. Of course, in the history of political and social thought it is possible to find a number of purported general theories of power but none of these has achieved any real scientific respectability.[7]

Theories of power are often divided into those that emanate from the political science discipline and those that come from sociology. This is a convenient distinction since, although both approaches might claim to be in the empiricist tradition, they have produced significantly different conclusions as to the nature of power. The sociological approach tends to stress the *centralisation* of power thesis, namely the theory that in every society there will be a small group that can dictate all major decisions. Political science has been associated with *pluralism*, the view that in society there is a number of influential political groups, not one of which can determine *all* decisions.

One of the most famous of the sociological models of power was C. Wright Mills's *The Power Elite* (1959). Mills claimed that the picture of the United States of America as a democratic pluralist society, characterised by decentralised decision-making and the separation of powers, was false. Beneath the veneer of constitutionality there was in reality a unified class or power elite which could always get its way on important decisions. The personnel of this elite were drawn from three interlocking elements in American society – business, politics and the military. The elite displayed group consciousness, coherence and, implicitly, conspiracy. Mills claimed that his was a work of empirical sociology in that he thought he had identified certain key sociological factors underlying the cohesiveness of the group, such as identical family and class backgrounds and the fact that the members of the group were educated in similar schools and colleges. Mills presented a picture of elite group domination which belied the openness, pluralism and individualism traditionally descriptive of American society.

The pluralist reply to this turns mainly on methodological considerations. A sociological *description* of the properties that may unite a collection of people does not constitute a *theory* which predicts that the group will get its way on a given range of disputed decisions, where interest conflict. Political scientists of the pluralist school maintain that whenever power elite theories have been cast in a scientific form they have been easily refuted (Dahl, 1958; Polsby, 1963).

However, it is in just this area that the pretensions of power studies to be scientific has been attacked and the weaknesses of a straightforward positivist version of empiricism exposed. The two key (and interrelated) claims of pluralism – that power exists only in situations of observable conflict and that people's interests are simply what their overt preferences reveal – have been specifically criticised. The critique has summed to a position which holds that the existence of an apparent consensus in society – that is, the absence of observable conflicts – does not mean that power relationships are absent. Furthermore, it is claimed that the satisfaction that individuals appear to reveal with their present social and economic arrangements does not mean that they are exercising autonomous choices.

The more modest of those criticisms of the pluralist model is that presented in P. Bachrach and M. Baratz's (1970) discussion of the 'two faces of power'. They claim that the pluralists see only one face of power, in cases of observable conflict. However, in reality certain issues, often to do with race and minority interests, although they are characterised by power relationships, do not appear on the political agenda: they are 'organised out'. In this view, 'non-decisions' are given a political significance which is neglected by the pluralists. It is not that people are compelled to do things – as losers in a pure conflict situation are – but rather that their wants are not counted. Issues are not raised because, presumably, it would be pointless to raise them. This neglect, it is claimed, is largely a consequence of the pluralists' behaviouralist methodology; an approach to the study of power which is exhausted by observations of overt conflict.

In a more radical theory, however, Lukes (1974, pp. 21–33) posits a 'third face' of power. This analysis goes further than that of Bachrach and Baratz in completely rejecting the behaviouralist approach and claiming that a proper theory of power must take account of the way interests (preferences) are formed by prevailing social structures which give opportunities to covert persons (or groups) to exercise power. It is the presence of (unobservable) power that prevents individuals becoming autonomous agents capable of realising their true interests. Power exists in the form of manipulating people's desires, not simply suppressing them. Lukes, notwithstanding his avowed anti-positivism, still maintains that his theory is an empirical one in that it is possible to ascertain what people's real interests are and what conflicts of interests exist, even though they are latent.

He makes use of a famous study by Crenson (1971) on the politics of air pollution to illustrate his argument. Crenson was interested in the fact that Gary, Indiana (a one-company town dominated by US Steel) had been much later than other American cities in securing anti-pollution regulations, despite the fact that its steel industry was notorious for generating dirty air. Yet there appeared to be no overt pressure for pollution control and the company had no direct influence in the local political process. It appeared to be the case that US Steel's *reputation* of power was sufficient to prevent the issue emerging in the conventional political arena. The power exercised by the company was then the power of omission rather than commission.

Although this looks very much like a 'two faces' of power account, Lukes sees in it the germ of a theory that acknowledges the decisive influence that groups operating through social structures may have over the forming of individuals' preferences. The apparent consensus in the community over the absence of anti-pollution regulations was illusory for it is, he claims, obvious, that their real interests would be advanced by such measures. There was a 'latent conflict ... between the interests of those exercising power and the real interests of those they excluded' (Lukes, 1974, p. 24)

However, he puts the matter in a way too favourable to his case when he writes: '... there is good reason to expect that, other things being equal, people would rather not be poisoned (assuming, in particular, that pollution control does not necessarily mean unemployment) – even where they may not articulate their preference' (Lukes, 1974, p. 27). The assumption here seems to be that autonomous agents would realise their true interests but for the existence of a power structure that systematically distorted them. But it is surely plausible to suppose that there was a genuine conflict between equally 'real' interests over the issue of pollution control (see Gray, 1983, p. 86) in the resolution of which US Steel may have only been one of a plurality of social forces. Furthermore, pollution, by raising production costs, *does* have an effect on employment prospects: this cannot be assumed away. Hence, it is not implausible to suggest that the local political system of Gary reflected people's preferences for jobs over clean air. The outcome might then have been undesirable on other grounds but not because a power system had distorted the people's real interests. However, the whole issue could be redefined and re-analysed as a classic public good problem. Anti-pollution measures are public goods which it is in no one's interests to produce. Transaction costs could have prevented the citizens collectively suing U.S. Steel for environmental damage, or property rights in the environment were ill-defined: the citizens lacked 'power to'. In this context it might be plausible to say that the market system as a whole exercised influence but it is less convincing to attribute direct power (and responsibility) to US Steel, which is what Lukes wants to do.

Irrespective of the truth of all this, it is clear that the simple dichotomy between power as a sociological concept and authority as a philosophical concept is somewhat misleading. For it is not the case that our knowledge of power is advanced by ever more sophisticated empirical enquiries. Just what 'power' is, and what phenomenon is being measured, are themselves philosophical questions that cannot be solved by mere observation.

5

Political Principles

1 Political principles and political philosophy

In earlier chapters we examined some of the major concepts used in the description of social and political phenomena. While we have touched upon some of the normative questions central to social and political philosophy, especially those to do with the nature and role of the state, we have done so without any explicit consideration of the principles that must underlie such questions.

Values and principles are the traditional concerns of the political philosopher. This is true if the activity of philosophising about politics is regarded as a purely second-order activity concerned with the clarification of the concepts used in political discourse or if, as is more often the case today, its major role lies in the evaluation of policies, law and institutions. In the latter case clarification is still an important exercise which must precede the (doubtless) more interesting task of justification.

Principles are peculiarly important in relation to the role of the state. In Chapter 3 we were mainly concerned with the task of elucidating some important differences between the notions of the *public* sphere and the *private* sphere and trying to see what specific institutional facts about the state made it peculiarly well equipped for the delivery of certain kinds of goods and services. But when we talk of the state in relation to principles we are asking a slightly different, although related, question. This is the question of the justification for the use of the state's authority to promote such things as equality and social justice or to protect human rights. Since principles are always likely to be in conflict, the philosophical arguments about politics will

108

turn on the justification of the use of the state's coercive power to implement policies derived from these principles. Of course, not all questions of principle depend on the justification of the use of coercion: a person desiring a more liberal society, in the older sense of the word 'liberal' which is linked with free market economics, demands that the state use less of its coercive power[1]. But this is itself a philosophical argument about the *illegitimacy* of the use of coercion; it is not necessarily an argument about the irrelevance of principles to political and social affairs. It involves a theoretical question: is the prohibition against coercion based on *efficiency* grounds – the claim that free markets generate more satisfactions – or is it derived from the inviolability of the individual (a rights argument?).

If principles are intimately connected to justification then it should be immediately apparent that the logic of statements containing normative political principles is very different from the logic of other kinds of statements in the social sciences. In positive social science, especially that of the extreme empiricist kind, the emphasis is on those statements which can be established as true or false by the method of observation. Even in those aspects of social science that are less empirical, such as the theory of law and certain parts of economic theory, the investigator would deny that her explanations entail any particular normative viewpoint or policy prescription. For an observer to describe a set of legal rules as normative does not involve her in a moral commitment to them.

In arguing about politics, we are not proving and disproving, or verifying and falsifying: we are justifying a policy by reference to principles. While people often appear to disagree strongly about particular laws or policies, such disagreement may be resolved if the particular policy prescriptions prove, under analysis, to be inconsistent with sincerely held principles. It is said, however, that some political disputes may be genuinely irresolvable if there is dispute at the level of ultimate principles, because there is nothing beyond this to which the dispute can be referred. Not all political theorists would entirely agree with this last point and some of the most interesting recent work is at the level of ultimate principles. It has been enhanced by the decline of Logical Positivism and emotivism (the claim is that ethical principles are non-cognitive, they merely convey feelings, not knowledge). While it is obviously true that political principles contain strong emotive elements, which are used in ways that appeal to our passions as much as our reason, it is not longer the case that political argument is completely disabled by such considerations.

2   Universalisability and ethical pluralism

The doctrine that the essential characteristic of principles is that they are universalisable is associated with the *prescriptivist* school in ethics but it is equally applicable to political principles. Recent important work in political philosophy relies implicitly (and in some cases explicitly) on this doctrine. Universalisability as a doctrine about the foundations of ethics is associated with the work of R. M. Hare (1963).[2]

The basic elements of the theory can be briefly summarised. The main function of ethical statements is that they are recommendatory; they are, in other words, guides to action. Unlike propaganda and psychological persuasion, however, there are logical relationships between ethical statements. A genuine ethical statement must be universalisable. This means that if one calls *x* good then all other similar cases of *x* must be called good, unless they differ in some relevant aspect. Universalisability, then, means that like cases must be treated alike. An example of universalisation appears in one version of the rules of justice, which states that 'people ought to be treated equally unless a morally relevant ground is produced for different treatment'. A person who commits himself to a moral principle is committed, as a matter of logic, to the universal application of that rule in all similar cases. This, of course, means that you must apply the principle to yourself if, on some hypothetical occasion, your actions fall under it. Therefore, moral rules and principles are abstract guides to conduct to apply to future unknown situations. This means that a principle would not be a moral principle if it contained proper names since then it would not be universalisable. Here is an important element of 'impartiality', in that one cannot exempt oneself from the application of a principle if the principle is to be universalisable. Rawls, in his famous derivation of the principles of justice (see Chapter 6 below), adopts a similar strategy when he tries to determine what principles would be adopted by rational moral agents to apply to future unknown situations under conditions of ignorance.

Hare, however, insists that universalisability is a logical feature of moral argument. It is not a substantive statement of impartiality, or fair treatment of individuals, because it is, as he says, logically possible to adopt any principles, as long as they can be universalised. Therefore moral argument for him is not deciding on principles because of their *content* but exploring the implications of holding whatever principles it is that we hold. Such explorations will take account of facts, since it is an empirical question as to what are similar cases, but moral argument itself is *deductive* in form (Hare, 1963, p. 30). An obligation to keep a promise, for example, cannot be derived from the fact of a promise alone but is deduced from this and the further premise that promises *ought* to be kept. Hare is therefore opposed to any kind of ethical naturalism – that is, the doctrine that words like 'good' stand for natural properties such as 'pleasure' – since this undercuts the prescriptive, recommendatory force of moral argument.

The decision to adopt a moral principle is a personal decision for which no rational justification can be given, and there is no limit, in logic, on the kinds of moral principle which may be adopted. Since consistency is the main feature of moral argument, quite appalling principles may be adopted, but Hare thinks that people are unlikely to adopt principles which when universalised harm their own *interests* (1963, pp. 86–111). Thus, in his famous example, a Nazi who believed that Jews should be exterminated would have to accept (logically) that he, or his family, should be exterminated if it turned out that they had Jewish ancestry. We eliminate appalling moral principles by seeing what happens when they are universalised. Hare thinks that 'fanatics' – who would consistently support an appalling principle even if, when universalised, it would act against their own interests – are extremely rare (1963, p. 172).

It has been suggested that the universalisability thesis is trivial in that it is almost always possible to point to a difference in a situation which makes a principle inapplicable. To put it another way, the rule of justice which states that 'like cases be treated alike' may be consistent with a great variety of treatment, depending upon what are counted as similar cases. When moral reasoning is characterised, if not exhausted, by universalisability, then at most it ensures a certain kind of fairness, albeit of a minimalist kind. However, the fact that the choice of a principle to be universalised is ultimately subjective is sufficient for the theory to be condemned as emotivist by those who would locate morality in concrete social experience.

However, the demand that moral argument be consistent is not trivial and may go a long way towards eliminating principles based purely on ignorance and prejudice. The universalisability thesis, since it asks us to adopt principles to apply to future unknown occasions, puts severe *practical* limits on the kind of principles that may be adopted. In Rawls's *A Theory of Justice*, rationally self-interested individuals, in a hypothetical state of ignorance, have to agree upon a set of principles to govern their future relationships. These principles are fully universalisable. In this procedure we have to imagine how a principle would affect us should we find ourselves in certain situations and the results of this enquiry have been shown to be far from trivial. Of course, Rawls's thesis is much stronger than the conventional universalisability thesis since he tries to show what principles would be adopted.

Another method of normative reasoning is *pluralism*. Although it is not formally inconsistent with universalisation, indeed both are similar in accepting that our ultimate moral and political principles cannot be given a rational justification, it does constitute a significantly different style of moral and political reasoning.

In describing this approach we must first distinguish the use of the word pluralism here from its use in a sociological sense to describe political activity as a process of adjustment between competing groups. In relation to principles, pluralism means that for the purpose of evaluating policy a *variety* of principles may be held; it is not possible to order or rank them under one supreme principle. Whether a particular policy is justified or not depends on how a person weights these competing principles. A person may value both freedom and equality and therefore, in any policy evaluation he will have to weigh the benefits of a more equal distribution of income and wealth that egalitarian taxation brings against the loss in the freedom of the individual to retain income. The ultimate source of these principles and the weightings attached to them must be simple intuition.

A clear statement of the ultimate plurality of values, and their irreducibility to one single principle, can be found in Sir Isaiah Berlin's *Two Concepts of Liberty* (1969, p. 125): 'Everything is what it is: liberty is liberty, not equality or fairness or justice or culture, or human happiness or a quiet conscience.' A loss of liberty may be compensated for by an increase in equality but it must be remembered that it is equality that has been increased, not another version of freedom, or even 'social utility'. The most fully worked-out version of this approach is to be found in Brian Barry's *Political Argument* (1965). In this important work Barry explained the rational basis of the pluralist approach to principles by an analogy with indifference curve theory in microeconomics. A person can show, by his preference map, that he is indifferent between various combinations of, say, liberty and equality, in exactly the same way as a consumer can be said to be indifferent between amounts of grapes and potatoes. The map will simply show how much liberty he is prepared to give up for increases in equality (it being assumed that principles are substitutable at the margin) and still remain equally satisfied. All that is required for rationality is that people be consistent in their choices.

Barry regards this pluralism as a reasonably accurate account of most people's attitudes towards principles. They are not normally *monists* – that is, they do not subordinate principles under one supreme value but are prepared to make trade-offs at the margin. Perhaps the most controversial trade-off in political argument in the contemporary world is that between efficiency and equality. It is accepted that the aim of increasing equality in the distribution of income can only be secured by a loss in efficiency.

It is to be noted that in Barry's approach policies are related to people's wants. His most frequent examples are concerned with the conflict between policies that maximise total want-satisfaction in a community (aggregative principles) and those that distribute want-satisfaction in a certain way (by promoting more equality, for example). This is different from the varieties of universalisation which ask us to adopt a set of principles to apply to future unknown occasions – when we are ignorant of *specific* wants and needs.

While pluralism has secured some considerable support amongst political theorists, and while it may also be a good *description* of the way people approach policy problems, it has serious drawbacks as an evaluative procedure. The problem is that individuals' weightings for various principles are likely to be dissimilar – that is, their indifference curves will be of different shapes – and there is no way of choosing between them. The rationality of individual consumers is easily demonstrated by this method, but the *justification* of government policy is quite another thing. The government must inevitably select one particular set of weightings when making policy and Barry offers no reason why any particular set should be preferred. It is no coincidence that advocates of both 'left' and 'right' economic policies can claim rationality for their programmes by the pluralist technique.

It is also the case that the rejection of this approach does not necessarily imply monism, as Barry (1973, p. 6) has conceded. Rawls offers a *set* of principles in his *A Theory of Justice* and by the use of a *priority rule* tries to demonstrate how the individual component principles will be ranked (see Chapter 6, below). Barry himself is curiously silent about the nature of ultimate principles and implies that they cannot really be argued about; rationality consists of making choices consistently from a given set with subjectively assigned weightings. Yet political theorists do maintain that some things can be said about them. Someone may weight equality very strongly and would therefore be prepared to sacrifice large amounts of liberty for small increases in equality, and here surely a question could be asked about the normally unintended *consequences* of adopting such a policy. Furthermore, some notion of universalisability may very well be needed if arbitrariness is to be avoided in normative political theorising. However, it would be misleading to deny the pluralistic nature of morality. Values do appear to be incommensurable in that there is no one that can secure universal assent, no measuring rod that can adjudicate between rival conceptions of the good or the right. In one sense this is a distinctive feature of liberal societies in that their rule structures, either through design or evolution, protect this diversity. Nevertheless liberalism, in all its versions, has been proposed as a value system that has a compelling hold on our reason. Yet from Berlin's perspective it is simply one doctrine amongst a plurality of competing ones. From within the doctrine itself no decisive reason can be produced to show why its emphasis on liberty and equality should theoretically rule as inadmissible orders that might value traditional hierarchy (Gray 1989). Liberal writers may have identified a kind of generic or basic morality (as in H. L. A. Hart's 'natural law with minimum content') but this is perfectly consistent with competing and often illiberal ways of life. But even if one accepts liberalism there is still the question as to what its components might imply for particular policy decisions: the seemingly irresolvable conflict between the rival liberal theories of justice is simply one example of this.

The above considerations have been about the 'meta-ethical' aspects of normative theorising. Meta-ethical questions are about the ultimate foundations, or logical status, of value judgements and answers to them do not entail any particular set of moral or political principles. To establish principles, additional arguments have to be advanced. Hare and Rawls's meta-ethical theories are not dissimilar, but while the former opts for a version of utilitarianism as his substantive moral theory, one of the latter's major concerns is to refute utilitarianism. How do we choose if moral decisions are ultimately subjective?

3 Contractarianism

The effect of the varieties of non-cognitivism and positivism was to produce this impasse in normative political philosophy; and the conclusion was that ultimately reason was incompetent to discriminate between rival value systems. The subjective nature of value judgements seemed to preclude the possibility of political philosophy itself. However, in recent years there has been a revival of a traditional method of political philosophy which acknowledges the personal nature of the moral decision while at the same time trying to show how discriminations between rival social and political orders can be made. The method is *contractarianism*: a method that demonstrates what structure of rules (including moral ones) would be chosen by individuals to advance their subjective interests, under specified circumstances.

Although contractarianism is mainly methodological (indeed it has produced a variety of substantive political philosophies, see, for example, Rawls, 1972; Buchanan, 1975; Gauthier, 1986) its exponents espouse some controversial views about the nature of man, reason and society. It provides, therefore, a useful link between the purely conceptual problems of normative politics and the substantive doctrines to be considered later in this chapter.

The contractarian method has, of course, a long history and although contemporary exponents of it are a little less concerned with the traditional problem of *political obligation* (the main moral question for Hobbes, Locke and Rousseau) they use assumptions that differ only in degree from those of their predecessors. In principle, it presupposes that legitimate moral rules emanate from agreement: that we are bound not by the dictates of an (alleged) objective morality but by commitments voluntarily made. In some contractarian theories particular moral rules and economic and political institutions arise out of specifically non-moral contexts: they emerge, or are discovered, through a process of bargaining. In others, the social contract is a device to protect a pre-existing moral structure (often couched in the form of individual rights). The former view is the more prevalent one in contemporary thought.

The idea of a 'promise', in which promisees are bound by their own wills, becomes the model for political and economic order rather than some objectively desirable state of affairs. No contemporary contractarian, of course, supposes that such promises were ever actually made, or that they can impose obligations through historical time; nevertheless, it is hoped that by this method of abstraction appropriate rules, quite often those to do with the distribution of wealth and income in society, can be constructed which accord with the choices of rational individuals unencumbered by motivations arising out of their present (and often privileged) circumstances.

In modern welfare economics the method is frequently used to solve public good problems (see above, Chapter 3). These difficulties occur because, if the assumptions about individuals are true – that is, that they are governed by rational self-interest and *immediate* calculation (see Hamlin, 1986) – then these individuals can have no incentive to generate those laws, institutions and policies that are in their long-term interests. By a contract (imaginary or otherwise) people may pre-commit themselves to forms of action which advance their goals. In all cases of potential collective benefit, constraint on individual action is required.

What these brief considerations show is that the contractarian method is quintessentially *liberal*[3] in a methodological sense, although specific political forms that emerge from it may not be liberal in the substantive sense (as the example of Hobbes shows in a spectacular way). It is also rationalistic, but in a rather special sense. It is obviously not so in the sense that an objective 'reason' can prescribe forms of conduct irrespective of history and tradition but in the sense that individuals may be said to construct, by the use of *their* reason, appropriate institutions. It is, then, subjectivist in approach.

The difference in the substantive political views that come out of the contractarian perspective derive largely from the different assumptions that are said to govern the contractarian setting. The most famous contemporary contractarian, John Rawls (see below, Chapter 6) produces a generally social democratic state with a heavy redistributive element largely because he believes that risk-averse people, imbued with a sense of morality, and ignorant of their particular talents, would not contract into a society which involved the smallest possibility of their being disadvantaged. On the other hand James Buchanan, who is much more Hobbesian in his foundations (see Barry, N., 1984), argues that individuals would choose a set of rules that would protect their property (which may have been acquired by force in a necessarily amoral state of nature) and which would authorise the provision of public goods.

If the contractarian method is to be a purely 'neutral' device for generating rules, institutions and policies out of people's subjective choices, then whatever does emerge must be, for procedural reasons, legitimate. Thus a particular outcome, say in the matter of social welfare, depends entirely on the distribution of moral sentiments across the contractors. The temptation for some contractarians, there-fore, is to describe the contractarian setting in such a way that certain inherently desirable outcomes are likely to occur. Indeed, it is the case that some political theorists, such as, Rawls, derive certain value conclusions from *intuition* and then show how they would emerge from the rational choice setting described by contractarianism. The result is that a certain plausibility in relation to values is achieved but at the cost of introducing an impurity in the supposed neutrality of the contractarian method itself.

Despite its clear drawbacks the contractarian method has one advantage: it asks us to look at existing social practices in the abstract and in ignorance of those particular interests that distract us from making decisions that would advance our long-term ends as rational maximisers. Classical liberals have found it particularly useful in surmounting those 'Prisoners' Dilemmas' that inevitably occur in market society.

In political philosophy, however, the tendency is still to emphasise particular substantive doctrines and it is to those that we now turn.

4 Utilitarianism

This is superficially the most appealing of moral and political doc-trines (see Sen and Williams, 1982). Since it has always been concerned with the maximising of human happiness it seems free from the dogmatism of those alternative doctrines which stress the importance of following rules, even when the following of such rules might result in human misery. It is also a forward-looking doctrine concerned with bringing about future desirable states of affairs and is not concerned with putting right past wrongs. It has for this reason always attracted social reformers and progressive thinkers, who often bring scientific techniques to bear on the process of policy formulation. To this extent it is a 'rationalist' doctrine; its advocates believe that social problems are capable of scientific resolution and that social harmony can be engineered. But it would claim to be free from the narrow dogmatism of other ideologies, which are often designed to advance class interests, in that utilitarian judgements are made from the standpoint of the 'ideal' or impartial observer and are designed to advance the *general* interest. Utilitarianism is also said to be derived from individualistic premises.

In the past utilitarianism was a meta-ethical doctrine *and* a body of substantive principles. Utilitarians identified the 'good' with pleasure, and hence committed the 'naturalistic fallacy' (Moore, 1903), by identifying the desirable with what is actually desired. The most famous of them, John Stuart Mill, tried to demonstrate some sort of 'proof' of the utility principle. However, their significant achievements lay not in the foundations of ethical judgements but in the political applications of those values in which they believed. Nowadays utilitarians are almost purely concerned with a kind of practical ethics and politics.

There is an important distinction between the utilitarian ethical doctrine, that a person ought to act so as to produce the general happiness (in the sense of beneficial consequences) on every possible occasion, and the economic, social and political doctrine which justifies government action, and therefore coercion, on the benevolence principle. Our main concern will be the economic and political doctrine since this was the primary interest of the classical utilitarians and the doctrine persists today mainly in this form. It is also important to note that the significance of utilitarianism does not lie merely in the fact that it evaluates human action, and political and social policy in general, in terms of its generally beneficial consequences but also in the very special way in which it interprets the notion of consequences. It assumes that society at large has a 'utility function', which is observable and measurable, and which consists of a sum of individual utility functions. To understand what this means we must go back to the founders of the doctrine.

Bentham provides us with the first systematic theory of utilitarianism: his basic ideas are formulated in *A Fragment on Government* (1948) and *An Introduction to the Principles of Morals and Legislation* (1970). Bentham's first aim was to found a 'science of ethics' based on some observable property in human action which could be maximised so that evaluation of action and policy did not depend on abstract, metaphysical principles which were purely subjective. An action was not right because it was in conformity with a rule of natural law: it was right only if it produced happiness. Pleasure, or happiness, was for Bentham the only good, and therefore actions and policies could only be evaluated by their *consequences*, in terms of the production of happiness.

Bentham is said to have attempted to combine two contradictory ideas in his ethical and political theory – utilitarianism and psychological egoism. He said that 'man is under the governance of two sovereign masters, *pain*, and *pleasure*, it is for them alone to point out what we ought to do, as well as determine what we shall do'; this implies both that men ought to seek happiness (in fact, the *general* happiness) and that each person can do no other than seek his own happiness. It may be possible to say that under certain circumstances maximising the general interest by the individual also maximises his personal interest, but it has always been thought that there is considerable tension between utilitarianism and egoism. In fact Bentham did attempt to resolve the tension by providing each person with a motive to promote the general happiness through the sanctions of the law.

Bentham assumed that there was an objective property of pleasure attached to every action, so that the effectiveness of a policy could be measured by reference to how much pleasure (or pain) it produced for each individual. Pleasures varied only in quantity, and Bentham produced a 'felicific calculus' to show how pleasure could be measured in seven dimensions (1970, ch. IV). There was no *qualitative* distinction between different people's desires: no individual's desire had a prior claim to satisfaction on grounds of its supposed superior quality. There is then an element of 'impartiality' built into utilitarianism.

Furthermore, Bentham was a methodological individualist. Words like 'state' and 'society' were fictitious entities and statements containing them had to be broken down into statements about individual behaviour if they were to have any meaning. Thus the community's interest could only be an arithmetical sum of the interests of the individual members. An ideally informed legislator could, with the objective yardstick of pleasure, compute the effect of, say, policies *A* and *B* by assessing, with the aid of a felicific calculus, the net balance of pleasure over pain that each produced and implement that policy which yielded the highest amount of net pleasure. Pleasure was thought to be an objective measuring rod which tells how much better policy *A* is compared to policy *B* in exactly the same way that feet and inches, for example, enable us to compare the lengths of physical objects. In determining the policy for punishing criminals the legislator must fix penalties (pains) just sufficient to prevent future outbreaks of crime so that the community is thereby better off. Punishment must not, for example, be too excessive since this would inflict more pain on the offender than it would generate pleasures for the community. In this process questions of 'desert' and moral guilt are inadmissable since they are entirely subjective concepts, and relate also to *past* actions which are in themselves irrelevant to a future looking, policy oriented, legislator.

The importance of *statute* law should now be apparent. While a legislator could derive a social utility function for the whole community from individual preferences, there was no guarantee that this would come about automatically since each individual could do no other than pursue her own pleasure. Therefore the sovereign, by the use of sanctions, had to generate artificially the coincidence between private and public interest. It is true that in economic matters Bentham believed that private actions would naturally lead to an optimal allocation of resources, and he was therefore a qualified advocate of *laissez-faire*[4]. But here the logic seems to be that if the legislator could make an improvement on the private market there would be nothing in principle to prevent the use of command/statute law to bring this about. It is certainly the case that abstract concepts of individual liberty or rights, since they are not capable of being put on the utility scale, would not be allowed to stand in the way of the production of *social* utility.

It is not difficult to demonstrate some major deficiencies in this attempt to formulate a science of policy. Pleasure is not an objective property which can be summed up and put on a scale, so that policy *A* can be said to yield so many more units of happiness than policy *B*. It is a *subjective* property inhering in each individual. The whole idea of a felicific calculus, by which pleasures can be measured on a unitary scale, is now regarded as being little short of absurd. But perhaps an even more decisive objection is the fact that the construction of the Benthamite 'social welfare' function requires that the ideal, fully-informed legislator be able to make interpersonal comparisons of utility. This means that to say that state of affairs *x* is preferable (yields more utility) than state of affairs *y* requires that there be some way of comparing the gains and losses to individuals that accrue through the implementation of the policy. To say that, for example, a tax policy is justified on utilitarian grounds requires that the pleasures of those who gain outweigh the pains of those who lose, in terms of utility – but there is no *scientific* way of making such a comparison. The fact is, though, that utilitarians do make such comparisons, and there can be no objection to them provided that it is recognised that they involve moral judgements.

It is no doubt the difficulties involved in measuring pleasure that has led utilitarians to associate the doctrine not with maximising a sum of pleasures but with generating preference or want-satisfaction (Pettit, 1980, ch. 12). Making the same assumption of orthodox utilitarianism, that equal consideration should be given to each person's wants or preferences, the injunction to the legislator is to maximise as many individual satisfactions as possible. The equal consideration point would preclude the most blatant cases of interpersonal comparability, where one person's interests are deliberately overridden on behalf of the collectivity. However, this approach is not without its difficulties.

Are mere wants to be maximised or should the legislator consider only fully informed ones? What information is available about various wants? As we have seen in the public good problem (see above, Chapter 3), in certain situations individuals have every incentive not to reveal their true preferences (if they can take a free ride). In such circumstances, the legislator may have to make a judgement about wants, thus destroying the original claim of the doctrine that it makes no judgement about the quality of preferences.

But there is a further, even more serious, problem with preference-satisfaction as a normative theory. If we are to take account only of expressed wants does not this mean that those which would be condemnable on other moral grounds, such as the wants of the racist or sexist, are to be given equal consideration with others? The utilitarian could argue that to do this would undermine the interests of others, but the point here is that to disallow such unpleasant preferences is to evoke principles, such as justice or equality, which are independent of utilitarianism; for these principles are not suscep-tible to the kind of calculation that the doctrine requires. If utilitar-ianism relies on a collective decision-making procedure (some version of majoritarianism would appear to be irresistible) for the transmis-sion of wants into public policy it is difficult to see how potentially immoral consequences can be avoided. Indeed, constitutional protec-tions for minorities, and other potentially disadvantaged groups, are founded on principles that sometimes defeat utilitarian claims.

Utilitarianism, however it is formulated, takes a narrow view of morality. It dismisses as mystical or metaphysical those ethical prac-tices that cannot be translated into preference maximising terms; most specifically those phenomena that impose duties arising out of past actions and which hold irrespective of any calculation of future benefits. The binding nature of promises and agreements are the obvious examples. It is inadequate for the utilitarian to say those should hold because their breach would disappoint legitimate expecta-tions; the reason why the breach of an agreement is condemnable is because it is wrong, not merely because such action generates dis-utility. As soon as we say that the injunction to maximise utility should be qualified by the admission of rules that will potentially conflict with its demands, we need some other principle to adjudicate such conflicts and therefore utilitarianism loses its claim to provide determinate solutions to moral and political problems.

It has often been pointed out that there is something almost totalitarian in classical utilitarianism. Despite its supposedly individualistic premises it does entail the imposition of a collective value judgement on society as a whole. If that cannot be derived from individual choices then it must emanate from the subjective will of the legislator. But if Bentham's psychological axiom is true, that every individual maximises his own utility, then the legislator will maximise his interests rather than social utility. In fact, Bentham was constantly aware of this problem. His first proposed solution was that a benevolent despot might implement the utilitarian utopia but later he was to argue that only a version of representative democracy would promote the general interest. This proposal will be considered in Chapter 11.

The Benthamite formula has also been severely criticised because in its original version it is easy to show that it is internally *incoherent*. We are told that the standard of value for a community is utility, or the Greatest Happiness of the Greatest Number, but, as has frequently been observed, this is capable of at least two interpretations. Are we to maximise the greatest possible amount of happiness or distribute happiness in such a way that it is enjoyed by the greatest number of people? The following example illustrates the way in which the two aims of utilitarianism can be in conflict. Consider two utilitarian policies, *A* and *B*:

	Policy *A*	Policy *B*
Person one	60 units of happiness	30 units of happiness
Person two	50 units of happiness	30 units of happiness
Person three	0 units of happiness	40 units of happiness

Under policy *A* more happiness is produced than under policy *B* but in the latter more people enjoy happiness. The point is that utilitarianism does not give a *decisive* solution to policy problems and therefore loses its claim to superiority over its rivals. In fact, it is probably the case that Bentham himself interpreted the Great Happiness principle in an *aggregative* sense (that is, policy ought to be aimed at producing the greatest total happiness), and abandoned his own quasi-distributive criterion (the greatest number principle). This is how utilitarianism is normally interpreted today, and it is certainly a more consistent view, but it is still open to the very serious objection that, because it is solely concerned with consequences in terms of the production of beneficence, it obliterates some important elements in our moral and political vocabulary, namely equality, justice and rights.[5]

Critics of the purely aggregative aspects of utilitarianism often point to some rather disturbing implications of the doctrine. Does not its deterrence theory of punishment sanction 'punishing' an innocent person, if that is the only way that others can be effectively deterred from committing crimes? On the assumption that interpersonal comparisons of utility can be made, does not utilitarianism allow slavery if the satisfactions of the slave-holders outweigh the pains of the slaves? In a popular example we are asked to imagine a healthy person going into a hospital ward where there are three patients, one requiring a heart transplant and the others kidney transplants. Does not utilitarianism require that the healthy person be made to give up his organs, as this would clearly bring about the Greatest Happiness of the Greatest Number? While utilitarians might justifiably claim that these are rather fanciful examples, they do indicate the clear deficiencies of a doctrine that is concerned solely with maximising future, collective want-satisfaction.

The most famous utilitarian, John Stuart Mill, was deeply disturbed by Bentham's concern with *mere* want-satisfaction as the sole criterion of political and moral value. In *On Liberty*, he appeared to suggest that freedom of action was a value in itself irrespective of its contribution to utility in a simple quantitative sense. Indeed, in *Utilitarianism*, he undermined the foundations of the doctrine by drawing his notorious distinction between 'higher' and 'lower' pleasures. By this Mill meant that certain activities were of a higher quality than others, even if they appeared to yield lesser units of happiness in a quantitative sense. Desires for intellectual contemplation, scientific and artistic enquiry and so on, therefore have a claim to satisfaction in a utilitarian society, and their value cannot be assessed by the crude hedonistic calculus. Mill insisted that the satisfaction of such elevated desires was consistent with utility, but it was a 'broadened' utility 'grounded upon the interests of man as a progressive being' (1974, p. 70). The pursuit of higher pleasures would yield more satisfactions in the long run.

We can see considerations not unlike those of Mill at work in some areas of public policy, notably in tax-funded aid for the arts. If a local authority subsidises the price of theatre or opera seats it is in effect selecting particular wants, out of the whole range of individual wants, for preferential treatment, since without such aid the intensity of wants felt by opera and theatre-goers would not be sufficient to keep the activities going. Such subsidies would be quite inconsistent with pure Benthamism.

Mill's ideas certainly represent a more 'civilised' version of utilitarianism and his commitment to personal freedom (see below, Chapter 8) qualifies him for admission to a broader liberal tradition. But he failed to solve the problem of the conflict between utility and justice.[6] Although he claimed that a properly articulated conception of utility would include considerations of justice and distribution, such a conception is in fact so broad as to be vacuous and can offer little or no guidance for the problems of policy.

Some contemporary utilitarians have developed the doctrine of *rule-utilitarianism* to counter some of the traditional objections to consequentialism, and have contrasted it with *act-utilitarianism* (see Mabbott, 1956; Lyons, 1965; Smart and Williams, 1973). Act-utilitarianism suggests that morality requires the individual to act, on every occasion, so as to maximise the sum of human happiness. This means that moral rules, such as the rules of justice and promise-keeping, are provisional only and may be breached if the strict adherence to them would diminish the sum of human happiness. Act-utilitarianism is normally addressed to those *deontological* ethical theories that define morality as the strict following of moral rules for their own sake (see Mackie, 1977, ch. 7). Often such theories prescribe the following of moral rules which may cause great suffering. An act-utilitarian like Bentham would say that there was no rational foundation for the principles of deontological ethics; they depend on intuition.

It is easy to think of examples which lend a superficial plausibility to act-utilitarianism. There are many occasions when to tell a lie (for example, to a Hitler or a Stalin) would actually increase human happiness, and when to enforce quite rigidly the rules of justice, in some types of criminal cases, would be quite gratuitous. It is also true that a morality, the rules of which bore no close relationship to human needs and wants, would have little to recommend it. But these rather trivial observations do not save act-utilitarianism from the main charges levelled against it.

In a political and economic sense, the consequences of a thorough-going act-utilitarianism are likely to be highly suspect. It seems to grant governments the discretion to act on behalf of what they think is the general interest. Since a Benthamite demonstration of the general interest requires the summing up and interpersonal comparison of individual utilities, its implementation could involve considerable arbitrariness. Yet act-utilitarianism would seem to exclude binding constitutional rules which limit arbitrariness. The Benthamite system, characterised by sovereignty and statute law, does grant the legislator great discretion. But the two great problems here are, firstly, the impossibility of the legislator calculating and comparing the consequences of alternative policies, and, secondly, the design of procedures to ensure that the legislator will promote the general interest rather than her own.

Rule-utilitarianism evaluates not the consequences of particular acts but the consequences of following rules. General rules, such as promise-keeping, telling the truth and the rules of justice, are justified on utilitarian grounds. Thus the breach of a rule, which might produce an increase in happiness, would not be tolerated because it is the following of rules themselves that contributes to human welfare. The virtue of rule-following depends partly on the claim that rules embody a kind of collective wisdom which is unavailable to the legislative calculator. Indeed, the presence of an established rule relieves people of the burden of calculating consequences that act-utilitarianism seems to require of them.

This is the kind of utilitarianism that Hume had in mind. While stressing the importance of rules it does not found them upon 'intuition' or an abstract metaphysic that is not related to human wants and social survival. In the Humean model rules are not so much planned and designed but develop almost spontaneously, and people adopt and retain those rules that prove to be useful (Miller, 1981, ch. 3). The rules of justice were not rationally demonstrated from an abstract notion of a 'social contract' but emerged as devices by which individuals could make their relationships predictable (Aiken, 1948, pp. 42–69). Thus rules acquire a validity which is independent of immediate consequences but is linked to utility and welfare in the long run.

However, rule-utilitarianism shows a tendency to slip back into act-utilitarianism whenever rules conflict. For here, a choice between rules would have to be made in terms of immediate consequences. Furthermore, if a rule is so formulated that exceptions are permitted, as any utilitarian is likely to recommend, then decisions as to whether the exception is to be allowed will turn on exactly the same considerations that influence the act-utilitarian.

The kind of exceptions to the utility-maximising imperative that rule-utilitarians have in mind are those that involve the protection of basic rights. However, if rights are admitted into the utilitarian calculus (by way of a rule) what will be produced is a somewhat weak form of restraint on maximisation but if rights are given full strength this will seriously attenuate the utility-maximising goal (Frey, 1985, p. 65). Certainly, collectivist utilitarians would never permit the rights of private property to stand in the way of some maximising goal.

Though rule-utilitarianism is a plausible social doctrine, it is difficult to see what it has to do with traditional utilitarianism. First, there is no attempt to define some utility function or collective welfare statement for the whole community; the rules, although they are justified by reference to consequences, do not embody a collective purpose. Second, and following on from the first point, there is no attempt to measure utility at all. Third, rule-utilitarians are sceptical of discretion, either at the personal or the political level. This has provoked the charge that rule-utilitarians are 'rule-worshippers'.

In contemporary political theory utilitarianism has suffered some serious setbacks (see Sen and Williams, 1982): almost all of those derive from its original commitment to 'pleasure' as the standard of value and its attempts to derive an aggregate social welfare function from individual utilities. All such attempts have been condemned as destructive of the 'separateness of persons' (Rawls, 1972, pp. 22–7). Almost all of the criticism derives from the original Kantian notion that individuals are 'ends' in themselves who ought not to be treated merely as *means* to the ends of others or a 'fictitious' entity called society. In this ethic, questions of justice are always prior to questions of utility or welfare. All this points to an unbridgeable gulf between those ethical and political theories that point to justice and individual rights as the main focus of value and those that stress consequentialist considerations.

5 Individualism

In contemporary political argument individualism has been an increasingly influential voice. But it is a complex word which covers a wide variety of normative positions. In a sense all liberal doctrines (as outlined in Chapter 1) are individualistic since they start from the basic proposition that individuals are in a sense the main focus of moral theory and that familiar social institutions should be neutral between differing conceptions of the good which persons will have: rules are in effect morally empty procedures which enable a pluralism about values to prosper. There has to be an agreement about just rules and practices but this consensus is consistent with a divergence of opinion with regard to particular ends and purposes. However, the individualism to be considered here is significantly different from conventional liberalism on the ground that the latter doctrine has become specifically associated with a form of redistributivism. As we shall see in Chapters 6 and 7, in conventional liberalism individuals have only a qualified claim to resources so that arguments from social justice and equality are used to justify a reallocation of assets in society. Indeed, egalitarian liberals argue that if the state is to be properly neutral between differing conceptions of the good, and if it is to treat people as equals, it is morally obligated to engage in significant redistribution because otherwise certain individuals and groups will be arbitrarily disadvantaged. The differences between the various liberal individualist doctrines turn on how they interpret the equality principle, though none rejects it.

However, a more rarefied form of individualism, deriving primarily from traditional liberal political economy, disputes the redistributivism associated with conventional liberalism (and its associated welfare institutions) in favour of a more austere doctrine that elevates the market to a pre-eminent role in the allocation of resources. The major claim is that if the state takes the dominant position here it will seriously attenuate genuine individualism. This is because political activity undermines property rights and the rule of law, and threatens liberty. For this form of individualism (perhaps more accurately called economic liberalism), personal achievement and self-fulfillment are realised through market exchanges rather than politics. Although excessive political activity in the private economy was in the past objected to on the ground of its alleged inefficiency, contemporary individualists have added a moral gloss to what was previously an almost exclusively economic argument. Although the morality of market individualism has not been fully developed, it also has a kind of metaphysical slant in that strict economic liberals assume that the only meaningful focus of attention for social analysis is the behaviour of individuals abstracted from their social circumstances and treated as more or less rational maximising agents. It is this methodological bias that gives individualism some claim to universalism in its prescriptions and has, of course, provoked the hostility of the communitarians.

No doubt, the collapse of communism, the perceived dissatisfaction with almost all forms of central economic planning, the dissatisfaction with some aspects of the welfare state and the spreading of market arrangements throughout the world have all contributed to the partial revival of this doctrine (a resurgence that is, however, less noticeable in Western liberal democracies than elsewhere). In America and Britain, economic individualism has been associated with conservatism. This is perhaps an unfortunate and inaccurate identification since the theoretical implications of the doctrine are decidedly unconservative and, as many traditionalists have noted, to some extent pose a threat to what have become accepted activities of the state. Individualism is not a party political doctrine but a way of analysing laws, policies and institutions from a distinctive theoretical perspective.

The individualist may be a rights theorist, who objects to state intervention because it seriously undermines personal autonomy and free choice irrespective of the inefficient (in a technical economic sense) outcomes of such action, or she may be more or less consequentialist in pointing to the adverse effect on individuals that state activity is claimed to have. The latter position is more conventional and has been effective in the questioning of public policy that has been such a feature of individualist thought. However, it should be distinguished from orthodox utilitarianism. For individualists object to the construction of utility functions for society as a whole, since these seriously compromise the separateness of persons and they treat individuals as means to the ends of society. The commitment to subjectivism which individualists display means that there are no objective purposes that can be attributed to society; its institutions are necessary mechanisms for harmonising individual desires and they are not the purveyors of a social good arithmetically summed up from individual goods. This is why individualism has been inextricably bound up with the objections often made to the imposition of plans, redistributive patterns and rational schemes on society. Its arguments have been addressed as much to conventional liberal egalitarianism as to the more spectacular experiments of socialism and communism. The arguments here are not merely economic, they also derive from the philosophical and ethical claim that there are no social purposes as such, only individual endeavours and goals. Economic individualists tend to argue that the liberal egalitarian's commitment to redistribution is the pursuit of a social purpose not reducible to individual plans and intentions: although most believers in social justice would insist that policies in its name are actually designed to enhance the well-being of identifiable individuals.

There is a connection between individualistic subjectivism about value and emotivism in ethical theory. In the absence of objective moral standards, individualists tend to claim that social rules are devices, agreed-upon procedures, to enable essentially private persons to pursue their goals. Thus the state is an agency or conduit for transmitting private desires for public goods from individuals to an artificial collectivity. The contrast between individualism and communitarianism here could not be clearer, for the latter doctrine specifically transcends subjectivism by locating objective moral standards in those shared meanings that a study of ongoing communities reveals.

Despite the vaguely formulated ethics of economic individualism, and its distinction from utilitarianism, it cannot be denied that its major political achievements derive from its consequentialist and quasi-empirical critiques of various public policies. The literature is replete with demonstrations of the counter-productive and disco-ordinating effects on the market process of such things as protectionist trade policy, rent control and indiscriminate welfare payments (see Friedman, M., 1962; Barry, N., 1987, chs 2 and 3). However, these arguments are primarily about efficiency and do not have much to say about matters, such as the foundations of justice, of rights and of liberty, which are germane to political philosophy. This lacuna stems again from that subjectivism in ethics which is such a feature of individualist thought. The only things that distinguish the economic liberal's public policy arguments from utilitarianism are the refusal to make interpersonal comparisons of utility and the rejection of the ideas of a 'welfare function' for society as a whole. But only in a few individualists, notably the extreme libertarians briefly discussed in Chapter 3, do these objections derive from moral statements about individual rights.

However, in a curious way individualist social theorists make use of the Pareto principle as a kind of surrogate for a rights doctrine. It will be recalled that this principle is really about efficiency – it shows how market exchange systems allocate resources according to individual desires and demonstrates that the state can only make improvements on the market in the supply of public goods. But the prohibition it places on the making of interpersonal comparisons of utility makes it a suitable alternative to aggregative utilitarianism for economic individualists. After all, utilitarians often justify progressive income tax (on the ground of the diminishing marginal utility of income principle) because it maximises total social utility. However, this is excluded by the Pareto principle because that rules out any change which makes at least one person worse off. The reference that the Pareto doctrine makes to the impermissibility of harming (however minutely) the interests of any one person in the construction of social welfare functions has therefore been a convenient way in which economic liberals have hoped to incorporate the moral claims of individualism in the basic structure of welfare economics. The same reasoning explains the preference that individualists have for various forms of unanimity and weighted majority rule procedures for the making of public decisions in democracies. Although these arguments exclude the cruder kinds of economic redistributivism, they do not constitute a satisfactory substitute for a genuine moral philosophy of individualism.

This is so for a number of reasons. The most important is that the Pareto principle makes no comment on the distribution of resources from which market trading begins. This, in fact, puts the *status quo* in a privileged position. Yet a fully-fledged moral argument for market individualism cannot leave matters there. For however morally acceptable, and efficiency-enhancing, the exchange process is it must begin with objects which are not acquired through mutually advantageous economic interaction. The obvious examples here are land and certain natural resources. Indeed, since Locke, liberal individualists have been obsessively concerned with the right to the ownership of scarce resources. The 'morality' of the Pareto principle relates only to exchange from a given set of resources. Indeed, many Paretians argue for a redistribution (on moral grounds) of initial resources and then endorse the efficiency improvements that consequent free exchange produces. It is incumbent then on an individualist to produce arguments that demonstrate the morality of a given distribution of resources. This clearly would necessitate some consideration of the rights of inheritance, of the problems that occur with the monopoly ownership of a scarce resource and all of the other issues that occur in connection with property. The Pareto principle neither approves nor disapproves of the initial distribution of resources, it is silent on the matter.

Furthermore, some liberal individualists (see Rowley and Peacock, 1975) have expressed dissatisfaction with the Pareto principle because it is not founded upon the principle of liberty. This disquiet arises from the fact that it is purely an efficiency criterion and for that reason could theoretically sanction considerable state intervention. For example, for a market to be truly efficient it is required that certain strict conditions be met. Consumers must be fully informed of all options so that suppliers cannot exploit their ignorance (this is important in the delivery of such services as health care), and there must be no externalities. These considerations could justify state intervention that goes beyond the supply of the conventional public goods. Liberal individualists might often find themselves upholding the principle of personal liberty against the claims of efficiency: making the market more efficient, in the Pareto sense, does not make it more free in a moral sense. Moral arguments for liberty may point in different directions from Pareto-efficiency considerations. Indeed, the fact that the Pareto principle could allow intervention on the ground of potentially limitless market failure makes it an unreliable guide for individualists.

As we shall see in succeeding chapters, individualism has to engage in moral arguments about liberty, justice and, especially, the right to property. Although in its pure economic guise it has contributed much to the understanding of the way that free markets work, especially their role in the co-ordination of knowledge (see Hayek, 1960), this is only one aspect of political theory.

6 Feminist ethics

We have already noted that feminism has produced new elements in the language of political theory. The distinction between the public and the private (and the arbitrary restriction of the latter to domestic life) has demonstrated that traditional political concepts have an application that goes beyond the conventional realms of politics and law. In many policy issues, the recommendations that feminists make could be incorporated into a gender-free liberal philosophy, though they do involve some possible conflicts with the ethics of that tradition. It is still true that when it comes to political evaluation feminists often make use of the principles described above but do so in a way which causes theoretical as well as practical problems.

Most important here is the extended use made of liberal principles, especially justice and equality. For what feminists do is to go beyond the gender and race 'blindness' of traditional liberalism and demand that special account should be made of the position of women, whose social deprivation is often the result of historical male domination. Thus feminists are normally in the forefront of demands for 'affirmative action' in the workplace and other measures to correct past injustices.

All this means that some feminist demands look as if they would conflict with the universalisability criterion mentioned above. If special account is taken of the position of women it means that moral rules will be less general and made to fit particular circumstances. Rules cease to be impartial guides to conduct but become weapons in the gender war. For the application of a kind of moral particularity is bound to lead to the claim that certain other groups, using liberal principles, can claim to be victimised; young white males in the United States argue that they are unjustly made to pay for past discrimination against women and blacks. This clearly involves contested questions of justice and fairness and, also, the problem of whether it is permissible to submerge individuals into whole groups and subject them to certain prophylactic policies which often harm their interests.

It is also argued by feminists that the roles which are assigned to women are not natural[7] to them but are 'socially constructed' (Okin, 1989). Biological differences do not dictate that women can find their highest fulfillment in being wives and mothers; these roles are assigned to them by social structures that make it more difficult for them to achieve success in the public world, which includes the private economy. Indeed, the Marxist notion of 'false consciousness' is frequently applied to women who choose the domestic world and submit themselves to its 'natural' morality. To feminists this is an ersatz voluntariness for it does not take account of the social factors that underlie women's choices. The liberal ideal of equality of opportunity is formally acknowledged but prevailing social arrangements make its substantive realisation impossible. What is required is a revolution in our customary way of thinking about evaluative issues so that we must take account of various social structures and developments which are not recognised by liberalism, communitarianism or any other male-orientated doctrine.

But there is another line of reasoning in feminist thought which might be thought inconsistent with the above observations. This is the view that traditional political morality is male-biased in a different way: it attempts to capture the whole of ethics in a narrow way and in doing so ignores equally important aspects of the moral experience. Male morality tends to be structured in general terms; it stresses duties and rights as features of rules which are indifferent to particular circumstances (Gilligan, 1982). Its feature is not benevolence, or even an awareness of special circumstances that might generate needs not capable of being subsumed under a universal rule, but is the coldness of a purely formal impartiality. Its stress on responsibility for action makes it entirely appropriate for the public world. In contrast, a feminine morality is peculiarly attuned to the peculiarities of a situation and is therefore capable of making moral judgements independently of, and on occasions superior to, those that follow from an understanding of the requirements of a rule.

On the face of it, this analysis looks very much like a reaffirmation of the separate roles for men and women that traditional political theory had implicitly assigned to them. Men have as their focus rationality and responsibility while women are concerned with care, altruistic predispositions and an intuitive understanding of those moral demands that transcend formal rules. However, it does not follow from this that women are to be forever confined to the traditional social roles. What is here being suggested is psychological, or even epistemological. It is a claim that morality is not exhausted by conventional, communicable principles.

It is not clear, though, that the depiction of typical morality as mere rule-following is entirely accurate. After all, even the most abstract of moral theories require individuals to accept rules that are to apply in particular circumstances. Indeed, people choose rules largely on their understanding of how they will affect them in special ways. Those theories that stress the element of impartiality in moral decision-making are not thereby excluding the relevance of particular circumstances, they simply insist that no one person or group should occupy a privileged position. Some theories specifically ask the moral decision-makers to put themselves in other people's shoes. Hume, in fact, made *sympathy*, an understanding of other people's predicaments, the basis of his utilitarian ethics. In the theory of justice, differences in treatment must be justified by differences in circumstances that are appropriate to the decision. So, although the rules of justice look formal and universalisable, the making of a just decision requires the taking account of particularities. Utilitarian calculations of the social good are invariably structured out of an appreciation of particular wants (Kymlicka, 1990, p. 273). Indeed, utilitarian policies, if they are to work, depend on the legislator's knowledge of special facts and circumstances.

Furthermore, the neglect of principles in the evaluation of conduct may leave the individual vulnerable to the potentially unreliable judgement of an observer motivated only by an appreciation of the particularity of a situation. Rules are important for political argument because they at least provide a necessary degree of predictability for human conduct: it is important to know why some action, of a person or of a government, is right or wrong – and this will depend on the invocation of a principle. Indeed, the most plausible of feminist arguments often result from an exploration of the meanings of conventional principles: an exploration which had not been undertaken by conventional political theorists, hidebound as they were by the orthodoxies of the discipline.

6
Justice

1 The problem of justice[1]

Despite more than 2000 years of political theorising the notion of justice still has no settled meaning: it is the paradigm case of an essentially contested concept. It is not simply that there are fundamental disputes at the normative level (it is only to be expected that individuals will disagree as to the justice or injustice of particular laws, policies and institutions), it is the fact that there is so little agreement as to what the concept stands for that causes serious problems.

The difficulty with the meaning of the concept has been exacerbated in recent years by the dominance of *social justice* as a moral and political value. In the last 30 years progressive social thinkers, alienated from Marxism both by the practical examples of tyrannical communist regimes and by more fruitful intellectual advances elsewhere in the social sciences, have justified radical social and economic policies by an appeal to social justice within the general framework of Western liberal democratic value systems. As a consequence the concept of justice has been perhaps irredeemably associated with problems of the appropriate distribution of wealth and income. The protagonists of social justice have therefore been concerned to demonstrate the criteria by which social justice sanctions certain distributive policies. The criteria are usually desert, merit and need, or sometimes merely more equality for its own sake. The emphasis placed on these different, and often conflicting, criteria may vary but the members of the school of social justice are united in their belief that the concept authorises a positive role for the state. That this view is more than just a declaration of policy or the justification of a substantive set of values but involves the *appropriation* of the *meaning* of justice to the radical view can be seen in a comment by one of its leading proponents, Brian Barry. In criticising the views of David Hume, who defended a conservative, rule-based explanation of justice, Barry said: 'although

Hume uses the expression "rules of justice" to cover such things as property rules, "justice" is now analytically tied to "desert" and "need", so that one could quite properly say that some of what Hume calls "rules of justice" were unjust' (Barry, B., 1967a, p. 193).

However, traditionally most users of the word justice were not necessarily radical, and nor is the contemporary usage necessarily tied to a reformist moral and political outlook. Those who are sceptical of social justice do not regard themselves as antithetical to what they would regard as a properly articulated conception of justice. In ordinary speech generally we talk of justice and injustice, where the words do not refer to the desirability or otherwise of states of affairs or particular income and wealth distributions but to the rules and procedures that characterise social practices and which are applied to the actions of individuals who participate in these practices. In this narrower conception justice is normally seen to be a property of individuals. When in the context of the common law we speak of a breach of the rules of 'natural justice', we are referring to an arbitrariness suffered by an individual in a rule-governed process. This latter concept has undoubtedly legalistic overtones but it should be sharply distinguished from a purely formal concept of justice. Justice is not merely conformity to law and it is certainly permissible to consider a law to be unjust without committing ourselves to the radical view.

The use of the term social justice in contemporary thought explicitly incorporates the notion of *welfare* into a concept which had traditionally been associated with rights and duties: to act justly was to give each man his 'due' or 'entitlement'. While there might be some dispute about what 'dues' and 'entitlements' were in particular cases, justice was not linked to an individual's (or society's) well-being or welfare (except in a trivial sense). The use of coercive law was limited to the restorative or corrective task of putting right a past *injustice*. Indeed, a person could act justly by simply sitting still. As Adam Smith wrote in *The Theory of Moral Sentiments*: 'Mere justice is, upon most occasions but a negative virtue, and only hinders us from hurting our neighbour' (1969, p. 160). What was peculiar about justice, for Smith, was the permissible use of force to guarantee it.

The connection between justice and welfare began with utilitarianism, especially Bentham. For in his work, no moral notion could have any meaning detached from aggregate well-being or welfare. Perhaps for the first time in political thought a rule of justice required some *further* justification, that is, one that went beyond the guaranteeing of a person his due. Thus utilitarianism is a monist doctrine in which individual claims to justice are necessarily submerged in a social calculus. A sceptic might well claim that what appears to be an essentially contested concept is not really so. It is not that these are two competing claims to a common exemplar, justice, but that there are two conflicting concepts, justice *and* welfare.

The word is part of a family of concepts which are intricately related.The concept most often used in the same context as justice is that of equality and the connection between the two ideas is a complex one. While there are clearly uses of justice which do imply equality – we speak of equality before the law and often regard certain forms of inequality as arbitrary and unjust – more often than not there is tension between the concepts. For example, justice would not sanction equality of reward to individuals who render widely different services. Traditional liberals have been associated with the view that the attempt to impose *material* equality on unequal people is destructive of the rule of law and necessitates totalitarianism and consequent injustice towards individuals. It is impossible to separate entirely the concepts of justice and equality but for the sake of convenience some of the particular problems to do with equality will be considered in the next chapter.

The contemporary interest in substantive theories of justice is not accidental and there are good philosophical and political reasons which explain it. We can deal briefly with the political reasons first. It is significant that the most important book on political philosophy since the Second World War, John Rawls's *A Theory of Justice* (1972), should appear in the United States of America when it did.[2] Its publication coincided with the culmination of the movement for equal rights for minorities (of whom blacks were the most important example), and with the heyday of other forms of political dissent. In addition, however much people might agree that capitalist and mixed economies deliver goods and services that people want more efficiently than other systems of production and exchange, there has been a persistent complaint that they do so at the cost of unacceptable inequalities of income, wealth and possibly power. There seems no reason *in justice* why some of the bizarre distributions of income and wealth in the West should be regarded as legitimate. Those political radicals who demanded political action over the questions of minority and individual *rights* and the distribution of income and wealth were explicitly appealing to the concept of justice. The publication of

Rawls's book provided, for perhaps the first time in a hundred years, a direct link between a fairly abstract, philosophical theory and particular policy recommendations in both the areas of rights and distribution.

The philosophical interest in justice is related to the special significance of the concept itself in social and political theory. As Rawls himself says, 'justice is the first virtue of society' (1972, p. 3) and most people would agree that, although a society may exhibit other moral values than justice, a society characterised by injustice would be especially blameworthy. The rules of justice, whatever they are, are thought to have a special obligatory force which other moral virtues do not have. Not only is it right to act justly, it is also specifically wrong to act unjustly. Other moral actions, such as giving a large proportion of one's income to charity, would certainly be regarded as good or morally praiseworthy but they would not be regarded as obligatory and it would not be wrong not to perform them. There seems to be a strong connection between rightness and justice and Rawls has persuasively argued that in moral and social philosophy the right is prior to the good. It could also be argued that some recent radical, egalitarian concepts of justice have so inflated the notion that there is a danger of the once strong connection between justice and rightful obligatory action being seriously weakened. It is possible that when conservatives in social philosophy today suggest that there are things that a society ought to promote other than justice they have the radical concept in mind.

It is for this reason that moral and political theorists distinguish justice from morality in general so as to elucidate its peculiar characteristics. Justice is a distributive concept. This means that it is primarily concerned with the way that rewards and punishments and so on are distributed to individuals in a rule-governed practice and its intimate connection with *fairness* indicates this. For example, we may criticise certain social practices such as child marriage, polygamy and so on as immoral but we would be unlikely to say they are unjust. We describe a particular rule or policy as unjust when it arbitrarily discriminates against a named group, such as blacks or women, or when it imposes unequal burdens on individuals and groups for which no relevant reason can be given. A society's laws and economic policies may produce general benevolence but at the same time allow gross disparities of income and wealth, and even an unfair allocation of civil rights. This, of course, is the traditional objection to utilitarianism.

But it would be misleading to suggest that justice refers solely to the fair application of a rule. Some rules, although fairly applied, may produce results which are repugnant to our intuitive conceptions of justice. And, of course, there are rules which, although they do not discriminate, we would hesitate to describe as just. One can think of less fanciful examples than this suggestion, from William K. Frankena: 'if a ruler were to boil his subjects in oil, jumping in afterwards himself, it would be an injustice, but there would be no inequality of treatment' (1962, p. 17). J. R. Lucas claims that laws of strict liability, while being perfectly general and non-discriminatory, may be unjust in some familiar senses of justice as they clearly do not 'give every man his due' (1972, pp. 230–1). Rules of justice can be given some content, however, which does not tie the concept to morality in general and which does preserve its connection with the distribution of rewards and punishment, rights and duties, and liberties.

2 The meaning of justice

We have already indicated some aspects of the meaning of the concept of justice and we must now fill out its basic features. The conventional accounts of justice normally begin by stating a fundamental rule that derives from Aristotle. The theory is that justice means treating equals equally and unequals unequally, and that unequal, treatment should be in proportion to the inequality. This is no more than a version of the idea implied in the universalisability criterion of ethics – that like cases be treated alike. This has been correctly described as a formal rule, or the principle of rationality which holds that some reason must always be given for different treatment. It does not in itself contain any elements of what might be termed intuitive or common sense notions of justice because it does not indicate in what ways people may be treated differently. It does not, of course, assume some fundamental equality of man because it is a purely formal rule.

This formal rule is not, however, completely useless since consistency is a necessary feature of moral and political argument. There is quite likely to be substantial agreement in some cases on what counts as relevant differences in justifying differential treatment. Differences in race, religion and sex are *not* thought to be relevant to the granting of civil and political rights, the assessment of written work in academic institutions, the selection of sports teams or in the appointment of personnel in commercial and other enterprises. However, it is not difficult to devise rules which do make such properties relevant and which are universalisable. Aristotle had no difficulty in making slavery consistent with justice: certain people were 'naturally' unsuited to citizenship.

The formal principle which tells us to treat like cases alike, even when supplemented by equality, should not be confused with the substantive egalitarian principle of justice which assumes that all departures from equality have to be morally justified. This *presumption* in favour of equality is found in Rawls's claim: 'All social values – liberty, opportunity, income and wealth and the bases of self-respect – are to be distributed equally unless an unequal distribution of any, or all, of these values is to everyone's advantage' (1972, p. 62). This latter view is a contestable value judgement and, in Rawls's case, implies a distinction between production and distribution so that what is produced in society is regarded as a common asset to be distributed unequally only when good grounds are produced. In Rawls's case, as we shall see, inequalities in distribution are justifiable only when they are to the benefit of the worst off. This presumption in favour of equality can easily be countered by the equally valid moral principle that an individual is *entitled* to what he produces.[3] In this latter view the inequalities that emerge from a market society, however bizarre they appear to the egalitarian, do not have to be justified by some relevant difference.

The formal principle assigns individuals to categories and requires merely that the rules which apply to the categories shall be adhered to consistently; it is therefore compatible with any substantive morality. The prohibitions on discrimination mentioned above are compelling only to the extent that the principles which underpin them are themselves acceptable. At most the formal principle may be described as a principle of equity and particular rules and laws can be assessed *internally* to see if the principle that 'like cases be treated alike' is rigorously maintained. Indeed many provisions of the tax laws in Western countries can be shown to be inconsistent with the principles that underlie them.

If the theory of justice is to be more than a purely formal principle that rules must be consistently applied, there has to be some under-lying concept of human equality. However, the relationship between justice and equality is a hotly disputed matter. Some social theorists would agree that justice requires that people should in some respects be treated as equals but they would reject the idea that a substantive social equality is itself desirable and also the dominant contemporary view that justice requires the justification on rational grounds of all existing inequalities. It is important to distinguish therefore between a strong and a weak sense of equality in normative discourse about justice. The more conservative theorists of justice admit only a weak sense because they maintain that any other sense involves a threat to liberty, rules and social stability. These theorists would probably maintain that this idea is best expressed by the proposition that people have property rights which would be violated by an application of equality in the strong sense.

The weak sense of equality contained in the concept of justice implies that for certain purposes individuals ought to be treated as if they were equal, although this prescriptive statement does not depend on the truth of some factual proposition asserting equality. It simply means that for the purposes of law no person is entitled to preferential treatment by virtue of some irrelevant property, such as wealth, birth, sex, race or religion. It would require public authorities not to discriminate on such grounds when making appointments (although some libertarians would object to the legal enforcement of non-discriminatory employment practices in the private sector). In the political sphere it would guarantee equal constitutional rights so that no one would have a prior claim to office over anyone else. However, this point should be qualified by the fact that justice does not entail a commitment to (democratic) political equality. Fair rules may be impartially enforced in regimes which allow little political participation and majority-rule democracies may generate arbitrary treatment of individuals and minorities.

Perhaps the minimal sense of equality described above is best captured in the principle which states that all men are entitled to 'equality of respect'. This means that whatever differences individuals display in their natural aptitudes, law and government should for certain purposes ignore these differences. To what extent governments should acknowledge this equality of respect in the area of welfare, for example, is, of course, a controversial subject which requires consideration of other principles. A not dissimilar idea is expressed in Kant's famous injunction to treat people always as ends in themselves and never as means only. It is for this reason that slavery is always unjust. On similar grounds the injustice of punishing an innocent man can never be compensated for by an increase in the well-being of society at large. It must be stressed that this argument alone cannot be used to justify any egalitarian social policy, rather it puts a prohibition on state action that abrogates individual rights.

The concept of justice in contemporary social philosophy has more to do with the justification of inequalities than it has to do with equality. The familiar concepts that belong to the family of justice are desert and need. It would clearly be *unjust* to treat people equally who differed in deserts and needs. While desert obviously provides a ground for differential treatment this is a little more complicated in the case of need. Some political theorists take need to be an aspect of the principle of equality and maintain that men are *equal* in having certain basic needs which call for government action, while others maintain that since men *differ* in these needs this justifies unequal treatment. We shall then have to consider need both as a part of justice and of general egalitarianism.

It is important, however, to make an analytical distinction between desert and need. The concept of desert refers to those properties of a man's actions that are worthy of special treatment. To say that a person deserves reward or punishment is to say that actions, efforts and results are the things that are relevant to the way that he is treated. However, to say that a person needs something means that she lacks certain things – money, an adequate diet, clothing and so on – which are thought to be essential to the realisation of a certain standard of well-being, however defined. But need cannot be a basis for desert because it does not relate specifically to a person's actions or efforts. Thus a person may still need certain things even though she has not deserved them by her actions, efforts or results. It would not be inaccurate to say that the concept of need has virtually replaced desert in recent egalitarian welfare social philosophies. The delivery of 'welfare goods', housing aid, health care and so on, is entirely justified in terms of need. However, attempts have been made to integrate needs into the idea of desert. It has been argued that if a person should experience distress through no fault of his own he should deserve welfare rather than merely need it (Campbell, 1988, p. 158). It would be an entitlement rather than an act of benevolence.

These features of desert-based justice make it a 'backward-looking' concept because, in proposing answers to questions about the distribution of punishment and reward, it directs us to look for those qualities in an individual's past actions which are relevant to the way he is treated. This is obviously so in the retributivist theory of punishment which rests entirely on the notion of desert and contrasts strongly with the 'forward-looking' doctrine of utilitarianism. A utilitarian has no interest in the past actions of an individual, or his moral guilt, for the assessment of punishment: he justifies punishment, or more strictly, any form of penal measure, solely by reference to its deterrent effect.

When it comes to justifying differential reward the concept is a little more complicated. We have already said that desert refers to past actions, efforts and results but this requires some elaboration. Clearly, we would not relate desert to efforts alone because, however praiseworthy a person's efforts might be, they cannot be rewarded in isolation from what she produces. Desert must in some sense be related to the value of the product but how a product is valued will depend upon a whole network of social principles and practices. It may be the case that because of some rare talent an individual may be able to produce something that is highly valued with very little in the way of effort. Yet we would not say that she did not deserve the differential reward that her talents enabled her to earn. Nevertheless, there is a problem here in that some social philosophers might say that some high rewards, although legitimately acquired, are not deserved because they are the result of no *merit* on the part of the fortunate individual. The earnings of popular entertainers, property speculators and financiers might fall into this category. By the same reasoning, inherited wealth would be regarded as undeserved. In this view, wages are not related exclusively to the value of the product but are a kind of compensation for the effort and disutility of work. This has radical implications for the wage structure of a modern economy since higher-paid occupations tend to be the least laborious (at least in a physical sense).

The traditional classical liberal conception of desert solves the problem by detaching the notion of desert from *moral* desert (although as we shall see, some extreme *laissez-faire* liberals clarify the issue by eliminating completely the use of the word desert in the economic sphere). In a liberal market society a man's desert is entirely a function of the value of what he produces and this value is determined by the preferences of individuals in exchange relationships. This has nothing to do with the moral quality of his efforts, which is regarded as a purely subjective matter. This rigorous idea of desert, associated with social philosophers such as Herbert Spencer, precludes the state from meeting people's needs.[4] It follows from this, of course, that the state has few justifiable claims against the individual.

Those who interpret desert in a moral sense, however, insist that it is the business of the state to correct the outcomes of a market society when they are the result of luck or ingenuity rather than the cultivation of special skills and virtues. In fact, even in a competitive market economy, recourse may have to be made to a subjective evaluation of a person's pay and prospects since in large-scale enterprises it may be difficult to determine objectively the value of a person's contribution. A more important point, perhaps, is that this view of desert underlies some justifications (although not all) of the confiscatory taxation of inherited wealth and steeply progressive income tax. Those who advocate permanent incomes policies presumably have a notion of moral desert in mind which they feel should be decisive in the determination of rewards for different occupations.

The concept of desert features strongly in the traditional version of the liberal creed, although it requires careful clarification when applied to the economic sphere. To the extent that it stresses personal *responsibility* for actions and favours rewards for efforts and results rather than need, it typifies a rather tough-minded social philosophy. It is individualistic in that it evaluates a person's actions as products of an autonomous will rather than as the outcomes of a form of social causation. In the question of punishment the notion of desert precludes the view that crime is a kind of disease which can be 'treated' since this view abrogates individual responsibility. Indeed, not to punish a criminal according to his deserts is to degrade him as an individual and make him a mere object of social policy.

For political theorists, the important questions about justice turn upon its connection with social and economic policy. Questions of justice in social affairs crop up in circumstances of 'scarcity', which we can take to be more or less permanent features of the human condition. In situations of abundance the question of who should get what, and why, would not arise. We are, however, all too familiar with vexing questions as to how the supply of kidney machines should be allocated, or what the appropriate distribution of incomes should be. In these questions the members of the family of justice – equality, desert and need – play their most important roles.

Theorists of justice have produced many answers to these questions and to simplify the issue we can make an important distinction, which is now commonplace in social and political theory, between *procedural* justice and *social* justice. Although there are many variants of both approaches the main features of each can be briefly summarised. In procedural theories the demands of justice are satisfied if certain rules are satisfied. Therefore no comment, in terms of justice, may be made about the outcomes of such procedures. Justice is only a property of individual behaviour within rules and cannot be a feature of 'society' or 'states of affairs'. In theories of social justice, however, justice is precisely a property of some social sate of affairs. A society is just, for example, if the distribution of income satisfies a certain criterion, and the state is morally entitled to use the apparatus of coercive law to bring this about. David Miller, in an influential book, expressed this view nicely when he said: 'it is impossible to assess the justice of actions without a prior identification of *just states of affairs*' (1976, pp. 17–18, italics added).

3 Procedural justice

In its rejection of social justice the school of procedural justice is firmly within the tradition of methodological individualism. Only the actions of individuals can be morally evaluated in terms of justice and fairness and it is absurd to praise or blame social processes or patterns of income distribution. However, procedural theorists of justice are most definitely not emotivists; propositions about justice are meaningful and are not merely expressions of emotion. They have meaning, however, only in the context of systems of general rules such as the traditional common law. Actions are just if they are consistent with those general rules which protect property rights and prohibit the use of fraud or force in the making of contracts. Procedural justice is exemplified in competitions, such as races. A fair race is not one in which the person who wins morally deserves to win but one in which there is no cheating, nobody jumps the gun or has an unfair advantage through the use of drugs (Barry, 1965, p. 103).

Procedural theorists are hostile to the distinction between production and distribution which is made by collectivists. There is no 'social pie' which can be divided up according to abstract distributive principles, there are only individual entitlements which it would be *unjust* to interfere with by coercive laws. There is clearly a connection between procedural justice and the market economy. The market functions as a signalling mechanism to attract the factors of production to their most efficient uses: any attempt to disturb this process, by way of an incomes policy, for example, will lead to an inefficient use of resources which ultimately makes everyone worse off. Also, it is argued that the pursuit of social justice must eventuate in totalitarianism (Hayek, 1944) since it requires an ever-increasing use of coercion in economic and social life.

Procedural theorists maintain (Hayek, 1960 and 1976) that all non-market criteria of income, such as those based on 'desert' or 'need', are necessarily subjective and can only work in a regimented, oppressive and illiberal society. While most procedural theorists are concerned about 'welfare' and accept that the state has some responsibility for those who cannot earn an adequate income in the market (Hayek, for example, believes that payments outside the market should be made to the poor), they deny that this has anything to do with justice. Hayek adopts a basically Humean view of justice: they are the rules that govern the acquisition of property, its transference by consent, and the inviolability of contract. Furthermore, they tend to emerge spontaneously if people are left more or less free to conduct their affairs. The role of the state is simply to enforce them, a necessity brought about by the familiar public good problem – that there is always a temptation for a particular person to breach a rule for short-term advantages even though widespread repudiation will make everybody worse off. The state is not, therefore, primarily responsible for the content of the rules of procedural justice.

Acts of injustice are simply wrongs committed against private persons. There are in essence two reasons why it is improper to attribute the terms justice and injustice to the distribution of income. First, markets are unpredictable, services that are highly valued in one time period will be replaced by others at another so that it would be impossible for the state to determine some just income, and then enforce it, without doing irreparable damage to the market (leaving aside the effect such action could have on personal liberty). Second, social justice theories presuppose a distributor who can have detailed knowledge of deserts and needs and can therefore make authoritative judgements about distribution. But judgements about desert and need are essentially subjective and it is this absence of agreement about them that leads Hayek to label social justice as a 'mirage', suggesting that they have no coherent meaning. While income determined by the market is ultimately a product of people's subjective evaluation of goods and services, it is in an important sense objective since it is not the product of the opinion of centralised authority. It is the unplanned outcome of the opinions of innumerable, anonymous, and decentralised agents. Thus no one person can be blamed for a particular distribution of income in the way that identifiable agents can be held responsible for the breach of a contract or the violation of a property right. According to Hayek, the market is about *value*, it has nothing to do with justice (apart from the rules in which it is embedded).

A number of points can be made about this doctrine. At a practical level it is simply not true that social justice rests upon a kind of linguistic confusion. People do have coherent views about desert (Hochschild, 1981) and although there may be some disagreement it would appear to be no greater than that about other political concepts. If some views are wrong they must be shown to be so, not dismissed because they rest upon an alleged misuse of the word. All Hayek has shown is that the implementation of social justice policies might (probably will) lead to technical inefficiencies but that has nothing necessarily to do with justice or injustice in the moral sense. Of course, Hayek denies that market outcomes have anything to do with justice, but this is no more than assertion. Furthermore, the rejection of popular beliefs about justice could have disturbing implications for the sociology of markets. They are only sustainable if they have some generalised legitimacy and if there is too great a disjuncture between the market's determination of income and accepted views of rightness the whole system could come under threat (Kristol, 1972).

But there is perhaps a deeper problem with Hayek's theory: it is not so much a theory of justice as a theory of the rules of co-ordination. It is undoubtedly true that a market process needs such rules if there is to be any predictability and security for the transactors; that is why we have rules of contract and titles to property. However, the theory of justice is by no means exhausted by a description of these rules. Even within the terms of Hayek's own theory some important questions remain unanswered. The most important of these concerns the justice of the claim to original property titles. Before an exchange process can begin there must be some explanation of the legitimacy of original holdings. From Locke onwards there has been a serious debate within all branches of liberal theory about the justice of the acquisition of property. Is a person morally entitled to the possession of, for example, land which is a good in finite supply? The unequal ownership of this can, and does, severely restrict the opportunities for many to participate in exchange. The same consideration would apply to other scarce resources, the possible monopoly ownership of which can lead to injustice which is not accounted for by a simple description of procedural rules. Even in less dramatic examples, such as normal inheritance, questions can be raised about the supposed *impartiality* of rules which arbitrarily advantage some people against others.

At most, Hayek has given us an account of the efficiency properties of certain rule-governed processes, and he is certainly plausible in his claim that egalitarian wage structures have a deleterious effect on the allocation of labour; but this has its major relevance only to centrally planned economies where incomes were fixed by arbitrary commands. In capitalist market systems, some of the rewards seem to be a product of sheer luck. It is, of course, true that there can be entitlements without deserts – that is, that people can have a just claim to something without deserving it in a moral, meritorious sense – but to say that the whole of justice can be described in terms of formal entitlements is to exclude from the argument considerations that appear to be highly relevant to the distribution of income and wealth. To say that someone is entitled to a reward because of a rule is not to say that the rule itself is just. All Hayek has shown is that markets need rules; he has not shown that the conventional market rules are just. One suspects that Hayek's argument is actually a utilitarian one, that free markets maximise total social welfare better than known alternatives. But this is only subsidiary to his original claim that justice can only *mean* conformity to procedural rules.

Even market theorists are prepared to say that entrepreneurs *deserve* their rewards because of their skill and foresight in correctly anticipating consumer demand. But even this modest moral claim is excluded by Hayek's threadbare definition of justice. Successful entrepreneurs don't deserve their rewards, they simply receive them as a consequence of the co-ordination process of the market. Notice that this criticism owes nothing to an evaluation of outcomes of market processes, as theories of social justice typically do; it is limited to the appraisal of human actions under general rules. Hayek's complete elimination of desert from justice makes it impossible for him to distinguish morally between the various activities that go into an economic process. Pure windfall gains, perhaps through inheritance or serendipity, are no different morally from genuine acts of entrepreneurial discovery and the creation of new value. In fact there is no *moral* justification for wealth accumulation in Hayek's theory, there is simply a set of co-ordination miles to make life predictable for transactions.

In his *Anarchy, State and Utopia*, Robert Nozick produced a procedural theory which attempted to elaborate on, and fill in some of the gaps in Hayek's analysis. He tried to give capitalist justice a more specifically moral foundation. In his theory he distinguishes between historical principles of justice and end-state principles. Historical principles hold that 'past circumstances or actions of people can create differential entitlements or differential deserts to things' (Nozick, 1974, p. 155). In contrast, end-state theories suggest particular goals to which a distribution should conform. Utilitarianism and theories of social justice are end-state doctrines. Nozick also distinguishes between patterned and unpatterned principles of justice. A patterned principle evaluates a distribution in accordance with some 'natural dimension' (1974, p. 156). A principle of justice which states that people are to be rewarded according to their needs would be a patterned principle. Not all patterned principles are end-state: for example, the patterned principle which states that individuals should be rewarded according to their deserts is historical because it directs attention to their past actions.

Nozick's own theory of justice is an *historical, unpatterned* theory. It is an entitlement theory in which the distribution of individual property holdings is just if it is a consequence of fair *acquisition* (without the use of fraud or force) or *transfer*. The only other aspect of justice is *rectification*, the principle which allows past injustices – that is, unfair acquisitions – to be corrected. The main point of the theory is to show that individuals have rights to their property holdings and there is no moral justification for a rearrangement of the spread of wealth in 'society'. Nozick, therefore, is a rigorous critic of the distinction between production and distribution; goods do not come into the world out of nothing but must be understood in terms of individual property holdings. The distribution of property holdings is therefore a product of people trading in their holdings. The *minimal* state protects individuals from invasions of their rights and if it goes beyond this to bring about a state of affairs which is *not* the result of free exchange it is in breach of their rights. Thus all compulsory welfare programmes are illegitimate. According to Nozick, the attempt to establish any patterned or end-state conception of justice must eventually lead to the destruction of liberty.[5]

The only restriction that Nozick puts on fair acquisitions and voluntary exchanges is that these must not violate the 'Lockean proviso' (1974, pp. 175–82); this means that they must not worsen the positions of others. But the proviso is interpreted very narrowly. For someone's position to be worsened someone else must appropriate the total supply of something which is *essential to life*; for example, 'a person may not appropriate the only water hole in the desert and charge what he will' (1974, p. 179). But the proviso would not, in Nozick's theory, prevent someone who discovered a cure for a fatal disease charging whatever price he liked for it since, unlike the monopolist who appropriates the total supply of something essential for life, he does not put others in a worse position to that which they are already in. This would only be so if he physically prevented others from trying to make the discovery themselves.

A still more important issue is Nozick's special explanation of the acquisition of property titles. It was noted earlier that Hayek's account of the justice of capitalism was deficient here and Nozick attempts to fill the gap by accounting for rightful possession. Before exchange and transfer can begin objects have to be legitimately owned. This legitimacy must consist of something other than Hayekian rules of exchange. How far does acquisition, subject to the aforementioned Lockean proviso, accord with justice? In one sense the creator of new value has a *prima facie* claim to possession, it could be said to be deserved in that it is a product of effort. Even though in an advanced capitalist economy there is no opportunity for creating value, in a Lockean sense, by mixing labour with previously unowned objects (for example land), it is constantly being generated, as Israel Kirzner (1973, 1989) claims, by entrepreneurial 'alertness' to the use to which goods can be put. In fact, Kirzner makes an improvement on Nozick by showing how this anticipatory action by individuals is responsible for most of the new value created. After all, oil in the ground did not exist as an *economic* good until someone correctly predicted that it would command a market price.[6]

Nozick attempts to get round the problem of the private ownership of finite resources, which appears to put non-owners in an unjustifiable worse position, by arguing that their well-being is actually improved by the greater productivity of private ownership (1974, pp. 178–82). This looks like a utilitarian rather than a rights argument, so the question of justice remains open. What is not absolutely clear is whether the kind of accumulation that Nozick permits does not leave people in a worse position. Even pure economic advantages may not fully compensate the loss of autonomy by individuals who are more or less compelled to work for monopoly resource owners. Also, much of the wealth owned seems to be a product of luck rather than effort. The rental income from the ownership of land is surely like this. It would be stretching credulity to suggest that ownership of land does not deprive other people of their rights (Barry, N., 1986, pp. 158–9). Should they not be compensated? In fact, in a later work (1989)[7] Nozick concedes this by suggesting that inheritance should be limited: only the first generation descendants may receive the full donation. The argument appears to be that although the owner of wealth should have the right to transfer it to whomsoever he or she wishes in the first instance, later people down the line, who bear no relation in justice to the original creation of the value, should have their inheritances taxed. This is a considerable modification of the earlier view where entitlements (legitimate claims to assets) were distinguished from deserts (as measured by the conventional moral criteria of merit, effort and so on) and were to be protected from invasion by the state.

It is not often realised that in *Anarchy, State and Utopia* there is some room for considerable redistribution by way of the rectification principle, the rule for correcting past illegitimate acquisitions. A person can only justly own something by exchange or transfer if the thing itself were justly acquired. It is quite likely that most of today's assets had their origins in an earlier unjust acquisition. Given that it would be impossible to trace back each claim Nozick recommends a general rule: since the worse off in present day society are likely to be victims of past injustice, they should be compensated (1974, p. 231). This would give quite a big role for the state and suggests that the original principles that Nozick recommends are difficult to sustain.

Many critics of the purely rule-based view of justice would say that it concentrates on only one aspect of justice and that it is always possible to say of a situation that, although the rules were followed, the outcome was nevertheless unjust. J. R. Lucas, who is himself a rigorous critic of social justice, nevertheless cannot accept the full implications of the minimal rules of justice contained in free market economics. He says that 'free exchange is not necessarily fair exchange', and describes the economic theory of *laissez-faire* as unethical (1972, p. 245). Of course, Hayek would maintain that it is simply illegitimate to describe the outcome of the market in ethical terms at all. But we do tend to evaluate the outcomes of a market process in ethical terms (and not always to propose some egalitarian distribution that owes little to just entitlement) since the concept of justice in ordinary speech is suggestive of criteria that extend beyond the enforcement of fair rules.

Even if the theorist wished to retain the relationship between justice and personal conduct, some modification of market outcomes is logically possible while preserving this language. If certain unpredictable dire results occurred it would still be possible to justify some intervention while still retaining the language of personal responsibility, such as by aiding the victims of such outcomes who were not morally responsible for their predicament. They would have a claim to redress *in justice*, while others, whose own recklessness led to distress, would have to depend on benevolence. Hayek, of course, would make no distinction between the two categories while still not denying the morality of extra-market payments to the needy, this would have nothing to do with justice. Sen (1981) has shown in stimulating detail how famines can occur, in systems governed by just procedural rules, when there is actually enough food to go round. It seems inappropriate morally, if not perverse, to insist that redistribution in such circumstances is not sanctioned by the principle of justice. Even Nozick conceded that 'catastrophes' can occur which require the suspension of his rules of justice (1974, p. 246).

4 Social justice

All theories of social justice are end-state or patterned theories since they propose that the process of exchange between individuals should be controlled and checked in accordance with abstract, external moral principles. Social justice requires that society as a whole, rather than just the actions of individuals, be evaluated for its justice and injustice. While most theories of social justice are egalitarian and socialist, there are exceptions. Some versions of conservatism, communitarianism and social philosophies based on religion, may make use of the concept in their descriptions of an ideal harmonious society based on unity, order and hierarchy. Such views on justice may belong in the same logical box as those of the socialists in that they are end-state and in nature collectivist, in contrast to individualistic conceptions. Nevertheless, the rest of this section is concerned with the radical arguments. There is also a problem in that most discussions of the question of social justice are bound up with a strong sense of equality and therefore there is some overlap with the next chapter. However, it is important to keep an analytical distinction between social justice and equality because, in some areas at least, proponents of the former wish to justify some inequalities. What is characteristic of radical theories of social justice is the presumption in favour of equality, departures from which are justified with reluctance.

An important feature of the approach of social justice requires special emphasis. The various theories do not propose sets of rules, or even principles, by which men can live *irrespective of their needs and wants* but instead take needs and wants, and their satisfaction, as the data by which a society can be assessed for justice. A society is just if it distributes want-satisfaction in a certain way. Social justice theories try to go behind the structure of rules to determine who is in need, say, of health care, educational opportunity, housing and so on.

Need is a particularly tricky concept in social theory. It is normally used by writers who claim that there is some *objectivity* attached to needs, in contrast to wants, which are purely subjective. The market system, it is conceded, is perfectly capable of satisfying wants; goods and services will be produced according to people's preferences so that the market is quite consistent with the individualism and pluralism of modern liberal theory. It specifically precludes the moral acceptability of a central planner determining what people should consume since that arrangement would simply lead to the production of the planner's subjectively determined array of goods and services. But the market cannot satisfy needs which are not specifically related to mere desires. Many market theorists believe that there is no distinction between needs and wants, that allegedly objective needs for food, clothing and shelter are really disguised wants. The argument is that there is no agreement about values, ends and purposes to justify the claim often made that needs form a special category, whose alleged objectivity justifies some special role for the state in their production, or to sustain the argument that need-satisfaction has a higher priority than want-satisfaction. None of this necessarily rules out an argument that, for various reasons, access to want-satisfaction should be increased, or even equalised. But certainly liberals who stress wants are objecting to the paternalism that seems to be implicit in the argument for the objectivity of needs.

Nevertheless, despite possibly illiberal overtones, there is a case for the objectivity of needs. The case depends on the claim that needs should not be seen as a category of desire at all but should be interpreted as part of *descriptive* statements about people's conditions of life. Wants do seem to depend exclusively on personal psychology; to want something is to imply nothing about whether or not that want should be fulfilled, or is necessary for survival. It depends entirely on subjective preference. But a person can need something and not even be aware of it: as when someone needs urgent medical treatment for a condition about which she may be completely ignorant. It would be extremely odd to describe that as a want because the truth of the statement has nothing to do with the person's psychological beliefs. Of course, in socioeconomic contexts people in need are often perfectly aware of their condition but that circumstance itself still derives its features from something other than inclinations or desires. The objective evidence of the need is readily available to an observer: 'What a person needs is a function of the real character of the object, not beliefs about it' (Plant, 1991, p. 194).

Needs may be considered so compelling that to leave them unsatisfied would be equivalent to harming a person, even though the situation is not characterised by the deliberation and intent that we associate with conventional harm. If needs are interpreted in this way then clearly they would constitute elements in the demand for strict justice, i.e. the meeting of needs would be a duty imposed on the state, logically equivalent to its function of enforcing the rules of procedural justice. Raymond Plant (1994) makes a related point in his critique of Hayek's theory of justice. Hayek had denied that there was a person who could be blamed for causing the distress that comes from unpredictable economic change. Plant makes two major points against this. First, that some of this change is quite predictable, so that a society can make plans to cope with it. Second, the fact that no one person is directly responsible for the distress does not mean that the duty to relieve it somehow disappears. For, as he persuasively argues, justice is a matter of how we *respond* to cases of distress, not merely a matter of identifying causal responsibility for it. Again, corrective action would not be aimed at mere want-satisfaction: it would be addressed to needs which arose independently of the deliberate actions of the person.

Still, perhaps the differences between Plant and Hayek, on this issue at least, are not as great as they appear. For in his attack on social justice Hayek was mainly concerned with refuting the argument that the whole spread of incomes in a society should be determined by a central authority in defiance of the verdict of the market. He never denied that there were welfare responsibilities; though he did distinguish justice from welfare and thence gave the impression that the duties to provide the latter were not of a compelling nature (still, his position is different from the Nozick of *Anarchy, State and Utopia*). Strictly, the satisfaction of basic needs, although a welfare demand, is not the same thing as establishing a welfare state (some of the provision of which is related to wants). Indeed, the admission of objective needs, carefully defined, would not affect the rigour of most procedural theories. In fact, most of the moral justifications of the welfare state do not depend solely on the existence of objective need, but on the egalitarian argument for some form of redistribution in the consumption of goods and services that are more correctly defined as wants. It should also be pointed out that the most pressing cases of need cannot be seen as a product of market processes at all but arise out of genetic and other more or less unalterable disadvantages.

Communitarian[8] theories of social justice are different alike from procedural theory and objective need arguments, for what these two doctrines have in common is a commitment to a certain universality.

They are not culture-bound. Procedural theorists assume that the claims that individuals have under just rules, although limited, derive from their humanity and not from their membership of a particular community. In a similar way, the entitlements to welfare that objective need theory accords individuals should be granted (where this is feasible) irrespective of the social origins of the recipients (Doyall and Gough, 1992). This would not necessarily imply a worldwide redistributive programme, just a recognition of morally legitimate demands that arise independently of particular social arrangements.

In contrast, communitarian theories of justice locate just claims in particular social value structures. They are a direct response to the subjectivism about values that is a feature of liberal theory of either the market individualist type or that which sanctions extensive redistribution. For although liberals may claim that just rules are objective, all other values are a matter of individual choice. An egalitarian liberal could then permit considerable freedom of choice in the consumption of typical welfare goods. However, Michael Walzer (1983) argues that questions about justice can only be answered by an exploration of the 'shared meanings' of a particular society. What this implies is that social justice does not require some general rule of redistribution, such as an income payment to the poor not tied to a particular service, but an appreciation of the fact that different human activities should operate under different principles of justice. For example, healthcare (Walzer, 1983, p. 10) should be distributed purely on grounds of need, while other goods and services should be allocated on quite different criteria. It is not so much the inequality of income in capitalist society to which Walzer objects, though the whole tenor of his argument reflects a certain, rather complex, egalitarianism, but the fact that it allows some individuals advantages in areas where money is entirely inappropriate. It is society, and its shared meanings, that gives goods their value and its verdict protects the community from a rampant subjectivism (even if that were accompanied by considerable redistribution).

All this implies that the shared meanings of the community may license the overriding of individual, market-based choice. But how objective are these shared meanings? Even in apparently uncontroversial areas like health, people put different subjective values on the service. Healthcare is not always about life or death but often involves choices about where expenditure should be directed. People may prefer to live unhealthy lifestyles, and in a free society would assume the risk via an insurance-based health system, but does the invocation of shared values authorise the community to lay down conditions and restrict choices precisely because medical care based on objective need would, presumably, be delivered at zero cost to the consumer? Of course, the existence of shared meanings does not close off debate, the meanings may not always be clear and much philosophical effort will be devoted to the exploration of them, but there is a clear implication in Walzer that justice is relative to particular activities. Society, under this theory of justice, could exercise a kind of power, however benign, over individuals and their choices which would be rejected by individualists of almost all types.

Walzer's apparent relativism would also preclude cross-cultural comparisons of social arrangements in terms of justice; or at least make them extraordinarily difficult. Justice is not a concept that governs the relationships between abstract individuals but is an idea the meaning of which is confined to particular cultures. As he reluctantly concedes: 'In a society where social meanings are integrated and hierarchical, justice will come to the aid of inequality' (1983, p. 313). He may well argue that in traditional class-based, or caste, societies the accepted, public shared meanings are misleading since they do not include the perceptions of arbitrarily excluded groups. Presumably radical social criticism, which indeed is part of Walzer's project, would be possible within this framework. But one cannot avoid the conclusion that the commitment to the community as the primary source of value is seriously disabling, and that the attention to *particularity* distracts the social critic from those more or less universal themes that have always concerned theorists of justice and, indeed, social justice.

5 Rawls's theory of justice

The first thing to note is that Rawls's theory is a type of procedural theory, but it differs from other procedural theories in several important respects. He wishes to show that justice is about the rules that should govern a social practice, and not about the evaluation of various states of affairs using criteria such as need and desert, but he attempts to counter the main criticism of this approach, which is that the meticulous following of rules may produce outcomes which are inconsistent with our common sense notions of justice. Therefore he wishes to show that under certain carefully specified conditions rational agents would choose a set of principles which are consistent with our intuitive ideas of distributive justice, and when which followed produce outcomes which, whatever they might be, are morally acceptable.

Despite its procedural features, however, Rawls's theory should be regarded as a contribution to the theory of social justice because he persistently stresses that all departures from equality have to be rationally justified: there is a presumption in favour of equality which contrasts strongly with various versions of the entitlement theory. Allied to this is an implied distinction between production and distribution. Even though Rawls makes great use of marginal productivity theory in the determination of wages, and indeed agrees that the application of it is the only way natural talents can be drawn into their most efficient uses to the benefit of everybody, he does argue that market criteria must always be controlled by the principles of social justice.

To elucidate Rawls's theory of justice we must start with his method of approaching moral problems, which is in the contractarian tradition of social philosophy (see above, Chapter 5). This involves abstracting individuals from their particular social and economic circumstances and reconstructing the rules, principles and institutions they would adopt in order to maximise their interests in any future society. Thus there are two essential parts of Rawls's programme: the description of the conditions under which rational contractors deliberate and the content of the principles they would choose.

The relationship between the conditions and the adoption of the principles is said to be deductive – that is, rational agents in the situation described by Rawls, will of necessity maximise their well-being through the choice of his principles of justice. Thus the principles will be unanimously agreed to and properly universalisable. Of course, it may be the case that the Rawlsian principles might be agreed to but the validity of the deduction denied, or that people may accept what Rawls calls the 'original position', in which individuals are abstracted from their environment, but deduce different principles.

The idea of 'reflective equilibrium' is central to Rawls's methodology (1972, pp. 48–51). This means that we must constantly check the conclusions of our moral reasoning against our intuitive moral notions and possibly readjust the conditions of the original position so as to derive principles which are consistent with these fundamental moral beliefs. There is perhaps a much greater reliance on intuition in the construction of the Rawlsian theorem than is apparent in the formal statement of Rawls's methodology. However, Rawls's method entails also that our intuitive notions of justice be modified by philosophical reasoning. This contrasts with others in the contractarian tradition (see Buchanan, 1975) who maintain that the rules of justice are those that would be agreed to in an hypothetical setting. There is no attempt here to check the agreed-upon rules against intuitive judgements in reflective equilibrium. There is no room, then, here for the kind of continuing redistribution that is implied in Rawls's approach.

We will consider first the description of the original position. Rawls places men behind what he calls the 'veil of ignorance' (1972, pp. 36–42). This is a hypothetical situation in which individuals are deprived of basic knowledge of their wants, interests, skills, abilities and so on. They are also deprived of knowledge of the things that generate conflicts in actual societies. Thus knowing that they are white or black, or Protestant or Catholic and so on, will not be of much significance since they do not know, for example, what particular patterns of discrimination operate in society. But they will have an elementary knowledge of economics and psychology, and also what Rawls calls a 'sense of justice'.

Behind the veil of ignorance, then, certain constraints are imposed and these are implied by the idea of having a morality. In Rawls's conception what is excluded is the 'knowledge of those contingencies which sets men at odds and allows them to be guided by their prejudices' (1972, p. 19). While Rawlsian men are self-interested, it is important to note that they are not, strictly speaking, egoists. Egoism, the doctrine that everyone should pursue his own ends on every possible occasion, is precluded by the notion of having one's life constrained by moral rules. A self-interested person can rationally adopt a set of moral rules to guide his conduct, even though the application of the rules may not be in his interest, in an egoistic sense, on every particular occasion. Egoism runs counter to Rawls's conception of the *right*, which is a 'set of principles, general in form and universal in application, that is to be publicly recognised as a final court of appeal for ordering the particular claims of moral persons' (1972, p. 135).

This can also be conveniently contrasted with utilitarianism, which takes all wants as initially entitled to satisfaction, including what might be thought of as morally undesirable wants, and then tries to maximise the total amount of want-satisfaction. Rawls excludes undesirable wants by the conditions of the original position and by the constraints of having a morality. The really significant difference between utilitarianism and Rawls is that his stress on the separate identity of persons precludes their desires from being conflated into a social utility function. Individuals are autonomous agents who ought not to be used as means to the ends of others.

People behind the veil of ignorance do not have to have a specially elevated conception of the good life; as rational maximisers they will wish to promote their 'primary goods' – liberty, opportunity, income and wealth, and self-respect (1972, pp. 90–5). The right is prior to the good and agreement about basic rules, and the guarantee of a certain level of resources, enables a plurality of conceptions of the good to be pursued. An increase in these enables individuals to pursue whatever rational plans of life they have. By constructing a theory of justice that allows only primary goods to be maximised Rawls hopes to avoid some of the traditional difficulties that arise when disputes about justice take the form of arguments about needs, deserts and so on; principles that are concerned with the maximisation of the primary goods preclude these sorts of comparisons. Yet it is this refusal to go behind the primary goods and consider particular needs that has provoked strong criticism. It is said that theories of justice have to involve some reference to want-satisfaction (Barry, B., 1973, pp. 49–51). For example, a given level of income means different things to different people depending upon their circumstances.

There are two crucially important assumptions that Rawls makes about self-interested rational agents. First, they are not *envious*. This means that they are concerned only with maximising their primary goods and are not affected by the positions of others. Thus non-envious people would rather secure the highest amount possible of primary goods for themselves, even if others have a much larger amount, than have a lower level on the understanding that others have much less too. Secondly, they can be assumed to have a conservative attitude towards risk. That is, since behind the veil of ignorance they do not know their propensity to gamble; in a situation of uncertainty they will opt for the least disadvantageous outcome in any choice presented to them.

Under these circumstances Rawls argues that the two following principles of justice will be chosen:

1. Each person is to have an equal right to the most extensive liberty compatible with a similar liberty to others.
2. Social and economic inequalities are to be arranged so that they are both
    (a) to the greatest benefit of the least advantaged and
    (b) attached to offices and positions open to all under conditions of fair equality of opportunity. (1972, p. 302)

The principles are arranged in *lexical* order under the priority rule (1972, pp. 40–5) which states that 1 is prior to 2, and within 2, 2(b) is prior to 2(a). The priority rule can be compared with the pluralist approach of balancing principles. We noted that in this theory there is no way of showing how a conflict between people who weight sets of principles differently could be resolved. Rawls wants to show that it is rational to opt for a rule which gives absolute priority of 1 over 2. To be more exact, he says that, given a certain level of economic development, it would never be rational to trade an equal liberty under 1 (for example, the equal right to vote) for some economic advantage.

The equal liberties under the first principle can be concretised as the familiar rights of liberal democratic regimes. They include equal rights to political participation, freedom of expression, religious liberty, equality before the law and so on. Rawls does imply that some equal liberties may be attenuated but only on condition that this leads to an increase in overall liberty.

Although 2(b) is technically prior to 2(a), Rawls spends a great deal of time on the latter and it is this which has aroused most interest. He calls this the 'difference' principle and it requires some elucidation. Rawls assumes an initial equality and argues that departures from this can only be justified if they result in clear gains. Obviously, the inequalities of income in a market system increase wealth, by drawing labour into its most productive uses, from which, ideally, everybody gains. Rawls's initial interpretation of the principle was that everybody should gain from inequality but this was later clarified to mean that it should be to the benefit of the least advantaged.

How does Rawls demonstrate that justice requires that all inequalities be acceptable only if they are to the benefit of the least advantaged? He reaches this conclusion in the following manner. He agrees that the Pareto or efficiency principle (see above, Chapters 3 and 5) is the criterion for the optimal allocation of resources in society. In the absence of externalities, free exchange will produce an efficient allocation in which no change can take place without making someone (at least one) worse off. An optimal position is reached when no further gains from trade are possible. However, an efficient allocation in this sense is consistent with any initial distribution of property holdings. Even a slave society is technically efficient if a move away from it would make the slave-holders worse off. Rawls therefore argues that since the existing distribution of wealth is likely to be determined by luck, political power and past injustices, the Pareto principle *alone* cannot be a satisfactory criterion of justice. Therefore, in the first instance, the competitive market must be regulated by the fair equality of opportunity principle. This principle then sanctions those social policies which are designed to mitigate the effects of social contingencies which give some groups and individuals unfair advantages over others. This is a clear departure from procedural theory since the fair equality of opportunity principle would eliminate all those advantages brought about by such things as inheritance.

This is quite an egalitarian argument in itself, but Rawls goes further and argues that the modified structure 'still permits the distribution of wealth and income to be determined by the natural distribution of abilities and talents' (1972, pp. 73–4). Any given distribution of *natural* talents, which enables some to secure high returns for their skills, is purely arbitrary from a moral point of view and Rawls thinks that the effects of this 'natural lottery' have to be mitigated by the difference principle. Those with natural talents are entitled to high earnings *only* if such inequalities are to the benefit of the least advantaged. However, once those conditions are met, the efficiency criterion can operate in a competitive economy, which Rawls thinks is possible under either private or public ownership, and the traditional principles of resource allocation will operate so that nobody will be made worse off in any economic outcome. However, to the extent that any given structure is unjust, the principles of justice sanction changes that will aid the worst off at the expense of the better endowed and therefore there will be a breach of the strict formulation of the Pareto principle.

The elimination of desert from the justification of earnings is worth considering further. Rawls is saying that since no one 'owns' their talents they have no moral claim to the income they generate. This is quite different from the procedural theorist's rejection of desert. In her theory, the market determines earnings in accordance with the value transactors create and moral merit may have nothing to do with this. Nevertheless, these transactors are entitled to their natural assets, society does not own the individual. Rawls, however, claims that individuals do not deserve their talents so society has a right to redistribute the rewards from their exercise. Though why such a fictitious entity should have any claim over them is not at all clear.

But even someone favourable to Rawls's redistributivist intentions would be highly sceptical of his methods. He makes no clear distinction between the possession of natural talents and the use which is made of them. While it may be plausible to suggest that no moral merit attaches to the former it is surely perfectly sensible, from an egalitarian perspective, to use words such as desert and merit in the descriptions of people's efforts, and in the judgements we make about their earnings. This argument is not merely utilitarian – in that some differential payments should be paid to those who work hard in order to bring their talents into use – but derives from justice itself. If the only justified inequalities are those that enhance the well-being of the least-advantaged then does not Rawls's doctrine unfairly penalise those who choose to exercise their talents?

Rawls has to show why his set of principles, and the priority rule, would be chosen by self-interested rational agents behind the veil of ignorance. Such individuals would adopt a maximin strategy and it is this that yields the principles of justice (1972, pp. 152–8). Maximin applies in situations of uncertainly when individuals have *no knowledge* of the probabilities of various outcomes occurring. Under these conditions rational agents, not knowing their propensity to gamble, will have a conservative attitude towards risk and will choose those principles which maximise the position of the worst off, just in case it should turn out that they are the worst off, in terms of talents and skills, in any future society.

Rawls's arguments here are directed against the various forms of utilitarianism. Since utilitarianism maximises total utility, irrespective of its distribution, an individual cannot be certain that he will gain from its implementation. If he knew his attitude towards risk and had knowledge of the probabilities of various outcomes it would be rational for him to gamble on the prospect of, say, turning out to be rich in a utility-maximising society. But in a situation of uncertainty he must assume that he has an equal chance of ending up at the bottom of the pile as at the top. While a slave society might maximise a high level of utility, a rational agent, under Rawls's conditions, must assume he has an equal chance of being a slave as a slave-holder and therefore will not take the risk. Of course, in Rawls's system the pleasures of the better off, however great, cannot compensate for the pains of the worst off.

However, it is certainly plausible to suggest that the circumstances in the 'original position' are designed so as to ensure that the principles of justice that Rawls favours would be chosen by self-interested maximisers. Indeed, Rawls concedes this with his notion of a 'reflective equilibrium' – the idea that there should be a kind of harmony between the conditions that govern rational choice and our intuitive moral and political judgements. Thus the setting is not a 'neutral' one which permits a system of just rules to emerge from pure subjective choice but one loaded in favour of a particular set. The veil of ignorance is drawn so thickly that people can have no knowledge (apart from elementary economics and psychology) at all of the facts that might influence their rational choices.

This approach is obviously aimed at ensuring that rational individuals will choose the maximin strategy. Yet it is surely plausible to suppose that individuals would be likely to have some knowledge of the probabilities of future outcomes. If this is so then they might well opt for a rule that maximised expected utility (a strategy rejected by Rawls).[9] The maximin strategy is such a 'safety first' approach to life that it is almost bound to generate the outcome Rawls desires. Yet a more 'natural' contractarian setting would be one involving some individual propensity to take risks. If this is so then the muted egalitarianism of Rawls's principles of social justice would seem less likely to emerge. The Rawlsian system can only work because of the assumption of ignorance.

There are, nevertheless, considerable advantages in Rawls's approach. He describes it as a system of *pure procedural justice*, which means that if the principles are unanimously agreed upon, whatever distribution emerges is necessarily just. Thus he can eliminate, in the evaluation of a distribution, interpersonal comparisons based upon desert and need. While individuals can agree upon basic principles they do not have the knowledge, nor can they be expected to have the capacity, to make these particular judgements. In fact, the only interpersonal comparison that Rawls makes is that involved in the identification of the least-advantaged representative person.

There is a particular aspect of the Rawlsian system which might be thought questionable. On what grounds is it reasonable for the better endowed to have their talents, in a sense, used for the well-being of the least advantaged? Rawls anticipates this objection and argues that social life cannot be reduced to individual transactions. It is a collaborative activity in which the most talented can only realise their opportunities in co-operation with those less able (1972, p. 103). This point would appear to put Rawls clearly into the school of *social* justice since it involves a collective dimension to actions which goes beyond the making of transactions between individuals within general rules of fair play.

The objections to Rawls's theory have turned partly on technical arguments about the validity of his deductions and partly on the content of his social philosophy. We shall be concerned here mainly with the general properties of the theory as a substantive theory of justice. There is a difficulty in that some critics have interpreted it as quite a radical egalitarian theory while others treat it as a particularly elegant restatement of the social principles of liberal capitalism. There is evidence for both views.

A great deal of attention has been paid to the nature of the difference principle. We noted earlier that Rawls hoped to devise a theory which is congruent with our intuitive notions of justice but it is not clear that the principle does this since it is consistent with some highly peculiar distributions. If inequalities are justified to the extent that they favour the least advantaged then this would logically permit vast inequalities between rich and poor as long as there is the slightest improvement in the prospects of the poor in comparison with any alternative. Yet intuitively we may wish to comment on the inequalities themselves, even though this means making the complex comparisons between individuals that Rawls forbids. By the same token a utilitarian would object to the conclusions of the Rawlsian theorem, which disallow great gains to the better endowed if that entails a minute loss in the expectations of the worst off. A utilitarian would be unhappy with this sacrifice of total social utility that the Rawlsian system enjoins.

Rawls tries to counter some of these objections by suggesting that such outcomes are unlikely to occur in practice because the application of his principles would bring about a natural tendency towards equality (1972, pp. 100–5). He argues that a 'chain connection' operates between the best and the worst off and that a rise in the expectations of the best off will have the effect of raising everybody else's expectations throughout the system. This has provoked great hostility from collectivists who say that it is a rationalisation of the traditional liberal-capitalist argument that, somehow, people can only gain from an economic process if the better off are allowed freedom to accumulate. Collectivists would argue that the better off are only able to be successful because of past privileges and class advantages which even a rigorous application of Rawls's fair equality of opportunity principle can do little to alleviate. There may, however, be something important in Rawls's idea here. The evidence suggests than an incentives-based market system does raise the well-being of the worst off, at least in comparison with all known and practised alternatives. While it is certainly impossible to eliminate all the advantages that some have over others, short of abolishing the family, it may be the case that the preservation of the more serious inequalities is a product of the granting of privileges by *political* authorities rather than an endogenous feature of the market system itself. In planned economies these privileges lead to very great inequalities of power.

A very difficult problem for Rawls is the identification of the least advantaged. This clearly cannot be literally *the* worst off person in any society and must refer to some class of persons: Rawls always refers to the representative man of the least-advantaged group. He gives two definitions of such a person (1972, p. 98), but his whole approach here has been heavily criticised. This is because his methodology precludes him from considering the actual disadvantages of individuals and groups and it is said that many people who are in real need because of special circumstances would be missed out if an abstract criterion based upon a particular measure of income or wealth were to be the lynchpin of social policy.

The nature and justification of the priority rule has been criticised. While in theory it provides a determinate solution to the possible conflicts between principles, the priority of equal liberty over economic advantage has been challenged. It is true that in liberal democratic regimes, an individual is not allowed to sell his vote, this, and other similar prohibitions, are a consequence of the *mores* of these political systems and it is difficult to see how they can be derived from the rational choice situation described by Rawls. It is certainly possible to think of cases where it would be rational to trade an equal liberty for an economic improvement.

Some penetrating criticisms of Rawls have come from economic liberals. They see it as a strongly egalitarian doctrine and presumably Rawls would not deny this. Specifically, they maintain that although it looks like a procedural theory of justice it does, nevertheless, pick out a particular end-state; that is, that distribution is just which maximises the well-being of the least advantaged. They also object to the presumption in favour of equality and the assumption that natural assets should constitute a 'common pool' to be distributed according to the principles of social justice. Indeed, Nozick's theory of individual self-ownership is a sophisticated refutation of Rawls's model (which in this respect seems unKantian).

Arising out of these considerations is an important point relating to Rawls's theory of the person. Since he makes a curious distinction between the person and the natural talents that she may (quite arbitrarily) happen to have it is difficult to see what is left once these talents have been stripped away and put into a common pool. But surely we, as persons, are primarily constituted by all our features, talents and so on, and moral appraisal is directed at the whole agent. If certain obvious features of personhood are detached from the agent then what kind of entity is left who is supposed to be the subject of praise and blame? Indeed, the approach undermines Rawls's original stress on the distinctiveness and separateness of persons, as a way of distinguishing his doctrine from utilitarianism, since all the significant properties of individuals which might be relevant to distribution, have now been conflated under the difference principle.

In his later work (Rawls, 1993) he seems to be departing significantly from the universalism that characterised *A Theory of Justice*. In that work individuals were informed by few facts about themselves or their communities; indeed, the agents were governed by the principles of rational choice and not by any prior notion of the good. But in his *Political Liberalism* the claim is that the theory of justice has a political not a philosophical justification and it would appear that it derives from a peculiarly American conception of liberal politics. While it is true that communities may be divided over rival conceptions of the good, especially where religious matters are concerned, Rawls now suggests that a well-ordered society will have 'an overlapping consensus' which allows for a toleration of these differences. This overlapping consensus is said to be consistent with the distributive principles which are retained from *A Theory of Justice*. However, the consensus itself seems to be little more than a restatement of John Stuart Mill's liberalism which owes as much to considerations derived from the American *community* as to rational choice. But once these deviations are admitted there seems no reason to suppose that other political communities will share what some might think are simply American liberal prejudices. One thinks of religions that simply do not accept that toleration that springs from Rawls's first principle of justice and there is little in communitarian thought that will persuade their believers otherwise. The 'public reason' to which Rawls (1993, ch. 6) constantly appeals turns out to be already informed by liberalism itself. Even a post-communist world is characterised by competing ideologies which are held with great intensity and American liberalism is merely one. The original Rawlsian doctrine may be as politically unrealistic as this but its derivation from rational choice gives it a certain grandeur and its method, especially the preclusion of contingent facts from the original position, does have a certain resonance with how we often think about justice.

An analysis of Rawls's theory reveals some of the familiar problems of justice.[10] The emphasis on justice as a system of rules provides a certain kind of rigour in the use of the concept while at the same time it seems to exclude some of our most deeply-held moral convictions about the way income and wealth should be distributed. Yet there seems to be little agreement about what a more expanded notion of justice should consist of, even amongst those who believe that all departures from equality are in need of justification. Such problems may be best approached by trying to understand what implications general distributive principles have for social policy. What is also required is some analysis of the other item on the agenda of social justice – equality.

7
Equality

1 The equality principle

In 1931, when R. H. Tawney first published his famous book *Equality*, he lamented what he called 'The Religion of Inequality' in British society. The problem for him, as a strong egalitarian, was not merely that extremes of income and wealth existed and that the system of social stratification preserved outmoded class distinctions, but that they were accepted as inevitable, and even approved of, by those who stood to gain most from their removal – the working classes. The people accepted the *mana* and *karakia* (Tawney, 1969, p. 35) of social and economic inequality in the same way that primitive people accept the ritual of tribal society. According to Tawney there was no rational justification for inequality; its survival was a matter of prejudice.

It would not be too inaccurate to suggest that today the position has been almost exactly reversed. There seems to be a new consensus, at least amongst *all* brands of socialist opinion, that every movement towards equality is necessarily a good thing, and almost all the social reforms in the welfare state are designed to promote by collectivist measures a form of equality that would not have emerged through private transactions. However, it is difficult to say how far the reverence for the equality principle extends throughout society at large.

The pace at which the progress towards equality proceeds varies from one Western country to another, as does the type of equality pursued. In the United States of America, for example, while there has been a considerable amount of legislative and judicial activity to promote social equality and create more equality of opportunity for minority races and groups, progress towards economic equality has been less speedy. Furthermore, many of Tawney's strictures on the British working class's acquiescence in the fact of economic and social inequality might well be true of the United States today. Arthur M. Okun, an egalitarian economist, conceded with regret the point that there is in that country a strong moral approval of the inequalities characteristic of a market economy, even by those groups in some considerable state of deprivation (1975, p. 128).

However, in recent years there has been a resurgence of serious anti-egalitarian thought (see Flew, 1981). A perennial debate between political philosophers concerns the relationship between equality and liberty and a long tradition in the discipline holds that the use of state power to bring about an equality that does not emerge spontaneously necessarily involves a reduction in personal liberty. This tradition has been reinforced in recent years by the resurgence of the school of political economy which argues that the imposition of egalitarian measures in the economic sphere necessarily disturbs those mechanisms that allocate resources efficiently in society, and that such disturbances will make everyone worse off, including those the egalitarian measures were designed to help. In this economic philosophy there is not just the familiar political theorist's problem of the tension between equality and liberty but also an exploration of the trade-off between liberty, equality and prosperity (Brittan, 1973, p. 128).

It is important to stress that in this chapter we shall be concerned with equality as a justificatory principle in its own right rather than equality as a part of justice. We have already noted that all theories of procedural rules justice contain a weak sense of equality which means that, whatever their differences, all people, on account of their common humanity, are entitled to be treated equally by the rules of a social practice. This is, of course, not especially egalitarian and is quite consistent with a great deal of social and economic inequality. It is also true that someone could accept this moral principle and still not accept the view that all inequalities have to be justified. As we have seen, most theories of justice do maintain that justice is precisely about justifying departures from equality (which is Rawls's procedure). Classical liberals maintain that a movement towards equality would be unjustified since it might entail paying the same income to individuals who make widely differing contributions to the output of an economy.

Equality can then conflict with the principles of justice (especially desert-based theories of justice) even though the strong sense of equality, or egalitarianism, is a basic component of social justice. The demand for equality is not a disguised demand for the removal of some unjustified inequalities so that all economic and social differences may have some rational foundation; it is an argument for the thing itself (Barry, B. 1965, p. 120). Political and constitutional rights, such as the equal right to vote in a democracy, are examples of the application of equality, just as laws prohibiting sexual and racial discrimination are. People may reasonably disagree on how far equality may be pushed but to say that egalitarian policies are reducible to policies that remove arbitrary privileges is to misunderstand the (prescriptive) meaning of the principle. Berlin makes this point when he says, of equality, that 'like all human ends it cannot be rationally justified for it is itself that which justifies other acts ...' (1955–6, p. 326). As a pluralist Berlin thinks that equality has to be traded off against other values. While accepting the independent status of equality as a political principle we shall not accept the view that 'ends' such as equality and liberty cannot be rationally argued about; indeed, some of the most interesting work done in social and political theory in recent years has been about ends.

The stress on equality as the essential feature of social justice means that egalitarians do not have to invoke the concept of moral desert to justify particular income distributions and in this they have something in common with *laissez-faire* liberals. An egalitarian who retained some belief in the importance of liberty should be highly sceptical of centralised institutions determining a person's worth subject only to political controls. The problem of need is more complicated since the satisfaction of needs is an essential element in the egalitarian's social programme. Yet there are grave problems in establishing what needs are and connecting these to equality. While it is true that people need food, clothing, shelter and so on, it is obviously not the case that they need equal shares of these things.[1] The most pressing cases of social justice are concerned with the justification of the satisfaction of quite different needs. The problem is that egalitarianism is a relational doctrine that makes comparative judgements about people's positions on a particular scale and is concerned to equalise them. But there is nothing intrinsically valuable about that. People's claims to deserts and needs can be met without an invocation of some comparative judgement based on equality.

2 Human nature and equality

Contemporary egalitarians are eager to make two disclaimers in the presentation of their doctrine. First, they deny that the demand for equality means a demand for absolute equality. In fact, this has rarely been demanded by any thinker in the history of egalitarian thought.

They think therefore that a more equal society would not be characterised by sameness and uniformity but by a certain amount of variety. It is simply argued that the removal of a large number of existing economic and other inequalities would represent a social improvement. Secondly, the argument for more equality is not normally justified by reference to a supposed natural equality in people. It is true that in the past egalitarian arguments did appear to derive from propositions such as 'all men are created equal', but it is generally agreed that such statements are of little use in the generation of egalitarian theories. In political discourse the word has little *descriptive* content because in all their most important aspects people are most certainly not equal. Therefore its use is mainly *prescriptive*; that is, policies are recommended because they promote the ideal of equality, and the justifications for them do not have to depend upon some descriptive properties of human beings.

Egalitarians would be unwise to base their arguments on human nature. Nothing follows logically about how men ought to be treated in an egalitarian sense from a statement about some supposed factual equality. There is an is-ought gap here, as in other problems of normative ethics. An egalitarian might say that men ought to be treated equally in those respects in which they are equal; they are equal in respect of x, therefore in respect of x they ought to be treated equally. But even if agreement could be secured on the prescriptive premise it is unlikely that the completed argument would generate the policies desired by the egalitarian since the ways in which men may be factually said to be equal are trivial. The temptation for egalitarians is to say that because men are equal in some respects they are equal in others and therefore ought to be treated equally (Lucas, 1971, p. 140).

The illegitimacy of 'is to ought' arguments also tells against inegalitarians who, from factual premises alone, attempt to derive policies that treat races and sexes differently. The claim (much disputed) made by some psychologists[2] that there is a strong correlation between measured intelligence and race, that on average certain races are superior to others in terms of natural abilities, does not entail in any way normative policy conclusions as to how individual members of the races and groups are to be treated. Policy conclusions with regard to matters of discrimination depend ultimately upon moral principles which cannot be derived from facts. The danger of making the egalitarian argument turn upon facts is that this invites the inegalitarian to produce evidence of natural inequality to give some bite to his argument that there is a case for treating people unequally.

This sort of reasoning underlies arguments for showing that a version of the equality principle does not depend upon natural equality at all. It is argued by some that the principle of equality before the law and the requirement that rules in a legal system should be general and non-discriminatory are the only procedures which can guarantee that fundamentally *unequal people* can conduct their lives with reasonable predictability and security. The inequalities of human beings cannot be a ground for government and the law treating them differently. In this context there is little difference between equality and liberty: the law protects both. This equality of treatment is, however, quite consistent with substantial economic and social inequality. In fact it is certain to be accompanied by such inequality since this ideal of equal liberty before the law enjoyed by individuals who are unequal in endowments must lead to some doing better than others. Yet to bring about a more substantial equality must involve treating them differently, which is contrary to formal equality. The most obvious example is in income, where if we wish to move towards the equalisation of incomes we have to treat people differently by the rules of the tax system. Here a problem of liberty emerges because an equalising tax rule must prevent some from spending their income as they wish.

While it is true that prescriptive uses of the concept of equality are more useful in moral and political argument than descriptive uses, nevertheless we still need to know something more about the right to equal freedom which is implicit in our discussion so far. Can this be supported rationally or is the commitment to the principle purely a matter of personal choice or is there some element of *impartiality* built into morality itself? Bernard Williams (1963) seems to imply that there is when he says that the distinction between fact and value cannot be used to smuggle in pure arbitrariness in the guise of moral argument. Thus he says that to argue that someone should be discriminated against purely on grounds of race is not to invoke a special moral principle but to act in an arbitrary manner, that is to say, in a way in which reasons are irrelevant.

The suggestion that morality itself implies an element of impartiality, while it does not yield substantive egalitarian conclusions, is not vacuous. From it we can derive the idea of a 'common humanity' – that minimal, but fundamental notion of equality that unites all men into one reference group for the purposes of moral argument. While people are different from each other in many important respects they are similar in comparison with other species. Thus we treat people equally, in the way that we would not (morally) treat persons and dogs equally (Wilson, 1966, p. 103), yet at the same time we recognise differences between persons.

For the egalitarian the price of agreement may be too high since a hierarchical society with no upward mobility or an extreme *laissez-faire* society would both be consistent with this principle. However, it is not trivial because clearly there are societies that do not recognise it and do not treat individuals as individuals but solely in terms of some category based on, say, religion, race or sex. Furthermore, the equality which is being referred to is not analytically tied to the entity 'man' because it is certainly possible to deny this property to those whom we would call persons on other grounds. What we are referring to in this notion of equality is that it is descriptive of those capable of making rational choices: people are at least equal in the sense that no one person's choices have an *a priori* right to superiority over another's. Yet we would not include within our reference group mental defectives and young children, precisely because morality seems to exclude those either incapable or not yet capable of making rational choices. Of course, this is not to say that we do not have very strong moral duties towards the mentally deranged and others whom we do not call rational choosers.

Despite some heroic attempts by philosophers, it is not possible to derive substantive egalitarian conclusions from the equal right to freedom implicit in the notion of a 'common humanity'. Arguments over equality of opportunity and the appropriate distribution of income and wealth take place between political theorists who accept the idea of impartiality in moral argument and that each human being is entitled to dignity and self-respect. Anti-egalitarians often argue that the imposition of socialist egalitarian measures undermines this dignity and self-respect and that the paternalism that often accompanies such measures negates the idea of persons as rational choosers. Therefore, the case for equality in the strong sense has to be argued for independently of appeals to 'common humanity'. The interesting problems centre on the connection between equality and other principles and the consequences of adopting egalitarian policies.

3 Equality of opportunity

While it is true that egalitarians disagree on the desirable level of equality in a quantitative sense, there is almost unanimous agreement as to the desirability of the qualitative value of equality of opportunity. It is a value which even some non-egalitarians have found appealing. Yet is it difficult to see what equality of opportunity has to do with equality at all, and, as has often been pointed out, if it were to be applied rigorously it might well produce a state of affairs with a much greater degree of economic and social stratification than exists at present in most Western democracies.

It is a strictly meritocratic doctrine which finds its most coherent expression in the authoritarian political philosophy of Plato. In his *Republic* all those factors which arbitrarily advantaged one person as against another were removed, including the family, so that the social position which men and women (Plato was an early and rigorous exponent of the equality of the sexes) found themselves in was entirely a result of their own abilities and efforts, all elements of chance having been removed from an individual's life-prospects.

While the modern exponent of the doctrine might claim that it is an aspect of the egalitarian creed because it entails the elimination of arbitrary advantages and a general levelling out of the social and economic system, the principle might also be interpreted as an example of the maximisation of an equal liberty. In this view to demand equality of opportunity is to demand the removal of impediments or obstacles that stand in the way of an individual realising her potential; an increase in opportunity is an increase in liberty. There is a certain plausibility in this view since, at least in the original formulation of 'the career open to the talents', the doctrine demanded the removal of *legal* and other unjustifiable privileges that reserved certain social, economic and political positions for classes, races or one particular sex. However, the modern exponent of the doctrine wants to do more than this; she also wants to remove those other factors that advantage some but which are the result of luck rather than legal privilege, such as being born the daughter of a successful entrepreneur. To remove these privileges is not to maximise equal liberties but to implement a general levelling out which would certainly involve the abrogation of certain liberties, such as the right to bequest.

The intellectual ancestor of modern thinking on equality of opportunity is undoubtedly Rousseau. In his *On the Origins of Inequality in Society*, he sought to explain the immorality of eighteenth-century European society by the inequality which made one man dependent on another. While Rousseau did not believe in absolute equality, and indeed on one famous occasion proclaimed the 'sacred right of property', he did say that when men establish extensive private property holdings they create conventional and arbitrary inequalities that reduce some to servility. Incidentally, Rousseau was certainly no advocate of equality between the sexes.

It is the supposed distinction between *nature* and *convention* that underlies Rousseau's egalitarianism. Natural inequalities of physical strength, intellect, beauty and so on, are acceptable: social inequalities, because they are a product of pure convention, are not. The distinction between nature and convention seems to turn upon the assumption that conventional inequalities are *alterable*, while natural ones are not, and it is this that seems to lie behind the contemporary doctrine of equality of opportunity (Rees, 1971, pp. 14–26). While Rousseau's solution to the problem of inequality created by commercial society was to retreat into a small agrarian community of equals governed by the popular will, the modern egalitarian is more forward-looking in that she hopes that society can be rationally planned so that all artificial advantages are removed: the only acceptable inequalities are natural, unalterable ones.

The difficulty with this superficially appealing idea concerns the distinction between nature and convention, which is not as clear-cut as egalitarians imply. While there is an obvious distinction between natural inequalities of strength, beauty and intelligence, and the artificial legal distinctions, such as those that prohibit members of racial or religious groups from taking political office, there is a vast area of social life where the words nature and convention are quite irrelevant. Rousseau's argument that inequalities are created by 'society' is really absurd since we have no useful conception of man abstracted from society which can form a touchstone for the legitimacy or otherwise of various distinctions. What might be thought of as a relevant natural distinction, such as that based on intelligence, is relevant only because society has conventionally regarded it as such for many purposes.

In a similar way, what might be thought of as conventional laws and institutions are not *merely* conventional or the product of choice. Can it be said that the English common law system or the parliamentary form of government were deliberately chosen?[3] It is true that such conventions are not natural phenomena, like the weather, but they are certainly not arbitrary. David Hume described the rules of justice that authorise the possession and transfer of property as 'artificial', but he said that it would be perfectly correct to call them fundamental 'laws of nature' in that every society must have some rules of this type which cannot be cast aside or substantially altered at will.

The significance of this for the egalitarian is that while rules can be altered, the proposed distinction between nature and convention does

not provide an indisputable criterion for determining what the altera-
tions should be. The existence of government and the need to enforce
general rules means that there will be of necessity some political
inequality which may not inaccurately be regarded as 'natural'. It
may be said that disparities between individuals in income and wealth
are conventional and arbitrary since they rest upon artificial rules
which are alterable by will. This is possible but in doing so new rules
will have to be found to govern property holdings which may turn out
to be the source of new conventional inequalities. This is not to say
that there are no arguments for increasing equality of opportunity, but
only to suggest that the distinction between nature and convention is
an unsatisfactory ground for them.

It is in education that the most substantial arguments for equality of
opportunity have been advanced and it is in this area that the familiar
problems of the concept can be most easily illustrated. If birth or
wealth determine educational opportunity then, superficially, this
seems quite conventional or arbitrary (and therefore open to altera-
tion) because we have a perfectly good, natural, indeed highly
relevant, criterion in intelligence on which a 'rational' educational
policy can be based. But in logic intelligence is no better a qualification
for educational preferment, since those excluded by this criterion may
legitimately claim that it is as arbitrary as birth or wealth. Indeed, in a
socialised system of education the parents of less gifted children may
legitimately complain that they, as taxpayers, are being unjustly
treated since they are being forced to subsidise the unequal education
of the newly privileged class of children. It could also be argued that a
disproportionate amount of money should be spent on the less gifted
precisely because they are less gifted.

All this is not to deny that the advocate of equality of opportunity
has a point when she protests at the injustices of a system of education
that seems to preclude groups of people on arbitrary grounds. However, just what non-arbitrary or relevant grounds might be is not as
easy to determine as some people have supposed. The family is the
source of much educational inequality but much of this is unalterable
short of abolishing the institution itself.

Even if such a distinction could be made it is by no means clear that
it would produce a desirable society. As Michael Young has shown in
his brilliant parody, *The Rise of the Meritocracy* (1961), a meritocratic
society would produce a much more rigid, and sinister, system of social
stratification than Western democracies have at present. Such a system
is likely to be resented, and be the cause of disharmony, precisely

because it is so eminently meritocratic. People who finish up at the bottom do not have even the comfort of being justly aggrieved at their lot because that is where they deserve to be. As has often been pointed out, what chance would the notion of a fundamental equality of human personality have of being accepted in such a world?

There is also the problem that some of the 'natural' inequalities may prove to be alterable with the advance of medical science. Genetic engineering may soon make it possible to eliminate hereditary differences so that a genuinely equal starting point in life can be established for everyone. The least successful will no longer be able to complain at the injustice of nature in distributing talents so unfairly.

There is no need to speculate further on this theme to realise that there is something deeply unsatisfactory at the heart of the doctrine of equality of opportunity. It would be unwise to push the doctrine beyond justifying the removal of the most obvious type of arbitrary discrimination based on race, religion and sex, since most of the egalitarian's ideals can be presented in ways that do not require the precarious distinction between nature and convention. The problem with an over-rigorous application of the doctrine of equality of opportunity is that the spread of alterable impediments to a person's success becomes wider and wider. This has the effect of all but eliminating those desert-based grounds for the awarding of income, prizes and other social honours that are familiarly used. If a person's achievements can always be explained by some arbitrary advantage then we have ultimately no way of knowing what achievement is. We normally want some way of distinguishing between what a person has a claim to by her own efforts and what is a product of sheer luck (which may give entitlements but it does not give deserts). Some attempts to make such a distinction pose threats to liberty.

But even in familiar policy areas there are difficulties that raise philosophical issues. For example, it seems on the face of it absurd that university education should be accessible *only* to those who can afford to pay for it. It seems natural that those who reach certain educational standards should receive grants from the state so that opportunity is equalised. However, this clearly involves a breach of justice (procedural and social). This is because those with degrees who earn higher incomes than those without them are clearly being subsidised by the relatively worse off (Maynard, 1975, p. 51). Since anybody who enjoys three years at the expense of the state, that is the taxpayer, is clearly in receipt of a considerable privilege, it is often argued in Britain that loans should replace grants. What is not often realised is that this is an argument for justice. It is now conceded by some socialists that many interventionist measures designed to bring about more equality do the reverse (Le Grand, 1982). This is largely because they are provided in 'kind' – in the form, for example, of housing and educational benefits – which enables the politically influential to determine their form, and are often delivered to persons irrespective of their income. The equal provision of services does not necessarily produce equal consumption because the decision to consume (especially higher education) will depend upon a whole network of background conditions. One reason why middle-class children disproportionately consume higher education is that the opportunity cost, foregone income from work, is much lower for them than for poorer children. We provide a more detailed analysis of equality and welfare in Chapter 10.

4 Equality, markets and resources

It is clear that the problems raised in the concept of equality of opportunity cannot be answered until we have a coherent understanding of equality itself; especially in the economic sphere. The difficulty here is that though almost all political theorists take some conception of equality as pivotal to their normative arguments there the agreement ends. There appear to be competing conceptions which have radically different implications for social policy. The consensus over the concept seems to be limited to certain prohibitions against treating people as members of different categories, defined by such features as sex, race or religion. Though even here that might apply only to public matters and not private arrangements. People may discriminate privately on arbitrary grounds, and bear the costs, and still claim to be within the equality provisions of a limited public law. One may doubt that there is an uncontroversial concept of equality, there are simply competing conceptions.

A free market economist might claim that the exchange system honours perfectly well the equality principle. Each transactor is treated as an abstract agent, not identified in terms of irrelevant features such as sex or race, and is free to exchange with whomsoever she wishes. Any prohibitions of such exchanges (beyond those required for the protection of the public) would be breaches of the equality principle because they would involve centralised authority making certain unjustified discriminations. Indeed, market economists claim that, historically, inequality stems not from the market but the state; the cases of the southern states of America and South Africa being the best examples. It is inefficient to discriminate on the grounds of race or sex. Of course, the free market will not eliminate all discrimination on arbitrary grounds – people may be willing to pay the costs that *private* unfairness involve – but at least the *idea* of the market is not against a conception of equality.

Some market theorists go further and suggest that a competitive market can meet some of the demands of a more substantive conception of equality – that is, one that wished to reduce disparities in income but not to a level which would affect productivity. This conception would therefore accept 'rational' inequalities but would regard those in existing capitalist societies as based on power (or perhaps Tawney's sense of prejudice or mystique) which has no relationship to economic needs. Thus, in a perfectly competitive market economy each factor of production (labour, capital and land) is paid an income just sufficient to induce it into maximum productivity. Payment according to marginal productivity would eliminate 'profit', because this is payment in excess of that required to draw factors into use and is usually explained in terms of monopoly power. Of course, there are good reasons why some market economists claim that profit is actually a justified reward for the discovery that continually takes place in markets (see Kirzner, 1989) and that a perfectly efficient market, even if it were conceivable, would actually be static. Still, the market system does tend to whittle away profit, at least until some new discovery gives someone a temporary advantage. To eliminate profit would be to attempt to make price equal long-run production costs. But what creativity in markets could occur if this were made the standard of reward?

However attractive the theory of markets (if not the practice) might be for egalitarians, it is so badly flawed morally in their eyes that it is an unsatisfactory model. The major deficiency is that people enter it with unequal resources, not only in terms of the physical assets that they possess at the start but also the differences in natural talents (brute luck) that earn them continuously higher incomes than those not so well-endowed. There is also the serious moral problem posed by those so disabled that they can barely compete at all. The point is that markets can work quite well with an amount of inequality that some would regard as unacceptable.

We have noticed in Chapter 6 that Rawls was anxious to stress the arbitrariness of nature in endowing talents so unequally: he therefore eliminated desert completely from social justice. However, he did not distinguish fully between natural endowments and *efforts* so that there remained some distance between his theory and our ordinary moral language. He also said nothing about the grievously disadvantaged, so that their fate would rest solely on the working out of the difference principle. Would not egalitarianism require compensation for those whose unequal position came about through no fault of their own?

Contemporary egalitarianism (see Dworkin, 1981) is really aimed at completing Rawls's unfinished agenda. In answer to the question, 'equality of what?' (see Sen, 1992), it would say that social circumstances should be so arranged that starting points in life are not such that some have unfair advantages over others: that the resulting inequalities should reflect people's choices and efforts rather than (alterable) social conditions. Luck is not entirely ruled out since it is not proposed that all contingencies can be planned for, but the brute luck, of either material assets or natural talents and genetic misfortune, should certainly be remedied. The market is by no means excluded for it is recognised that to plan output independently of choice would be to breach a fundamental liberal principle, that is, no one's conception of the good should have priority over others.

In some important ways this approach is reminiscent of a classic problem in economic thought (although it is not recognised by Dworkin or other authors in this tradition): the question of economic 'rent'. If a certain factor has no alternative use then the income it earns could be taxed away with little or no effect on efficiency. Land was the obvious example and it was argued in the nineteenth century that landowners received an income (rent) through no entrepreneurial effort on their part. It was a product of the luck of ownership and there were a number of schemes for taxing it away (though not, of course, the income derived from any improvements that owners had made to the land). In a sense, modern liberal egalitarians regard payment to those who exercise natural talents as a form of rent which is not essential to draw those talents into productive use. There are many other factors involved, not the least of which are the moral duties we owe to the disadvantaged, but this rent element seems to be a significant part of the theory.

Dworkin's hypothetical egalitarian society is structured around a distinction between inequalities which are 'endowment sensitive' and those which are 'ambition sensitive'. The former emerge from the advantages that some derive from the purely arbitrary distribution of resources and are quite unrelated to the choices, efforts and achievements of persons, while the latter are not at all contingent since they flow from whatever actions of a person bring about her success. By making this distinction, and reserving moral appraisal for the results of ambitions, he is implicitly restoring the idea of desert to distributive questions. The distinction between deserts and entitlements, which is a feature of procedural justice, is abandoned because in Dworkin's scheme there will be no unjust entitlements. The argument is a development of an earlier claim of his (see Dworkin, 1977) that every person is entitled to 'equal concern and respect'; to deny people adequate resources would be to abrogate that right. However, that claim appears to be vague enough to accommodate a variety of liberal positions (including procedural justice).

There is, then, an initial commitment to equality, and while departures from it are clearly permissible they require moral justification. Dworkin imagines that in some purely hypothetical scheme people have to bid for available resources (these are somehow 'given') in an auction. The resources – land, materials and so on – are not distributed equally since people will want to do different things so that what one person may want to do with something will differ from what another will desire. Instead, people are given equal amounts of a token (clam shells) with which they bid for resources. The final distribution of resources will reflect people's subjective choices and will be 'envy-free' in that no one will prefer anyone else's bundle of resources to his own. What persons do with their resources is entirely up to them and they are responsible for their actions. There is no implication that people who make mistaken choices have a *prima facie* claim on society.

There is, however, another part of the process; that dealing with the unequal distribution of natural talents. For, according to the theory, inequalities arising out of the maldistribution of them are just as unchosen as is the arbitrary division of physical resources.[4] There can be no objection to the use that people make of their talents, and indeed society gains when they are drawn into these most productive uses but, like Rawls, Dworkin protests at the random initial allocation. There is also the question of the unfortunate people who have virtually no talents. Dworkin proposes an insurance market in which people have to buy premiums that, to some extent, protect them against the vicissitudes of nature. In effect, people born with talents will have to buy them back via the insurance market. Thus somebody naturally endowed with the skills that will yield a high income as a lawyer, accountant or doctor will have to pay for them. In this way society gains from the use of these skills without having to pay rent for them. Those anxious to be highly paid professionals will obviously have less of their clam shells left to spend on other resources. This approach contrasts remarkably with the self-ownership model of Nozick's.

All this looks like a piece of science fiction but it does have a remote analogue in the real world. After all, the higher taxes paid by the better paid could be interpreted as the price they have to pay for their abilities. Of course, the approximation will be rough and ready and in reality those born with severe disabilities are not compensated fully (unless part of the tax yield were paid directly to them). Still, it is not clear how exactly they would be compensated under Dworkin's scheme, though presumably they would pay no premiums and would benefit from comprehensive welfare schemes. Certainly, Dworkin believes that a properly designed tax and welfare system would be a surrogate for his theoretical proposals. In one respect, the talented would still do better despite their high premiums because the arrangements are ambition-sensitive and since society puts a value on skills their rewards could be considerable even if the rental element were eliminated.

However, from another perspective, having talents could be something of a burden (see Miller, 1990, pp. 90–1). The prices of the premiums will reflect the values that society places on certain talents. Highly talented people will have to buy back their abilities at considerable cost. But if somebody did not wish to use her talents in ways rewarded by society, she would still have to work to pay for the premiums. This would seriously distort the choices that people make between work and leisure. Someone who does not wish to use her mathematical ability in a socially useful way, perhaps she prefers the scholarly life, will still find herself paying high costs for that talent. We seem to have come a long way from the classical theory of rent, where that payment was felt to be unjust because land itself had little alternative uses. There may be some people who have little alternative use for the talents, so that part of their income could possibly be considered as rent, but it would be unwise to see that as a general feature of labour markets.

There is a more general objection to schemes which attempt to tax ability and it is to do with *knowledge* and *value* in the market process. With regard to both the distribution of physical resources and natural talents, it is impossible to say how much they are worth in advance of the actual operation of markets. Dworkin has proposed quasi-markets, not real markets. The latter are characterised by uncertainty and unpredictability, tastes constantly change and new productive techniques emerge in an entirely unplanned manner. Thus even if one accepts the assumption that people should start out with equal purchasing power in relation to physical resources it is very likely that the values of those resources would change very quickly so that new inequalities would be quickly generated. Dworkin has no objection to inequalities that emerge from individual choices but a great deal of inequality stems from changes in tastes of others, over which the individual has no responsibility. Is that to be considered an aspect of brute luck, hence requiring correction, perhaps by re-running the auction, or just treated as the unavoidable luck of the game? The value of assets, and our knowledge of it, is revealed by real markets, not imaginary ones.

A similar problem is apparent in the question of natural talents. The premium charged for them is bound to be arbitrary and very quickly a competitive market will establish new values. In such circumstances it will be very difficult to establish a distinction between inequalities that result from efforts, and in a sense are deserved, and those that result from the unfair bestowal of abilities. In fact, much new value is created by individuals who, with very little in the way of resources, just happen to hit upon a new discovery which turns out to have quite a high demand (Kirzner, 1989). Dworkin's scheme seems to imply that there is a kind of objective measure of resources (either of the physical goods type or of natural talents) so that the whole spread of inequalities in a society can be morally assessed in terms of whether they arise out of chance or genuine efforts. But resources do not exist independently of the human action necessary to create or exploit them. Whether they are deserved or not is such a complex issue that one wonders if any definite resolution could be reached in the terms set by Dworkin.

The conclusion might very well be that we should worry less about equality as a relational concept – when one person's well-being is assessed entirely in terms of her standing in comparison with others – and more about well-being itself. It is true that a guide to this can be found by locating someone's position on the income and wealth scales, those at the bottom will clearly lack resources, but it is not clear that equality is all that useful beyond this. Even possession of resources can be an inadequate measure; different things will have different meanings to people so that merely equalising them may not contribute to an equal maximising of welfare. But perhaps we should not aim at maximising equal welfare (Dworkin, 1981) either, since that could have quite perverse implications. What if someone's welfare depended on the cultivation of extraordinarily expensive tastes? The point is that equality itself, at least in its more substantive, egalitarian manifestations, may not be a feasible goal to pursue. We have separate and independent reasons for aiding people whose lack of resources seriously undermines their autonomy without invoking equality as a relational principle. People are badly off irrespective of comparisons with others and an obsession with equalising may distract us from a perfectly acceptable concentration on this.

The pursuit of equality also has an effect on other principles; notably liberty. It is not necessarily the case that they are always in conflict. After all, somebody from the free market end of the liberal spectrum would argue that an exchange system requires equal liberties so that the law should not discriminate in the freedoms it grants people to make the best of themselves through competitive co-operation with others. Somcone of a more state interventionist persuasion would maintain that the value and worth of liberty depends on resource availability and that a purely formal application of the equal liberty principle leaves many people without meaningful freedom. But taken in a substantive sense, the demand for equal liberty is not something that can be satisfied uncontroversially. How do we know when liberties have been equalised? Egalitarians may claim that a loss in the liberty of the rich is perfectly justifiable in liberty-maximising terms if it increases the liberties of the poor. But in the absence of a common and uncontroversial scale of values it is impossible to say whether such a trade-off is socially and morally optimal.

The issue concerning equality is always, 'equality of what?' Since the answers to the problem are invariably conflicting it might be better to ask a different question, one more to do with the conditions that make people's lives meaningful and worthwhile. Thus, the aim of social policy should not be to establish substantive equality *between* people but to alter circumstances so that some are not condemned to low levels of well-being. Egalitarians too readily assume that this can only be achieved by economic redistribution, that is, by dispossessing the successful. The attempts to establish equality in the economic sphere have not only been unsuccessful empirically (Phelps Brown, 1988) they have also generated new forms of inequality, especially in the political sphere. All too often egalitarians assume that the state is a neutral instrument which can be relied upon to implement, almost costlessly, supposed intrinsically desirable ends.

5 Equality, the family and feminism

Given the distinction made in Chapter 5 between public and private in feminist thought it is not surprising that some of the most original writing by feminists should be about the family, a subject largely neglected by traditional political theory. Susan Okin's *Justice, Gender and the Family* (1989) is a welcome addition to the literature. Despite its title, the book is really about equality because its recommendations are set in the context of a general argument for the extension of the equality principle to areas hitherto ignored by conventional political theory. Thus Okin is dissatisfied by the achievements of justice in employment, equal opportunities legislation and so on because although the rules here are formally fair and gender-free they operate in an environment which is already contaminated by inequality between the sexes: an inequality brought about by social practices. Many of these practices are not directly coercive towards women but their overall effect is to reinforce inequality and give it a veneer of legitimacy. Thus, although the law may not formally differentiate the sexes it is the case that women tend to get segregated into particular occupations and married women who have careers are especially disadvantaged in a gender-biased society.

Okin pays great attention to differences in human capital between the sexes; this clearly creates and preserves inequality. Men have higher valued human capital than women (women who devote part of their married lives to child-rearing suffer a significant decline in the value of human capital as a result) not because of their choices and efforts but because entrenched social practices prevent equality here. There is no reason at all to suppose that marginal productivity is different between the sexes (except for certain occupations that depend exclusively on physical strength). This is highly relevant to married women who will normally give up their careers to raise a family with the result that if they return to work their earnings will be lower than men's because of the fall in the value of their human capital. Because of institutionalised norms, it is almost obligatory for men to continue to work during the years of child-rearing while women stay at home, which introduces a kind of unnecessary dependency. Again, because of gender norms, women who do return to work after child-rearing are expected to assume also the burdens of domestic duties.

The few men who have written about the family tend to take an economic rationalist stance. Thus Gary Becker (1981) regards the family as an economically efficient unit. Accepting the division of labour, with women staying at home and men going out to work, he argues that both sides make the familiar gains from trade. This division is eminently rational because possibly for social reasons (rather than reasons of economic efficiency) women tend to earn less than men. This model, whatever its moral deficiencies (and presumably its proponents would claim that it is value-free), does generate some interesting predictions. One is that divorce rates tend to rise as women return to the workforce because then the gains from trade are not so easily available.

But is this model 'fair'? In a narrow sense it is since the arrangements it describes are undertaken voluntarily. It is as if couples had agreed to a set of rules (or accepted the implicitly gender-biased rules of society) and are, in a sense, bound by the outcomes, including inequality, that they generate. To a feminist, however, they are manifestly unfair: not merely because she wouldn't accept as genuine the 'voluntariness' described by the economist and would look for those social factors that implicitly produced the decisions, but also because the very economic structure of marriage generates power within the family. The very fact that the family relies on the husband's wage, however voluntary the arrangements that produce this, generates dependency for the wife.

The most egalitarian implications of Okin's analysis of the family comes out in her discussion of marriage and divorce: the law, in America especially, treats women as equals (in the traditional liberal sense) while the conditions of marriage renders them unequal. Again, the reason for this turns on human capital. After divorce women have a diluted claim over their ex-husband's income from human capital. Maintenance orders are difficult to enforce; alimony payments tend to be temporary in America so that once the value and division of such things as the house and other assets are settled the husband is more or less free of obligations. Since wives normally have custody of children, and their human capital is of lower value than men's, their post-divorce incomes fall dramatically (all this is confirmed by empirical evidence). Okin blames the way no fault divorce laws function for much of this.

What relevance does political theory have to all this? Okin is openly egalitarian in her claim that in principle 'both post-divorce households should enjoy the same standard of living' (1989, p. 183). Thus wives should have a claim on future, and possibly unexpected, increases in a husband's income in perpetuity. However, a traditional liberal's view of marriage, derived from a strict application of procedural justice, might wish to abolish no fault divorce laws and therefore allocate responsibility for the breakdown of the marriage (Barry, N., 1994b): the terms of the settlement would, to some extent, take account of wrongs committed by either spouse. Of course, the arrangements for the maintenance of children would operate independently of this. Whether this would achieve more equality for women is difficult to say, although the example does bring out the difference between an egalitarian and a justice-based approach to marriage and the family. The obvious, and unjustified, post-divorce economically inferior position of women, in America, could be tackled in various ways without endorsing Okin's egalitarianism (in fact, she doesn't specifically justify her commitment to equality in the broadened sense she favours).

From the perspective of political theory, it is difficult to know what is the best way to address the position of women's substantive inequality. From one view, this emerges from the spontaneous operation of choices and the development of social practices and institutions. But feminists are right to say that there is nothing *natural* about this: it may well have happened because roles are socially structured. Again, Okin is right to stress that sex should not determine lifestyles, people's well-being should be a function of the choices they make and not determined by logically irrelevant factors. However, to eliminate entirely all of the factors that determine sexual differentiation would involve the state in a great deal of intrusive activity (especially in relation to family life). This would be resented by many people, including women, who might very well regard such action as destructive of the integrity of the private world; accepting the feminist's definition of that phenomenon. Furthermore, it is a debatable question as to whether or not the positions of women in society are voluntarily assumed or the product of (alterable) social forces.

In fact, Okin's proposals are more modest than her analysis might suggest. She recommends changes in the divorce law so that post-divorce equality can be achieved, and the public provision of child care so that women can compete on equal terms in the labour market, rather than a wholesale attack on the pervasive, and perhaps unavoidable, influence of gender on social affairs. The traditional language of political (especially liberal) theory might be broad enough to cope with the phenomena feminists describe. The complaint might then be that historically the political theorists have failed to see the implications of liberalism outside the conventional fields of law and government.

8
Liberty

1 Liberty in political philosophy

The concept of liberty (or freedom, I shall use the terms interchangeably) is perhaps the most difficult of all political concepts to elucidate.
That its use is suffused with emotive appeal is obvious. No writer of a
political programme dare suggest that his specific proposals are not an
exemplification and amplification of freedom and few political philosophers in the history of the subject have resisted its allure (while at the
same time producing wildly different implications of its meaning). The
outcome of this is that liberty tends to become not a separate principle
or value, to take its place alongside others, but rather a shorthand
expression for a closely related and allegedly symmetrical set of values:
a surrogate term for a completed social philosophy.

It has been suggested (Dworkin, 1977, ch. 12) that it is simply
dissolved away once we specify the terms in which laws and institutions can be appraised. Thus there is no separate 'right' to liberty in his
liberalism, it is absorbed in the right each person has to equal
consideration. Hence political argument revolves around the merits
of this claim rather than the principle of liberty. Since any society will
have a whole range of perfectly justifiable restrictions on liberty, there
can only be particular arguments about specific liberties – political,
artistic, sexual and so on. These disputes can only be settled by a
consideration of how a proposed restriction affects each person's right
to equal concern and respect: traffic laws do not, racially biased rules
do. This, however, has the effect of making it rather easy to pick and
choose which liberties are to be protected. For example, economic
liberties are not valued highly in the contemporary Western world by
egalitarian liberal philosophers whereas personal liberties are. If there
were a general right to liberty this distinction would be difficult to
draw.

Some contemporary political philosophers (for example, Oppenheim, 1981) who retain an independent concept of liberty, have tried to
cut through the confused debate about liberty to locate a 'neutral'
definition. In other words, despite the differing values espoused by the
users of the concept it is claimed that it can be explicated conceptually
in a way that makes it indifferent between competing ways of life,
moral codes, notions of the self and of rationality. The question of the
meaning of liberty is to be sharply distinguished from its value and
purpose. Yet when we look at things like coercion it may be difficult to
define them in a non-evaluative way.

Still, in some branches of social theory liberty is used in a more or
less neutral way. In microeconomics, for example, the consumer is
treated as a rational agent who simply maximises her utility, as
revealed in her 'free' choices for various goods and services, and no
questions are asked about the origins of those choices or their worth,
beyond the fact that she makes them. Thus the drug addict, whose
actions might be thought, plausibly, in some sense to be 'unfree', is as
much a rational chooser as any other consumer; at least, for the
purposes of price theory. Internal constraints, to do with psychological factors that affect choice, are not relevant to liberty.

However, this procedure is a mere convenience designed to side-step
the philosophical questions about liberty in order to pursue a quasi-
predictive science. In fact, the final result of this approach might well
be to eliminate liberty, since if choices of consumers could be fully
predicted what interest would there be in the traditional problems
concerned with the concept? In fact, economics has never achieved this
state and most observers agree that it cannot: precisely because it deals
with human action, not conditioned behaviour, so that questions
about liberty remain. It is best seen as a science that explores the
consequence of choice, not as method for predicting choice. Still
questions of value and purpose that are germane to a philosophical
concept of liberty are not normally considered.

The major difficulty is whether there is one definition of freedom,
which analytical philosophy can reveal, or whether there is a variety of
meanings, each of which depends upon certain other theoretical
presuppositions. Certainly in the most discussed work on liberty since
the war, Sir Isaiah Berlin's 'Two Concepts of Liberty', first published
in 1958 (see Berlin, 1969), the author argues that each of his two
candidates evinces a particular political theory and conception of the
self, and other writers (see, especially, Connolly, 1983; and Gray,
1987) deny that one authoritative account is possible. However, it

might be valuable to discuss the conventional 'common sense', empiricist view of the concept as 'absence of constraint' and indicate the difficulties inherent in it before discussing Berlin's theory in more detail. The specific difficulties in this definition concern the nature of the constraints that are said to reduce liberty and the account of human agent who is the subject of liberty.

2 The meaning of liberty

In ordinary speech we understand liberty or freedom to mean the absence of constraints or obstacles. A person is free to the extent that her actions and choices are not impeded by the actions of others. While most liberal thinkers maintain that it is the *deliberate* actions of others that inhibit the liberty of the individual – and in familiar social and political contexts examples of unfreedom are of this type – this is not *necessarily* so. It has been suggested that a person's liberty can be accidentally limited by the actions of another, as when someone may inadvertently lock another person in a room; the unfortunate victim certainly is unfree although this is not the result of anyone's deliberate contrivance (Parent, 1974, p. 151). However, such cases are not of great interest to the social and political theorist since his main concern is with the justification of the limits on liberty posed by political and other authorities, and clearly intention is involved here.

The cases of unfreedom that illuminate the concept most clearly are imprisonment, slavery, severe restrictions on the choice of consumer goods and any action deterred by a law backed by sanctions. Thus people not actually in chains, or directly caused to act in a physical sense, are still unfree if the environment is so arranged that they will likely respond to the will of another. The types of constraints are numerous and various, so that statements about liberty are seriously incomplete if they do not specify particular prohibitions. While in political argument people demand 'liberty' itself or a 'free society', these are incoherent slogans until it is indicated what particular restraints it is desirable to remove. Since all societies are characterised by a variety of restraints the demand for complete liberty is meaningless; unless it is the cry of the hermit who wishes to opt out of all social relationships and lead a completely self-sufficient life. But even if this state of affairs were possible the 'liberty' enjoyed in it would be of no interest to the political theorist.

We think of freedom in the context of particular constraints occurring in social relationships. While it is sometimes meaningful to speak of *physical* constraints limiting personal freedom this is not normally at all helpful. One does not normally say that a person is not free to fly like a bird or that one's liberty to travel to the United States of America from Britain is impeded by the existence of the Atlantic Ocean (Lucas, 1966, p. 146); in such cases it is the *power* that we lack. The point of labouring this rather obvious fact is that it directs attention to the most important aspect of freedom, which is that it is concerned with circumstances that are *alterable*. We speak of individual liberty being constrained when the particular constraint is removable. If certain features of social life can be altered then freedom may be increased. But what is or is not alterable is highly disputable, especially in the economic sphere.

Free action is then voluntary action. It is action which is a product of individual choice and not dictated or determined by threats and other forms of coercion. Of course, this does not take us very far since there is the vexed question of what is to count as a constraint. Do the examples of influences in the form of psychological pressures on individuals, in the case perhaps of advertising, count as causes of unfreedom? Also, although most theorists of liberty say that the existence of law implies the absence of freedom, it is undoubtedly meaningful to say that people do *freely* choose to break the law and are therefore, strictly speaking, not impeded. By reasoning which appears odd to the modern mind, Hobbes maintained that freedom and 'threat' were not antithetical, that someone motivated by fear was nevertheless free.

When freedom is understood as voluntary, uncoerced action it enables some kind of ethical evaluation to be made of human conduct: there is an intimate connection here between freedom and responsibility. It would be meaningless to distribute praise or blame to actions that were not voluntary. To say that a person's action is the product of choice is to say that he could have acted otherwise than as he did, and to say that is to attribute rationality and responsibility to agents. There are severe difficulties in the notion of a responsible rational agent but without such a notion the idea of a free society would be incomprehensible. Of course, all theorists of liberty exclude certain categories of persons, children and mental defectives, for example, but they restrict this to as small a number as possible. But where is the line drawn between rational and irrational conduct?

A most important feature of freedom as the absence of constraints is that it distinguishes free acts from right or virtuous acts. Unlike some 'positive' theories of liberty which imply that the only proper freedom is doing the right thing or pursuing worthy aims, the common usage conception of freedom is not concerned with the *content* of an action, but only whether it is prevented or not. A person who wastes her freedom on worthless activities is just as free as a person who develops her potentialities to their highest point. The traditional liberal was concerned precisely to stress the fact that freedom necessarily involves the freedom to do wrong and to make mistakes. The justification for so wide a range of freedoms in his doctrine depends upon the idea that people can learn from their mistakes and that social progress depends upon this. The problem here is that freedoms can conflict, that one person's liberty to write, publish and display certain kinds of literature may collide with another's freedom to suppress these things. Just what the relationships should be between law and liberty is one of the most complex and delicate problems for liberal theorists.

It is, then, true that a free society will contain a myriad of restraints on liberty. The owner of property can prohibit others to use it, and will be protected by the law. This obvious point has led some writers (such as Cohen, 1979) to conclude that a capitalist society must necessarily restrict the freedom of the proletariat because (it is assumed) they are non-owners. They are always subservient to owners because, from a Marxist perspective, freedom means effective power and this in turn depends on property and the protection that the legal system gives it. In a sense it is true that a free society allows people to accumulate property and hence exclude others from its use, but this only indicates that freedom is being used in a moral sense. What is being referred to is a *right* to liberty rather than a description of various social phenomena. It is quite meaningful to claim that the right to liberty can be universally held without implying that it should have equal value for people. Indeed, a person could be free, in the sense of not being subject to anyone's commands, without owning anything. The contrast is frequently made between the penniless wayside traveller who, though poor, is free, and the well-fed conscript who is continually subject to orders.

In a world of scarcity there has to be some rule for the allocation of the right to use property, whether it is public or private, and the application of that rule must diminish freedom for some in the sense implied by Cohen. There is no evidence that the transfer of ownership from private to public increases liberty, unless some arcane schemes could be devised which somehow allocated equal time to each person for the use of a collectively owned good. All experience of collective ownership indicates that it brings about considerable reductions in liberty. To say this is not to deny the complexities of the relationship between liberty and property. It is by no means the case that the existence of private property is a sufficient condition of personal freedom, there are too many cases of authoritarian regimes that allow it while forbidding other forms of free expression, for that to be plausible. However, experience suggests that some private property is a necessary condition for freedom and independence.

The account of freedom given so far should not be confused with a superficially similar definition. This approach identifies freedom with the absence of impediments to the *satisfaction of desires*. In this view a person is free when she can do what she wants to do, when she is not frustrated. This identifies freedom with contentment or want-satisfaction.[1] It is misleading because it implies that a person is still free even though there are impediments preventing her from doing that which she does not want to do. From this it would follow that a slave was free simply because all his desires were satisfied and he had no wish to be burdened with the kind of choices that a free person has to make. We can only make comparative judgements about freedom by looking at the range of alternatives available in one situation or another; whether individuals actually want the liberties that exist is not strictly relevant to the analysis of freedom.

It would also follow from this mistaken definition of freedom that freedom could be increased by actually suppressing or manipulating desires so that only desires which can easily be satisfied remain. The important point about freedom as the absence of constraints is that it accommodates a *potentiality* for the satisfaction of desire. A person may be forbidden from doing that which he does not want to do anyway but we do not describe him as free, however contented he is, since the prohibition cuts off a possible future course of action. A free society is not one which allows individuals to have their desires satisfied but one which, by reducing coercive law to the minimum, allows for an ever-widening range of choices. For this reason, it is sometimes said that freedom may not always be congenial; the necessity of making choices may indeed be burdensome to some. We can distinguish between 'feeling free', a state of contentment, and 'being free', a state in which the major impediments of making choices have been removed. The old lag may deliberately commit a crime in order to recapture the security of prison life, but it would be absurd to describe his resulting condition as one of liberty.

A distinction is commonly made, although not universally accepted by political theorists, between being *free* to do something and being *able* to do something. To be free to do something is not to be restrained, while to be able is to have the capacity, financial or otherwise, to do something. Thus I am free to go to France if there is no law preventing me from travel but I am unable to take advantage of this freedom if I cannot afford to do so. Liberals who uphold this distinction want to make clear a conceptual distinction between liberty (not being restrained) and the conditions which make liberty worthwhile.

Those who oppose this maintain that there is a distinction between freedom *from* and freedom *to*. It is not merely the fact that a starving person who is not *legally* prevented from eating in an expensive restaurant enjoys only a derisory liberty, but that freedom itself requires positive action by the state. It is this reasoning that has been used to justify social legislation designed to increase the opportunities of individuals. State action is said to increase liberty and not merely to reduce inequality. Undoubtedly there is an attempt to capture the favourable overtones that freedom has for some policies which may in fact involve a loss of liberty. It must be stressed, then, that those who object to the assimilation of being free with being able are not necessarily objecting to the policies but to the description of their purpose. They are welfare-maximising rather than liberty-enhancing.

It has often been pointed out that one of the disadvantages of this assimilation is that it destroys the special significance of freedom. How are we to describe a situation in which a rich black person is denied entry to a restaurant in a country where a colour bar operates, if freedom *means* having a certain capacity? Freedom is intimately connected with rights and in one important sense (see Chapter 9) rights are held against governments and individuals. These rights may very well be lost sight of if intervention to correct an unacceptable inequality is presented as an increase in liberty. The same argument applies to attempts to treat liberty as a type of effective power – persons' freedoms increase to the extent that they have greater powers or abilities to do things. This has only a superficial plausibility. It is true that the purely formal account of liberty as absence of constraint gives us no clue as to how effectively people may be able to use their liberties, but the conceptual identification of freedom and power leads to the bizarre conclusion that the perfectly free agent is someone of unlimited power. Being able to do something is important to freedom but it is not freedom itself: a lack of power may be a regrettable fact of life but it is not necessarily a lack of liberty.

It is also important to examine the connection between liberty and political liberty. Many writers do not clearly separate the two concepts but it is certainly the case that many important freedoms could obtain in the absence of political liberty. We normally associate political liberty with democratic regimes, and it includes the right to vote, to participate in politics and to influence government. While it would be odd to describe a society as free which did not grant political liberty, it is true that democracies, characterised by participation and responsive to the popular will, may suppress individual freedoms. But it is also true that non-democratic societies, and even mild dictatorships, may leave their citizens well alone in certain important areas. The connection between democracy and personal freedom is a contingent and not a necessary one. However, it is important to note that the *competitive* party democracies in the West *must* grant some considerable freedom to people to associate, communicate ideas and to oppose government if they are to survive and this of itself ensures the maintenance of important freedoms (including a free press).

We understand freedom to mean the absence of coercion. The actions of free persons are actions that are not determined deliberately by others. One of the clearest cases of a person's unfreedom is when she is limited and restricted in her behaviour by the existence of laws backed by sanctions. Law and liberty are commonly thought to be antithetical. The precise relationship between law and liberty is, however, in need of some clarification.

We say that someone is not free to do *x* if a law, backed by a sanction, prohibits it, but if freedom means the absence of impediments it seems, paradoxically, that the existence of a law does not render a person unfree. One can still choose to break the law and it would indeed be most odd to say that criminal acts are not free acts (Benn and Weinstein, 1971, p. 206). Also some laws hardly limit freedom at all since the penalties that accompany them are so slight that they function like taxes rather than instruments of coercion; parking fines may be viewed in this way. Similar problems arise in the case of someone who obeys the law because the penalties of disobedience are extremely painful. In such a situation a person still chooses to obey when he could have done otherwise; is he not therefore free? From this it would follow that if freedom means the absence of impediments or obstacles to actions and choices imposed by others, then the only genuine case of unfreedom would be where a person is imprisoned, or, to put it more exactly, when he is literally bound and chained. This seems to be the position taken by Hobbes in his attempt to demonstrate the consistency of freedom and threat.

The theory embodies a kind of 'physicalist' view of liberty (see Steiner, 1974) which maintains that a person is free to the extent that he remains in motion. It is the most extreme of the 'absence of constraint' accounts of liberty since it puts virtually no conditions, except physical ones, on the exercise of freedom. It presupposes that there is a fixed quantity of liberty available in society which cannot be augmented by the removal of an impediment; the effect of this removal would only be to redistribute liberty across the range of relevant agents. However, this is somewhat implausible for surely the presence or absence of certain laws, especially criminal laws, can be evaluated for their contribution to liberty all round in the sense of removing impediments to the exercise of choices. We can surely compare societies in terms of the aggregate amount of liberty they permit. It is more realistic to say that communist society reduced liberty all round rather than claim that it redistributed it from the people to party officials.

The important point about the relationship between freedom and threats is that the existence of a threat reduces liberty by making certain courses of action unavailable without excessive costs. While it is true that I technically am free to disobey, for example, an armed robber's commands, I cannot do so *and* stay alive. If it were a genuine exchange of goods I give up one item for something I prefer and my liberty is preserved. In obeying threats, however, my preferences are determined by overwhelming power. It might be better, then, to describe freedom as the 'non-restriction of options' (Benn and Weinstein, 1971) than merely absence of restraint (where the nature of the restraint is unspecified). Freedom is not *merely* choosing but deciding on a course of action in the context of expanded opportunities. Sometimes external conditions have been so manipulated that to describe a choice as free would be to distort the meaning of the word. This is not to deny, though, that there can be possible intractable disputes about what does and does not reduce my range of options.

It is obvious that for the benefits of liberty to be enjoyed there must be a legal framework within which action can take place. To avoid disputes being settled by recourse to violence a legal system grants *A* liberty to do *x* and this is only meaningful if *A* has a right against *B*;

that is, *B* is under an obligation not to impede *A* in the exercise of his liberty. The existence of a legal system means that one person's liberty is another's restraint. Bentham believed that law and liberty were antithetical, that every law was 'an infraction of liberty', and thought that a necessary balance between freedom and restraint could be reached by reference to social utility. A legal restraint could only be justified if it produced a net increase in utility for the community as a whole. However, the absence of a common measuring rod of utility, along which pleasures can be calibrated, means that differing restraints cannot be compared. There is a case, then, for comparing various government actions in terms of their effects on individual liberty rather than their contribution, or otherwise, to overall utility.

There is, however, a different liberal tradition that does not necessarily understand law and liberty as being antithetical; at least, not when the two concepts are understood in certain specified ways. This tradition derives from Locke, who, in a famous phrase, said that: 'The end of the law is, not to abolish or restrain, but to preserve and enlarge freedom' (1960, p. 348). In an equally notable passage he said, of law, 'that ill deserves the name of confinement which hedges us in only from bogs and precipices'. Thus not every law is an evil, and a legal framework is a logical necessity for freedom since free action is only possible within a framework of known rules (see also Hayek, 1960).

The modern versions of this doctrine hold that an individual's liberty is only limited to the extent that a coercive law dictates that she perform a particular action. A legal system such as the common law, which merely sets necessary limits to individual action, does not inhibit freedom because an individual can plan her life so as to avoid its prohibitions. If the rules are perfectly general, non-discriminatory and predictable they can be treated as equivalent to natural phenomena and are therefore not destructive of liberty. Laws couched in the form of commands, which direct individuals to do certain things are, however, inconsistent with liberty since they are not impersonal but proceed from particular wills, and cannot be planned for and avoided in the way that general rules can. To the extent that general rules are predictable, more or less unalterable and not the deliberate product of centralised authority, they are consistent with liberty even though they prohibit certain courses of action.

This theory is clearly directed at the command theory of law and utilitarianism. It holds that since freedom is limited only by particular commands these should be reduced to the absolute minimum and also that, because no social utility function can be derived from individual preferences, the justification for law cannot be that it produces more utility. Since liberty is the highest principle, laws and policies are evaluated for their consistency with this and not with utility.

It is true that in some respects the existence of general rules does not appear as a restraint on individual freedom and 'free societies' do exhibit the major features of the above theory, but the claim is defective. By defining freedom as not being directed towards particular ends it ignores the fact that freedom is still limited when courses of action are closed, even though the individual is not actually ordered to do anything.[2] There are many examples of perfectly general laws in Western democracies which impose severe constraints on individual liberty. Any theory of liberty must take account of the range of alternatives that are open to the individual, so that the wider the range the more free an individual is.

While threats posed by others constitute the standard case of constraints on choice, attention in recent years has been directed to a different type of limitation on individual liberty; that which occurs when an individual's choices are determined by psychological forces over which she has no control (see Chapter 4). Since freedom and rationality are so closely connected it would indeed be disturbing for the traditional concept of liberty, which deals mainly, but not exclusively, with external, observable restraints, if, say, the effects of advertising were to make consumers subservient to producers. In fact, the effects of psychological pressures have probably been exaggerated and, indeed, an important element in the liberal's creed is that rational agents should be able to resist such pressures. However, the existence of psychological techniques, even those which fall short of brainwashing, should always be considered as one of the many possible ways in which the autonomy of the individual may be undermined (Benn, 1967).

In fact, it is the problem of internal constraints that is the most intractable for the common sense view of liberty. For it is the case that we sometimes say, quite plausibly, that a person's liberty is limited by the presence of psychological compulsions and 'irrational' desires even if there are no external and coercive forces compelling an action. The drug addict, the kleptomaniac, and the person driven to do uncharacteristic things by sexual jealousy are frequently cited as examples. The account of freedom in terms of the non-restriction of options can accommodate such behaviour as types of unfreedom since it does not confine the ways in which options can be restricted so narrowly as the simple absence of constraint view.

But to say this, however, is to depart (significantly perhaps) from a purely neutral definition of liberty. For we now have to take a stand on what is to count as a 'rational' desire. Although all proponents of the common sense, empiricist concept of liberty wish to distinguish the idea from 'rational freedom' (freedom as the pursuit of a special sort of rational end for man) the admission of even a 'minimalist' concept of rationality seems to compromise it. Free action may be interpreted as action conducive to a person's subjectively determined ends, reached after due consideration and rational reflection, as distinct from merely impulsive *behaviour*, but what would we say of the heroin user who had seriously contemplated the consequences of his action but, nevertheless, reasoned that it was still worth continuing? Can we describe his action as unfree without invoking some objective, rational end? One can surely think of less extreme examples.

The point of this is that it indicates that the concept of freedom is suffused with perhaps irresolvable disputes about the nature of constraints and what it is to be a rational agent. This can be seen in a brief analysis of Gerald MacCallum's (1972) attempt to produce a neutral definition of liberty. He argues that freedom must always be understood as a 'triadic' relationship. When we talk of an individual's freedom it is always a question of what constraints she is free from in order to do or become something. Claims about liberty have to be analysed in the following form: x is (or ought to be) free from y to do or become (or refrain from doing or becoming) z. Differences between theories turn upon how the three 'term variables' are filled – indeed, economic conditions, such as poverty, could count as a constraint. What is not at issue, it is claimed, is the meaning of liberty itself; which is always capable of a single explication.

If this is meant (as it surely is) to explicate the concept of liberty and to distinguish it from the various conceptions (for an excellent discussion of these, see Gray, T., 1987) its success is merely at the formal level, for all the interesting arguments about liberty turn on how the term variables are filled. This is most obvious in the case of the y variable, that is, the range of impediments that can count as genuine constraints on liberty. Coercion seems an uncontroversial candidate but apart from the case of physical causation, what is or is not coercion leads to endless disputes. This is never more so in the question as to whether economic deprivation limits liberty. Market theorists say that it does not (they try to distinguish liberty from welfare) since in exchange systems no one identifiable agent can be held responsible for the distress, in the way that, say, a gunman can. Collectivists naturally take the opposite view. Again, feminists would argue that the socially structured roles to which women tend to be assigned undermines their liberty despite the veneer of choice which the liberal legal order offers them. Similar things could be said about the other term variables. What all this demonstrates is that a coherent account of liberty will draw on the theorist's conception of the person and on the particular way of life, social, economic and political, in which human action is understood. The problems generated by such diverse accounts are not resolvable by a supposed uncontroversial definition of liberty.

3 Negative and positive liberty

We have seen how a common sense, more or less empirical account of liberty, as absence of constraint, is difficult to maintain in the face of fundamental disagreement about the social phenomena with which the concept is associated. There is, however, an attempt to reduce the rival accounts to just two: that these encompass nearly all that can be said about this seemingly intractable political idea. This interpretation is expressed in Sir Isaiah Berlin's now classic *Two Concepts of Liberty* (1969).[3]

Berlin distinguished between a 'negative' and a 'positive' conception. The negative sense is contained in the answer to the question: 'what is the area within which the subject – a person or group of persons – is or should be left to do or be what he is able to be, without interference by other persons?' (1969, p. 121). The positive sense is concerned with the answer to the question: 'what, or who, is the source of control or interference that can determine someone to do, or be, this rather than that?' (1969, p. 122).

The negative conception is clearly not dissimilar to the account given in the preceding section. It is characteristic of the strongly anti-metaphysical utilitarian tradition in English political thought and is a marked feature of the writings of Jeremy Bentham, James Mill, John Stuart Mill (although he was not an entirely consistent spokesman of negative liberty), Henry Sidgwick, Herbert Spencer and the classical and neo-classical economists. It flourished at a time when individuals were struggling to be free from the unnecessary restraints of arbitrary government and when individual choice determined the allocation of resources. The main political axiom of the negative liberty doctrine was that 'everyone knows his own interest best' and that the state should not decide his ends and purposes. It involved, therefore, a 'minimalist' view of the self.

Essential to the doctrine was the sanctity of contract. In Sidgwick's uncomplicated view of the 'self', for example, a person who freely negotiated a contract, even if the terms were particularly onerous to her, thereby expressed her individual choice. The law must enforce all contracts (with some exceptions, such as contracts of slavery), since not to do so would imply that the state knew what was good for the individual. A person's liberty was a function of that area in which she was left alone and not related to the *quality* of the action.

This is best understood as a doctrine about the *meaning* of liberty. Although negative freedom is often condemned as 'freedom to starve', this is somewhat misleading. It does not necessarily put a prohibition on state intervention but merely holds that this cannot be justified on the ground that it increases freedom; although arguments from equality (or more often utility) might well sanction such action. However, the historical connection between negative liberty and *laissez-faire* economics cannot be denied, and most of its advocates favoured a minimal state (though Berlin does not). The concept does, though, *appear* to be neutral, in that its use is compatible with a wide range of policies. It claims to describe the condition of liberty without indicating whether it is good or not.

Positive liberty, on the other hand, does not interpret freedom as simply being left alone but as 'self-mastery'. The theory involves a special theory of the self – the personality is divided into a higher and lower self and a person is free to the extent that his higher self, the source of his genuinely rational and long-term ends, is in command of his lower self, wherein lie his ephemeral and irrational desires. Thus a person might be free in the sense of not being restrained by external forces but remain a slave to irrational appetites; as a drug addict, an alcoholic or a compulsive gambler might be said to be unfree. Since true freedom consists in doing what you ought to do then law, if it directs an individual towards rational ends, may be said not to oppress but to liberate the personality. If a law that appears to restrain us meets with the rational approval of the individual then positive liberty appears to retain a toe-hold on our ordinary concept of liberty. The main feature of this concept is its openly evaluative nature; its use is specifically tied to ways of life held to be desirable.

Of the many political theorists who have held this doctrine, Rousseau (1913) may be briefly mentioned. Rousseau maintained that true liberty consists in obedience to a moral law which we impose upon ourselves. We are not free by maximising selfish interests but by promoting those interests which we share with others. Rousseau's argument does not depend upon a naïve altruism but rather on democratic institutions being so designed that we have an incentive to impose laws on ourselves that advance common interests. One essential requirement is a significant measure of social and economic equality. The problem is, of course, determining what these common interests are, and ultimately Rousseau has to admit that if, even after participation in a democratic assembly, an individual finds himself at odds with the General Will he must be enslaved by his lower self and therefore unfree. The individual may be 'forced to be free' by coercive laws.[4]

T. H. Green introduced the idea of positive liberty to English political thought with his famous essay, 'Liberal Legislation and Freedom of Contract' (1888, vol. III). Here he specifically rejected the negative concept of liberty and argued that state intervention – for example, in the form of factory legislation, which appeared to breach liberty of contract – actually expanded positive liberty. This was so because Green identified liberty with worthwhile ends; ultimately they were communal ends (see Weinstein, 1965). Proper liberty was absent in the market because exchange relationships maximised mere subjective choice.

It is an approach that has had great influence on the philosophy of the welfare state. By increasing people's opportunities, state intervention also increases their liberties. Again, the objection to the market is not derived solely from the inequality that it is said to promote but also from the claim that the more a society is contaminated by commercial instincts the more our communal instincts are squeezed out. Titmuss (1970) claimed that this contamination denied individuals the liberty to consume collective goods.

A particularly influential modern version of positive liberty, not considered by Berlin, can be found in the philosophy of the neo-Marxist, Herbert Marcuse. In a number of works (Marcuse, 1964, 1967, 1969), he maintained that although Western capitalist democracies have removed traditional impediments to liberty they have managed to stifle freedom and rationality by new forms of *repression* and *domination*. The masses do not enjoy 'true liberty' since their tastes and wants have been manipulated by the techniques of modern capitalism. Furthermore, their revolutionary zeal has been blunted by a constant supply of consumer goods. The formal provision of civil liberties does not indicate that genuine freedom of expression exists since opinion has been successfully moulded by the 'system'. Indeed, dissent is tolerated precisely because it is no threat to capitalist domination. True 'freedom' would appear to consist not in the making of choices but in the pursuit of 'rational' ends.

While it is true that many of the consumption habits of individuals in liberal societies may not be desirable, this in itself illustrates an essential property of freedom; that is, freedom involves the making of choices, many of which may turn out to be mistaken. Marcuse merely equates freedom with pursuing activities which he regards as desirable. Furthermore, his intolerance of other philosophical and political ideas removes the essential element required for human progress – rational criticism. Equally sinister is his critique of the freedom of expression and opinion in Western liberal democracies as a system of 'repressive tolerance' since it removes the distinction between societies which have clear and genuine impediments to freedom of thought, discussion and communication, and those which do not. His identification of freedom and 'truth' prevents that competition between ideas which is the mark of a free society.

Berlin easily exposes the dangers involved in some arguments for positive liberty. It depends crucially on a special interpretation of the self; it assumes not just that there is a realm of activity towards which the individual ought to direct herself but that she is being liberated when she is directed towards it. The route to totalitarianism is plainly laid out when the higher purposes of the individual are made equivalent to those of collectivities such as classes, nations and races. According to Berlin, a belief in positive liberty entails a *monist* social philosophy; the idea that all other values – equality, rights, justice and so on – are subordinate to the supreme value of higher liberty. However, it is not clear that positive liberty *necessarily* implies monism, although the examples chosen by Berlin do exhibit this feature.[5] Positive liberty could simply refer to those conditions which are necessary if choice is to be meaningful.

A further implication of positive liberty exposed by Berlin is the argument that liberty is increased when sovereignty is put into the 'right hands' (1969, pp. 162–6). Negative theorists correctly maintain that liberty is reduced whenever the circle within which individuals are free to choose is diminished, and it can be diminished by democratic as well as despotic government. Indeed, a great deal of personal freedom is possible under authoritarian regimes. For Rousseau and Marx, however, it appears to be the case that freedom is a function of the will of the enlightened people or exists only when the rule of the bourgeoisie is replaced by that of the proletariat.

While Berlin has produced convincing arguments to show that certain political theorists have misused the concept of liberty, and indeed blurred obvious differences between restraint and autonomy, it is open to doubt as to whether he has distinguished two *different* concepts of freedom. He says himself that the two terms 'start at no great logical distance from each other' (p. xii): the difference is that theories built on them develop in different directions and reveal strikingly different attitudes to social and political life. But true though this is it does not follow that statements about 'self-mastery' and 'self-realisation' may not be reinterpreted as statements about removing restraints on individuals. As we have noted earlier, one person may be as constrained by internal factors, such as uncontrollable desires, as another is by external laws.

Berlin himself does concede that theories of individual liberty which do depend on a certain view of the self, rationality and the ends that we ought to pursue, are not necessarily incompatible with our ordinary notions of freedom. This is apparent in his introduction to a later edition of 'Two Concepts of Liberty' (1969, p. xxxvii) where he points out that the contracted slaves who had no desires that were frustrated, could not properly be called free. However, concessions such as this do suggest that a *purely* negative account of freedom is deficient, and that a 'neutral' definition of the concept is impossible to achieve without doing considerable damage to ordinary language.

Hence, an important criticism of negative liberty is that in the attempt to drain the concept of morality most theorists miss some important features of freedom. What is crucial is that when we assess a particular community for its liberty-enhancing properties we must take account of the *values* of particular liberties that are available. In an intriguing example, Charles Taylor (1985) suggests that from the perspective of negative liberty communist Albania was actually freer than Western liberal democracies. The reason is that, however repressive the regime, it had fewer restrictions, in total, on human conduct than in the West. For example, there were no traffic laws (private car ownership was forbidden) and none of the irksome restraints on behaviour that exist whenever a wide range of opportunities is available. The implication of the argument is that negative liberty theory invites us to make quantitative comparisons of liberty restrictions without reference to the qualitative aspects of the remaining liberties.

Whatever the truth of Taylor's comments on Albania (he was writing before the collapse of communism), his point is of some theoretical significance. But it seems to apply to a particularly narrow conception of negative liberty. Most theorists do make distinctions between various liberties and assess them in accordance with how far they advance human well-being. A lack of free speech, or the liberty to acquire property, would be regarded as serious restrictions even if they were accompanied by few restrictions elsewhere. Conventional liberal democracies are relatively free because the liberties they nourish are morally important. To say this is to import specifically moral features into the concept of liberty, but it is not clear that conventional accounts of negative liberty exclude them. All that Taylor has shown is that meaningful accounts of liberty cannot be neutral between varying ways of life. Berlin's own theory of negative liberty is embedded in a notion of pluralism that specifically values variety and choice.

4 Liberty as autonomy

A related criticism of negative liberty focuses on the fact that to describe freedom as the absence of coercive law does not tell us anything about what a person can do. Negative liberty is only important insofar as it contributes to something that is valuable and the favoured candidate for the critics is *autonomy*. Liberty as autonomy is much more than the absence of restraints for it refers specifically to the range of options that is open to a person and to the conditions necessary for the achievement of a variety of goals. According to John Gray (1992), negative liberty has no intrinsic values, it is merely a necessary prelude to a description of what is valuable in life. Liberty as autonomy does not, as in the more extreme theories of positive liberty, require the complete obliteration of individual subjective choice by the state but it does demand that institutions provide a range of facilities that turn abstract choices into real opportunities. Gray writes that: 'It is patently obvious that autonomy is far more than the mere absence of coercion by others, since it is self-evident that that condition may co-exist with a complete inability to achieve any important objective or purpose' (1992, p. 23).

Gray is following in the footsteps of Joseph Raz (1986) who had launched an attack on negative liberty mainly on the ground that the priority of the right over the good, in orthodox liberal theory, distorted the morality of freedom by suggesting that rights against coercion were the only important preconditions of liberty. It is the pursuit of value that is itself a necessary aspect of freedom and value cannot be confined to subjective desire: 'The provision of many collective goods is constitutive of the very idea of autonomy and it cannot be relegated to a subordinate role, compared with some alleged right against coercion ... ' (1986, p. 207). There are undoubtedly communitarian elements in liberty as autonomy.

It might be thought that this is simply a demand for redistribution to increase people's capacities, so that liberty becomes valuable to those hitherto unable to enjoy it, and indeed Gray's suggestions for an enabling welfare state (1992, ch. 5) are consistent with this project. But it is clear from his other work that Gray has a more ambitious conception in mind. In 'What is Dead and What is Living in Liberalism' (Gray, 1993, pp. 282–398) he appears to prefer a form of human flourishing which is by no means reducible to the satisfaction of subjective desire and he claims that a liberal order is deficient if it precludes the idea of 'perfectionism'. In other words, there are collective goods, quite unlike the public goods of subjectivist classical liberal economic theory, which have intrinsic value – that is, they have worth even in the absence of anyone expressing a want for them. It is argued that autonomy 'presupposes as one of its constituent elements a rich public culture containing a diversity of worthwhile options' (Gray, 1992, p. 42). Raz is even more openly favourable to the idea that persons can express liberty and morality only as members of particular social groupings that embody the idea of the good: 'A person can have a comprehensive social goal only if it is based on existing social forms, i.e. forms of behaviour which are in fact widely practised in his society' (1986, p. 308). Naturally, the specific significance of coercion diminishes in this perfectionist context; indeed Raz (1986, p. 417) subverts the standard classical liberal argument by suggesting that for a state not to provide the conditions for autonomy would be harmful and liberty-reducing for some people.

Gray and Raz are not adopting some kind of positivist account of liberty which would involve highly controversial concepts of rationality and the (possibly) coerced pursuit of a higher end, an approach of which Berlin was so rightly critical. Their conceptions of liberty are consistent with pluralism to the extent that they identify freedom and autonomy as the ability to choose from a variety of ends. However, the model of choice exercised in the market place would seem to be a morally inadequate understanding of freedom because it maximises subjective choices rather than intrinsically valuable things. Though Gray does concede that the market does encourage some freedom as autonomy.

There are problems, both conceptual and normative, with the concept of autonomy itself and the dismissal of negative liberty as empty or meaningless. It is simply not true that the absence of coercion has no value independently of a consideration of the ends and purposes that an individual may pursue. The fact that one is not coerced means that whatever is done is a product of choice, irrespective of whether it is directed to one's long-term ends, the value of which may be in dispute. There is surely some value in the fact that in a free society opportunities exist for individuals to be authors of their own actions, and the only important moral point is whether their actions impinge on the liberties of others.

It is possible to say that a person acted freely even though he or she did not act autonomously in the rather rarefied sense described by Raz and Gray. It is not that absence of coercion is merely a condition for the exercise of autonomous choice. Negative liberty is not merely instrumental. People can and do protest about unjustified limitations on their liberty irrespective of the projects they wish to pursue. In fact, they may not even know them. A free society, with a vibrant economy and a predictable legal order, is the only social arrangement in which people can come to terms with their ignorance: and lack of information here refers not just to economic knowledge but also to one's personal plans and projects. One cannot know what it is to be an autonomous agent until one has experience of freely choosing amongst alternatives. And this requires that each individual should have a sphere immune from the intrusions of coercive law. It is not that autonomy defines liberty but rather that one has to be free before one can be autonomous. To define liberty exclusively in the context of given social forms, as Raz appears to do, precludes the moral legitimacy of a person breaking out of those forms. The innovator (perhaps regrettably for a conservative) succeeds largely because she upsets existing social arrangements.

None of this is meant to imply that there can be human agents completely abstracted from social forms who are understood solely through the calculus of their desires (that would be to discount foolishly the value of spontaneously developing social rules and practices), nor is meant to endorse the kind of mindless and deliberate non-conformism recommended by John Stuart Mill. However, it does rest on the idea that under conditions of non-constraint, individuals are the makers of their own lives, whether or not they lead them as fully autonomous agents. To accept that individuals are necessarily understood partly by their social natures is not to endorse the moral priority of social forms.

One can go further and challenge the importance of autonomy itself. Many people lead their lives unreflectively, they follow traditional rules and practices and they make choices of a fairly trivial kind. To what extent are they unfree? Like everything else which is valuable, autonomy has an opportunity cost, the time and other resources needed to acquire it could be spent on something else. One could complain about people's foolishness in not becoming autonomous, they may indeed become willing victims of consumer fads and fashions in market society, but not their lack of liberty (if they behave in an uncoerced manner). Furthermore, the promotion of autonomy does involve the state (Raz, 1986, p. 161) in an enhanced role: not merely to redistribute income but to provide valuable goods which would not be produced at all if wants were the only criterion. Thus the 'government has an obligation to create an environment providing individuals with an adequate range of options and the opportunities to use them' (Raz, 1986, pp. 417–18).

Among the many difficulties with this position is the obvious fact that autonomy as interpreted by Raz and Gray is an indeterminate moral ideal; it is not like rights-protection or the supply of public goods, which, although controversial at the edges, are capable of being formulated as reasonably coherent tasks for a state to perform. And although Raz is insistent that the autonomous life involves choice between alternative projects he is equally convinced that market-based individualist society is incapable of fully meeting this demand. Why not? The answer is, apparently, that this order, because it is based on subjective choice, will fail to provide objective and intrinsically valuable goods; notably the maintenance of common forms of life. But since there is likely to be considerable disagreement about what these intrinsically valuable ends are, the state, in selecting one or more out of the range of possible candidates, is likely to generate the very tensions that undermine common forms of life. Although Raz's pluralism precludes the state promoting and privileging any *particular* way of life it is difficult to see how the authority he grants the state would not be used in this way. It is possible, surely, to modify the theory of negative liberty to take account of the differing moral values of particular liberties (to deal with Charles Taylor's criticism) and to supplement the idea by a redistributive rule that makes sure that negative liberties are not worthless to some deprived people, without endorsing the vague and ambiguous value of autonomy as the primary condition for the existence of liberty. It is true that the evaluation of particular liberties, and the determination of the redistribution required to make people's lives meaningful, are difficult tasks but are probably more tractable than those that emerge from the application of autonomy. None of this is meant to imply that autonomy is not an important moral ideal, when we talk of moral choices being autonomous we mean that they are valuable because they are not determined by extraneous forces. However, by making autonomy dependent on certain conceptions of the good, and embedding it in particular forms of social life, Raz and Gray have made it unnecessarily contestable. It can be understood in more modest ways.

5 John Stuart Mill and the value of liberty

On Liberty is justly praised as the most eloquent expression of the libertarian approach to morals and society and although it has been much criticised, and subjected to a great number of differing interpretations, it is still quoted today in arguments for individual freedom. Yet, curiously enough, despite Mill's contempt for custom, and for rules that could not rationally be justified, and his encouragement of spontaneity, individuality and 'experiments in living', his work had very little influence over those radical political movements which propagated these very same things. Mill's ideas were extremely influential in the academic debate in the 1960s over the relationship between law and morality, but elsewhere it was Marx's influence that was dominant. The reason for this must surely be that liberation in the latter's doctrine did *not* include the traditional economic freedoms of the free enterprise economy. Mill himself argued that in Victorian Britain business was the only outlet for individual expression which a stifling and conformist public opinion regarded as legitimate.

Mill has often been accused of thinking that any free action, no matter how immoral, at least had some value in virtue of the fact that it was freely performed. Against the view that liberty in principle is always a good thing many writers have echoed the views of Mill's sternest contemporary critic, Sir James Fitzjames Stephen, who said that fire and liberty could not be said to be good or bad but were 'both good and bad according to time, place and circumstance' (1967, p. 85). It is true that Mill thought that 'all restraint qua restraint is an evil' but he did not think it was unjustifiable; he merely thought that there was a presumption in favour of liberty and that the onus of justification always lay on those who would restrict liberty.

Mill is frequently cited as a theorist of 'negative' liberty (in Berlin's sense of the term) but this requires some explication since he was less interested in discussing the traditional restraints on liberty imposed by despotic governments – which had been removed in parts of Western Europe and North America in Mill's time – than new ones in the form of the pressures of public opinion and social convention. It was this that was severely threatening 'individuality'. By individuality Mill meant the property in human beings that made them *active*, rather than passive, and critical of existing modes of social behaviour so that they refused to accept conventions without submitting them to the test of reason. Freedom appears to be not simply the absence of restraint but the deliberate cultivation of certain desirable attitudes. It is because of this that it has been suggested that Mill had a rationalistic view of liberty and veered towards a positive conception. It is also said that he was an elitist in that on more than one occasion he said that only a minority were capable of enjoying freedom as individuality. Nevertheless, his conception of liberty is firmly anchored to the notion of *choice*: 'He who lets the world, or his own portion of it, choose his plan of life for him, has no need of any other faculty than the apelike one of imitation. He who chooses to plan for himself employs all his faculties' (1974, p. 123). Mill implies that freedom consists in actually challenging accepted rules, but one could argue that a person who follows customary rules of behaviour, even if he does so unreflectively, is not necessarily unfree. Indeed, customary rules may be indispensable conditions for the exercise of liberty and there are arguments, not necessarily utilitarian, to the effect that the cultivation of the personality traits favoured by Mill are not conducive to the *order* of a free society. It is the virtual identification between individuality and liberty that leads Mill to suggest that the great bulk of the population is incapable of appreciating it: 'they have no tastes or wishes strong enough to incline them to do anything unusual, and they consequently do not understand those who have . . . ' (1974, p. 134). The masses are unfree precisely because they are the slaves of custom.

There are, then, elitist elements in Mill's account of liberty, but the principle that he uses to determine the boundary between the individual and society seems, superficially, to be uncompromisingly liberal. This is the famous 'harm' principle. The *only* ground for interfering with an individual is to prevent harm to others; over actions that affect only himself the individual is sovereign (1974, p. 69). This rules out paternalism, the idea that law (and society) can intervene to promote what are considered to be a person's best interests, 'moralism', the idea that some acts are intrinsically immoral and therefore must be punished irrespective of whether they affect anyone else, and even utilitarianism, of the Benthamite kind, which would license interference in order to maximise the general happiness. Of course, Mill's principle is capable of a libertarian or an authoritarian interpretation. Since all but the most trivial acts affect somebody in some way, then, could this not allow the law to protect the public from certain immoral acts which, although they do not cause injury in a direct sense, nevertheless cause offence? Furthermore, Mill himself certainly believed that his principle did not imply moral indifference towards the self-regarding behaviour of others and that it was permissible to use persuasion (though obviously not coercion) to discourage someone from immorality.

To preserve the liberal elements in Mill's theory his principle has been interpreted in a number of ways. It has been suggested that Mill meant that intervention is legitimate only when an individual's actions affect the *interests* of another, as opposed to merely affecting himself, or that there is a distinction between *direct* and *indirect* effects of action. Modern versions of Mill's doctrine make a distinction between causing *offence* and causing *injury*. It is recognised that the effects of individual liberty may well cause offence, especially to people with strongly held moral beliefs about appropriate forms of social behaviour, but no one has a right to protection from this in the way that he has a right to the protection of his person and property. What Mill is clear about is that the repugnance that the majority may feel for immoral acts that do not cause injury could never constitute a reason for prohibiting such acts. This runs counter to Benthamite utilitarianism because the latter allows for the pleasures of *malevolence* in the measurement of social utility, so that the abhorrence the majority may feel for particular sorts of private conduct has to be considered along with the pain that would be caused to individuals if such conduct were to be prohibited. Mill, in effect, established the modern liberal view that there is a right to liberty which cannot be overridden by orthodox utilitarian considerations; an individual's freedom cannot be sacrificed in the interests of public policy, but only for some other 'right'.

Even if Mill's particular statement of the connection between liberty and individuality is not accepted by all theorists his argument for the instrumental value of freedom in the promotion of social goods features strongly in contemporary discussion. This is especially true of Mill's celebrated argument for the complete liberty of thought, discussion and expression (1974, ch. 11). Mill's major argument for freedom of expression follows from his empiricist epistemology. Since all knowledge is a product of experience, even our most firmly-held convictions as to truth and falsehood are corrigible and may be overturned. Therefore competition between ideas (and the prohibition of claims to infallibility) is the only means of guaranteeing that truth will prevail. Mill did believe that the number of disputed doctrines, including those in the social sciences, would decline but this could only come about through free intellectual debate. Mill argued that the suppression of opinion may blot out truth, that society benefits from even the free expression of false doctrines since truth is served by refuting them, and, perhaps most importantly of all, that truth is many-sided and likely to emerge from conflicting ideas (even the most obviously false theories are likely to contain some hidden truths) (1974, pp. 108–11).

These arguments are not strictly utilitarian. It is easy to show that there could be arguments for suppressing opinion if that would increase happiness (as would be the case in a society where the bulk of the population were of a particular religious persuasion). Even Mill's principle that progress is advanced by unrestricted freedom may not always be applicable in some aspects of scientific research, especially in such obviously potentially dangerous areas as nuclear research and microbiology. Of course, it is the harm that results from this misapplication of scientific discoveries that is wrong, not the activity of free scientific enquiry, but it is surely not difficult in some areas to establish a very strong connection between the two. What is true is that scientific truth can only be established on an *objective* basis in a community in which claims to infallibility are abjured and the canons of rational argument are accepted, but this is only one aspect of Mill's argument.

There are major problems of free expression in the question of the propagation of ideas which may have dangerous consequences and which deliberately treat certain groups in an insulting and degrading manner. Racist propaganda is a clear example of this. Should there be legal restrictions on the dissemination of such ideas?

In many cases there is no problem. The use of words which are deliberately designed to incite people to commit acts of violence would clearly be prohibited by most interpretations of the harm principle. In fact it is doubtful if special legislation is required to protect minority groups from insulting comments since the common law provides such protection for individuals. Some people have argued for a prohibition on the right of free speech to political parties whose doctrines may well stir up racial hatred, on the ground that freedom should not be extended to those who preach intolerance. It is true that a liberal society must take steps to protect itself from groups whose ideas, if put into practice, would destroy the liberal order, but the danger is that it may lose its liberal credentials in doing so. The main principle that liberals stress is that a person should only be punished for her actions if they breach the rights of others, and not because of the opinions she holds; also they would be wary of coercive legislation, the justification of which might depend only upon a contingent relationship between opinion and action.

The problem is particularly acute in connection with the right to free assembly and association. Are the authorities entitled to ban meetings of groups whose professed ends are antithetical to the idea of an open and tolerant society? The difficulty exists because such meetings are normally held in publicly owned halls and collective decisions therefore have to be taken on issues on which it is highly unlikely that there exist anything like unanimous agreement. Presumably, very few would deny the right of a private owner of property to let it to whom he liked. The danger is that the authorities may ban public meetings which are for the expression of views of which they disapprove, when the libertarian principle is that only considerations of harm and injury to private rights and public order should affect the decision. However, the danger in the interpretation of liberty in terms of property is that owners of property themselves could undermine freedom of action by simply excluding non-owners from certain activities. If freedom is interpreted in some sense or other as freedom of 'action' then it is surely plausible to suggest that a private property system could develop in such a way that individual freedom (in the negative sense) could be limited just as it is under more conventional (political) forms of constraint (Barry, N., 1986, pp. 181–2).

Mill was probably much too optimistic in thinking that all restrictions on free discussion should be removed because truth would emerge from the free competition of ideas since, in a utilitarian sense, much harm may be caused by the spread of dangerous doctrines before truth finally triumphs (if it ever does). Discussion and expression cannot be literally unrestricted (as laws against libel and slander indicate) but the rationale of restriction is difficult to formulate. The danger in the Benthamite justification for restriction is that it may reduce freedom to a vanishing point. A different way of treating free expression is to regard it as a type of personal and property right; the limitations on its exercise by one person being determined by the fact that others have similar rights. Questions of justifiable restrictions on liberty would then depend upon judicial interpretation within general rules rather than legislation.

Mill and later liberals have probably been far too sanguine about the social effects of more or less unrestricted freedom of expression. Feminists have been understandably concerned about certain features of pornography that systematically and deliberately degrade women. There may be a correlation between the spread of this material and the increase in sexual crime against women. It may be difficult to defend a purely abstract freedom of expression when some of its effects in the real world are disturbing. In other words, the act of saying or publishing something deeply offensive about women may be instrumental in the commission of certain offences. It would be going too far, I presume, to suggest that the graphical depiction of rape is somehow equivalent to the act but the connection between the two is closer than the somewhat starry-eyed Millian liberals ever realised. In this context feminists might find themselves at one with communitarians who protest at the threat to shared values which is sometimes posed by Mill's rootless individualism.

In today's 'catalogue' of liberties, freedom of expression is still probably valued more than economic liberty (when this is interpreted as freedom to exchange without direct government interference); indeed the connection between economic freedom and other civil liberties is seldom appreciated. Yet free exchange between individuals is undoubtedly an important exercise of liberty and a society which forbade all other liberties but allowed this would still be free to this extent. The market economy is the only social device man has developed which combines freedom, in the sense of personal choice, and efficiency. One argument frequently used to sever the connection between economic and personal liberty is that restrictions on, for example, the right to contract and the right to accumulate property, do not affect one's moral rights. In other words they do not involve the abrogation of the right to equal concern and respect (Dworkin, 1977,

p. 278) since, in a liberal society, they do not involve discriminations based on race or colour. And, unlike restrictions on free expression, they do not involve the state making judgements about what is valuable. They are simply aspects of public policy which can be judged purely on utilitarian grounds.

But conceptually it is hard to see that there is a distinction. The right to contract freely (within the constraints required for public security) and the right to free expression are both necessary features of personal well-being and to give the former no legal protection against state invasion (which is the case in most liberal democracies) is to deny each person the opportunity to make choices about his or her lifestyle. The excessive regulations of hours and conditions of work have severely undermined this freedom. Even so fervent an anti-classical liberal as Gray (1992, ch. 2) concedes that market freedoms are essential components in individual autonomy. What is important here is that economic liberty is a means for achieving a certain amount of independence. If our economic well-being were to depend solely on the state then no matter how efficient it was in generating welfare (which can be doubted) the citizens would to some extent have their autonomy compromised by the necessity to conform to political rules in order to become entitled to a level of well-being. In fact, economic liberties and the familiar personal liberties are inextricably linked for the grant of, say, the right to free expression would be meaningless if there were not the economic freedom to accumulate the means necessary for independent publication.

From a utilitarian perspective an important justification for economic liberty is that decentralised economic decision-making guarantees that a greater amount of knowledge is utilised than is the case under central planning (Hayek, 1960, ch. 2). The major *economic* disadvantage of centralised planning is that the planner does not have access to the knowledge of consumer tastes and production costs that is automatically signalled to the participants in a market process. Even if freedom is considered as an instrumental value only, rather than as constitutive of individuality, it is difficult to deny that it is essential for the handling of ignorance and uncertainty that characterise all social and economic processes.

Economic freedom does, however, throw up some interesting problems for the political theorist. One is that the process of exchange between individuals may not produce a state of affairs which would not be called 'free'. One example is the closed shop in industrial relations. If an employer voluntarily makes an agreement with a trade union to employ union members only, should it be prohibited by law? Is it consistent with liberty for the law to reproduce those character-istics of a free society which have not emerged through the voluntary transactions of individuals? It could be said that the conditions of employment are a matter for individual negotiation and not coercive law and that as long as a variety of employment prospects exists, individuals who do not wish to join trade unions would not be harmed. It is certainly not the case that voluntary closed shop agreements have the same coercive features as, say, some aspects of picketing.

6 Law, morality and paternalism

The issues raised by Mill in the defence of individual liberty have reappeared in the extremely interesting debate occasioned by the emergence of the 'permissive society'. In the last 30 years or so in many Western democracies, laws governing personal conduct have been significantly relaxed so that individuals now enjoy more freedom with regard to sexual habits, choice of literature and lifestyles than ever before. It is interesting that the debate on permissiveness illus-trates the point that the connection between democracy and personal liberty is a *contingent* and not a necessary one; for example, the Republic of Ireland has impeccable, democratic credentials yet it had illiberal laws in relation to divorce, contraception and censorship, which have only recently been relaxed.

In Britain the libertarian principles that should determine the relationship between liberty and the law were set out in the Wolfenden Report, published in 1957. Echoing Mill, the Report said that there ought to be a sphere of personal conduct which should be immune from the law. Alluding to a distinction between the *private* and *public* realms the Report maintained that the criminal law should only be concerned to protect the public from outward displays of immorality and with the prevention of corruption and exploitation. Thus it was recommended that homosexual relations between consenting adults be legalised and that while prostitution itself should still remain legal the law should be made stricter on the outward manifestation of the activity, such as soliciting.

The libertarian position with regard to law and morality is that where no harm is involved and all parties consent to the activity then the fact that the activity is immoral should not be a reason for legal interference (in fact, some libertarians would maintain that the activity itself could not be called immoral if it involves no harm). The application of the injury principle is restricted so as to exclude the 'injury' experienced by a bystander who might feel aggrieved at the thought of some immoral act taking place since if this were to be relevant then there is no limit to the reach of the law into people's private lives.

It is argued that all coercion requires justification and that the frustration and pain experienced by those denied the liberty to practice unconventional sexual activities, the risks involved in entrusting the police with the task of enforcing 'moral' laws, and the possibility of blackmail, all combine to make legal prohibitions of private immorality productive of great misery.

But this view has never been without its critics. In the nineteenth century, the great common law judge Sir James Fitzjames Stephen in his *Liberty, Equality, Fraternity* was of the opinion that certain sorts of immoral acts are so degrading that 'society' must express its disgust and abhorrence of them by punishing the perpetrators irrespective of the fact that the acts in question rest on consent and harm no one (1967, ch. IV). Punishment is required to 'denounce' certain crimes for their depravity. This particularly harsh view might be more plausible in relation to crimes involving victims and direct injuries. Stephen had a very much less optimistic view of man than Mill and was deeply sceptical of the value of personal liberty in the formation of character. His belief that moral standards had to be constantly reaffirmed by coercive law revealed a rather Hobbesian conception of social order.

The contemporary exponent of the Stephen argument is Lord Devlin, who, in his Maccabean Lecture *The Enforcement of Morals* (1965), challenged the rationale of the Wolfenden Report. Like Stephen he believes that society has an interest in preventing private immorality, that no clear distinction can be drawn between private and public, and that the proper relationship between liberty and law cannot be determined by the abstract principles of the rationalist philosopher. His justification for the law's punishment of immorality is, however, slightly different from Stephen's. Devlin maintains that society is held together by a belief in certain moral standards and that although departures from these may harm no assignable individuals a generalised flouting of them will lead to the collapse of society. In a famous analogy he likened immorality to treason in his justification for legal action against it. The analogy here, though, is somewhat forced since traitors *intend* to harm the interests of their country while immoral people are normally engaged in purely private activities.

Much of his argument rests upon the assumption that certain sorts of criminal offences can only be explained in terms of a moral principle. For example, the criminal law prohibits a person from consenting to his own murder, which reflects the principle of the sanctity of life; bigamy is a criminal offence because the principle of monogamous marriage (in Western societies) has to be enforced by law. Thus law is not merely a device to protect individuals from harm but represents the concrete expression of a set of *integrated* moral ideals, and seemingly minor disturbances are to be forbidden because they threaten the whole structure.

In a famous reply to Devlin, H. L. A. Hart (1963) presented a modern version of Mill's attempt to determine *theoretically* the limits of the law in personal morals and refute the argument that an act may be punished because it is immoral. He said that those cases where the law forbids an act even when consent is involved can be explained on other grounds than the enforcement of morality. His argument is that simple paternalism (a consideration forbidden by Mill) can justify the criminal law forbidding a person consenting to his own murder or the trade in hard drugs. Since the liberal philosophy of learning from mistakes can hardly be said to be appropriate in these cases the state has to take a decision to protect people from themselves. To disallow this, says Hart, would preclude the state from many areas such as welfare – where its presence is thought to be desirable.

In fact many libertarians would object to this precisely on the ground that paternalism could be as destructive of individual liberty as Devlin's legal moralism. Both justifications require the state, through its officials, to take a decision as to what is best for a person whose actions harm no one else. If paternalism justifies the outlawing of duelling does it also outlaw certain private sexual acts, such as sadomasochism? In fact, there are many acts about which it is impossible to make an unambiguous judgement within the terms of Hart's theory.

The example of the trade in and consumption of narcotics is interesting because Hart's justification of legal intervention on paternalist grounds could easily be challenged by strict libertarians *and* utilitarians. A libertarian might argue that even though the consequences of taking hard drugs usually mean a diminution of rationality and individuality (in Mill's sense), this does not justify the use of coercive law to prohibit what is, in a technical sense at least, a free act.

The more plausible utilitarian argument is that, whatever people's views about the morality or immorality of drug-taking, the consequences of preventing it are much worse for a society than the consequences of allowing it. This is because in the absence of a free market for a wanted good gangsters and racketeers will always provide it. Furthermore, the very high price of a banned good leads desperate addicts to crimes they would not otherwise commit. The additional suffering brought about by the small increase in addicts that undoubtedly would occur if restrictions were lifted would be easily outweighed by the increase in security that society would enjoy because of the removal of a major incentive to crime.

Hart is on much stronger ground when he makes an important distinction between immorality and indecency (1963, pp. 38–48). The law can intervene when someone's actions cause public offence, so that it is the public display of the act that invites legal sanction, not its immorality. Thus it would be punishable to display an obscene poster in a main shopping precinct but quite legal to enjoy the same picture in the privacy of one's own home. Under Devlin's criterion, if something is to be forbidden because it is morally wrong then it is always wrong, whether performed in public or private. The implications of this for liberty are alarming; it implies that the only limitations on the authority of the law to enforce moral standards crucial to society's existence are the practical ones of enforcement.

Liberals do not deny that a society's existence depends upon some agreement on moral rules but they insist that this agreement is compatible with a plurality of moral ideals and that there is no evidence that a society will collapse if people experiment with different moral practices. The freedom to indulge in minority practices should be limited by reference to a rational principle and not by popular opinion, no matter how deeply felt and widespread that may be. Devlin does not think that the decision as to what is morally right or wrong should be that of a majority; indeed, it must be a product of something wider and deeper than this. Nevertheless, he has been criticised, with some justification, for allowing brute prejudice rather than reasoned moral argument to determine the extent of legal interference with personal liberty (Dworkin, 1977, ch. 10). It is also misleading for Devlin to suggest that a society's morality is reinforced by the coercive sanctions of the law. The liberal, and more plausible, view is that rational argument and the critical discussion of values provide a surer basis for morality than the symbolic and denunciatory use of punishment.

9

Rights

1 Rights in political theory

Implicit in the preceding discussion of evaluative problems has been the notion of a 'right'. Underlying the arguments for equality, even in the minimal sense, is the proposition that individuals are entitled to respect as moral agents capable of choice, and that to use them for collective ends, as some critics maintain utilitarianism does, is to deny a basic right of equal liberty. While it is true that some systems of political philosophy make no use of human rights, and indeed may openly reject them, they feature prominently in all discussions concerning the individual and the state. In contemporary Western political theory the dispute is more likely to be about the purported *content* of the various statements about rights than about the intelligibility of the concept of rights itself. This is aptly illustrated by the differences between two sorts of normative liberalism. An extreme individualistic liberal (or libertarian) believes that individuals have rights, whether recognised or not by the legal system, which political authorities ought not to transgress, and uses a natural rights argument to limit severely the role of the state. By contrast, the liberal who recommends a more active role for government in society and the economy frequently justifies this by reference to a revised and more expansive conception of human rights[1]. In the history of political theory, natural rights have often been linked to the concept of natural law. As we have seen, natural lawyers maintain that there is a moral order against which positive laws can be tested for their validity, and it is a short step from this to assert that individuals have rights against political authorities which are sanctioned by natural law. John Locke, perhaps the earliest modern exponent of rights, connected these to natural law, and the famous eighteenth-century political statements of the rights of man were rooted firmly in this tradition. However, the link is not a necessary one. The medieval concept of natural law, best exemplified in the jurisprudence of Aquinas, while it presented a framework of morality by which the realm of politics could be justified, did not grant rights to the citizen against political authorities; rather it imposed on everybody, including rulers, a coherent set of moral duties. It is only with the secularisation of natural law that we find the emergence of the potentially revolutionary doctrine of the rights of man. Modern moral arguments for the rights of man can be presented independently of natural law arguments of the traditional type.

Historically, the doctrine of natural rights has suffered from the vagaries of political and intellectual fashion. It was popular in the seventeenth century but suffered at the hands of utilitarianism and Marxism in the nineteenth century and in the early part of the last century. Utilitarians always thought that the logical structure of the arguments for natural rights was fallacious and that the social values implicit within the utilitarian calculus were an adequate foundation for normative politics. Marxists have specifically criticised the ahistorical and absolute nature of statements of rights and argued that they can only be properly understood within the context of particular economic and social circumstances.

Furthermore, conservatives have objected to natural rights on the ground that their alleged possession by individuals presupposes that the identity of the individual can be established in abstract terms. In effect, natural rights liberal individualism poses an *a priori* threat to authority. Implicit in it is the idea that the actions of duly constituted, legitimate political authority are always open to challenge by an abstract reason. Yet to the conservative not only does this undermine the foundations of political order, the validation of which is always derived from the values that are immanent in an ongoing social system, but philosophically it rests upon the error that the identity of persons can be established outside particular communities.

In this century statements about natural rights suffered at the hands of the Logical Positivists. Their explicitly normative character meant that they were vulnerable to the charge of being 'meaningless' and therefore of no interest to the analytical philosopher. Politically, however, the horrific experience of the last war, and of various brands of totalitarianism, heightened interest in natural rights and brought about a new sense of urgency in the desire to see some form of international protection of them. Furthermore, the demise of Logical Positivism and the renewed interest shown in the meaning of statements of rights and the implications they have for other values, and in the possibility of rational justification (as opposed to absolute demonstration) has brought about a nice combination of practical and theoretical concerns for the political philosopher to handle.[2]

The history of theoretical speculation about rights reveals significant changes in their character. In the traditional doctrine rights were always asserted *defensively* against some invasion of the individual's private interests. The invasion of most direct concern to the rights theorist was that brought about by the state. In the theories of limited government that invariably accompanied the doctrine of natural rights the state was morally forbidden to cross the boundary lines around the individual established by these rights. In Locke's theory the state was not the creator of rights but was limited to the enforcement of those pre-existing individual rights which were inalienable. The authenticity of these rights – in Locke's case, the rights to life, liberty and property – could be demonstrated by reference to natural law and reason. Indeed, the essentially negative nature of traditional rights meant that they changed from being radical anti-statist claims in the seventeenth and eighteenth centuries to rather conservative ideas in the nineteenth century, when they were used to disallow a more active role for the state in economic and social life. This is especially true of the right to property in American political thought and political practice. Also, libertarian anarchists, who certainly believe that individuals have rights, have been eager to point out the danger of granting the state a monopoly in the enforcement of these rights.

In contrast, in the last 30 years there has been a marked tendency to inflate the notion of rights. Rights are now not merely asserted defensively against state action but are interpreted as legitimate claims on government to satisfy human needs. Whereas traditional rights statements consisted of the right to life, free expression, property, free association, free movement and so on, they are today likely to include the right to medical care, a minimum wage and holidays with pay. The Universal Declaration of Human Rights, issued by the United Nations in 1948, consisted of both the familiar 'negative' rights and the new economic and social rights. The controversy surrounding this will be considered later in the chapter. Furthermore, not only has the content of rights changed but the range of entities considered as rights-holders has been significantly extended so that we now read of animal rights, where once only human beings were considered capable of possessing rights.

2 Analysis of rights

While there are a number of types of rights any analysis must begin with a simple distinction between legal and moral rights (Cranston, 1973, pp. 9–17). The existence of legal rights can be established quite easily by reference to a system of law; indeed, positivists maintain that the only genuine right is a claim which can be enforced by a court and that any other account of a right is entirely subjective and metaphysical. In contrast, moral rights cannot be established by reference to an ongoing legal system (although some moral rights are given specific protection in the law) but depend for their validity on their consistency with social and moral practices and on how they can be morally justified.

There is a great variety of moral rights, the most familiar being those that occur in social relationships; parents have rights against their children and patients have a right to be told the true state of their health by their doctors. The paradigm case of the creation of rights and duties is a *promise* (Melden, 1977, ch. 2). Promises are made by rational moral agents, capable of choice, and they create entitlements to persons such that they have the right to limit the freedom of other parties. To break a promise is then to deprive a person of his rights and undermine his status as an autonomous moral agent.

Human or natural rights are types of moral right in that they do not depend for their validity on enforcement by the legal system, but they are a special sort of moral right in that they do not emanate from specific promises or agreements but are said to belong to all persons, irrespective of what nation, community or social practice they may be a member of (Hart, 1967, pp. 63–4). However, this claim to universality which is made by theorists of natural rights poses some problems in the justification of rights.

Of course, some countries have incorporated the traditional rights into their legal systems and made them immune from ordinary political and legal change. Thus the actions of government are limited by the existence of these constitutional rights. It is the aim of active movements for human rights to turn all universal moral rights into positive rights, and to secure international institutions that protect the rights of the individual against the invasions of the state. While the differences between legal and moral rights are clear, it must be stressed that *all* statements about rights exhibit structural similarities. There are some common features of rights which must be elucidated before we can consider the specific political philosophy of human rights.

Political and legal theorists are interested in the many different senses in which the word 'right' is used. In jurisprudence, the classic analysis of the complex nature of statements about rights is to be found in Wesley Hohfeld's *Fundamental Legal Conceptions* (1919), and, although this work is concerned exclusively with the meaning of rights in legal systems, much of what Hohfeld says is of relevance to a wider context of 'rights talk' (see Raphael, 1967, pp. 56–7; Feinberg, 1973, ch. 4; Weale, 1983, ch. 7; Freeden, 1991). Hohfeld distinguished four types of rights: liberties, claims, immunities and powers. A liberty-right is a right that imposes no specific duties upon anyone else, a claim-right depends for its existence on there being a duty on someone else, an immunity is a specific exemption from a law granted to persons –such as diplomatic immunity or the immunity granted to trade unions from tort actions under the 1906 Trades Disputes Act – and powers are those rights that (typically) political institutions (such as a sovereign parliament) have to determine the rights of others. Of this classification, liberty-rights and claim-rights are the most interesting for the political theorist.

To have a right in the sense of a liberty means that one is under no obligation *not* to perform a certain act and the existence of the right does not depend on the performance of correlative duties on the part of others. Thus in the case of exploration of the earth for valuable natural resources each person has a liberty-right to proceed and none is under an obligation to another to refrain from so doing. In Hart's famous example of two people walking down a street and seeing a coin, each has a right to the coin in the sense that neither is under a duty to allow the other to pick it up (though each is under a duty not to use force in the process). Where rights are understood as liberties, then, the possession of a right by one person does not entail the restriction on the liberty of another in the sense of that person being under a correlative duty.

Hobbes's 'right of nature' is an example of this from the history of political thought. In a state of nature, characterised by the absence of law and government, each person has a right to do anything which is conducive to his own survival (Hobbes, 1968, p. 189). Since the right of one man cannot infringe the liberty of another, the state of nature is highly insecure. For Hobbes, this necessitates the existence of an absolute sovereign who is the source of all positive law. In Hobbes's system the right of nature is the only natural right and its exercise, under the conditions described, would make orderly social life impossible. Other political theorists, who do not share Hobbes's assumptions about human nature, deny that his is the only possible version of a natural right.

Since most important uses of the word 'right' occur in situations where the holder of the right is entitled to limit the freedom of others it might be thought that the isolation of a right as a liberty is not very significant. All theories of rights 'fill out' the notion of a right with an account of the conditions under which one person's right entails a duty upon another. However, the idea of a liberty does indicate that individuals have a *prima facie* right to have their desires satisfied and that the violation of this requires justification (Flathman, 1976, pp. 42–4). It is perhaps best exemplified in a competitive market economy, correctly described as a system of 'natural liberty', in which each person has the right to maximise his interests, in the sense of not being under a duty to refrain from doing so. But these systems require structures of rules which allow individuals to make legitimate claims against each other, and which supplement liberties. It is these that provide some predictability in a competitive system.

In the more usual sense of the word 'right', it is understood as a type of claim. Claim-rights entitle their holder to limit the liberty of another person. *A* has a right against *B*, deriving either from a moral or legal rule, which puts *B* under a duty. It is not the moral quality of the act that entitles *A* to limit *B*'s liberty but simply the fact that he possesses the right (Hart, 1967, p. 56). Indeed, there may be occasions when some other moral consideration may compel *A* to waive his right against *B*. Situations can easily occur in which it would be right to break a promise and therefore violate someone's rights. It is crucial, then, to distinguish between doing the right thing and having a right, since these usages describe different moral situations.

Claim-rights possessed by persons are quite different from favours or concessions granted to individuals by authorities. A person may be allowed to do something by another, and indeed her welfare may be significantly improved by the actions of others, but that is very different from saying that she has a right, in the sense of a claim. When someone has a right, by the rules of a practice, by an agreement or promise and so on, he acquires a kind of sovereignty over another, against whom she has a legitimate claim. It might be thought that *A* is in a privileged position with regard to *B* by virtue of her possession of the right, but a system of rights receives some justification from the fact that, at least in the liberal-individualist system, everyone is likely to be the possessor of a right on some occasions (Flathman, 1976, pp. 81–2). To say that someone has a right is to acknowledge her autonomy as a moral agent capable of making choices, and while it is possible that moral and legal systems may exist which do not recognise rights, such systems are deficient, from the individualist's point of view, for this very reason. The individualistic feature of statements about claim-rights is revealed by the crucial point that only the holder of a right can waive it or suspend it (Melden, 1977, pp. 99–101).

To use the language of rights in political discourse is to use a *distributive* language (akin logically to the concepts of justice and minimalist equality). Its rationale derives not from any connection it may or may not have with the maximisation of social welfare (or any other aggregative consideration) but from the moral argument that individuals have claims against others not to be treated in certain ways. Again, the conferring of rights on individuals is not to say that they are the likely beneficiaries of some duty (although it may, in the positive law, look as if this is the case) on others but that they have a certain sovereignty over their own persons. It is this that gives the peculiar *force* to statements about rights; and it is this notion of a right as a kind of possession that gives substance to the argument that only individuals may waive them.

A perennial question asked of rights is whether duties and rights are always correlative in a logical sense, as the Hohfeldian analysis of claim-rights implies. We have already shown in the analysis of rights as liberties that a person can have a right without there being a corresponding duty upon anyone else, but we must also consider the question of whether all duties imply corresponding rights. In the case of claim-right, the argument that duties and rights are logically linked seems to be watertight, but there are uses of the word duty which do not imply correlative rights. We can speak of individuals being under duties without there being corresponding rights against them held by others. This is especially so in non-legal contexts. We speak of duties to relieve suffering, to be charitable and so on where it would be odd to speak of others having a right in the strict sense. This is because in moral discourse the word duty has come to have a wide range of application, one that extends beyond the simple duties-rights correspondence that is characteristic of legal relationships. This is not to deny that the moral demands of duty may be extremely pressing but only to suggest that this describes a logically different situation from that in which one person, through the possession of a right, may legitimately limit the freedom of another. It might be better, for the sake of clarity, to distinguish between obligations and duties. Rights and obligations seem to be correlative because they arise, in the familiar context of agreements, contracts and promises, in a self-assumed manner. This is not so of moral duties, which can be owed by some persons to others in the absence of any specific agreement that created them.

This distinction becomes crucially important in considering whether it is permissible to attribute rights not only to infants and animals but also to adults who may not satisfy the minimal criteria of rationality normally associated with the possession of rights. It seems more plausible to speak of our duties towards infants than to say that they have rights. This is because the attribution of rights depends upon a certain concept of a person that incorporates autonomy, rationality and the faculty of making choices and entering into agreements within the confines of rule-governed relationships. That infants obviously have the potentiality for conduct appropriate to this concept of a person seems insufficient a reason for saying that they have rights as infants. The same reasoning indicates that it would be improper to speak of the rights of the higher animals, even those that may satisfy some minimal criteria of rational behaviour and towards which human beings have strong feelings of affection. One of the important aspects of someone having a right is that she, and only she, can choose to waive the right, and it would be odd to attribute rights to species manifestly incapable of this.

More difficult problems are posed by the case of the mentally ill, especially as the definition of insanity is itself in dispute. There are many cases of people being forcibly detained in institutions who are quite capable of shouldering the responsibilities that necessarily accompany the possession of rights.[3] It would, however, be difficult to say that psychopaths have rights, for example, since their mental condition does not seem to include those properties of the human personality which are essential to the concept of a moral agent. If the mentally deranged do not have the capacity to understand the purpose of rules, the meaning of promises and agreements, and to feel guilt and remorse, it severely undermines the possibility that they may behave in accordance with the dictates of morality.

A social and legal order in which individuals have rights to that extent recognises their autonomy and self-respect as moral agents. A society that recognised the needs of individuals and promoted policies that maximised their welfare would be a benevolent society but it would not for that reason alone accord them rights. Indeed there are many examples in history of minorities being favourably treated by a dominant class but not granted the freedom which comes with having rights (Wasserstrom, 1971, pp. 109–22).

So far we have been talking of moral and legal rights in general but natural or human rights have certain features which distinguish them from other sorts of rights. The logic of rights that derive from institutional frameworks, moral and legal practices, family and personal relationships, and promises and undertakings seems, on the face of it, to be different from that of the traditional declarations of human rights. In these documents individuals are said to have rights in whatever society they may find themselves. These are thought of as claim-rights but they belong to persons as persons and not as members of particular states, societies or social groupings, and do not derive from promises and undertakings.

Although many political theorists would accept that individuals have natural rights, the justification of the more general rights has always been difficult. Central to many discussions of this problem is the argument that implicit in the idea of a morality is the notion of rights. While it is certainly possible that a moral code can be coherent without such a notion, one that recognises individual autonomy is scarcely conceivable without the idea of rights, the violation of which requires considerable justification.[4]

H. L. A. Hart distinguishes between *special* rights and *general* rights (1967, pp. 60–4). Special rights, which arise out of specific undertakings and agreements between individuals, presuppose the existence of general rights because one needs a special right (or claim) to justify a limitation on another's freedom, and in the absence of such a right everyone has the general right not to be coerced. If there are any natural rights, he says, then there is at least the equal right to be free, a right which is possessed by all persons capable of choice. The recognition that there is such a right is implicit in the moral justification of its abrogation. Of course, justifications have always been found for the violation of this right but it is a significant practical point that many tyrannical regimes while systematically violating rights nevertheless formally acknowledge their existence. If the public interest is invoked whenever a right is violated this implicitly recognises that there is a prima facie claim to non-interference.

When social and political theorists maintain that human beings possess rights as human beings rather than as members of a social practice, or as participants in a moral or legal relationship, they actually mean that there is a minimum concept of human equality at work in moral argument. This view was considered in a previous chapter and can be restated here in the context of rights. When we say that each person has an equal right to freedom, to be left alone (unless there are substantial grounds for interference), to choose her own course of action, to exchange values with others, and not therefore to be used as a thing or instrument for the advantage of the 'community' or 'society at large', we mean that irrespective of her merit as an individual in her personal and moral capacity, she is at least equal to others in human worth (Feinberg, 1973, pp. 94–7). Even convicted criminals, who have violated the rights of others and therefore do not score highly in moral grading, still have the right not to be treated in cruel or humiliating ways by their gaolers.

The equal right to freedom, however, needs to be filled out by other considerations in political argument. It might be used by extreme liberals as a barrier against interference in freely negotiated contracts between individuals and against the state using the property of individuals to advance social purposes. But since morality permits the justification of limitations on this right, a more collectivist conception of society would be consistent with it. However, the argument then would be about the justification of the proposed intervention, not about the existence of the right itself.

There are differences amongst political theorists concerning the content of rights and their supposed 'absolute' nature. The concept of human rights has been expanded in recent years to include economic and social rights and the controversy surrounding this topic is of major importance today. However, the traditional statements have not differed greatly; rights to life, liberty, property, free expression, freedom of movement and a fair trial figure prominently. All of them appear to require little positive action by the state. Political authorities do not create rights and are limited to the enforcement of those rights that already exist. The argument now, however, is that just as it would be impermissible for the state to invade someone's protected sphere it would be equally wrong for it to deny someone those economic facilities which are necessary for a moral life.

A criticism often made of the traditional statements about rights is that the rights listed conflict, and that in the absence of some ordering principle or priority rule, they present a somewhat incoherent and muddled set of demands. Does not the right to property conflict with the right to life in a famine, when a person might justifiably claim that another individual's property rights are not inviolable? In fact, in this particular example, Locke would maintain that there is no conflict; since there is a strict duty (obligation) on everyone to preserve society, there is a right of the poor and indigent against the rich to secure relief from their suffering. Locke's real problem is that of making his belief that a man's property cannot be taken from him without his consent consistent with the obvious fact that there has to be coercion in order to raise taxes for essential government services, including the enforcement of rights.

Contemporary exponents of Locke's doctrine of natural rights do argue that statements about rights can be constructed without any inconsistency between the various rights. In fact, they would argue that rights do not have to be *specified* or enumerated but that all the basic rights can be derived from the equal right to freedom where that is interpreted to mean that each individual has an inviolable right to person and property. Restrictions on one person's freedom would not count as violations of his rights if they were designed solely to prevent the use of force or fraud against someone else. Similarly, libel laws would not count as a limitation on anyone's rights to free expression since they protect what are, in effect, property rights that individuals have in their personal reputations. The state would then be limited by the existence of one basic human right.

Collectivists argue, however, that this interpretation of human rights is far too narrow in that it merely gives an ideological justification of the existing set of property rights, which is quite arbitrary from a moral point of view. Instead of being a universal set of claims which are not necessarily tied to any political ideology, rights end up as outgrowths of the social philosophy of individualism. In the radical collectivist view, truly human rights must include a welfare element (see below, Section 4).

The other main difficulty with the doctrine of human rights is over the question of whether they are absolute, where this means that they are to be honoured *without exception* (see Feinberg, 1973, pp. 94–7). For example, does the right to life put a prohibition on capital punishment? The statement that each person has an equal right to liberty offers little guidance here. It is possible to argue that an absolute right to life does not preclude the taking of life if that action is essential to secure the protection of life generally. Clearly, the killing of a terrorist, if that is the only way that he can be prevented from indiscriminate slaughter, would not be thought of as a breach of rights. The case of capital punishment is more difficult but it could be maintained by a natural rights theorist that the institution is morally permissible since it is the convicted murderer who has breached the right to life. It might be argued, however, that there are no absolute rights as such and that situations can be envisaged in which a human right may be overridden. There is nevertheless a meta-ethical right, the right to equal consideration, which requires that justification must be given when individuals are treated in certain ways if they are to be accorded the status of moral agents. But of course this right has no specific content in the way that typical human rights have.

Human rights are also thought to be *inalienable*, that is, they cannot be given up or traded away. Thus slavery is always illegitimate since it violates a person's right to freedom, and makes him a tool of another (no matter how beneficently the slave-owner treats the slave). Unlike non-universal moral rights, which can be waived, the rights that every person has against unjustified interference cannot be simply re-nounced. The point of saying that certain natural rights are inalienable is that if a person voluntarily gives them up he, in a sense, resigns from the moral community and puts the determination of his future into the hands of somebody else. Voluntary contracts of slavery involve the attempted surrender of the right to freedom and choice. To argue that natural rights are inalienable is to argue that such contracts do not take away the right: a person may, for various reasons, wish to abandon his control over his own future, but this does not mean that he has extinguished a right in the way that one might waive the right to be repaid a £5 loan to a friend. In the former case, the right can be reclaimed. Still, there is a problem for those who believe in the morality of self-ownership, for that does seem to imply that a person may trade away rights.

A perplexing problem that concerns the supposed inalienability of rights is that of euthanasia. In effect, does a person have the right to renounce his own right to life? If this is so, it implies that perhaps the most fundamental of the specific rights is, in principle, waivable. In fact there are many cases, involving painful and terminal illnesses, where the legal *impossibility* of the patient choosing to end his own life itself constitutes an abrogation of his rights. Indeed, to allow the person to decide whether to continue living or not is to pay tribute to him as a rational moral agent capable of choice. Of course, it has to be established that a person is a rational agent when he makes such a decision and is fully aware of the consequences, but to prohibit euthanasia, and in doing so prolong needless agony, seems to reflect the dominance of a particular sort of moral code over the sanctity of individual autonomy and the rights that go with it.

3 Critics of rights

The doctrine of natural rights has never been without its critics and it has been rejected both on philosophical and political grounds (see Waldron, 1987). It has been suggested that statements about rights are incurably metaphysical and that the social and political ends of the theorists of rights can be formulated in more philosophically respectable concepts. Politically they have been interpreted as radical ideas potentially subversive of the social order, or as reactionary obstacles that prevent the radical transformation of society based on 'scientific' principles.[5] The basic point that underlies all collectivist criticisms of human rights is that they consider them to be excessively individualistic and ahistorical. There are other important refutations of the doctrine but those provided by utilitarianism and the varieties of Marxism and communitarianism are perhaps of most interest to contemporary political theorists.

Bentham's (1843) objection to natural rights was both philosophical and political. As a legal positivist of the command school, Bentham could not accept that statements about natural rights were even meaningful. Rights were correlated with duties and to be under a duty was to be liable to sanctions in the event of failure to perform an action. To ascribe a right to someone is to say that he stood to benefit by the performance of a duty on the part of someone else. Thus statements about rights, duties and obligations could be reduced to statements about the facts of a system of law. In Bentham's philosophy it would also be possible to speak of moral rights and duties where failure to perform an action is met by the sanction of popular disapproval. But it would not be possible to speak sensibly of the abstract rights of man which are said to exist independently of legal systems with sanctions. In a famous phrase he described them as 'nonsense upon stilts'. At most, Bentham would concede that natural rights were no more than expressions of what legal rights men *ought* to have; but even here the justification for such rights must be in terms of social utility and not in terms of any other moral principle.

Bentham's political objection to natural rights was that they were in fact reactionary, and that their alleged existence retarded the application of science to social reform. Armed with the felicific calculus, the sovereign could derive a collective welfare judgement from the (observable) preferences of individuals, and policies could therefore be evaluated according to their consistency with this rather than their conformity to abstract principles of rights and justice, the validity of which depended on intuition and subjective opinion.

We have seen earlier how utilitarianism fails to provide an objective morality because the derivation of a collective welfare judgement from individual preference requires that utility can be measured and that the legislator can make interpersonal comparisons of utility. Since these things cannot be done, statements about utility are logically no different from statements about natural rights in that they rest upon sentiment, intuition and subjective judgement. We do, of course, make utilitarian-type judgements about the interests of the community but these are ultimately moral judgements and must therefore be evaluated on moral and not scientific grounds.

By concentrating exclusively on the beneficial consequences of action as the source of value, utilitarianism ignores the rights that come from the past actions of individuals, and the rights that arise independently of social utility from the agreements they made and from their dignity and autonomy as human beings. To say that someone has a right to something entails quite a different justification from that involved in utilitarianism. In pure Benthamism the individual disappears once his preferences are known and incorporated into the utilitarian calculus: and since in a Benthamite legal order the legislator is unlimited in his authority, individual rights may well be abrogated in the construction of the social welfare function. In fact, rights are most often asserted defensively against the general interests of the community. If people do have rights which do not depend upon political enactment for their existence then these cannot be violated merely on grounds of utility for, apart from the difficulty of determining what the general interest is, this would destroy the whole purpose of rights, which are the possessions of individuals for their protection against the 'public'. It is possible to conceive of situations where utilitarian arguments which justify the abrogation of a right might be compelling, but the strong conception of rights involves the idea that the individual can be coerced only when her actions threaten or damage the *rights of others* and not merely when they appear to be against the interests of the community.

It is misleading to suggest that Marxists are as systematically hostile to the idea of natural rights as some utilitarians have been. In fact, contemporary Marxists and collectivists are ambivalent towards human rights, as Marx himself was. On the one hand, for example, they are eager to wage revolutionary struggle against colonialism on behalf of the rights of man, but on the other they are extremely critical of the individualism of the traditional theory of rights, especially its commitment to personal property.

Marx, in *On the Jewish Question* (1971, pp. 85–114), saw the rise of human rights in historical context. The liberation of man from the oppressive and restrictive feudal economic and social structure was a stupendous achievement which realised the major aims of the natural rights thinkers. However, he was insistent that the so-called rights of man 'are nothing but the rights of the member of civil society, i.e. egoistic man, man separated from other men and the community' (Marx, 1971, p. 102). True to historical materialism, Marx rejected the claim to universalism made by liberal theorists of rights. The emancipation of man required the transcendence of *all* oppressive social and economic institutions, not merely those of feudalism; and the bourgeois period of history, for all its many virtues, established mainly legal and political protection for the individual right to appropriate property. For Marxists rights are anti-social, individualistic and divisive.

Nevertheless, formal acknowledgement of the universal importance of human rights was a feature of most communist regimes. The 1936 Soviet constitution, a product of Stalinism, while including economic and social rights, did also include the traditional liberal rights to freedom of association, free movement, a free press, a fair trial and so on, as did its 1977 successor. However, even these formal concessions are qualified by the existence of strict social obligations. Even in Soviet theory the familiar civil rights could only be exercised in the interests of the proletariat and could not be held against the socialist state.

In practice, of course, the history of the Soviet Union was characterised by a persistent and systematic violation of human rights.[6] During the height of the Stalinist terror Soviet cruelty is thought to have been unequalled outside Nazism. It may be the case that such occurrences were historical aberrations, or that they proceeded from the personality of Stalin and other Soviet leaders, but it is worth asking whether some explanation can be found in the Marxist conception of human rights. A conception that puts them purely in a historical context and rejects their universal features, in effect, makes individuals the instruments of society.

Ironically, a conservative who rejected the notion of natural, universal and inalienable rights would do so on not dissimilar theoretical grounds to those of the Marxist. For it is the case that traditionalists from Burke onwards have regarded the attribution of rights as kinds of possessions of individuals abstracted from particular communities as untenable. If rights are to exist meaningfully they must derive from certain sorts of relationships that exist prior to the notion of individuals as abstract choosers. Thus it is not just to the political effects of natural rights theory to which conservative political philosophers objects but to the notion itself. Indeed, some have detected a *reductio ad absurdum* in the argument that to have a right means the possession of a kind of sovereignty over one's own body: surely, this implies that it would be legitimate to trade away one's rights – for example, if a person is the owner of one's body, what could be the objection to voluntary slavery or any other form of an onerous labour contract? Thus, in this strong sense of a right, some traditional rights would not be inalienable. Indeed, there is a tradition in political thought (see Tuck, 1979) which did view rights in this way and, of course, Hobbes derived the legitimacy of the authoritarian state from a not dissimilar idea.

However, in the liberal conception of rights the notion is not derived from pure choice alone but rather an account is also taken of the circumstances in which choices are made. Thus although it may be linguistically permissible to say that submission to a sovereign power is an exercise of a person's rights, since she could have acted in other ways, the existence of 'threat' itself constitutes a violation of rights. Nevertheless, the possibility of voluntary slavery is something of a theoretical puzzle for rights theorists, if not a likely practical problem.[7]

Communitarians have been the most vigorous contemporary critics of rights theory. Their critique is partly philosophical but mainly political. Alasdair MacIntyre writes that· 'There are no natural or human rights and a belief in them is one with belief in witches and unicorns' (1981, p. 67). This stark claim presumably derives from the objection to liberal individualism that it abstracts persons from the social circumstances and illegitimately supposes that their political arrangements can be reconstructed so as to give effect to their preferences (subject only to the rules of justice, whether distributive or procedural). To communitarians, however, since the good is prior to the right, it is only pre-existing social forms that can give meaning to people's lives: to endow them with abstract rights simply ignores those shared values and understandings. Only the latter can resolve inevitable conflict between individuals and groups. The invocation of rights, in fact, exacerbates disagreement.

Rights theorists have to some extent provoked this response by failing to articulate an uncontroversial set of rights and seeming to downgrade the claims of community. In a famous expression Dworkin (1977, ch. 5) has argued that rights 'trump' all other considerations in political argument. In fact, he slightly modifies this by claiming that rights can be overridden by urgent considerations, without exactly specifying the rationale for the overriding. But the right he stresses, to equal concern and respect, is capable of a variety of interpretations. For him, it does not include economic rights, which can always be trumped by public policy considerations, but for others these are just as valuable as the traditional civil liberties. The communitarian's position is that these issues are irresolvable outside a body of shared values, the exploration of which gives us objective answers to pressing questions. Whatever rights we have cannot be held against the community.

At the more practical level, the communitarian's argument is that rights talk is disruptive of those political mechanisms that are essential if harmony is to be fostered. This can be seen from the fact that the essentially legalistic language of rights presupposes that right answers can be found to questions which are necessarily indeterminate. The abortion question in America is a classic example: both sides to the dispute address it in absolutist terms and both can make an appeal to rights (the woman's right to choose and the rights of the unborn child) embodied implicitly in the Fourteenth Amendment to the Constitution. To a communitarian the question should be settled politically by the invocation of values not expressible in absolute rights form. In a federal system, this would lead to a variety of legal rules on the issue. This would be unacceptable to the rights theorist.

A further criticism would focus on the fact that the list of rights tends to expand. This is most noticeable if we look at the growth of welfare rights (see below), but it is observable in other areas – for example, the demand for the widespread regulation of working conditions in a market economy is now formulated in the language of indefeasible rights. The point here is not to pre-empt a solution to these difficulties but merely to say that when they are put in the rights form it clothes the alleged answer with a peculiar form of absoluteness. For example, seeing economic regulation as a matter of rights precludes consideration of cost–benefit analysis which might be thought highly relevant to the issue.

There is, then, a danger that the language of rights might drive out other forms of evaluative argument. But as long as we value individual claims against collective organisations (as well as against other persons) we will find it difficult not to use rights. The fact that there has been an undue expansion of rights claims is not a reason for submitting to relativism, which is certainly an implication of the anti-individualism of some communitarian doctrines.

4 Human rights, economic and social rights, and welfare

Since the Second World War there has been an expansion in the concept of human rights: there has been a change from what may be called 'negative rights', that is, rights held against the state which require little in the way of public, collective action beyond the establishment of a legal order guaranteeing liberty and security, towards rights which require more positive political action. These latter are called economic and social rights, welfare rights or rights to well-being. This widened concept of rights was given great political impetus by the United Nations Declaration of Rights of 1948. This declaration consisted of two parts, one concerned with the traditional civil rights and the other with things such as medical care, education, political participation and the now notorious right to 'periodic holidays with pay'.

However, the whole concept of welfare rights has been highly controversial, for both political and philosophical reasons. The political reason stems from the fact that the second category of rights was included in the UN Declaration under pressure from the Soviet Union. Some Western writers argued that the satisfaction of economic rights by communist governments would distract attention from their abrogation of the more basic rights. The philosophical objection was that economic rights were not properly human rights and that a different moral language was appropriate to the welfare aims of the second part of the Declaration.

The general philosophical objection to welfare rights takes the following form. Rights are in principle derived from the right to freedom and are rights held against others who have correlative obligations not to interfere; they are grounded in the idea that individuals are entitled to dignity, respect and autonomy. This philosophy puts the concept of a right into a different moral context from the duty of benevolence, to which the idea of welfare is said properly to belong. In Hart's theory the morality of rights is about the justifiable limitations on liberty; to have a right against somebody is to be entitled to have a claim *enforced* against that person, who in turn has an obligation to honour the claim. To have a right against the state is to have a strong claim not to be interfered with. But in relation to rights to welfare it is often said that no party can be legitimately coerced to honour them. Who is under an obligation to recognise rights to well-being? Those who think that there are rights to welfare normally think of the state as being responsible for the satisfaction of such claims, but they would also argue that individuals may be in positions in which someone has a right against them derived from considerations of the other person's well-being rather than from a contract or an agreement. An example of this might be a patient with blood of a rare group having the right to a transfusion from someone else with blood of the same type (Peffer, 1978, pp. 74–5). The important point is that theorists of welfare rights wish to capture the special obligatoriness of the concept of a right so that coercion is legitimate for meeting claims to well-being.

Maurice Cranston (1967, 1973) has been very critical of the attempt to elevate social and economic rights to the status of human rights proper by the authors of the UN Declaration. Cranston argues that the only genuine *universal* human rights are the traditional negative ones and that the inclusion of economic rights in the Declaration involves a 'category mistake', that is, the error of assigning something to its wrong logical 'box'. In Cranston's view, economic rights belong to the category of ideals, not of universally realisable human rights. Thus rights have ceased to be barriers against unwarranted interference but have become social goals.

He reaches this conclusion on two grounds. First there is the 'ought implies can' argument. This holds that for any action to be morally obligatory it must be possible for the agent to perform it. Thus, if a child is in danger of drowning in a pond, a bystander who is able to swim and can easily rescue it, *ought* to do so; but the same cannot be said, say, of a person who is ten miles from the scene of the accident and unable to do anything about it. By the same reasoning it is absurd to suggest that all citizens have economic and social rights since in most countries of the world economic conditions make it impossible to implement them seriously. Things are different, however, in the case of the traditional civil rights since a recognition of them normally requires *inactivity* on the part of government; political officials merely have to desist from interfering with the free movement of individuals, imprisoning them without trial, censoring the press and so on. Thus negative rights are genuine universal rights of man while economic rights are ideals, or, at the most, rights that belong to members of particular societies at particular times. Negative rights are said to be 'compossible' (Steiner, 1979), which means that a set of rights can be so designed that there is no conflict between the various rights. Thus the argument is that if welfare rights exist then this imposes an obligation on others to satisfy them. If they are compelled to honour them then their rights are violated: rights are then no longer 'equal' and the set is not compossible. Cranston's second argument is that negative rights are more important in a moral sense than economic rights. It is simply more vital to individual autonomy that governments refrain from cruel and arbitrary action, and from measures that destroy liberty, rather than provide 'free' social services or holidays with pay.

There is considerable intellectual weight behind the objections to the assimilation of welfare rights to universal rights. One problem not discussed by Cranston is that even if societies can afford to implement economic rights this may have unanticipated consequences for other rights. If a welfare state guarantees individuals incomes higher than they can earn in the market, then it is bound to attract more immigrants than it otherwise would, and thus lead to highly illiberal immigration laws. Similarly, if the state pays for the education of doctors out of general taxation then this may lead to the demand physically to prevent them from leaving the country in order to earn higher incomes abroad. These examples show how the existence of welfare rights may lead to the denial of the right to free movement.

Strict libertarians argue that considerations such as these, plus the general fact that the implementation of welfare rights abrogates the rights of others because of the increased power it entails, tells heavily against the expansion of the traditional rights. They might suggest that people's incomes *ought* to be increased (on grounds of general benevolence) but deny that individuals have a right to this in the strict sense of the term.

Proponents of economic and social rights (see Plant, 1991, ch. 7), deny the logical distinction that Cranston makes between the two sorts of rights. They say that even the implementation of negative rights requires some sort of positive government action; this is especially true of the right to life and the right to a fair trial, both of which require a considerable range of publicly provided protective services. Indeed, it may be the case that under certain circumstances governments may not be able to implement the customary civil rights. Thus in some cases the application of Cranston's 'ought implies can' criterion may have curious consequences. If a country is rich enough to provide for welfare rights but finds it difficult to guarantee basic negative rights, do the former then take precedence over the latter?

Furthermore, as Hamlin (1986) has pointed out, the alleged distinction between negative and positive rights does not logically entail a minimal state, as many of its proponents favour. For if there is a strict obligation to protect negative rights this could justify unlimited expenditure on defence and zero expenditure on welfare: a surely counter-intuitive result. Indeed, there may be conflicts between the supposedly compossible negative rights. There are competing claims for protection, since not every legitimate demand can be met in a world of scarcity, so that choices have to be made which must lead to a ranking of the rights. The claim that negative rights are costless is only theoretical. Of course, if people honoured them they would indeed be costless but in a practical sense they are subject to a special kind of scarcity – goodwill. But as Raymond Plant (1991, pp. 270–1) has shown, that is logically no different from the scarcity to which economic and social rights are prone – that of resources.

For those reasons it is maintained by theorists of welfare that there is a symmetry between the two sorts of rights. The conditions of well-being, what it means to be an autonomous agent, requires both that negative rights, in the sense of there being entitlements to forbearances from invasive action on the part of others, and welfare rights, some guaranteed minimum, be recognised by the state (although welfare rights theorists do often claim that the obligation to provide minimal welfare may lie on non-political agencies). Thus Raymond Plant claims that to be a moral agent capable of making autonomous choices requires that the person has a claim to welfare in the strict, enforceable sense, otherwise moral action would not be possible: 'Basic needs have to be satisfied to do anything at all' (Plant, 1986, p. 29; see also Gewirth, 1987). This is not a claim to *specific* resources, but a general claim to that welfare which is necessary for agency.

However persuasive these arguments may be, there are other reasons which indicate that there is no *exact* symmetry between negative and welfare rights. These hold apart from any practical reasons that tell against the assimilation of one to the other. The reasons cover the following issues: *indeterminacy*, *justiciability*, and *responsibility*.

Indeterminacy is a problem because welfare rights theories say potentially conflicting things: that a positive right to well-being is *more* than the entitlement to the minimum required for mere survival and that the needs on which it is based are objective. Thus even if it is agreed that well-being is essential to a developed morality it is hard to see how its demands can be translated into the precise language of rights if it is to be a legitimate claim to more than a bare minimum. If one believes in the incommensurability and diversity of values it is strictly impossible to incorporate the various 'well-beings' into one authoritative pattern. Even the right to life is not always a conclusive claim (apart from the prohibition it puts on the taking of life). After all, the demand does not entail that vast resources should be devoted to preserving any life. Judgements have to be made about the value of life and these involve peculiarly delicate choices, especially in socialised medical systems. This problem is becoming acute as advanced medical technology enables life to be preserved (at great cost) but at a fairly low level of quality. It is not clear that the talk of welfare rights is all that helpful here.

Indeed, the subjective nature of well-being may well mean that the only way it could be honoured would be by unequal distributions of resources; which would be condemnable on other moral grounds. This question is crucially important when we consider the connection between the welfare rights that are owed to us as human beings and those social (welfare) rights that belong to us as members of particular communities. For generous interpretations of the former would sanction an international redistribution of resources, which would be precluded by the latter.

This problem of indeterminacy leads directly to the question of justiciability. It is understandable that welfare philosophers should demand the constitutional protection of welfare rights since it is almost certainly the lax political rules of majoritarian democracies, and the discretion granted to officials, that have caused the failure of postwar welfare policies aimed at both equality and the relief of deprivation (see Goodin and Le Grand, 1987): coalitions of group interests have submerged the widespread desire for some form of welfare for the needy that exists in a community. Yet the demand for strict constitutional standards, to prevent phenomena such as the middle-class capture of the welfare state, is not the same thing as the demand for a 'list' of welfare rights (as in the UN Declaration of Human Rights). It is difficult to see how one could claim in a court of law that one's right to well-being had not been upheld by a government. No doubt the same thing could logically be said of some of the negative rights but the difference in degree between the two types has great significance.

The last difference between negative and positive rights centres on the question of personal responsibility for action. Does the fact that a person may act in such a way that he becomes entitled to welfare make a difference to his moral claim? This point has some practical application as contemporary welfare policies are known to encourage people to adjust their behaviour so as to secure an advantage. Alan Gewirth, who certainly believes in the symmetry of negative and positive rights, nevertheless stresses the fact that the agent 'cannot rationally demand of other persons that they help him to have basic well-being unless his own efforts to have it are unavailing' (Gewirth, 1987, p. 68). David Harris, a proponent of social rather than universal rights, similarly argues that: 'The fact of need, independently of how the need was created, does not provide a sufficient ground upon which a normative defence of need-meeting policies can be founded' (Harris, D. 1987, pp. 60–1). Both these writers imply that questions of causal history and the direct attribution of responsibility for action are relevant to the moral status of welfare rights. In contrast, we would not say that a person who behaved foolishly by walking in an area known to be plagued by muggers had thereby forfeited his negative right to forbearance. The point is that we do not grant a welfare right automatically and the distinction between the two sorts of rights it alludes to has a practical application as well as a theoretical significance. For those critics of the welfare state who claim that it creates dependency rather than individual responsibility are challenging, often in a regrettably vulgar way, a basic tenet of welfare philosophy, that is that welfare institutions help to foster a less acquisitive agent than that which inhabits the apparently amoral world of competitive markets.

It would, of course, be argued by a communitarian that the negative rights themselves are accompanied by social duties, logically equivalent to those pertaining to economic and social rights. Membership of a community and consuming the collective goods that it provides imposes certain duties on individuals that go beyond mere forbearance from negative rights-violating action. Such social responsibilities may include jury service and military duties but are also likely to encompass acting for the common interest in less tangible ways. Voting, participating in community affairs at some personal cost and refraining from egoistic action (even when this involves no illegality) are possible candidates.

Whatever is said about the cogency of welfare rights arguments, it does not follow that a rejection of them entails a rejection of the welfare state and we shall be looking at specific arguments for the welfare state in the next chapter. At this point it is enough to argue that it is possible to maintain that there is a duty, even of a compelling kind, for public institutions to relieve suffering. If the claim is put in this form, rather than in the form of indefeasible rights, some preconditions on the receipt of welfare of the type specified by Gewirth and Harris, could be made. The point here is that statements about rights are not all that helpful until we know the interests they are designed to protect. A specification of these interests, which may derive from demonstrable needs or claims for the provision of conditions that make for a worthwhile life, may be more useful than the stark and quasi-legalistic form in which rights statements are normally put. Only in this way can the dispute between negative and welfare rights theorists be resolved.

There is, unfortunately, a tendency to put a lot of political demands in the rights form; largely because the use of that language gives them a particularly compelling force. To have a right to something is to defeat all competing claims, perhaps derived from utility or some notion of the public interest; and goes along way towards weakening that pluralism which is a feature of all forms of liberal politics. To claim a right is often to put a 'stop' on moral argument. Since many of the contemporary rights demands are not really claims that defeat all rivals, the use of the term should be restricted to the overwhelmingly important, or ultimate, political values such as free movement, fair trials and free speech. The plea for welfare rights therefore is a plea for the recognition of some *interest* which can be handled by the regular political process, and while it is true that rights claimants do have interests, it is not the case that all interest demands are rights.

5 Animal rights and animal welfare

The language of rights has extended in recent years not merely in that the range if human demands that may be couched in the form of rights has widened but also it is the case that the entities who may be considered as rights holders has expanded. Traditional rights theorists regarded only human beings as the subjects of rights, and even here the category was sometimes qualified by things like rationality and the capacity to form life plans and embark on exclusively human projects. It was often thought that children were not proper rights bearers, although potentially so, precisely because they were not considered to be appropriate for the responsibility that is demanded of rights holders; they were not capable of recognising duties or taking on the burdens of relationships of reciprocity. It was felt that the morality that we have towards babies, mental defectives unlikely ever to reach maturity and others who did not meet a fairly demanding criteria of rationality was covered by a notion of strict duty. This, of course, did not in any way weaken the moral entitlements of those agents, the notion of a duty was by no means optional and indeed could override some competing right that a person might have. Such duties that are owed to these entities were not waivable, as a right could be. Bentham, whom as we have seen was hostile to the notion of rights in general, still thought that animals should be considered in the utilitarian calculus. The important question regarding animals was not 'Can they reason, nor can they talk. But can they suffer?'

The question of the relationship between utility and rights is, in fact, no better illustrated than in the question of the morality of human conduct towards animals. It is philosophically significant that those who have been most concerned with the interests of animals are sharply divided between rights theorists and utilitarians. In terms of policy the difference between them does not matter too much, the utilitarians (see Singer, 1993) are no less committed than the rights theorists (Regan, 1984) in their demand for a radical re-examination of the way that we treat animals. Both these schools of thought insist that certain animals have a moral status equivalent to human beings and they are equally critical of that 'speciesism' (logically equivalent to racism, class discrimination and sexism) which allows human beings a privileged place in the moral universe. Indeed, the presuppositions that we make about moral thinking, and the consideration of who are entitled to moral agency, are apposite to the utilitarian or to the rights case for animal liberation.

The first point to make here is to determine the facts that are relevant to the moral argument for animals. It is true that some philosophers in the past thought that animals had no claim to moral consideration at all, that they were 'objects' entirely at the service of man, who was unconstrained by ethics in the way he treated them. It is unlikely that anyone seriously takes that view today and most legal codes contain rules against the cruel treatment of at least the higher forms of animal life. But does this imply that they are proper moral agents?

Most theorists, whether they are for or against animals as fully fledged moral persons, concede that they are *sentient*, they can feel pleasure and pain and react to the external world in predictable ways. That in itself is a constraint on the way we treat them. But can we go further than this? Of course, it would not be true that animals have the kind of rationality that many rights theorists consider to be relevant for full moral agency but that is to beg the question about what qualities are required for this. Animals may not be able to communicate through language as effortlessly as humans can but philosophers (Singer, 1993, pp. 114–17) have been impressed by research which indicates that chimpanzees, especially, can understand simple instructions, they have a memory and seem to act from intention. It is clear that something more than sentience is at work here. But is this enough to make the higher animals moral agents? Does the fact of sentience, and the minimal of communicative ability, make these animals moral *persons*, either in the sense that they may be treated as rights holders or entitled to the equal consideration that the utilitarian calculation requires?

The two features that are normally required for these demands to be satisfied are that animals should be capable of having legitimate interests and that they possess autonomy. Raymond Frey, the most sophisticated opponent of animal claims, concedes that they are sentient, and these constrain humans in some (limited) ways, but denies (Frey, 1980) that they have interests in the full sense. They have no interests in plans, purposes or future projects in the way that humans have. This is perhaps a strong claim because animals clearly have an interest *in* not being killed. But it would seem that this interest would not of itself be sufficient to justify compulsory vegetarianism, which is presumably the ultimate aim of animal liberation movements.

Frey is on stronger ground when he argues that animals lack a vital ingredient in moral personhood, and one that has been discussed in this book, and that is *autonomy*. We think of a moral agent as autonomous when she is author her own actions, when no extraneous forces (such as poverty or dependence on others) determine her choices and when she is capable of taking full responsibility for her decisions. It seems absurd to describe even the higher primates of being autonomous in this sense, even though biological research (Singer, 1993, p. 110) suggests that they do exercise some of the main features of an independent life, they form elementary societies with internally recognised hierarchies and may even establish 'property' in some form. However, as Frey (1980) argues, they do not appear to have that *control* over their own destinies that autonomous humans do. Their behaviour seems to be biologically determined for the purpose of survival, and, however efficient their methods may be may be, animals do not display that choice from a variety of futures which human action typically involves.

Perhaps the most persuasive argument for either animal rights or for their incorporation into the utilitarian calculus derives from 'marginal cases' (Garner, 1993, pp. 14–16). It is the claim that since some human beings (mental defectives or very young babies) lack these very qualities, and yet we do not treat them as mere objects for our own convenience, or eliminate them if they are burdensome, but accord them the same features of moral personhood that we grant normal adults, why should we treat animals differently? Is this the classic example of speciesism? In fact, some utilitarian opponents of animal claims, such as Frey (1980, p. 59), are prepared to consign people whose lives are so miserable that they are not worth living to the same category as the higher animals. There is, of course, the conventional utilitarian constraint that unnecessary suffering must be avoided, which also applies to animals as sentient beings, but neither group is awarded any special moral status. Thus the claim for moral consistency is bought at what some people might think is a very high price. The argument about exactly what is a moral person remains uncomfortably indeterminate.

Animal liberationists, as has been noted, are split between rights and utility. Animal rights theorists tend to slip into the 'argument stopping' mode mentioned above; they avoid the sometimes delicate calculations that have to be made on the salient issues by simply asserting that animals have rights not to be treated in certain ways. Thus complex discussions about whether, for example, it is permissible to use animals in experiments which might save many human lives, are simply ruled out by definitional fiat. All we can safely say of animal rights is that, if there are any, they must be of the general or unacquired type, according to Hart's classification quoted earlier in this chapter. For the most enthusiastic animal liberationist would not claim that even the higher primates could make those contracts or agreements which generate what Hart calls special rights. But if they are unacquired rights, or general constraints on the way we treat animals, it is up to the theorists to demonstrate that they do genuinely exist. The elusive search for such a conclusive demonstration tends to distract attention from some of the more tractable features of the debate.

In this context, the arguments of Singer are much more interesting. He is a preference utilitarian in the manner discussed in Chapter 5. The purpose of this form of moral appraisal is to establish conditions by which as many preferences as possible can be satisfied and this approach avoids complex, and probably unanswerable, questions concerning the measurement of pleasures and pains. This enables Singer to avoid the problem presented by the claim often made, that if utility is to be maximised then meat eating is perfectly acceptable, indeed is to be encouraged, since it leads to the breeding and consumption of animals which, under the right conditions, can have short but happy lives. Animals are merely 'receptacles' (Singer, 1993, pp. 120–6) of pleasure and in the absence of meat eating there would be fewer pleasures since few animals would exist, and some species might even die out. However, Singer's preference utilitarianism leads him to say that animals, as moral persons, have intrinsic value; they have biographies just as humans do and have every claim, under the Benthamite 'equal consideration' principle, for inclusion in the utilitarian calculus.

Furthermore, Singer's utilitarianism prevents him slipping onto some of the wilder, implausible claims of the rights theorists. While he is quite open in his admission that a healthy chimpanzee is worth saving, in preference to a human being whose life is of little or no value, he also concedes that it might be permissible to use some animals in experiments which could lead to the cure for some dangerous human illness: although the conditions here are very stringent and might rule out much conventionally acceptable scientific research. Again, Singer regards some animal species as not moral persons (fish, for example) and here the only constraint is that we do not inflict unnecessary suffering. Perhaps these species are mere receptacles. He is a little uncertain about chickens but is severely critical of modern factory farm methods of production; they are totally unacceptable whatever type of utilitarianism we are talking about.

10

Welfare and the Welfare State

1 The origins and rise of welfare theory

The twentieth century has seen a dramatic increase in the role of the state in the social field. In defiance of Marx's claim that the state could act only in the interests of the bourgeoisie, it has expanded its activities in the fields of social security, unemployment benefit, old age pensions, health, education and in many other policy areas which were hitherto left to individuals themselves or, more likely, to those intermediary institutions, such as churches or community and ethnic groups, which stand between persons and the state in the structure of civil society. The property-owning classes seem to have acquiesced in the payment of the redistributive taxes needed to pay for much of this.

The distinguishing feature of these historical earlier welfare arrangements were that they were (and some remain) *voluntary* whereas state actions are typically coercive; whether the favoured policies are delivered through compulsory social insurance or through taxation. Thus philosophical questions immediately arise: what is the rationale for the deprivation of liberty that this involves? Or perhaps it is not a deprivation of liberty at all but an increase in power, in the sense of creating opportunities for individuals to do things they could not otherwise achieve? Furthermore, even if it does increase coercion, is not the diminution in freedom validated by the reduction in inequality that the welfare measures are said to produce? As we shall see, all of these propositions are contestable.

There is a great variety of justificatory principles, ranging from straightforward consequentialism through to egalitarianism and natural rights (as we have seen earlier in relation to rights theory), at work in the case for the welfare state. Indeed, the anti-collectivism of its opponents depends on similar principles. Still, the beginnings of a social welfare philosophy, and a theory that provides an explanation of the concept of welfare and an explicit and principled justification either for or against state involvement in the delivery of whatever is decided to be the welfare 'good', originated in the eighteenth century and the doctrines adduced then were more or less uniformly utilitarian. The historical origins of welfare theory are in the 'Scottish Enlightenment' and it is no coincidence that the idea was derived from the progress that was made in economics, notably by David Hume and Adam Smith, although some of the main elements in this utilitarianism preceded these writers. With the triumph of the 1688 'Revolution' and acceptance of the Whig settlement agreed in the 1690s questions of law, state and political obligation became less pressing and social theorists became very concerned about more mundane things such as individual and social well-being and the conditions felt to be necessary for its promotion.[1] Economics replaced politics on the social agenda and 'republican'[1] ideals of community and the common good were relegated. Most of the concepts used in the original welfare debates are still used today.

The crucial advance in welfare theory occurred with the discovery that human well-being, however defined, was not a function of *deliberate* political action but rather a consequence of the equilibrating properties of free markets, of free international trade, of the division of labour and all of the other social institutions that give rise to the operations of Adam Smith's 'Invisible Hand' (see Barry, N., 1982). Implicit in this was a downplaying of the role of morality. It is not that ethics were absent in the philosophies of Hume and Smith, it is that human well-being was held to depend on motivations, notably self-interest, that were eschewed and condemned by traditional Western (normally Christian) morality. Indeed, in the outrageous 'anti-ethics' of Bernard Mandeville[2] it was specifically claimed that commerce and virtue were antinomies and that if a society wanted economic prosperity it would have to encourage greed and other anti-republican sentiments. With regard to welfare, a subtle use is made today of an argument pioneered by Mandeville. He claimed that the frivolous and wasteful expenditure of the rich actually improved the welfare of the poor, it led to an increase in employment and human well-being; and all without any government involvement at all. This is now known as the 'trickle-down effect' (Barry, N., 1999b, p. 18) of free markets. The basic point is that social welfare cannot be designed by conscious planning but emerges naturally from the free play of individual striving.

In the beginning of welfare theory the phenomenon itself was uncomplicated: it simply meant well-being, satisfaction and contentment and it was held that it was not the responsibility of the state to produce it. It is true that an early rights theorist, Tom Paine (1984), was in favour of a form of welfare rights but this itself was not anti-commercial or socialistic and his belief in welfare was attached to or derived from the normal functioning of market society. But by the end of the nineteenth century social welfare theory became associated with the critique of capitalism. Welfare became connected to redistribution and this was justified in other than classical utilitarian and individualistic terms. People began to conceive of a form of social or public welfare which was not reducible to the sum of private experiences. Welfare ceased to be exclusively connected with utility and although economists[3] continued to write in this language, the 'New Liberals' (see Barry, N., 1999b, ch. 5) of the late nineteenth and early twentieth centuries thought that a strong state could more effectively generate welfare than would the unaided market.

However, it should not be assumed that societies had failed to generate welfare outside the market; there was a developed form of welfare outside the exchange system and the state (Green, D., 1993). Churches, local groups based perhaps on ethnicity and other charitable organisations performed valuable welfare functions independently of these two rival social mechanisms. Since they form part of the intermediate institutions of civil society they have always been admired by critics of the welfare state who would prefer a more localised and voluntary welfare system. But there had always been rudimentary welfare institutions of a public kind in England, this was the Poor Law, which began in Elizabethan times. The Poor Law Amendment Act, which seriously – and controversially – reformed the prevailing system in 1834, introduced practical and conceptual problems which remain to this day (Barry, N., 1999b, ch. 2). But other European countries, and nineteenth-century America, had similar arrangements. The experience of the Poor Law is not of historical interest only for the intellectual debate it aroused has resonance in all welfare arguments and the concepts it spawned remain serviceable for the welfare controversy.

The designers of the 1834 Poor Law Amendment Act (Barry, N., 1999b, pp. 24–8) were Benthamite utilitarians and really did think that utility could be measured in cardinal terms and that interpersonal comparisons were perfectly feasible. They were the first theorists to introduce what are today known as welfare functions as targets for government. The old Poor Law system was condemnable because it was intolerably expensive, just as critics today complain of the current welfare system. In addition, it caused dysfunctional behaviour, notably defection from work, and it upset the normal functioning of the labour market by its subsidy to wages. But the early utilitarians also believed that overall satisfactions would be promoted if some aid were given to the poor; the well-being of the donors (in those days, local ratepayers) was increased if avoidable suffering were eliminated. There was also the fear, which has resurfaced in the twentieth century, that civil disorder would occur if no aid were given to the distressed.

But what was theoretically and practically significant was the discovery by the utilitarians of what is now known as 'moral hazard', the phenomenon of aid to the deprived encouraging the numbers of the deprived group to rise. From the pessimistic assumptions of market economics one would predict that welfare payments cause unemployment and family breakdown by making leisure more attractive than work. The authors of the original Poor Law Report put the matter bluntly: 'Every penny bestowed on the poor and indigent is a bounty on indolence and vice' (Checkland, S. and Checkland, E., 1974, p. 36). Hence the harsh conditions that were imposed on those who were in receipt of Poor Law benefits[4]. Of course, the permanent welfare problem is that attempts to discipline the workshy inevitably involve unpleasant conditions for the genuinely needy, who are in distress through no fault of their own. The intellectual legacy of the nineteenth century was the rigorous theory of human nature on which their policy prescriptions rested.

Questions of social justice, which have little to do with utility, entered the welfare debate as the nineteenth century progressed. The issue was seen not merely as a problem of helping those who would have otherwise not survived but a general concern amongst social philosophers that access to a range of welfare goods and services should be widened; policies that included old age pensions, unemployment insurance and health care were developed. The philosophical debate between individualism and collectivism was reflected in public policy initiatives that went far beyond the Poor Law and, in Britain, old age pensions were introduced (1908) and unemployment insurance (1911). Many of the policy initiatives were derived from Bismarck's social insurance in late-nineteenth-century Germany.

What we now call the 'institutional welfare state' emerged gradually and this system eventually included almost all citizens in social insurance and was not exclusively aimed at the poor. Although these policies now find their justification in communitarianism and egalitarianism they were originally validated by doctrines which derive from liberal economics. A rationale for *social* insurance can be justified from the 'adverse selection' problem of private insurance markets (Barry, N., 1999b, p. 133). This means that only those likely to experience a misfortune – such as unemployment or bad health – would insure against it. Thus, it is said, all the advantages from 'pooling' resources would be lost and private insurance could not survive, or be prohibitively expensive. The extent of adverse selection may have been exaggerated but it certainly provided a justification, within the broad tradition of liberal economics, for the typical welfare institutions and policies. Nevertheless, it was persuasively argued that at the time of the introduction of compulsory social insurance, welfare problems were being adequately handled by the intermediary institutions of civil society, such as friendly societies, churches and trade unions. Thus the voluntary welfare examples show that societies should not be exclusively analysed in terms of atomised individuals, who owe no social duties to anybody apart from the ones that they had contracted into, versus the all-powerful collectivist welfare state which is compulsory for all citizens.

One important change in the meaning of social welfare occurred as the state got more involved with policy initiatives: that is, welfare seen as partly pure redistribution from the rich to the poor, for which many moral reasons can be given, and welfare understood to be a goal of a collective insurance system. The latter interpretation of welfare is crucially important, for as welfare states develop the government begins to nationalise the insurance industry because of adverse selection and this model is not supposed to be directly redistributive; people have paid for their healthcare and their old age pensions through their social insurance contributions and they have genuine entitlements to the benefits. Although this model is not necessarily inconsistent with economic liberalism, historically it has rarely been properly funded, like a proper insurance system, and citizens come to rely on payments for which they have not strictly paid yet to which they have a legal entitlement.

2 Contemporary welfare arguments

The meaning of welfare might seem straightforward but it has become quite complicated. Does it refer to a state of well-being which is measured in terms of satisfactions, perhaps understood in monetary terms only or does it have an ineradicable social aspect? The former understanding would make welfare a purely subjective phenomenon, one which makes voluntary market exchanges the benchmark of satisfactions. But almost all social theorists, apart from extreme libertarians, put qualifications on such subjectivism. Market choice, it is said, must be informed so that the chooser is fully aware of the consequences of her preference. Welfare theorists often imply that ordinary consumers have too high a time preference, that is they value present satisfactions too intensely and do not save for the future. Perhaps it would take an extraordinary high interest rate to persuade them to forgo present consumption and save. That, presumably, is the major justification for compulsory state insurance schemes to pay for health care and old age pensions. The argument for compulsion in welfare would hold even if people were perfectly informed of the consequences of their choices; they might be too myopic to act in such a way that guaranteed their welfare over the long run. In that case the argument for state compulsion in the institutional welfare state is simple paternalism; no government is prepared to see people pay the adverse consequences even of their informed choices. There might even be an argument here for state compulsion from moral hazard: if people realise that they will be helped from society at large if they act short-sightedly they might very well raise their time preferences.

The arguments against subjectivism in welfare have been refined so that nowadays it is claimed that certain needs are *objective*. We have already noticed that some forms of redistribution are justified because such benevolent action is not addressed to satisfy possibly frivolous wants but is aimed at meeting with needs for which the person does not choose to have. Welfare goods are pre-eminently of this type. The demand for health, education, pensions and so on are not mere wants but are essential elements in a reasonable life so that it is rational for them to be supplied via the tax or compulsory social insurance mechanisms. There is certainly some plausibility for this in relation to health since there is clearly the possibility, indeed likelihood, that someone could be in need of medical treatment about which she could be completely unaware. The foundation for the institutional welfare state rests then upon the belief that it is not merely lack of funds that puts people in need of certain kinds of state aid (the traditional classical liberal approach to the welfare problem) but that the familiar social positions that people occupy entitle them to such (see Barry, B., 1990) aid. These positions give rise to objective needs. Thus the unemployed have a claim in justice to redistribution from the employed, the old from the young and those with children from the childless. If the only criterion were lack of a minimum income, which would be met by some sort of residual payment, it is argued that the real costs of being in a certain economic situation, such as those mentioned above, would permanently disadvantage them. In this conception of welfare, a person's well-being is not a function of basic income alone but by a measure that is bound up with the rewards that should go to observable social positions. This is the rationale of collective welfare (Goodin, 1988).

It is a conception of welfare that derives from social philosophies that have dominated mainland Europe for most of this century, and to a very great extent it is that which emerged from the Beveridge 'revolution'[5] in Britain after the last war; though the social insurance foundations of the latter began, as we have noticed, in 1911. It is egalitarian to the extent that it assumes an equal entitlement of all to certain welfare goods. The treatment of disablement is the best example of this approach to welfare; for those unfortunate to suffer from a disability that precludes their full participation in civil society are, in effect, compensated for their unavoidable disadvantage. The welfare they should receive is not something that merely prevents them falling into destitution but is sufficient enough to put them in a position which approximates to that which they would have enjoyed but for their disability. It is an approach which differs considerably from what may be called the Anglo-American attitude to welfare problems which is concerned primarily with the relief of poverty. It concentrates on income as the measure of social deprivation. The system is often referred to as the 'residual welfare state'.

The philosophical predisposition behind the European view is not crudely egalitarian – since presumably income inequalities would remain as long as the welfare imperative to aid the disadvantaged is satisfied – but has obviously much more connection with social justice than does the classical liberal conception of a free society. Like political liberalism in general it is more concerned with the creation of equal liberties than with the maximisation of choice. But its connection with a Rawlsian notion of justice is harder to fathom; indeed, Rawls's imperative to maximise the well-being of the least advantaged seems to bear superficial similarity to this position but in reality it is concerned with redistribution to the poor, as measured in simple income terms. Still, there is no clearly worked social policy in *A Theory of Justice*. If anything the welfare doctrine under consideration seems to have much more in common with the communitarian theory of justice espoused by Walzer (1983), than Rawls's position. Certain goods, and healthcare is an obvious example, ought not to be distributed by the market mechanism precisely because they are special enough to be *shared* by all members of the community and their delivery should in no way depend on income, or even choice. They are not examples of mere wants and having to pay the market price for healthcare might well financially drain an otherwise reasonably well-off family.

Furthermore, such an institutional theory of the welfare state is not concerned with negative liberty. The reduction in choice that natio- nalised welfare produces seems clearly to reduce personal liberty but communitarian welfare theorists would argue that this is too super ficial since the provision of functionally necessary welfare goods and services actually increases freedom all round (Raz, 1986; Gray, 1992). The security that they provide leads to an expansion of freedom as autonomy; the fact that they do not depend on the ability to pay (though they are, of course, financed by tax and social security contributions) means that important obstacles to well-being are removed or overcome. A person cannot be fully autonomous if she is incapable, through lack of resources, of making decisions that reflect her long-term values and purposes. Choices that are made in the absence of the security provided by institutional welfare become responses to immediate events, such as a dire emergency, rather than being conducive to a rational life plan. The apparent reduction in liberty that the welfare state causes is said to be deceptive, since it really creates a form of liberty as 'empowerment'; without resources the individual is at the mercy of, for example, the accidents of the market, the business cycle or any other contingency that might randomly effect people in ways that harm their well-being. Though if freedom is increased by empowerment it is difficult to conceive of any limit to the role of the state in providing welfare in the guise of its promoting liberty. Indeed, the proponents of this view rarely consider market-based solutions, which depend on individual rational choice, to the above problems. The insurance market is the obvious mechan- ism and, although there might be a problem with adverse selection, the disincentives here have been much exaggerated. What the market does is to provide opportunities for experiments in welfare provision.

3 The market and welfare

While economic or classical liberals favour private insurance, they are not indifferent to the problems of the poor. Most, but clearly not all, classical liberals believe that *some* state welfare is justified, though its type is remarkably different from the conventional social democratic view. The first point to make is that economic liberals reject the main features of the institutional welfare state outlined above. They maintain that some public provision for deprivation is possible without the resource allocation process of the market being disrupted; though they are well aware of the moral hazard problem created by too generous welfare arrangements. What is more important is the fact that classical liberals also maintain that such aid to the deprived does not necessarily involve redistribution from rich to poor but can benefit everybody: it is a Pareto improvement.

This looks like an odd claim since much of the argument is addressed precisely to the egalitarian intent, if not practice, of the modern welfare state. But the classical liberal theory here is addressed mainly to one form of welfarism, the compulsory institutional welfare state, to which all individualists are opposed. But if there are altruistic sentiments in a community, a version of welfare could be achieved which does not involve redistribution or the creation of more or less monopoly welfare services. The better off may want to help the poor and would experience an increase in utility were this to happen. Furthermore, a particular form of welfare, cash aid for the deprived, may be made consistent with negative liberty if the compulsory features of the welfare state were wound up and people were allowed to spend their money on goods and services of their choice; those who could not, for financial reasons, survive in the market would receive a cash subsidy to raise their disposable incomes. They would not be compelled to spend this money in any particular way.

Milton Friedman (1962, p. 191) expressed this view when he claimed that:

> I am distressed by the sight of poverty; I am benefited by its alleviation; but I am benefited equally whether I or someone else pays for its alleviation ... we might all be ... be willing to contribute to the relief *provided* everyone else did. We might not be willing to contribute the same amount without such assurance.

In other words, welfare provision is a type of public good, like clean air or national defence; its compulsory nature is a response to market failure or, in this particular case, the assurance problem – that is, uncertainty about other people's behaviour which affects an individual's choice. But it might well be asked: if people care about each other, why is this not expressed through voluntary charity? Indeed, Friedman (1962, p. 190) comments favourably on the significant amount of eleemosynary activity that does take place in capitalist societies. Furthermore, what kind of altruism is it which has to be provided compulsorily? How can coercive taxation be made consistent with a fundamental belief in liberty?

All these questions could be satisfactorily answered if, and only if, welfare were a genuine public good. But one can doubt that it is. After all, one person's generosity does make a difference, albeit small, to the relief of poverty. This is not like pollution, where co-operation is required to eliminate free riders. The logical implication of Friedman's argument is that eleemosynary activity would not occur at all, yet it clearly does. However, a better explanation of benevolence is that people regard such action as the fulfilment of a moral *duty* rather than the production of a public good.

As has been noted (Sugden, 1984; Barry, N., 1995a), Friedman's theory has an odd prediction. Since the important point is that it does not matter who contributes to the alleviation of poverty (the important thing is that poverty is relieved), it would imply that, if people knew that the income from a charity is about to fall, they would contribute more as their income rose, subject only to the constraint that their original consumption of private goods remained the same. It is only the assurance problem that prevents this happening. Yet it is difficult to imagine that it is this alone which prevents charitable donations. It is much more plausible to suppose that it is the charitable impulse itself which is weak. People would not give all of their extra income if it were needed to supplement the charity's income, though they might well give some. It would follow from Friedman's theory that the converse should hold, that people would give less to the charity if they knew that others were giving more. But, again, it is unlikely that a person's charitable motivations are influenced directly by what other people are doing. It is a question of moral duty and the motivation to be moral is not a function of other people's behaviour.

It is true that people's benevolence may be influenced by some extraneous forces – for example, voluntary donations tend to be higher the lower the tax rate and people probably do give a little more as their incomes rise. But it is unlikely that there are sufficient altruistic motivations to generate even the minimum level of income that Friedman himself would be prepared to tolerate. The point is that, with regard to public policy, the demands of welfare conflict with the demands of liberty (in this case the freedom to spend as much as possible of one's own income), and there can be no overriding principle that can adjudicate between these two competing moral imperatives. As a classical liberal Friedman is confident that the liberty principle should take precedence.

This is, of course, why he rejects all features of the institutional welfare state. He is against any form of paternalism so that even those in receipt of welfare should be permitted to spend it as they wish. He is not at all worried that they might not invest in pensions, healthcare insurance, education and so on. His view is that the problem of poverty is lack of cash, not the inability of people to spend their income wisely; and that moral imperative would hold irrespective of any efficiency problems that may or may not occur with the public delivery of the conventional welfare goods.

However, it would not necessarily be inconsistent with economic liberalism to put restrictions on what welfare beneficiaries can do with their money. Should not the donors, the taxpayers, have some influence on how their money is spent? The use of a mild compulsion here does not represent a complete loss of liberty, like a direct command or a system of the direction of labour, since people only have to obey orders if they take advantage of the welfare system. It seems that some mild restriction on what recipients of welfare do with their money is not at odds with the main features of a free society. It would make the donors better-off.

Still, there is a further foundational problem with the classical liberal theory of welfare. If the supply of welfare is to be in cash (in Friedman's case through the operation of the Negative Income Tax), how much money should that be? Should it be limited to the avoidance of destitution alone, in which case it would be quite low even in a rich society, or should it be fixed relative to the wealth of a community? If it is the latter it might well generate the problem of moral hazard, which already happens in the richer Western societies. In any case, in the vote-maximising processes of a democratic society, the Negative Income Tax is quite likely to be bid up.

But not all classical liberal and conservative critics of the welfare state follow Friedman. Many of them are worried by the behavioural problems associated with it. Most of these writers are very much concerned with the moral hazards caused by excessive welfare payments. Charles Murray (1984), although remaining a classical liberal, produced a penetrating study of the American welfare state which indicated that serious social dysfunctioning occurred through easily obtainable welfare. Although poverty was technically reduced in the 1960s and 1970s, this masked a great increase in 'latent poverty' (Murray, 1984, ch. 4), that is, the poverty that would increase were it not for the extensive welfare services and cash payments that became available in President Johnson's 'Great Society' reforms (see Barry, N., 1987, ch. 6). Marital breakdown increased, as did defection from work. In an implicit critique of Friedman, Murray argued (1984, ch. 11) that evidence indicated that in two American cities where a version of the Negative Income Tax had been tried the problems of dysfunctional behaviour were worst of all.

Still, Murray remains broadly in the classical liberal tradition. He believes that most of the welfare problems would be solved if the welfare state, in its present form, were to be dissolved. He thinks, almost in a deterministic manner, that good behaviour would be produced by the correct incentive structures. The more conservative critics of welfare are not so optimistic and maintain that people do not behave so mechanistically. Lawrence Mead (1986) maintains that the size of the welfare state is not the major problem; the difficulties that emerge stem from an almost permanent change in attitudes that the prevailing form of welfare form has produced. In a later work (Mead, 1992, ch. 4) said he could find little evidence that dysfunctional behaviour was positively correlated with declines in the value of welfare, which actually occurred in the US in the late 1970s.[6] The problem with the welfare state, Mead claims, is that in the US, it was grafted on to a society which was already characterised by a great deal of liberty. America does not demand a great deal of its citizens, beyond obedience to law and a basic loyalty to the flag. But this liberal state of affairs, with the minimum of social duty, proved to be disastrous in the context of a generous welfare system. People have become, Mead maintains, recipients of generous welfare and owed no duty to society, in terms of good behaviour in return. The welfare predicament that faces America, Mead maintains, cannot be resolved by liberty but by a mild form of coercion: 'The solution to the work problem lies not in freedom but in governance' (1992, p. 81). There could not be a greater contrast between Friedman's optimism about people's capacities and Mead's pessimism regarding human nature.

Undoubtedly, this approach has great resonance with conservatives who can talk of a decline in social standards brought about by a welfare system which demands little in the way of reciprocity: the welfare beneficiaries therefore are almost automatically tempted into dysfunctional behaviour. This is why Mead (1992, ch. 4) favours 'workfare'; a system which requires that welfare recipients perform some service, in the public sector if the private sector cannot create enough jobs to absorb the unemployed.[7] Mead concedes that such schemes may be costly but his solution to the welfare problem does not turn on efficiency but on the enforcement methods which equip welfare claimants for civil society. Both Mead and Murray are worried about the rise in unmarried motherhood in the United States; and there is evidence that a similar phenomenon is happening in Britain (Murray, 1996).

Perhaps this is less of a problem in European Union countries were citizens are in more comprehensive, though costly, social insurance systems. For example, Sweden, the most socialist of the European welfare states, has always had a workfare scheme. It is the case that behavioural difficulties tend to be more a feature of countries like Britain and the US that have welfare systems which depend more on residual payments to the poor than on arrangements which integrate people more fully into civil society. It is often claimed that residual welfare states reproduce the anonymity of the market, and indeed its egoism, in the welfare world, where it is clearly more harmful. The more communitarian welfare systems produce that social discipline which appears to be absent in the more libertarian regimes.

However, the more conservative critics of the welfare state argue that in whatever form it takes, it replaces genuine voluntary and local action, which is directed toward the relief of poverty, by vast, bureaucratic and impersonal administrations. As Nathan Glazer (1988, p. 7) said: '... every piece of social policy substitutes for some traditional arrangement ... in which public authorities take over, at least in part, the role of the family, of the ethnic and neighbourhood group, of voluntary associations'. It is true that welfarism in its statist form in effect captured whole areas of social life which in earlier times had been dealt with by spontaneous, self-governing processes. Social insurance, which was introduced in Britain in 1911, simply replicated the roles of friendly societies and trade unions, with all the disadvantages of centralised bureaucracy which that entails. The relief of poverty was often left to voluntary bodies.

These arrangements are genuinely communitarian in that they rely exclusively on ethnic groups, religious bodies and other non-state organisations to deliver the welfare good. It is much easier for them to prevent the emergence of moral hazard. They have the local and tacit knowledge to distinguish genuine claimants for welfare relief from opportunists and 'free riders'. Furthermore, they are less prone to rent-seeking by their employees: those who work in state bureaucratic welfare systems have every incentive to expand them. Unfortunately, orthodox communitarians look to the state to care for the unfortunate victims of market society. The exchange system may be cold and impersonal but there is little evidence that centralised government is any the less soulless.

4 Equality, liberty and the welfare state

The rise of welfarism and the welfare state has undoubtedly led to a re-examination of some traditional concepts used in political theory. The welfare idea itself originally came from economics, especially that associated with the rise of market society in the eighteenth century and the original justification for welfare lay entirely in utilitarianism; the market was valued because it maximised aggregate welfare but, as we have seen, it might occasionally fail. What is important here is that the production of welfare is entirely a consequence of our normal, self-interested motivations. It is the natural and unplanned outcome of the market. The followers of Bentham (and originally Mandeville) had little interest in distributive questions, or in changing human nature; although these two features would not be true of John Stuart Mill's brand of utilitarianism.[8]

But by the end of the twentieth century welfare had become more associated with justice and equality. Furthermore, the welfare state was understood to be quite consistent with liberty. This last point seems paradoxical given its foundation in paternalistic, indeed coercive, governmental activity. It is, of course, true that no social democracy has ever actually forbidden the private consumption of the traditional welfare goods but their supply is made difficult, and subject to intense state regulation; and if a person still chooses to go private he is, in effect, paying twice.

From a pluralist point of view this loss in negative liberty can be compensated by another principle, or complex of principles. The favoured ones are, naturally, social justice and equality. A loss in liberty could be tolerated if it led to an increase in overall welfare or if it were the unavoidable outcome of efforts to maximise the principles of a fair society. Since, on utilitarian grounds, it has been shown to be impossible to beat the market in the production of aggregate welfare, the emphasis by socialists now is on the promotion of social justice, equality and general virtue through state welfare. It is legitimate to sacrifice freedom in the pursuit of these goals, which are primarily redistributive. Also, it is claimed that a welfare society promotes communal and non-egoistic values.

The original advocates of state welfare really did believe that the establishment of a welfare society would bring about a change in human nature, that the self-interested striving of market participants would be replaced by more altruistic and less individualistic citizens if they shared common goods and services. They have resisted the 'privatisation' of welfare programmes precisely because they feared that the penetration of society by the commercial ethic would undermine our altruistic and communitarian sentiments. This claim was vividly illustrated by a debate that took place in the 1970s and 1980s over the supply of blood. Some economists had argued that if blood were priced by the market its supply would automatically be increased so that 'excess' demand would not be a problem. The opponents claimed that voluntary donations would be sufficient for human needs (although it was pointed out by market theorists that under a donor system the supply was not quite voluntary since much-needed blood was taken from prisoners). Although the argument was partly empirical, in that rival claims were made about the efficiency properties of the pricing system and the donor system, it was really philosophical: the opponents of the pricing of blood were dismayed that so precious a commodity should depend on the self-interested motivations of, in effect, market traders (Titmuss, 1970).

There is some evidence on both sides of the argument; voluntary donations of blood have been known to decline once people are aware of the fact that it is being priced. And there are other examples of good or virtuous motivations being 'crowded out' (Frey, B., 1996) by the presence of market incentive structures. According to the anti-market welfare theorist, R. M. Titmuss, the obligation we have to give blood is a 'gift to a stranger' which in no way depends on price or even on reciprocity; the conservative doctrine which regards people as being held together in a series of mutual pacts, in which a person's generosity is rewarded by similar acts of his fellow citizens. The claim of Titmuss is that the welfare state is underpinned by pure altruism, which is very different from reciprocity.

Still, the rather specialised examples of the flourishing of altruistic motivations are not sufficient to found a welfare state, which is normally based on mild coercion. Indeed, there is ample evidence that the Mandevillian impulse is dominant across all the standard areas of the welfare state. It has been revealed by significant research that the middle classes exploit the welfare state. Although the standard services it supplies in kind, such as health and education, are supposed to be equally available for all citizens, the middle classes consume them disproportionately. For instance, the National Health Service in Britain is supposedly founded on egalitarian principles, yet it is not equally available to all. As Julian Le Grand (1982) has shown, the better-off visit their doctors more frequently than the poor and generally enjoy better health. As we have noticed, this phenomenon is explained by a simple economic principle – opportunity cost. Poorer people have to give up more in terms of wages when they visit the doctor than do the normally salaried middle class. With almost zero priced higher education higher the differences in consumption are even more startling. Obviously it is more likely that children from poorer backgrounds will leave school early to take up paid employment, while richer families will be in less need of an extra income. As Le Grand (1982, p. 46) says: 'Policies involving subsidies whose distribution is dependent on peoples' decision to consume the good or use the service favour the better off'. He thinks that the only way to achieve more equality is through straightforward cash redistribution because that precludes the better off from beneficial participation (Goodin and Le Grand, 1987) in the welfare schemes. Yet such a cash redistributive policy defeats the major object of the institutional welfare state.[9]

If there is then serious doubt about the propensity of welfare states to produce equality there is less doubt about their tendency to reduce liberty, unless that concept is defined in counter intuitive ways. Supporters of collective welfare provision either have an overt paternalist attitude which doubts the capacity of individuals to make rational choices or they resent the inequalities that private provision generates (which are likely to be greater than those produced by collectivist schemes). Furthermore, there is an increasing dispute over the efficiency properties of the welfare states, in the sense of their ability to produce, by the political mechanism what people actually want. If we take two areas of welfare, healthcare and pensions, we can see the rival principles at work.

There are two competing methods of producing a health system; private insurance (or even direct payment 'over the counter') and collective delivery via social insurance, with 'rights' to treatment irrespective of ability to pay (Robinson, R., 1990). In practice they both tend to suffer from deficiencies: oversupply in the part of the private insurance system (as well as the problem of the uninsurable) and undersupply by the public or collective method of delivery. In the US about 14 per cent of GDP is spent on health while in Britain it is only 6.5 per cent. In continental Europe it is a little higher than in Britain, for, although it is mainly publicly provided, there are no quasi-monopoly suppliers equivalent to the National Health Service.

The major political and economic arguments for socialised medicine arise out of the alleged failure of the market (Barry, N., 1999b, ch. 4). Although healthcare is clearly not a technical public good it has certain features that make it amenable to state corrective action. There is supposed to be an imbalance of knowledge between doctor and patient which might lead to the medical profession deceiving the helpless patient about her true needs. Again, once a patient has paid his insurance premium he has every incentive to demand more, and perhaps unnecessary, healthcare (which the medical profession has every incentive to supply) since the marginal cost to him will be zero. However, the patients are in a dilemma, each one has no incentive to curtail his demands since he has no assurance that others will be so prudent. All this produces an increase in the price of health insurance premiums which prices poorer people out of the market. A further factor that raises costs in insurance-based systems is litigation. America is a liberal and a highly litigious society and expensive malpractice suits may well be an important factor in rising health costs.

This facts may explain health costs in the US and they could be seen as further examples of market failure; but this may be too rapid a conclusion. It may be the case that people in the US actually want to spend more on health. Even though infant mortality rates and longevity data are pretty much similar in Britain and the US, when it comes to the quality of ancillary services and speed of treatment American citizens enjoy a much better service than the British do. They are prepared to pay for it. Anyway, insurance companies have become better at monitoring health care over the years and, furthermore, a variety of different models of private healthcare have been developed which significantly curtail increases in costs.[10]

Nationalised welfare systems suffer from the fact that the political mechanism is not as good as the market at transmitting people's wants for things such as healthcare. The vote motive (see below, Chapter 11) drives politicians to underestimate (rationally) people's wants and despite the adverse publicity that is generated by well-advertised problems of underfunding, the political mechanism is slower to respond to them than the market is. In fact, if any good or service is delivered at effectively zero price the demand will be infinite; rapid technological progress will only exacerbate the problem. Thus healthcare will have to be rationed, either by price, as in a market system, or by administrative decisions, as now is the case in public systems. And as we have already seen, the original aim of equal consumption has not been achieved not only because of the significance of opportunity costs but also because of the fact that the better off are able to manipulate the system to their own advantage. The similar social background of both doctors and middle-class patients enables them to 'jump queues'.

The most severe problem that awaits maturing welfare states is that of pensions (see Barry, N., 1985), which has been exacerbated by a declining birthrate and improvements in medicine which have enabled people to live much longer. In theory, there should be no problem of market failure here; pensions are simply deferred wages and the amount people save should depend only on their time preferences (the rate at which they discount the future). People with a high time preference do not care too much about their retirement and prefer to spend now rather than save. Those with low time preferences value the future greatly and therefore will save (though how much will, of course, also depend on the rate of interest). As we get older, we all tend to lower our time preferences. But problems arise in nationalised pensions schemes over intergenerational injustice, which occurs because sometimes one generation has to pay the pension costs of an earlier one.

Presumably the original justification for state provision of pensions derived from paternalism: governments did not trust individuals to save for their future and rather than governments having to face a catastrophic welfare bill from the aged, people were compelled to save during their working lives. This is normally done through various forms of social insurance (British help for the aged began in 1908 as a pure welfare and redistributive scheme but the policy was later incorporated into the national insurance system). Now if certain facts about the social world could be known with certainty and were repeatable, a nationalised pension system would be feasible. These facts include a stable and predictable rate of economic growth, virtually unchanging deathrates and constant birthrates. Then a pension could be paid as a transfer between the working and the retired populations with no problems of intergenerational injustice.

However, the difficulties arise because these certainties do not exist: economic growth varies, birthrates tend to decline in prosperous countries and longevity increases through improved medicine. In a purely private system workers would save in a fund which would generate enough income for their retirement. The problems of a declining birthrate would be catered for in the market by a deepening of the capital structure; the shortfall in workers which may occur produces a more capital intensive economy. Workers would directly own their own savings for retirement and if governments were really worried about people having too high time preferences, they could compel them to make some saving without actually taking part in the process itself; just as they compel drivers to insure without being involved in the insurance business.

However, with some rare exceptions,[11] governments have not done this but have incorporated pensions into compulsory social insurance schemes. Worst of all, they have not rationally planned the system. It should be self-financing like a regular private pension scheme but governments have financed their pensions obligations by the 'pay as you go' method. This means that pensions are paid for by the current working generation to the elderly and a hypothetical 'contract' between the generations is legislated which authorises the taking of current workers' contributions on the implicit promise that they will be cared for by the next generation when they retire. The problem is that the facts mentioned above, which are necessary for a viable state scheme, do not hold. What has happened in Western countries is that longevity has significantly increased while the birthrate has fallen. Since the pension schemes are not properly funded, one generation will have to pay for the pensions of the current retirees with no guarantee that its members will be so rewarded when they retire. In fact, if most peoples' social security contributions in the US had been invested in the stock market, they would have been assured of a much greater return than the value of their state (federal) pensions. In fact, the paternalistic justification for state pensions is invalid. It is governments, not individuals, that have too high time preferences, they spend the social security income on other public projects and do not build up a proper fund. This is why all Western countries, with the possible exception of Britain which reformed its system in 1986,[12] face a potential pensions catastrophe in the twenty first century.

From a political theorist's point of view, what can be made of the 'contract between the generations'? It is certainly true that in less well-developed countries young people assume without thinking about it that they will look after their parents in their old age. It is a moral duty. The contract may be implicit rather than explicit, but it is no less binding for that reason. However, in the highly mobile and increasingly anonymous industrial societies of the West, such intergenerational obligations are unlikely to be self-enforcing and the idea that there was ever an implicit contract looks increasingly implausible; especially so for the generation which turns out to be the victim of the whole system. Rawls's abstract contracting model is no help (Barry, N., 1985). People behind the veil of ignorance are risk-averse (or at least they do not know their attitude to risk, which will impel them to be ultra-cautious); they would not sign a contract which left them with the slightest possibility of being in the one generation that gets burdened with the pensions bill from an unfunded scheme.

There would not be such an intellectual or moral problem if the aged, as a class, were the poorest in society. The welfare given to them could be treated as a pure welfare transfer, justified, perhaps, on grounds of need. But, especially in America, they are not the most impecunious members of society in *need* of welfare but are a group which thinks it has an entitlement through a lifetime's payment to a fund. Which in a legal sense it has, though not in an economic sense since in most welfare states the retired receive more than they have put into the system. Even in Britain, while it is true that a fraction of the aged in society is in the greatest need, it is not true of the aged as a whole, most of whom have built up assets over a lifetime's earnings (Barry, N., 1993, pp. 260–3). The poorest are the minority who depend exclusively on the meagre basic state pension.

11
The Public Interest and Democracy

1 The Public Interest

One of the most pressing and theoretical problems of modern politics is that of devising procedures and institutions by which collective interests may be advanced. At one time it was argued that 'democracy' would be adequate for this since it was thought to be, in principle at least, a system in which the 'people', as opposed to an irresponsible minority, ruled. However, theory and experience indicate that there is no *necessary* connection between democratic procedures and the advancement of common interests. Not only is there the problem of the oppression of minorities under a democracy, but the likelihood also exists that the system encourages the pursuit of sectional and group interests to the ultimate destruction of the public interest. Before this can be considered, however, an understanding of the concepts of public interest and democracy is required.

The concept of the public interest can be interpreted not too inaccurately as a contemporary version of those 'aggregative' concepts, such as the 'common good' and the 'general will', which are found in traditional political thought. These concepts are now to some extent discredited, mainly because they elevate aggregates such as the 'group', the 'community' and 'society' to a position where they stand for 'higher' values than those of individuals. These metaphysical entities are thought to represent the 'true' or 'real' purposes of individuals and, indeed, many writers have claimed that the influence of these notions was responsible for the oppression of individuals and minorities by collective organisations in the twentieth century. Classical advocates of the doctrine of the public interest, however, argue that the concept describes the *shared* interests of a community and that its promotion, so far from oppressing individual interests, actually enables individuals to secure advantages which they could not otherwise enjoy. The existence of 'government' itself is justified on these grounds. Statements about the public interest can then in some views be firmly anchored in the methodological individualist's framework.

Nevertheless, as we shall see below, it is not the case that all meaningful statements about the public interest are interpreted in this rigorously individualistic way. Some writers suggest that there are policies that do advance the interests of the public but that these cannot be derived from the abstract choices of individuals, and indeed are often imposed against some private interests; they are implemented by suitably *disinterested* governments that are aware of the collective welfare of the community taken as a whole. This dichotomy has important political implications for it indicates that the classical liberal individualist concentrates on the design of special institutions and procedures (in effect, constitutions) that encourage people to maximise their shared interests in some public activity while, in contrast, the non-individualist believes that utilitarian legislators (benevolent dictators?) or ideal observers *ought* to pursue this task. However, both approaches would deny that the concept of the public interest is *necessarily* essentially contested, that its meaning is a matter of intractable dispute, and that its invocation has no relevance for public policy.

Nevertheless, the concept is not without its critics. Political theorists of an emotivist frame of mind still maintain that the concept has no 'operational' meaning, that is, there is no such thing as the 'public' which can be said meaningfully to have an 'interest', and that the concept is used emotively to add honorific overtones to policies which are, in reality, merely to the advantage of individual or private group interests. In this view, to say that 'policy x is in the public interest' is logically equivalent to saying 'I approve of x.'[1] This charge has particular force in modern democracies where strategically placed pressure groups almost invariably attempt to legitimise their sectional claims in terms of the public interest.

It does not follow from this, however, that appeals to the public interest are devoid of meaning. Also, it is important to note that the refutation of the normative aspect of the concept does not depend solely upon a demonstration of its supposed non-existence in an empirical sense. It is logically possible that a proposed policy is in the public interest but that it ought not to be promoted – perhaps because the advantages it has for the 'public' are accompanied by some undesirable consequence. Yet all too often political argument is impoverished by the assertion that the concept is either operationally meaningless, or that its implementation involves highly controversial assumptions about people's 'true' or 'best' interests.

Following Brian Barry we can say that something, for example a policy or a law, is in a person's interest 'if it increases his opportunity to get what he wants – whatever that may be' (1967b, p. 115). Thus 'interests' are means towards the attainment of ends; something is in a person's interests when it enables him to satisfy future wants. Interests are therefore distinct from wants. A person can be mistaken about his interests in that something that he thinks may advance want-satisfaction may turn out under analysis not to do so. Whereas it would be an example of *moralism* to tell a person that his wants are mistaken, as when people are told that they *ought* not to spend their incomes in certain 'undesirable' ways, this is not the case with interests. People hire experts to handle their interests, and this can only mean that by so doing they hope to put themselves in a better position to satisfy their own subjectively determined future wants.

It does not follow from this apparent self-denying ordinance about personal ends or wants, however, that the political theorist is completely disqualified from commenting on their plausibility. Individuals, as purely self-interested maximisers, or as members of the public, may want things that are simply infeasible or mutually incompatible (see Oppenheim, 1981, p. 126). For example, the public, in some form or other may express a 'want' for full employment *and* zero inflation, or for maximising economic output *and* an equal distribution of income and wealth; yet the empirical and theoretical arguments that these policies are incoherent are surely compelling. Nevertheless, that still leaves a very wide range of subjectively determined wants which the (broadly) liberal political theorist has to accept as 'given'.

While it is easy to see how a policy may advance an individual's private interests, it is not so clear that a policy can unambiguously be said to advance the public interest without invoking a metaphysical, organic notion of the 'public'. In fact, further analysis shows that this is quite possible, for there are interests which individuals share as *members of the public* which cannot be promoted except through some kind of public decision-making procedure. We saw this in Chapter 3 in the discussion of public goods. A person increases his opportunities to satisfy his wants when certain things are provided publicly because they would not be provided at all, or perhaps underprovided, through a system of purely private transactions.

It should be clear what the word 'public' means. 'Public' is always contrasted with 'private', so that when we say that the public is affected by an act we mean those 'non-assignable' persons who in various situations cannot be defined as private individuals or as members of private groups (Barry, B. 1965, pp. 190–2). Thus in a rail strike the public consists of those persons adversely affected by the actions of the members of a private group, the railwaymen's union. A public park is so called because it is available to *anyone* indiscriminately. It is obvious, therefore, that the composition of the public will vary from issue to issue, and that individuals will find themselves sometimes as members of the public and at other times as members of the groups opposed to the public. The difficulty is that in many policy disputes an individual may find that he has interests both as a member of the public and as a member of an organised group smaller than the public, and it is not always clear whether his *net* interests lie with the policy that affects him as a member of the public or that which affects him as a member of the group. Only rarely, for example, in the case of the *existence* of law and government, can it be more or less unambiguously said that an individual's private and public interests are identical.

Furthermore, without some sort of formalised constitutional procedure there is normally no incentive for individuals to promote policies that advance their interests as members of the public. In the absence of sanctions it will always be in the interests of an individual to renege on an agreement to pay her share of a publicly provided benefit since, from her point of view, her not paying can make little or no difference to its supply. For libertarian political economists this is the primary justification for the state, but the reasoning is applicable to any group containing large numbers (Olson, 1965).

The English utilitarians were very much aware of the problems of the public interest and tried to solve them with the conventional utilitarian calculus. Proceeding from an individualistic framework, Bentham argued that the community is a 'fictitious body, composed of the individual persons who are considered as constituting as it were its members. The interest of the community then is, what? – the sum of the interests of the several members who compose it' (Bentham, 1970, p. 12). The utilitarians had a strong sense of the public interest, that is, they assumed that there was a wide range of public policies which were prevented from being implemented by the existence of 'sinister interests', mainly the aristocracy and the unenlightened. Unfortunately, this 'class' was in control of the political system of nineteenth-century

Britain and therefore prevented the advancement of the community's interests. An example was the ability of the aristocracy, through its control of the unreformed Parliament, to retain the Corn Laws: protective legislation which prevented the import of foreign wheat until the home supply reached a certain price. Since the aristocracy owned the land on which the corn was grown, their rent (that is 'unearned income') was automatically increased because of the protection. Employers and employees, of course, had a common interest in cheap food. The problem for utilitarians, therefore, was to ensure that public and not sinister interests were maximised (their proposed solution will be considered later in this chapter).

The difficulty with all this is the familiar one of deriving a collective judgement from individual preferences. Since there is no objective measuring rod of pleasure, any aggregate result of a utilitarian calculation must, in a logical sense, be quite subjective. Since individual interests are almost certain to be in conflict, the definition of the public interest as a 'sum' of interests is incoherent. As we have seen, the public interest is only meaningful in the context of the evaluation of policies which affect individuals in their capacity as members of the public and it cannot be simply computed from their private interests. This makes it logically possible to say that there can be a public interest while at the same time individuals and groups may have an interest in opposing it. Examples of public or common interests that exist in a reasonably stable and integrated community are those that people have in a common system of law, defence against external aggression and the whole range of public goods that was discussed in Chapter 3.

A way of getting over the problem of identifying what the public interest is in public policy problems might be to ask a different question: is a particular proposal *against* the public interest? Thus in British takeover law the initiator of an acquisition or merger does not have to show that it will benefit everybody (it is quite likely that it will cause some harm in the form of job displacement) but only that it will not adversely affect the public by, say, creating a monopoly or restricting competition in some other way (see Barry, N., 1991, ch. 4). But this approach would be too feeble for communitarians who argue that in such processes the shared values of particular groups in society are subordinated to the profit motive. The fact that beneficiaries of efficient market methods are the 'anonymous' members of the public, and those temporarily harmed are easily identifiable, means that communitarianism is at a great moral advantage. For these and other reasons, there is likely to be a conflict between market efficiency and the non-individualistic values of social harmony and non-economic co-operation.

An example of the failure to analyse carefully the relationship between public and group interests comes from the 'pluralists' and this failure leads them to eliminate mistakenly the public interest from their political vocabulary. The sociological pluralists, or group theorists of politics, are sceptical of the applicability of the public interest to political and social affairs. They argue that it has no use in empirical work in that there is no such thing as a public interest, beyond the minimal notion of a 'consensus' about fundamental values which every stable society must have, and that in normative political argument it cannot function as a standard for the appraisal of policies. The interesting thing about pluralism is that not only do some of its adherents describe politics as a process of conflict between groups but they also go on to recommend that 'politics' itself, where this means both the voting system in a democracy and the negotiation and bargaining that takes place between organised groups at the stage of policy-formation, ought to be valued as a decision-making process. As long as the decisions made in a community reflect the relative strength and importance of groups then stability, freedom and efficiency are likely to be better promoted by a regime characterised by 'politics' than, say, a liberal market economy or a full-blooded socialist system. In this argument there can be no public interest, only group interests: the crucial point that an individual may evaluate a policy from her position as a member of the public *and* as a member of a group is lost.

It is easy, however, to show that the persistent pursuit of group interests through the political process leads to a reduction of freedom and efficiency and a failure to promote genuine shared interests, so that each individual member of the community is worse off than he would have been without 'politics'. As Mancur Olson puts it:

It does not follow that the results of pressure group activity would be harmless, much less desirable, even if the balance of power equilibrium resulting from the multiplicity of pressure groups kept any one pressure group from getting out of line. Even if such a pressure group system worked with perfect *fairness* to every group, it would still tend to work inefficiently. (Olson, 1965, p. 124)

It is important to remember that unlimited pressure group activity may produce results that are favourable to the members of a group but which are unfavourable to *society as a whole*, to which, of course, each group member belongs. To illustrate this simple but often misunderstood point we can take the case of protectionism (see Barry, N. 1995b, pp. 77–9). Now from the point of view of the consumer and society as a whole, it is clear that free trade between nations is the optimal economic policy since citizens gain from the efficiencies brought about by the international division of labour. However, from the point of view of any single producer group it would be better if its products were protected by tariffs from foreign competition while all other goods were allowed to come in freely. But for a government to protect merely one group would be bad politics, leaving aside the question of fairness, since it would presumably mean ignoring other groups equally essential for the welfare of the community. Yet to satisfy all the groups by protective measures would make society as a whole, that is to say, the group members taken individually, worse off than they would be under free trade.

There is another area of contemporary importance which involves an application of the public interest yet it has received little attention from political theorists. This is the problem of the rapid depletion of scarce resources. While each individual has an interest as a member of the public in the conservation of certain vital resources, she does not have any incentive to contribute to this by her actions as a private citizen, since these can have only a negligible effect on the determination of economic events. The two solutions to this problem are the reformulated classical liberal position that only a wider use of the price mechanism and a redefinition of property rights can bring a movement towards a harmony between individual and public interests; and the interventionist arguments that centralised planning by government is required in order to maximise the public interest.

Classical liberals argue that the price system automatically conserves resources since as a good becomes more scarce its price will rise; this naturally 'rations' its use and also stimulates the search for new supplies or close substitutes. All this may seem obvious enough, but what is interesting is the incorporation of a theory of property rights into the argument. It is argued that the price mechanism will not generate the public interest if property rights are inadequately defined. If a system of property rights does not include the right to exclude people from the use of a resource then wasteful consumption will become endemic and a rational allocation of resources will not emerge, the community as a whole being worse off.

Three types of rights are delineated: communal, state and private[2]. A communal right to use a resource exists when any person in the community is entitled to use some resource without restriction. This resource might be a common piece of land, the produce of which is available to all indiscriminately. This will, under certain conditions, lead to overuse and what is called the 'tragedy of the commons'. Since communal rights do not exclude anyone from the use of the resource we can expect the rapid depletion of the game and stock of common lands, so making everybody worse off in the long run. Only if rights to restrict the use of property develop will this be prevented. A developed property rights system may give the state, through its officials, the right to exclude, or this may accrue to individuals through a system of private ownership.

The classic example of how the 'tragedy of the commons' was averted by the development of property rights is that of Indian tribes whose members habitually hunted animals only for their immediate needs; the existence of communal rights to the stock did not therefore bring about its depletion (Demsetz, 1967, pp. 350–3). However, the advent of the fur trade meant that there was a much greater use of the stock: had the system of communal rights remained, no individual would have had any incentive to economise and the animal resources would have been quickly depleted. Fortunately, a system of property rights developed which included the right to exclude so that stocks could be conserved despite the change in their use brought about by the fur trade. However, such a development did not occur in other tribes, which accordingly suffered a depletion of stock.

Present-day economic liberals have applied this concept of property rights to a number of areas such as pollution, the preservation of fisheries, and the continuing struggle to prevent 'desertification' in Africa (Burton, 1978, pp. 84–8). Not surprisingly they stress the advantages of a system of private property rights over a state system. The argument is that individuals have a greater incentive to be informed about economic conditions than the officials of the state and that the market is a better restraint on the squandering of resources than is the political system (which is what the public officials are accountable to). There is also the not inconsiderable point that economic liberals claim that state action is an inherent threat to liberty.

While this approach still retains a concept of the public interest, and shows how a public interest may exist even when groups and individuals appear to be in conflict with it, it is a somewhat limited conception. The idea seems to be that people have a common interest only in relation to rules and that the potential conflict between an individual's private and public interests can be resolved if institutions are designed which give individuals an incentive to promote their shared interests. What is excluded is the idea that governments ought to be permitted to promote the public interest where this exceeds their traditional function of enforcing general rules. This follows from the psychological premises of economic liberals; they assume that the officials of state, if not bound by strict rules, will maximise their own interests rather than those of the public.

Other writers, however, take a less gloomy view of government and argue that under classical liberalism many policies which are in the public interest would not get promoted at all because the requirements for that system are quite strict (the details of various procedural schemes will be discussed later in this chapter). Many schemes to do with welfare, the environment, the arts and so on, which might be said in some sense to be in the public interest, in that an individual's interests as a member of the public would be advanced if they were implemented, would fail under a system of strictly limited government since they would always find some opposition[3]. In modern societies it is difficult for such shared interests to be organised, compared to private interests, and therefore those who favour a more expansive concept of the public interest maintain that only the state can promote it.

It is here that we get a genuine political argument over the public interest: one side, the individualist or classical liberal, interprets it in a narrow sense while opponents have a more expansive view in mind. The difference really depends on the notion of how interests are to be interpreted. For the individualist, expressions about the public interest must be ultimately reducible to the subjective choices of individuals (see Barry, N., 1984, pp. 584–5). Thus, the justification for a policy being in the public interest is not strictly speaking utilitarian, at least in the sense in which that doctrine involves the construction of a utility function via the adding and comparing of utilities, but rather that it is that policy which people would *choose* (especially in relation to the supply of the conventional public goods). This does not preclude policies being enacted for the public which meet with some opposition from private interests being legitimate. They would be so if the procedure itself had more or less unanimous support. It is argued that over a range of issues individuals would be unlikely to find their preferences thwarted regularly.

Oppenheim denies that statements about the public interest are always reducible to statements about individual preferences. He claims that 'a policy, to be in the public interest, must promote the welfare of the public as a whole rather than the personal welfare of each, or any of its members' (Oppenheim, 1981, p. 132). The public interest is what would emerge if people acted benevolently, rationally and disinterestedly. Thus something can clearly be in the public interest, from a utilitarian point of view, even if it does not emanate from some collective choice procedure (a process which is assumed to be entirely governed by self-interest). It is clear that this utilitarianism opens up the possibility of a wider range of public interest policies than does the individualistic view.

The difficulty in this attempted detachment of the public interest from individual self-interest is that it leaves the substantive content of the public interest vague and ambiguous. If the public interest is not the subjective choice of individuals, mediated through a constitutional procedure, then is it not merely the subjective choices of governors? Obviously, Oppenheim would want to avoid this, indeed he does say (1981, p. 133) that policy-makers should be guided by the collective welfare preferences of all, or most, of the members of the public, but it is not clear how it can be done in the absence of collective choice rules. Furthermore, any judgement about the public interest derived from utilitarianism faces the familiar problem of the incommensurability of individual utilities.

The narrow and expanded versions of the public interest come into conflict over the interpretation and evaluation of democracy. Exponents of the narrow version maintain that democratic institutions tend to promote group interests in the guise of the public interest with the result that those *genuine* shared interests that individuals have can attract little electoral support. They therefore recommend severe restrictions on majority rule to protect individual rights from harmful collective decisions. Their opponents take a more optimistic view of 'political man' and argue that rulers do not necessarily use public office to maximise private interests. Party competition under the majority-rule procedure is not only adequate to hold government to account, but is also a means of advancing measures for the public welfare which go beyond the mere enforcement of general rules, property rights and the maintenance of stable economic conditions.

However, a discussion of this issue, which is perhaps the most important in contemporary political theory, must be prefaced by an analysis of democracy itself. This is pursued in the following section and the main themes explored here are returned to in Section 3. In the final section of this chapter we will consider some of the issues in democratic theory which fall outside our main analytical framework.

2 Democracy

As is the case with so many words in the political vocabulary, the word 'democracy' has acquired remarkably strong emotive overtones. Its use is often as much designed to provoke a favourable attitude towards a political regime as it is to describe particular features of it. Today political systems that differ widely are almost always described as democratic and the word is used in a bewildering variety of contexts[4].

Thus we have 'liberal democracy', 'social democracy', and 'totalitarian democracy'; the word is also used in non-political contexts, as when people speak of 'industrial democracy'. It would appear from this that the word has little descriptive content and is merely an honorific label attached to those forms of political and economic organisation of which the utterer approves and wishes his listener similarly to approve. But this was not always so. In the nineteenth century democracy had a fairly precise meaning; it described regimes that today would be called liberal democracies and opposition to such political systems was conventional rather than exceptional. However, not since the fascist and Nazi tyrannies of the 1930s have political writers (and leaders) openly declared their hostility to democracy in principle.

As the above examples indicate, it is customary to give propositions containing the word democracy some descriptive content by adding an adjective to indicate what *type* of democracy is being discussed. Liberal democracy might then mean a political system in which individual rights are given special constitutional protection against majorities, and social democracy would describe a political system in which, in addition to conventional liberal rights, there exists a considerable measure of collective action to create social and economic equality. In Marxism, the traditional political rights that are associated with liberal democracy have no intrinsic value, they are no more than the superstructure of power that presides over a society characterised by bourgeois economic relationships and vast inequality. The disintegration of the capitalist order would, presumably, render political democracy redundant: it would be replaced by economic democracy – equality.

While this 'adjectival' approach has some obvious advantages in the way of clarity in political argument it secures these at the cost of assuming away some of the traditional problems that occur with the use of the word democracy. In fact, the word need hardly be used at all: all that a person wanted to express about political systems could be encompassed in the words such as 'liberal' or 'socialist'.

Yet the apparent contestability of democracy presents analytical problems no less severe, indeed probably more so, than we have encountered with other concepts in the political vocabulary (for a thorough contemporary analysis, see Sartori, 1987). The myriad of competing theories and definitions can be crudely reduced to two major ones: the 'classical' theory and the 'elitist' theory. Almost all discussions revolve around the question as to whether democracy should be seen, in the classical sense, as an ideal form of self-government characterised by active involvement of the citizenry in decision-making or whether, given certain realistic assumptions about man and society, it can be no more than a system of competing elites in which the public merely confirms or validates through infrequent elections a particular minority's title to govern. Indeed, as we shall see below, some elitist theorists of society doubt that democracy is even possible however 'open' elites might be.

A further distinction of some significance should be mentioned here, although it does not quite fit into the above dichotomy. It is between 'rationalist' and 'empiricist' democratic theories. Rationalist theories derive, *a priori*, models of democratic government from certain abstract ideals, irrespective of specific political experience. The democratic theory implicit in the French Revolution, with its notion of the fundamental 'rights of man', is an example of rationalism. In this model, democratic systems derive their authority from direct appeals to the people, understood as equal citizens. The democratic system that emerged in Britain through the development of constitutionalism and the rule of law is perhaps the best example of empiricist democracy. This form traces democratic authority not from abstract ideals but from legal rules and practices that, to an extent, exist independently of the will of the people. An analysis of these two types of democracy has important implications for normative democratic theory.

There is then a case for subjecting 'democracy' itself to further analysis beyond delineating the main features of political systems that happen to call themselves democratic. The fact that the word has been appropriated by thinkers who represent widely different ideologies is no reason for denying that the word has meaning or significance. In fact, some of the more eccentric users of the word reveal inconsistencies and contradictions which the political theorist has a professional duty to expose: analysis of this kind is not dependent upon there being a peculiar 'essence' of democracy, knowledge of which can be discerned by the philosopher.

The first step in such an analysis is to dispel the illusion that the term democracy always stands for that which is good or virtuous about a political system. If democracy is used to describe the 'good society' then there will indeed be as many types of democracy as there are visions of utopia and the word will lose all descriptive meaning. However, once we can recognise the legitimacy of saying that, for example, 'decision *x* was arrived at democratically but its implementation involved the violation of an individual right', then it will be possible to develop a 'critical' theory of democracy. Such a theory includes both an analysis of certain descriptive features of democratic regimes and an appraisal of those features from a more general normative standpoint.

Another way of saying the same thing is to distinguish between democracy as a certain kind of procedure, to be contrasted with monarchy and various forms of oligarchy and closed elite rule, and democracy as a particular form of society, characterised by such things as extensive popular participation and social and economic equality. It is this latter that the 'classical' theorists of democracy had in mind. While some of the latter features may be relevant to a critical theory of democracy (they will be discussed in a later section of this chapter), too great a concentration on them may distract the attention of the political theorist away from some important analytical problems. It is surely legitimate to describe some regimes as democratic which do not have these attributes, however desirable in an ethical sense they may be. The remainder of this section will thus be concerned with the problems of procedural democracy.

When we speak of procedures we mean simply those rules of a social practice which determine the legitimacy of courses of action; we distinguish these from the results or outcomes of such actions (see Chapter 6 for the discussion of this in connection with justice). Democratic procedures are special sorts of political procedures which are designed to involve the 'people' in decision-making and the making of laws, in the way that monarchical or autocratic procedures are obviously not. Indeed, such an involvement was thought by some political philosophers, notably Rousseau, to solve the problem of political obligation, since individuals would not regard obedience to laws they had imposed upon themselves as restrictive of their liberty.

The origins of the idea of democracy as 'rule by the people' go back to the ancient Greek experience where rule by the *demos* was obviously contrasted with monarchy and aristocracy, but the modern meaning of this phrase is significantly different. In Greek times the *demos* was a section of the population (the poor and numerous) and all types of government were thought of as sectional government. But in modern times purely sectional rule is frowned upon and democracy has come to mean rule by the whole people. In fact, the peculiar virtue of democracy is thought to lie in the fact that it is the only form of government that can, in principle, advance the interests of all the members of a politically organised community. Of course, democratic procedures are often used to advance sectional interests and economic theorists of democracy have produced sophisticated arguments to show that under certain conditions this will invariably happen, but the normative arguments for democracy now turn largely upon the idea that it is uniquely concerned with shared values.

Taken literally, the phrase 'rule by the people' presents an impossible ideal for democratic theorists. This is not only because of the commonplace observation that *direct* democracy, a system in which decision-taking and law-making is a function of the whole community unmediated by any form of representation, is impossible to realise in all but the smallest societies, but also because 'ruling' implies ruling over someone or some group, and if all the people rule, over whom is it that they rule? What is surely meant is that in a democracy legitimacy is a function of laws being a product of a *majority* decision, where access to that decision-making process is not restricted to some particular class or group. This last point implies that democracy entails some commitment to political *equality*; not an absolute equality, since any form of rule necessarily involves some political inequality, but in the sense of no race, class or individual being arbitrarily deprived of the opportunity of participating in the political process. It is, of course, almost a truism to say that democracies will vary in the extent to which the ideal of equal political participation is approached.

If democracy is defined in terms of majority rule, where the composition of a representative assembly and decisions taken in that assembly are determined by a majority vote, it poses severe problems both at the normative and descriptive levels. Are people really prepared to accept majority rule procedures as legitimate in all cases? Of course, they are not and there is no reason why they should. The problem is that in any community characterised by divisions which are of a permanent kind, for example, divisions of race or religion, majority rule procedures simply entrench the position of the dominant race or sect. The example of Northern Ireland demonstrates the poverty of pure majoritarianism. Both Protestant and Catholic communities can appeal to the majority principle: the former has a clear majority in the six counties while the latter would be substantially ahead in an all-Ireland context. However Ireland is politically constituted there will always be a potentially alienated minority. The distressing fact is that in terms of world politics the Irish case is the norm rather than the exception. Majority-rule procedures are only acceptable when the *major* interests of particular groups within the community are not at stake. There is also the problem, to be considered below, that the majority principle may not reflect the *public* interest even in a reasonably homogeneous community. Thus for a variety of reasons political theorists are reluctant to define democracy in terms of pure majoritarianism alone (Barry, B., 1979).

A further problem is that even if a majoritarian voting procedure is consistent with stability and the protection of minority interests, the necessary qualifications for participation in the political process are by no means clear (Dahl, 1979). All democracies impose some conditions for participation, but there is by no means universal agreement on what these should be. There cannot be an unrestricted franchise since no one has recommended that minors or the severely mentally deranged should be allowed to vote, but beyond this opinions vary. Until recently countries which disenfranchised women would not have been denied the title of democracy and theorists of liberal democracy have often excluded some categories of people, or given special weightings to others. John Stuart Mill, who favoured extra votes for the educationally qualified, is a clear example of the latter[5]. It is no answer to say that Mill was therefore not a 'true democrat' because, since all theories of democracy include some qualifications for participation, it is incumbent on Mill's critics to say what these are and why they are better than his. There will always therefore be an element of arbitrariness about electoral qualifications even though most people would agree that for a system to be democratic all same adults should be entitled, as of right, to participate.

At the descriptive level it is argued persuasively that the majority principle is inadequate for marking off democratic regimes from non-democratic ones. The most casual observations of Western democracies reveal that governments rarely satisfy the majority principle. This is clearly seen in Great Britain whose 'first past the post' electoral system virtually ensures that most governments are minority ones; indeed, the sometimes eccentric (by the strict standards of egalitarian democracy) relationship between votes cast and seats won means that occasionally the major opposition party may have a bigger share of the popular vote than the government.

For these and other reasons some democratic theorists have suggested that majoritarianism is not a decisive feature of democracy and that consequently the fear of the 'tyranny of the majority' has proved to be unfounded. In this view, which is a version of 'pluralism', democracy is characterised by 'minorities rule' in contrast to the minority rule of non-democratic, one-party states (Dahl, 1956, 1971). What is distinctive about pluralist democracy, or 'polyarchy', is the presence of a multiplicity of competing interests and groups in a system in which power is decentralised so that no one interest can dominate. While democracy is in an important sense rule by elites it is not a system of closed elites, as was argued by the Italian anti-democratic elitist theories (see below).

The system is thought to have considerable normative value precisely because it is *not* majoritarian and because the competitive nature of the process, and the fact that access is open to all, enables it to approach a rather modest standard of political equality. Against this it is often said that it falls a long way short of political equality in that it clearly favours established political groups and militates against the poor and unorganised; and also that the struggle for power between powerful organised groups means that shared interests are not always promoted (see Section 1 of this chapter).

It seems curious that the majority principle, which appears to be one of the defining characteristics of democracy, should, on analysis, turn out to play such a small role in the system, yet it would be unwise to eliminate it entirely. It is honoured, albeit imperfectly, in many Western democratic systems and, superficially at least, it seems to meet some of the requirements of political equality. Where collective decisions have to be taken it seems more reasonable to go for a quantitative judgement than for a qualitative one, since any departure from the former implies that certain people are especially qualified to make such judgements. It is this that marks off a democracy from a meritocracy. While it is true that in areas where collective decisions have to be taken some theorists dispute that majority rule procedures will maximise the public interest, the main disagreement amongst political theorists is the range over which majority decisions should be decisive. As we have noted already, when a community is divided along ethnic or religious lines, a genuine constitutional democracy will include procedures that maximise the interests of all rather than numerical majorities, and even in relatively homogeneous communities democracy is thought to be consistent with the constitutional protection of individual rights.

It could be said that this account is descriptive of liberal democracy only, and that other ideals are worthy of the title. There is some truth in this, but it should also be noted that its properties may, as a matter of fact, meet the more general standards of 'democracy', such as political equality and participation, better than any existing alternative. It is doubtful if one-party democracies or 'people's' democracies can ever reach these standards, even though such regimes, it is said, are legitimised by 'popular enthusiasm'. This is because the absence of genuine choice between political alternatives removes the possibility of there being even the minimum of control by the people over government.

The prevailing problem in traditional democratic theory is that of reconciling the aim of 'government by the people' with the obvious fact that government itself is a minority activity. However much the development of democracy may take account of representation, of competition between groups and accountability of governments through periodic elections, there have always been social theorists who have argued that democracy of *any* type is impossible because of the inevitability of *elite rule*. Those who take this view are not making the trivial observation that the exercise of government must be in the hands of a minority – even Rousseau was insistent that democratic *government* was impossible (although the making of democratic general laws was not) – but the potentially more damaging point that elite rule is necessarily *irresponsible*, in that elites are not accountable to the people and that genuine choice between alternatives is impossible. In this general view, democracy is not the name of a specific form of government – since all governments are in principle the same – but is a 'political formula', or 'myth' designed to deceive the masses into thinking that they can have some influence over government.

The elitist thesis is generally associated with the Italian writers, Pareto (the mathematical economist whose ideas we have already discussed in relationship to the role of the state) and Mosca, whose sociological theories were formulated earlier this century.[6] While the conclusions each writer drew about the possibility of democracy were not markedly dissimilar, their foundations were rather different and worth a brief discussion. Pareto's demonstration (see Meisel, 1967) of the inevitability of elite rule was based on the psychological premise of the fundamental inequality of people; while his argument looks historical, it was profoundly ahistorical in that he interpreted the whole of human history in terms of the 'circulation of elites'. Elite leadership was a function of the predominance of certain psychological attributes, which he called 'residues'. The most important of these were those of 'courage' and 'cunning' and a ruling elite would be composed of individuals who possessed one of these properties: put metaphorically, elites would consist of either 'lions' or 'foxes'. The circulation of elites occurred through changes in these residues. The egalitarian premise of democracy was fallacious because individuals would display the qualities necessary for ruling to a vastly unequal degree. In fact, outside purely economic relationships, Pareto thought that individual behaviour was irrational so that responsible self-government was an impossibility. Elites would only change through changes in 'residues' and democratic procedures could in no way affect this. Democracy was no more than a slogan.

Pareto's distaste for democracy, or rather his attempt to prove 'scientifically' that it cannot exist, arises then from his belief in the necessity of 'natural aristocracy' in society. A society is in an equilibrium when there is a harmony between the exercise of power and a particular aristocratic quality (residue). Disequilibrium (the fall of one elite and its replacement by another) occurs when there is a disjuncture between power and 'right'. History is simply a record of this never-ending process. Also, it is a process that was largely uninfluenced by 'ideas'. Thus the rise of the democratic ideal, especially its egalitarian element, could not affect the operation of psychologically-derived 'laws' of society.

Mosca's elitism (see Meisel, 1965) was more historical and socio-logical than Pareto's. The dominance of elites, and the consequent rigid division of society into two strata, were explicable in terms of social developments rather than deduced *a priori* from a small number of slender propositions about human nature. In comparison to the masses, who will always be unorganised, elites will be organised and, if not exactly cohesive, will present a unity which will guarantee their survival irrespective of democratic electoral processes. The qualities that sustain an elite will vary from one historical period to another, but in modern industrial society wealth, knowledge and bureaucratic skills predominate. In fact, the elite consists of two layers, the higher stratum of leaders who control the machinery of the state and a second stratum of trained administrators and technicians – although the latter body must not be relegated to secondary importance, as it is essential to the survival of the state. While Mosca was more favourably disposed than Pareto to representative democracy, and even hinted at the possibility of competition operating so as to restrain rulers, his general conclusion – that the democratic idea functions largely as a myth – was not dissimilar from that of his compatriot.

What characterised both Pareto and Mosca's critique of the possibility of democracy was that its target was really the classical (and perhaps rationalistic) theory of democracy. The idea that democracy consists of direct participation and active self-rule with little difference between governors and governed was obviously vulnerable to their anti-egalitarian strictures. However, it is less clear that a more procedural conception of democracy, with its emphasis on constitutional rules, and the accountability of *competing* elites to a free electorate, is similarly unrealistic. The assumption that power is necessarily concentrated in any form of government, and incapable of diffusion, is more of an assertion than a proven proposition.

Of equal interest is the anti-democratic thought of Robert Michels (1958). He made an extensive study of the German Social Democratic Party, one of the earliest of democratically organised political parties, and claimed to have discovered the 'iron law of oligarchy'. This holds that in any formal organisation, whatever its structural arrangements, a small minority will hold office, decide policy and so on, irrespective of the wishes of its members. Indeed, it is a feature of all organisations that they become dominated by minorities who have the time and energy to invest in administration. Of particular importance in this is the acquisition of *knowledge*. It seems to be a sociological truism (although of some significance) that most people are not prepared to devote as much of their time to the public world that an activist theory of democracy requires. Michels' strictures are particularly relevant to contemporary participatory theories of democracy (see below).

Nevertheless, what may be true of the bureaucracy of a democratic political party (which is what Michels was really studying) may not necessarily be true of *democracy* (see Sartori, 1987, pp. 148–51). Once again, the force of Michels' arguments seems to be more directed against certain ideal conceptions of democracy than against the *competitive* democratic systems with which we are familiar. The trouble with the kind of elitism propagated by Pareto, Mosca and Michels was that it made it extremely difficult conceptually to distinguish one form of government from another.

It was J. S. Schumpeter (1954) who managed to construct a theory of democracy that was compatible with a certain kind of elitism. What made some of the traditional theories of democracy so vulnerable to the elitist criticisms was that they set impossibly high standards. They assumed that democracy required that government should reflect the 'will of the people', so that the outputs of the democratic machine simply represented the desires of the electorate.[7] Schumpeter easily showed that such a picture was highly unrealistic; it assumed that there is an homogeneous people's will when in fact all large societies are characterised by a multiplicity of conflicting wills; it assumed that in public affairs people's behaviour is likely to be rational (in matters affecting their private interests Schumpeter maintained that people have a very much greater incentive to behave rationally than they do in politics); and it took no account of political leadership, the fact that all government involves action taken independently of the 'people's will'.

Despite this profound scepticism Schumpeter still thought that the word democracy had descriptive content and that a democratic system had much to recommend it. In effect, he turned traditional democratic theory upside down and argued that a democratic system was not characterised by the translation of the people's will into government action but by competing parties offering alternative programmes to the electorate; the voters having little direct influence over the content of such programmes. The people were in fact limited to choosing a government, and what marked off democratic from non-democratic regimes was nothing so pretentious as 'government by the people' but the fact that, in the former, political competition existed and provided some minimal degree of accountability. It also necessitated some basic freedoms since a competitive party democracy required the freedom to form associations and propagate ideas. In a celebrated phrase Schumpeter defined democracy as 'that institutional arrangement for arriving at political decisions in which individuals acquire the power to decide by means of a competitive struggle for the people's vote' (1954, p. 229). Indeed, Schumpeter was one of the first democratic theorists to draw a direct analogy between political and market behaviour.

In Schumpeter's rather meagre account of democracy, participation is strictly limited and the influence that voters have over government policy is minimal; furthermore, a system with a severely restricted franchise would count as democratic as long as competition determines the party that is to govern. His was a purely procedural account of democracy; it is no more than a method for producing a government and is compatible with almost *any* kind of society. Schumpeter did, however, believe that under certain conditions it is likely to be a benign form of government, or at least less malign than the known alternatives. These conditions include a relatively homogeneous and 'open society', a professionalised and experienced bureaucracy, and recognised restraints on 'politics'. This last point is most important and Schumpeter insisted that if too many economic and social activities become subject to democratic politics the system will come under great strain. This would follow from Schumpeter's belief that the level of rationality achieved in political activity is very much less than that in economic behaviour. This insight has been confirmed in many sociological studies of voting behaviour which have revealed evidence of ignorance on the part of the electorate which would have alarmed the 'classical' theorists of democracy.

While Schumpeter's theory has had a significant influence on the development of democratic thought, it is not at all clear that it is an accurate account of the concept, either in a descriptive or normative sense (see Graham, 1986, ch. 7). Certainly the level of participation that it requires would fall some way short of contemporary demands. If people are too incompetent to decide policy issues one wonders if they are equipped even for the minimal task of choosing leaders. There is no attempt to link up democracy with the public interest which, one assumes, Schumpeter regarded as just another emotive slogan. His refusal to consider such facts as social and economic inequality in his construction of a workable democratic system leads him to a kind of passive acceptance of existing liberal democratic forms as embodying the only viable conditions for political choice.

There is some doubt as to whether he is prescribing or merely describing liberal democracy. It is true that in practice participation is limited but it is also clear that Schumpeter did not disapprove of this. He in fact argued that the citizen becomes 'a primitive again' as soon as he enters the political arena. The whole argument is coloured by as much a cynical view of human nature as it is sober analysis. It is, nevertheless, a valuable corrective to those heady ideals that have tended to dominate democratic thought. Indeed, the economic theory of democracy builds essentially on Schumpeterian premises.

Those who share Schumpeter's contention that democracy is to be interpreted as a 'method' of government stress that its connection with liberty is instrumental rather than conceptual. While we have just noted that party competition requires some liberties if it is to work at all, this does not mean that the outcomes of democracy may not be illiberal in a general sense. In fact, liberal individualists insist that *all* forms of government should be restricted by general rules and that protection of freedom cannot be guaranteed by putting government into the 'right hands' but by carefully limiting the range of collective action.

3 Procedural democracy and the public interest

In the preceding section we were concerned in a very general way with the major characteristics of procedural democracy. In recent years there has been a growing body of knowledge on the workings of this system, much of which casts doubt upon whether it is possible for democracy to work in the way that the early enthusiasts for the ideal intended. Of most importance is whether it can produce the public interest or those values which individuals share as members of the community. Of course, many people think that democracy should do more than this (see the next section of this chapter), but one important justification for democracy is that it is a desirable form of government precisely because it is concerned with general rather than sectional interests.

The first systematic attempt to demonstrate that democratic procedures would generate the public interest was made by the utilitarians, Jeremy Bentham and James Mill. As we have seen, the utilitarians mistakenly thought that the public interest could be summed up from private interests, but if their argument is re-interpreted to mean that the public interest represents those interests which individuals have as members of the community (in fact, there is some evidence that Bentham on some occasions took this view) then it is possible to see if their constitutional proposals will lead to the maximisation of community interests.

James Mill's *Essay on Government* (1955), first published in 1820, was the simplest utilitarian demonstration of the case for democracy. In methodology the *Essay* resembles contemporary economic theories of democracy in that Mill attempted to 'prove' the case for democratic government by reasoning deductively from some simple axioms of human nature which are assumed to be universally true. In no way did his case depend on experience or empirical knowledge of the various forms of government.

Mill took an extremely gloomy view of human nature. He assumed that man is motivated purely by self-interest, by the desire to maximise pleasure and minimise pain. Labour is a painful activity and therefore Mill believed that each person will seek naturally to appropriate the product of another man's labour. While people need government to enforce contracts and provide the general conditions for economic activity, Mill assumed that government, unless prevented, will become a 'sinister' interest which seeks to exploit the people. Mill, somewhat implausibly, took it for granted that capitalists and workers had a common interest in opposition to the land-owning class which controlled government at the time he was writing.

According to Mill, 'checks and balances', or the separation of powers, could never restrain the actions of government since one part of government would naturally seek to accumulate all power in its own hands. He was firmly wedded to the necessity of the 'sovereign power' idea and maintained that, on *a priori* grounds, the only way for the people to be governed in their interests was for the people to govern themselves. Since 'direct democracy' was impossible in a modern state, he designed a system of representative democracy in which government itself could never emerge as a sinister interest. This was to be achieved by universal suffrage (in fact, Mill restricted the vote to men over 40, but this inconsistency can be ignored for our purposes), the mandating of representatives, provisions for their recall, and annual parliaments. All these devices were for the purpose of making the governing class exactly reflect the interests of the people. Under these conditions majority voting and the secret ballot would produce the public interest out of the purely self-interested actions of individuals.

Criticisms of James Mill have normally centred on his methodology, his conception of man and his complete lack of interest in democracy as anything more than a method of government. However, it may be more useful to comment on the internal logic of his system. It is clear that there is no reason why the majority procedure should generate utility and critics, including Macaulay and Mill's son, John Stuart Mill, eloquently expressed a fear of majority tyranny. James Mill's only fear was the political power of the aristocracy and he assumed a harmony between the middle and working classes. He failed completely to anticipate the rise of party and class politics under democratic rules. He was aware that the working class might vote against their long-term interests but, somewhat inconsistently, argued that education would prevent this. He seemed unaware of the possibility of coalitions of private interests dominating under democracy, and his own belief in the necessity of a concentration of power at the centre further increased the possibility of the system producing undesirable and unintended consequences.

Problems of this type have exercised the minds of contemporary economic theorists of democracy who follow Mill's methodology but dispute his conclusions. Their main concern has been to suggest certain institutional arrangements that extend beyond equal voting which will ensure the maximisation of genuine public interests in a democracy. It is true, however, that most of these theorists interpret the public interest in a particularly narrow way, and their critics maintain that under simple majority rule a great range of shared values may be promoted. But before we discuss this some mention must be made of a specific logical problem that has perplexed economists and political theorists for the past 40 years. This is the problem, associated with the work of Kenneth Arrow in the field of welfare economics, that, under certain conditions, constitutional procedures for the making of collective decisions, of which majority rule is one type, produce inconsistent outcomes.[8] The argument here is not about the moral problems of majority rule, or the likelihood or not of it maximising shared interests, but about the impossibility of any collective decision-making procedure reproducing the same logical features as an individual decision does.

Arrow argued that for a collective choice procedure to be rational, it has to exhibit the same properties as an individual's rational choice. The most important of these is transitivity; this means that if an individual prefers x to y, and y to z, then he must prefer x to z. An individual's set of preferences will then exhibit an *ordering*. Now if we impose some fairly mild conditions on a collective choice procedure (such as majority rule) it can be shown that a collective ordering of preferences cannot be derived from all the possible individual orderings where there are more than two preferences. The conditions imposed are collective rationality (a social choice must exhibit the same logic as an individual's choice); the 'Pareto principle' (if alternative x is preferred to alternative y by every single individual then the social ordering ranks x over y); the 'independence of irrelevant alternatives' (the social choice must not be affected by alternatives not within the feasible set); and 'non-dictatorship' (there is no one individual whose preferences always take precedence over the preferences of other individuals).

The 'impossibility' of democracy can now easily be shown. Imagine three individuals, x, y and z, whose preferences are transitively ordered between three alternatives, A, B and C, in the following way. Person x prefers A to B and B to C; y prefers B to C and C to A; and z prefers C to A and A to B. Now in a series of pair-wise comparisons a majority prefers A to B, a majority prefers B to C and a majority prefers C to A. There is no determinate solution. Thus while individual preferences are transitive the collective choice procedure of majority rule produces not a clear decision but merely 'cyclical majorities'. The disheartening thing for the democrat is that for a result to occur it will have to be imposed by a 'dictator'. This entails a breach of one of Arrow's undemanding conditions.

On the whole, political theorists have not been unduly perturbed by Arrow's results. The conventional answer is that where democratic systems involve a straight choice between two alternatives, as in orthodox two-party systems, no 'paradox of voting' occurs. But where a choice is required among three parties (as is the case in Britain), voters are not normally given the opportunity to rank their preferences and vote in a series of comparisons so as to determine the winner. If they were it is quite likely that 'cycling' would occur.

In a choice situation the 'Arrow problem' is said to be avoided if the preference orderings of individuals are limited to those that are 'single-peaked' (Arrow's work showed that for a social decision procedure to be valid it must be able to handle *all* possible individual preference orderings). Single-peaked preference orderings are those that exhibit a consistency or pattern (which can be represented on a graph) so that, in political terms, a left-wing person will consistently rank policies from left to right (or right to left for a right-wing person). The 'moderate' will consistently rank policies falling to the right and left of his preferred policy, those further to the right and left being the least preferred. It is also assumed that political parties are fully informed about voters' preferences. In general elections in Britain the paradox could be avoided if the third party's voters (Liberal Democrats) switched their votes in a consistent manner on a second ballot, producing what is known as a 'Condorcet winner' (after the French theorist who originally discovered the problem). However, in conventional liberal democracies there is only one choice and no possibility of ranking preferences. It is quite likely that voters' preferences will be single-peaked on separate issues but the paradox is almost certain to occur in a democracy because voting takes place on an *amalgamation* of issues (party platforms). Nevertheless political theorists often argue that party competition in a democracy does produce determinate outcomes.

However, in a famous example, Anthony Downs, in *An Economic Theory of Democracy* (1957), assumed that voters' preferences are single-peaked and represented opinion in a uniform spread on a left-to-right continuum with 'extremists' at both ends and 'moderates' in the middle. In a straight fight the party whose platform nearest approaches the preference-ordering of the 'median' voter (the voter exactly in the middle of the continuum) will win. Competition for votes between the two parties will therefore lead to their convergence around the middle. Under these conditions there is a kind of 'invisible hand' in democratic politics which produces correspondence between government policy and the opinions of the electorate. Of course, there is no guarantee that government policy will represent the 'public interest'; whether it does or not will depend on the opinions of the median voter, and, in the absence of constitutional restraint, a majority will in principle be able to oppress a minority. However, where there is a stable left-to-right continuum, defenders of competitive party democracy argue that it works tolerably well in producing at least 'moderation'. Where a community is deeply divided (as, for example, Northern Ireland is), it is quite obvious that unrestricted party competition of this kind will simply produce policies that reflect the interests of the dominant sect.

The radical economic theorists of democracy have, however, seriously questioned the claim that competitive party democracy always works to the public's advantage, even in the more favourable political systems of, say, Great Britain or the United States of America. In the real world of democracy there are a number of reasons this may not be so (reasons which are in fact explored in Downs' book). There is the technical point as to whether the world is single-peaked or not. In fact, the existing empirical evidence suggests that voters do not order their preferences in a consistent manner. If they do not, then there is no one platform which will beat all other platforms and a range of winning majorities will be possible (Wittman, 1973). Thus the winning platform will not necessarily represent the preferences of the median voter. It will be impossible to predict how the winning majority will be constructed and the suggested virtue of a two-party system – that it encourages a convergence around the centre – will be lost. The absence of single-peakedness means that the outcome of a democratic election will be quite arbitrary. It has been suggested that the only way that the opinions of the median voter could be reflected in the outcome of a democratic vote would be for each issue to be decided *one at a time*, on the assumption that vote-maximising in a party democracy distorts preferences.

Of equal significance is the fact that parties will not be fully informed about voters' preferences and will have to rely on organised groups to transmit this information. In the process preferences will be distorted, and perhaps moulded to suit the interests of the group. Strategically placed interest groups can press upon government policies which may not be to the advantage of the community at large. Lastly, in most working democracies it is not necessary for a party even to secure a majority of votes to gain office so that it becomes much easier for party strategists to put together winning coalitions.

The political market consists of parties (entrepreneurs) and voters (consumers). To get elected, political entrepreneurs will put together programmes that appeal to voters as members of private groups rather than as members of the public. There is no incentive for entrepreneurs to offer policies that maximise the public interest because the benefits of these are likely to be spread thinly throughout the population at large, and are long term in their effect, while those that favour private groups are tangible and immediate in their impact. It is in the public interest that no private groups be privileged by the tax system yet it is in the interests of, for example, mortgagees that their tax relief should continue and that measures should be taken to protect the mortgage rate from the upward movements of all other interest rates. It is not in the public interest that public expenditure on services should be significantly increased above the level at which individuals would be prepared to pay for them voluntarily, but party competition for votes inevitably tends to push up public expenditure because there are more votes to be gained from such a policy than are to be gained from a policy of restraint. This is because the benefits of the latter, although they accrue to the public, are indirect. The absence of a budget constraint means that, whereas excessive individual expenditure is automatically curtailed in an economic market, government can pursue its vote-buying policies by running a budget deficit, which may be financed by inflation since taxation to pay for excessive government services is a vote loser. But once again policies of 'no inflation' and balanced budgets are public goods for which there is no incentive for the individual elector in the competitive political process to vote. Of course, there is a constraint somewhere since governments cannot pursue inflationary policies for very long without the collapse of the currency; and a return to economic prudence will be brought about by international factors. Financial prudence will be dictated by international monetary institutions and these will lay down strict conditions for their support of the currency (this, in fact, happened in Britain between 1976 and 1979). This ultimate restraint is, however, long term and indicates, in effect, the failure of democratic political institutions to generate those policies that are in the interests of the public.

It might be thought that voter rationality, as discussed by traditional democratic theorists, would operate so as to prevent such unintended consequences of the vote-maximising process, but it is obvious that, in the economist's sense of rationality, the opposite is the case. No one individual or group can have any incentive to promote the public interest in a democracy since he (it) cannot be sure that others will do likewise. This is just another example of the 'Prisoners' Dilemma' discussed in Chapter 3. It is for this reason that democratic governments are peculiarly prone to the pains brought about by the scramble over distributive shares between powerfully organised groups (see Usher, 1981). Schumpeter and others have stressed the fact that people cannot be expected to be as rational in the public world as they are in their private affairs where the costs of various courses of action are more clearly evident. In fact, economic theorists of democracy have had great difficulty in explaining why people vote at all given the vanishingly small value of the vote in most constituencies, and the sometimes not inconsiderable costs expended in the act of voting.

This is in essence the economic theory of democracy. It is thought to have a special application to Great Britain because the British political system imposes virtually no constitutional restraint on government, and it has a 'first past the post' electoral system. This latter point means that normally parties do not have to secure the support of even a majority of electors in each constituency in order to win and therefore have a great incentive to produce policies that directly favour determinate groups rather than the public at large. The absence of a written constitution means that the elected government, which rarely has the support of a majority of the voters, is unlimited in political authority. Two related points have been stressed in this context: firstly, the abandonment of the former conventional rule that governments ought to balance their budgets; and secondly, the removal of traditional restraints, such as the gold standard, on the government's exercise of its monopoly of the supply of money (Buchanan, 1978;

Rowley, 1979, pp. 17–18). It is argued that the operation of all these factors has threatened freedom in Britain and will ultimately destroy democracy itself. Economic theorists of democracy maintain that competitive party democracy works effectively only when the behaviour of political actors is subject to strict rules. In this way they are following the insight of Schumpeter, who argued that democratic stability was only possible when the range of social and economic affairs subjected to political resolution was narrowly circumscribed.

Radical individualists are doubtful if a simple majoritarian collective decision-making procedure can be made consistent with liberty, even conventional liberal democracy operating under ideal conditions. They maintain that attention should not be directed toward designing some procedure by which individual preferences can be translated into collective choices, but towards designing institutions which protect individual voluntary exchanges. In effect, the 'Arrow problem' is sidestepped by severely reducing the range of collective choices. This seems to be the approach of James Buchanan and Gordon Tullock in their important work *The Calculus of Consent* (1962).

The authors argue that under majority rule public expenditures will always be higher than the sums individuals would pay if they were to finance the activities by voluntary exchanges. This means that people have costs imposed on them which make them all worse off in the long term. They postulate that if there is agreement on an initial distribution of property in a community then each individual's interests would be advanced under a system which required something approaching unanimous agreement (of representatives, for practical reasons) for any collective expenditures. Buchanan and Tullock do not eliminate the public interest entirely – individuals do have interests as members of the community – but they reduce it to those issues where very wide agreement can be secured. This means that many shared interests would not be promoted because a minority whose private interests exceeded their interests as members of the public could always veto such proposals. However, under majority rule individuals will have costs imposed on them in that they will be forced to pay for activities they do not want undertaken.

However, even unanimity does not mean that nothing will ever get done. In fact, it will encourage bargaining and 'log-rolling' between political actors. A representative who wishes to secure the collective delivery of a good or service that affects only his constituency will have to attract the support of other representatives by agreeing to support their projects. This process allows for various 'intense preferences' to be expressed. Under orthodox democracy a relatively apathetic majority may stand in the way of a proposal for which a minority may have strong preferences, but under unanimity, vote-trading allows these preferences to be expressed without others having costs imposed on them. The trouble is that a strict application of the unanimity rule makes the cost of bargaining high: small minorities will almost certainly set very high prices for their agreement and Buchanan and Tullock therefore are prepared to modify unanimity in order to reduce bargaining costs. For most proposals they favour a weighted majority (two-thirds) somewhere between straight majority rule (which imposes 'external' costs on the minority) and unanimity (which involves such high bargaining costs that many desirable projects would not be undertaken).

Although Buchanan and Tullock's extremely individualistic solution to the problem posed by democratic decision-making has found favour only in the specialised world of Public Choice theory, the basic logic of their argument can be discerned in all those procedural theories of democracy that are more concerned with the placing of limitations on the exercise of collective choice than finding ways of implementing the people's will. They are part of a long tradition of political thought that, starting from pessimistic psychological premises, naturally assumes that those entrusted with political power will use it for their own advantage. The problem, therefore, is to place obstacles in the way of the exercise of political power. One reason why this approach has not been fashionable, despite the clear evidence that unrestricted political power almost always produces undesirable consequences, is that while limiting power protects individual rights it also places a veto in the hands of those already in a privileged position. The price of security against majority oppression is the preservation of economic inequality which becomes the cause of permanent resentment. It is true that Buchanan and Tullock's highly theoretical argument assumes that problem away by postulating an agreement on the distribution of property, but in reality the problems are likely to be formidable.[9]

A further objection to the various models of limited government is that in them the public interest – where that means something more than agreement on rules, referring instead to positive policies which advance the well-being of the community – will be neglected (Barry, B., 1965, ch. xv). In a reasonably homogeneous community, wide and amorphous interests may be better advanced by majority-rule democracy than by the bargaining process that occurs under the Buchanan–

Tullock type of system, as long as there is no single party domination. However, majority-rule democracy requires considerably more coercion because of the fact that it will rarely be in a person's private interests to act voluntarily for the public benefit. To say that governments ought to promote a wide range of public interests requires a change in the psychological assumptions that underlie the economic theory of democracy. Buchanan and Tullock and others carry over the apparatus of microeconomic theory into the political realm; they maintain that it is wrong to assume that because politicians and bureaucrats are not involved in private economic relationships they do not have the same motivations as market transactors. It cannot be assumed that they will maximise the 'public interest' merely because they are in public office.[10] The problem is that the acceptance of these assumptions involves the limitation of the public interest to the enforcement of general rules and the provision of the traditional public goods, while their replacement by a more optimistic view of 'political man' involves the risk that not only will individual rights be threatened by majorities but also that coalitions of private group interests may well damage those public interests that even the radical individualistic accept.

It should be stressed that the Public Choice school of political economy is by no means hostile to democracy. Nor are they elitists in the style associated with Pareto, Mosca and Michels. They do not regard the public as inert masses easily manipulated by adroit minorities. Indeed, political leaders in a competitive democracy do respond to voters' preferences but the problem is that simple majority-rule procedures distort individuals' preferences for public services. The presence of 'Prisoners' Dilemmas' in society, it is claimed, drives individuals to vote for policies that are not in their interests as members of the public, or even in the interests of a numerical majority. The type of democracy Public Choice economists recommend is 'constitutional democracy' of a more restrictive kind than is practised in Western countries today.

It is with some irony that the kind of economics practised by the Conservatives in Britain since 1979, and favoured by Public Choice economists in both their professional and private capacities, has been implemented under the very constitutional system they have been so adept at criticising. This in itself is a tribute to the economic theory of democracy which does show that election victories and public policies are not the outcome of some determinate and equilibrating system (as the median voter theorem implies) but of a whole range of phenomena, of which chance is surely one. It is also worth pointing out that those Conservative politicians (such as Hailsham, 1976) who pressed hard for constitutional reform in Britain in the 1970s were remarkably silent between 1979 and 1997. Despite the inadequacies of the British system by Public Choice standards, it did manage to drag Labour towards the centre and to deter inflation and high public spending.

Still, even from the perspective of the Public Choice school it is not clear how constitutional reform would achieve the end that its members ultimately desire – smaller government. This is because the models used have great difficulty in explaining voter rationality at all. Given that the likelihood of a single voter's decision affecting the outcome of an election is remote there is little incentive for her to be rational. Unlike the consumer, whose choice for a good is decisive, the voter knows that her choice will have no effect on the outcome (apart from in a tie). Thus even if voters wanted smaller government (as opinion polls suggest that American voters do), this is unlikely to occur when the political agenda is set by party activists, opinion leaders and bureaucrats. Their influence is made possible by rational ignorance of the voter. If she desires smaller government, she has no incentive to be informed about the policy stance of candidates since her vote will not be decisive. In contrast to the conventional theory of democracy, the economic theory more or less detaches the electorate from the outputs of government.

In an intriguing book, Geoffrey Brennan and Loren Lomasky (1993) take the story a stage further by stressing the 'expressive' function of voting. The sort of benefit a voter gets is not increased wealth, or some kind of utility maximisation, but is more like the satisfaction a football supporter gets through venting his feelings. This is not quite a perversion of an old justification for voting, that people do so from a sense of civic duty despite its opportunity costs, for the theory is concerned with *how* people vote. Thus Brennan and Lomasky suggest that a person who had an altruistic sentiment, but also a preference not to pay high taxes to benefit the poor, could happily vote the altruistic ticket because her vote wouldn't make any difference. She would, though, feel better. Even if it turned out that higher taxes were imposed, against her true preferences, this would not make her voting the way she did irrational since one vote cannot (normally) affect the outcome. However, it is just as likely that the voter will produce malicious expressions, even though the implementation of a whole string of them might actually harm her. The anonymity of the ballot box is, anyway, a good protective device against public criticism since its secrecy ensures that no one else can know that these attitudes are held.

Whether voters' intentions can be detached from outcomes in the way suggested is a moot point. It is surely just as plausible to assume that voters act as if their decisions had some bearing on the result. Indeed, Brennan and Lomasky write as if a normative support for democracy has to be structured around some association between intentions and preferred outcomes. The implication of their argument is that this connection can be achieved by procedures that draw a closer connection between voting and the outputs of government. The bigger and more anonymous a system is, the more likely it is that expressive functions will predominate (or lead to a decline in voter turn out). However, if decision-making could be decentralised, this might go some way to establishing a link between voting and outcomes, thereby overcoming 'rational ignorance'.

Interestingly, Brennan had earlier suggested (see Brennan and Pettit, 1990) that open voting could be a method of eliminating malicious preferences since people would be faced in public with the responsibility of defending, or explaining them. This is a clear echo of John Stuart Mill's opposition to the secret ballot, which he thought encouraged the propagation of purely selfish and anti-public motivations. The movement of Public Choice theory towards a consideration of how preferences are formed, and how they might be altered, is a significant departure from the earlier models in which preferences were simply given and various procedures were suggested for their aggregation into collective choices. It is a subtle step towards 'deliberative democracy' (for a description of this, see Miller, 1992) which requires open debate and discussion and encourages the changing of preferences.

4 The radical critique of liberal democracy

Not all objections to the utility-maximising approach are collectivist in inspiration. Some writers regard a democratic system as an ethical system of rights and duties which cannot be measured for success in terms of its satisfaction of individual desires. Even Rawls, who in many ways writes in the individualistic tradition, rejects the idea that even an ideally working competitive party democracy is sufficient to generate just legislation. He does not suggest that this might emerge

from improved institutions alone but maintains that legislators must
be imbued with a 'sense of justice' (1972, pp. 359–62). Other critics of
the utility-maximising approach object in principle to the application
of the methodology of microeconomics to the political sphere and
argue that a democratic society generates those values of co-operation
and fraternity that are said to be absent from the self-interested world
of economic markets.

Still, the most sustained criticism of the traditional liberal approach
is that of the neo-Marxist C. B. Macpherson. He claims that there are
two elements in Western democratic theory. One is the familiar one of
utility maximisation (a liberal democratic political system is the
essential complement of a free economy) and the other is concerned
with the maximisation of *powers*. This latter element, which Macpherson traces from J. S. Mill's modification of orthodox utilitarianism, is
an ethical concept which interprets man as a *doer* and a *creator* rather
than as merely a consumer. A truly democratic society will promote
these powers of creativity and social co-operation rather than maximise aggregate satisfactions. The utility-maximising model of democracy is ethically deficient because the exchange process conducted
within the capitalist economic system entails a transfer of powers (in
the ethical sense). Because access to the market is unequal and the
worker has to sell his labour power to capitalist owners, his powers of
creativity and free choice are thereby reduced. Macpherson concedes
that existing liberal democracies have conserved civil and political
liberties more effectively than existing socialist regimes but argues that
there is no inherent reason why a system of socialist ownership may
not develop in such a way as to end the transfer of powers that takes
place under capitalism while maintaining liberty. He argues that
welfare state institutions, which tend to some extent to make goods
and services available on the grounds of need rather than contribution
to the social product, do not fundamentally alter the characteristics of
liberal-democratic society.

Macpherson also denies that liberal societies – merely because they
grant universal suffrage, choice between political parties and civil
liberties – are exclusively entitled to the use of the word 'democracy'.
He claims that there are other, equally valid variants (1966, ch. 1).
Communist countries might qualify if they, for example, granted full
intra-party democracy and opened up their closed bureaucratic systems. Third World countries, which have no experience of Western
individualism, to the extent that their governments are legitimised by
mass enthusiasm, also fulfill the ideals of some historical theories of

democracy. The empirical evidence for all this is anything but encouraging.

The difficulty with Macpherson's argument is that he evaluates existing liberal democracy by reference to some 'ideal version' of democracy, rather than by comparing it directly to existing alternatives. It is not all that difficult to show that Western capitalist countries – with their considerable economic inequalities, remote governments, bureaucracies and absence of real opportunities for ordinary citizens to influence policy-making – do not meet the high standards of political equality and participation set by some traditional democratic theorists, but it is more important to make realistic comparisons between these countries and their socialist and former communist opposites in terms of more modest objectives, such as personal freedoms, civil rights, relief of suffering and general standards of living. It is difficult to conceive of any economic system which will not involve a 'transfer of powers' and a reduction of freedom, in Macpherson's sense, as long as there is scarcity and the consequent need for the division of labour and some form of ownership of resources (be it public or private). A more feasible reform programme for liberal democracies would be to work for a wider dispersal of private property and the removal of monopoly and other forms of privilege.

However, radical critics of liberal democracy have persistently turned towards collectivist solutions to the problems of modern democracy. Whereas individualists have suggested that some of the problems associated with collective choice can be coped with by reducing its extent, socialists have recommended that they are best solved by actually extending such choice and changing the way it operates. This is what lies behind the demand for more 'participation': it is said that the threats to equality and political liberty entailed by the existence of 'big government' and bureaucracy can be removed by decentralising government to smaller units, such as the region and locality, rather than by trying to dispense with government in certain areas. It is to be noted that individualists and socialists are often attacking the same problems but the former's solution is to reduce the area of social life occupied by government, whatever form government should take.

The advocates of participation[11] claim that political equality is denied in competitive party democracies since the activity of the citizen is limited merely to choosing his political leaders on periodic occasions. This is especially damaging in contemporary industrial societies since the ever widening range of government activities means that changes occur which seriously affect individuals and communities and yet these individuals and communities have very little control over government under conventional democratic rules.

Theorists of participatory democracy therefore recommend that politics should be a continuing activity and not just confined to elections at regular intervals. It is assumed that if decision-making is shifted away from the bureaucratic state into smaller communities this will enable individuals and groups to produce laws and policies directly related to their needs and interests. Participatory devices would also involve considerable use of referenda and other means of establishing close consultations between government and the people.

An important inspiration for this approach is the democratic philosophy of Rousseau, whose ideas are especially appropriate for small, closely-knit communities. While Rousseau felt that democratic government in an *executive* sense was an ideal highly unlikely to be realised in most societies, he thought that the people could be directly involved in the making of general laws. The legislative process would be characterised by discussion and debate in order to determine what laws are in the general interest. Rousseau's ideas can, however, be interpreted in a procedural sense because he thought that under certain conditions majority rule will produce beneficial outcomes for individuals as members of the community. This will be so if individuals are imbued with a sense of public spirit and are approximately equal: if these conditions hold, citizens acting self-interestedly will produce the public interest (or General Will). However, like some contemporary public interest theorists, Rousseau was very much aware of the likelihood that large and unequal groups will become sources of loyalty apart from the community at large.

Contemporary theories of participation, like Rousseau's, depend to a large extent on man's nature being 'moralised' by the process of democratic consultation and social interaction. Those selfish motivations which might lead to antisocial outcomes may be harnessed for the public good under the right conditions. John Stuart Mill, unlike his father, also viewed the democratic process as an 'educative' one: it was not just a machine for generating satisfactions but was an activity which helped to form a more desirable human character.

The difficulty with such doctrines is that if the necessary conditions cannot be satisfied and if human nature refuses to be 'moralised', there is no protection for the individual who finds himself at odds with collective decisions (although this particular criticism cannot be directed at John Stuart Mill). While it is true that collective decisions of small communities are likely to be less oppressive than those of centralised state bureaucracies, this is not necessarily so. If individuals are allowed to move freely from community to community, that will itself afford some protection – but modern states are not likely to allow these decentralised political entities the independence of action that is required for a variety of institutions to emerge.

Participatory democracy may display some affinities with direct democracy, a system in which individuals are regularly called upon to express, through referenda, a preference for alternative policies. But in this individuals are still uttering a private opinion (Sartori, 1987, pp. 110–12) and although it may be preceded by debate and information, or more likely propaganda, it is not quite what the participation theorists have in mind as the ideal form of democracy. The privacy of the judgement makes it more likely that it will display a 'selfish' interest rather than one directed towards the ends of the community. Whether 'deliberative democracy' can overcome this is still an open question.

However, such a notion of involvement comes right up against the problems posed by the elitist theorists, Pareto, Mosca and Michels, who would claim to have a much more realistic view of the way that regimes which call themselves 'democratic' work. Indeed, if people's tastes for political involvement vary, as surely they do, then a widened 'politicisation' of social and economic life will increase the opportunities for those people with a high taste for participation to dominate political life. Thus elites are just as likely to emerge under a participatory system as a simple choice system. This tendency will be reinforced the larger the size of the political unit: Michels' supposed 'iron law of oligarchy' may well be operative in these circumstances. Furthermore, although wide participation in political life may be a good thing, it could also be seen as a 'public good' (Olson, 1965) which few people have any incentive to supply precisely because the benefits it offers are minute, indeed often intangible, compared to the immediate benefits that can be secured through supporting a particular group interest.

It is remarkable that few participatory theorists of democracy consider decentralising more decisions down to the individual. It is true that there has been an increasing tendency for governments of Western societies in recent years to do so; but it has been for efficiency reasons (important though these are) rather than from considerations that arise from an affection for individuality as such. Yet, as has often been commented, the market is a continuous referendum in which no one person can be outvoted. It is, of course, true that the market is characterised by inequality of access (ironically, if people were truly equal they would have little need to exchange): but so is the political arena.

A further problem in non-individualistic theories of democracy is that they pay relatively little attention to the traditional machinery of constitutional democracy – the separation of powers, the rule of law, judicial review of legislation and so on. But if the unrestrained collective will were really allowed to determine all political decisions it might well result in illiberal policies that were at variance with the values of the participatory theorists. More conservative theorists of the community would not object to this precisely because they do locate moral value in concrete institutions rather than in the choices of abstract individuals, but this is a different argument from that of participatory democracy.[12]

Most contemporary theories of democracy insist on the primacy of politics, and a downgrading of economics, for the promotion of freedom. In a currently popular view, David Held (1996, p. 295) maintains that we do not have the option of 'no politics': he claims that individual autonomy is possible only in the public sphere, where wide, participatory action is the best mechanism for the reconciliation of diverse, and potentially conflicting, values. In an implicit modification of the traditional idea of civil society, which envisaged a world of truly autonomous associations *outside* the ambit politics and the power of the state, he recommends a kind of democratisation of civil society's economy which would specifically limit the power of private capital and the economic corporation. For Held, and other contemporary theorists, such 'economic power', so far from being a welcome source of independence from politics, undermines citizenship. In this view '. . . the realisation of the principle of autonomy would require . . . a system of collective decision-making which allowed extensive involvement of citizens in the diverse forms of political affairs that significantly affect them' (Held, 1996, 310). It is unlikely, however, that a form of democracy, however refined, can compete with the private market in the protection of personal liberty.

Held does recognise the need for a private world but in his conception of democratic autonomy that world would in fact be politicised: 'The right to a life of one's own within a framework of democratic accountability is indisputably important' (Held, 1996, p. 326). But one wonders what kind of privacy can be protected in contemporary majority rule democracies riven by pressure groups? The logic of democratic politics means that political agents rarely aim for the genuine public interest but almost always for group interests. All this has been assiduously analysed by public choice analysis and the economic theory of democracy but there has been little effect in assuaging the appetite for politics. In fact, there is a virtue of apathy in a stable society since the active cultivation of politics leads to group domination.

As in so many other areas in political philosophy, the differences between the various democratic theories can be explained to some extent in terms of different conceptions of human nature. Those with a more optimistic view of political man, or at least a belief that man has a potentiality for spontaneous virtuous activity, are eager to dispense with traditional restraints in the belief that a better society will emerge from positive political action, while the more pessimistic 'liberals' base their arguments for limited government and restraints on politics largely on what they regard as unalterable features of the human condition. If most people are 'maximisers', then institutions will have to be designed so as to prevent one individual's maximisation harming others, and liberals regard maximisation in politics as being potentially more harmful than in economics.

Notes

1 Political Philosophy and Political Thought

1. Analytic statements are true by definition and convey no information about the world. Synthetic propositions are empirical and give us knowledge about the external world.
2. It is now the orthodox view in the philosophy of science that no amount of confirmation can establish a scientific hypothesis. The correct procedure does not involve the constant verification of empirical generalisations but consists of rigorous attempts to refute or falsify hypotheses. See Popper (1957) for the application of this view to social science.
3. It should be noted that Gray has reduced significantly the importance of the essential contestability of political concepts in his later (1983) paper. Plant, Lesser and Taylor-Gooby (1980) make extensive use of the idea in relation to welfare.
4. Some writers, especially Gray (1978), argue that the notion of an 'exemplar' is irrelevant to the theory of essential contestability.
5. It must be stressed that this is no more than a convenient label for a common approach to social and political matters. Not only would many people object to the word 'liberal' in the label but also the word 'rationalist'. This is because 'rationalist' is used to describe the political theorist who believes in the reconstruction of the social world according to abstract rational principles. However, the word rationalist can still be used to describe a theorist who both stresses the importance of the evolution of rules and practices and takes a critical reflective attitude towards them.
6. This choice of lifestyles and the stress on rules rather than collective projects is common to all forms of liberalism.
7. There is a great variety of ethical liberalisms in contemporary political thought. From the anti-interventionist side, individuality is thought to put a prohibition on rights-violation; from the interventionist side, state action is permitted in order to expand equal liberty. What they have in common is a notion of the individual abstracted from particular social settings, and an (excessive?) optimism with regard to the role of *reason* in the conduct of human affairs.
8. Marxism survives as a rather specialised academic subject. It has little to say about contemporary economics and politics.
9. Whether Japan and East Asia will be able to resist the spread of Anglo-American capitalism is a moot point. But the remarkable flexibility of the latter model makes it better equipped to cope with the stresses and strains of 'globalisation'.

2 Law and Social Control

1. The problem of abortion and the right to life is the kind of issue that involves natural law.
2. While Bentham and Austin were legal positivists, there is a close connection between the command theory and the normative doctrine of utilitarianism (see Chapter 5).
3. The clause that guarantees equal representation for the states in the Senate.
4. In the constitutional history of the US since 1937 the Supreme Court has consistently upheld laws concerning economic regulation and private property even though such legislation had hitherto been struck down as unconstitutional.
5. European legal arrangements do, however, lack a clear and uncontroversial 'constitution'.
6. Liberals constantly stress that rules are needed because of the unalterable fact of man's ignorance. Since each person can only have a limited knowledge of the world about him, rules are required to set standards of behaviour so as to make social life predictable for individuals. It follows from this that it is impossible to *design* a set of laws which anticipate all possible cases. It is for this reason that some liberal-rationalists argue that certainty in the law is more likely to come from the gradual evolution of a common law system than one based on statute.
7. Postmodernism is the radical doctrine that denies the possibility of truth or objective knowledge, even in science. Modernism in scientific thought might represent the idea of progress in knowledge or a transcendence of primitive ways of thinking with empirical science as its epistemological exemplar but postmodernists believe that this is an illusion. It is equally true of Marxism and all forms of liberalism (see Harvey, 1989).
8. Both Critical Legal Studies and feminism seem to share the Marxist belief that a change in social circumstances will generate a change in human nature. Predictable legal systems are based on certain uniformities in behaviour.

3 The State

1. Moral freedom in the Kantian sense consists in following universal principles dictated by rationality and not immediate, empirical circumstances.
2. An extreme organic and authoritarian version can be found in B. Bosanquet (1899). This book was severely attacked by L. T. Hobhouse in *The Metaphysical Theory of the State* (1918). However, Hobhouse belonged to the same intellectual tradition.
3. This was because he thought that all social order was the product of sovereign power.
4. Although these are theoretically different justifications for the limits of state action, in practice they produce the same conclusions.

5. The successful surmounting of the Dilemma does not depend upon people becoming altruistic. All that is required for solutions to public good problems is that enough in a community are 'brave reciprocators', that is willing to co-operate in collective action but prepared to take retaliatory action against defectors. Since they will not co-operate with 'nasties' (regular defectors from agreements), a process of evolution through natural selection may well lead to the survival of co-operators (see Sugden, 1986, chs 6 and 7). But even Sugden concedes that large numbers may render the problem insuperable.
6. Coase was talking about efficiency solutions to public good problems; he was not interested in distributive questions.
7. In a later work Nozick (1989) has departed significantly from the relentless individualism of *Anarchy, State and Utopia*.
8. Free market feminists object to the state not because it is male dominated but because it enacts regulations which impede female advancement by reducing competitive conditions.

4 Authority and Power

1. Although it could be argued that this is unfair to Machiavelli, that he is really a political theorist of *republican* government and that this encompasses politics, legitimacy and the rule of law.
2. A better word here might be *wants*. The connection between interests and wants is analysed in Chapter 11.
3. This might be described more accurately as a curious case of psychological causality.
4. An example of this might be Franco's Spain.
5. Brian Barry's *Power and Political Theory* (1976) contains a number of important articles and an extensive bibliography.
6. For a critique of the conventional neo-classical view of monopoly power, from the perspectives of 'Austrian' economics, see S. Littlechild (1981).
7. In modern social theory the theorists of elite rule, notably Pareto and Mosca, might be said to be postulating certain very general propositions about power. There will be some discussion of their ideas in relation to democracy in Chapter 11.

5 Political Principles

1. However, it is the case that the withdrawal of state activity in certain areas could cause considerable harm, especially in welfare where certain entitlements have been created (see Barry, N., 1985).
2. Hare's metaethics has been quite influential in modern economics, especially in relation to the role of reason in welfare economics, see A. Hamlin (1986).

3. Contractarianism is a specifically liberal *method*, precisely because it treats individuals as rational agents rather than as members of communities.
4. Adam Smith's 'Invisible Hand' metaphor, which shows how private interests and public benefit are harmonised, is a quasi-utilitarian doctrine but is strikingly different from Bentham's.
5. For an argument to show how statements about rights can be derived from a utilitarian framework, see J. Gray (1984).
6. The nineteenth-century philosopher, Henry Sidgwick, in his *Methods of Ethics* (1874), argued that utilitarianism must ultimately rest upon intuition and that it should take account of justice as a separate principle.
7. D. Hume (1972) made a distinction between natural and artificial morality which feminists would not accept. Natural morality governs personal and family relationships, while the artificial was about enforceable rules, such as justice.

6 Justice

1. The bulk of this section is taken from Barry, N. (1979, ch. 7).
2. It should be noted that Rawls had been communicating his ideas in article form since the early 1950s.
3. For a valuable discussion of this distinction, see K.J. Arrow (1973, p. 247). It is worth noting that most objections to the type of approach adopted by Rawls centre on its supposed vacuousness rather than its conflict with the 'productivity' principle.
4. Of course, most adherents of this chilly doctrine do not deny that people have *moral* duties to the needy.
5. In his Wilt Chamberlain example, Nozick argues that if people are willing to pay money to Chamberlain, a famous basketball player, which gives him an income way above a 'socially just' norm, then the enforcement of that norm is quite incompatible with liberty. He writes that 'no end-state principle or distributional patterned principle of justice can be realised without continuous interference with people's lives' (Nozick, 1974, p. 163).
6. Kirzner argues that the justice of accumulation in this manner is validated by the invocation of the 'finders keepers' rule of conventional morality (1989, ch. 4).
7. In *The Examined Life* (1989) Nozick appears to have given up some of the ideas in *Anarchy, State and Utopia*: he even admits the relevance of communitarian principles.
8. Marxism has lost its attractiveness but an attempt to incorporate his theory into conventional ethics is contained in Zyad Husami's (1978) interesting article on distributive justice.
9. Some writers have derived utilitarian results from a methodology not unlike that of Rawls (see Harsanyi, 1976).
10. Hayek (1976, ch. 7) claims that because Rawls's rules deal with unknown situations they are similar to classical liberalism's doctrine of justice. However, the redistributive element in Rawls seems quite alien to that doctrine.

7 Equality

1. Though to acknowledge the importance of need is to recognise the relevance of equality, at least in a minimalist sense.
2. For a discussion of the philosophical implications of this see A. Flew (1981, pp. 32–40).
3. This line of reasoning is developed by Rees (1971, p. 22). The argument is similar to that of Hayek, who maintained that the distinction between nature and convention was misleading, and that many social institutions – such as law and money – are not natural (like physical phenomena) but they are not merely conventional, in the sense that they are merely optional. See his essay, 'The results of human action but not of human design' (1967).
4. It has been suggested, sardonically, that this whole procedure could be used to justify the redistribution of body parts.

8 Liberty

1. In Bentham's theory liberty existed by permission of the sovereign.
2. For a critique of this whole approach, see Hamowy (1961).
3. All references are from Berlin's *Four Essays on Liberty* (1969).
4. Though this paradoxical claim has some plausibility in relation to laws that prevent individuals taking actions that will destroy their future liberty (for example, restraints on drug consumption).
5. There would also be a monistic conception of negative liberty, as in anarcho-capitalistic theories in which any inequalities thrown up by the operation of untrammelled free markets are acceptable.

9 Rights

1. Nozick exemplifies the first type of liberal rights theorist, Dworkin the second.
2. Recent important introductory books on rights include D. D. Raphael (1967), M. Cranston (1973), E. Kamenka and Alice Erh-Soon Tay (1978), T. Campbell (1983) and J. Waldron (1984 and 1987).
3. Thomas Szasz (1961) is a vigorous advocate of the idea that there is no such thing as genuine 'mental illness' which justifies the forcible detention of individuals in institutions.
4. Some political theorists would argue that people's *interests* ought to be protected rather than vague abstractions called 'rights'.
5. Curiously, this judgement on natural rights is common to utilitarians and Marxists.
6. In the black economy, presumably, a kind of liberty right existed.
7. Nozick does concede, in a rather oblique way, that his conception of rights logically permits *voluntary* slavery (1974, p. 331).

10　Welfare and the Welfare State

1. Republicanism, from Machiavelli's *Discourses*, has referred to the anti-individualistic spirit that sustains a community without either a market or political coercion.
2. Mandeville's *Fable of the Bees* (1924) was first published in 1705. It shocked people by rejecting notions of civic virtue as impossible and hypocritical. Mandeville showed that commercial success depended on the cultivation of the baser motives; they, in fact, generate (accidentally) prosperity and social harmony.
3. Welfare economists concentrate on theoretical proofs of various forms of market efficiency.
4. The workhouse test, which required that conditions inside it should be worse than the lowest paid labourer outside, produced harsh conditions and a loss of liberty for the inmates.
5. The Beveridge social insurance system embodies, in theory, many classical liberal features. It is not supposed to be primarily redistributive; people should have paid for their benefits.
6. Important Supreme Court decisions exacerbated the welfare problem by making it easier to claim benefits (see Barry, N. 1987, ch. 7).
7. America's radical reforms in 1996 cut most welfare payments, including the wasteful Aid to Families with Dependent Children. Mead's ideas might have been influential in its design; it includes 'workfare'. There have already been dramatic reductions in welfare rolls.
8. Mill certainly favoured wealth, but not income, redistribution.
9. Many welfare writers believe in middle-class participation in socialised medicine and public education because, despite their inequalities, it is their 'strong elbows' that ensures a high level of service (Barry, N., 1999b, ch. 6).
10. Health Maintenance Organisations, by providing fixed price coverage, have constrained costs.
11. In the past decade Chile has privatised pensions. People are compelled to save but they have a choice of market schemes.
12. Britain significantly reduced the future costs of state earnings related pensions (SERPS). People were given incentives to join private schemes.

11　The Public Interest and Democracy

1. Among the most vigorous opponents of the idea that the public interest has any cognitive meaning is F. Sorauf (1973).
2. See H. Demsetz (1967, p. 54). Much of my analysis is taken from this article and A. Alchian and H. Demsetz (1973). See also Steven S. Cheung (1978).
3. See Brian Barry (1965, pp. 234–6). Barry argues for a much wider concept of the public interest than that favoured by the 'property rights' theorists.
4. There is an enormous number of books on democracy. The following are recommended: Jack Lively (1975), Barry Holden (1974), J. R. Pennock

(1978), W. Nelson (1980), G. Duncan (1983), K. Graham (1986), G. Sartori (1987) and D. Held (1996).

5. Mill was also an early advocate of proportional representation. For a comprehensive survey of Mill's ideas on democracy, see J. H. Burns (1957).

6. For an introduction to the social theories of Pareto and Mosca, see James H. Meisel (1965).

7. Schumpeter's account of what he called 'classical democracy' was something of a ragbag of utilitarian theories and 'popular' notions. For a criticism, see J. P. Plamenatz (1973).

8. Kenneth Arrow (1963). Arrow has also presented his theory in a number of articles, see especially (1967a) and (1967b). Of course the 'paradox of voting' discussed by Arrow has a long history.

9. Buchanan (1975, chs 1 and 2) discusses the problem of the distribution of property in a contractual model.

10. While bureaucrats obviously cannot maximise profits as entrepreneurs are assumed to do, their behaviour has been interpreted in terms of similar psychological assumptions by political economists. Bureaucrats are said to maximise the size of their bureaux, or some other phenomena which cannot be measured in monetary terms. See Niskanen (1973) and Tullock (1976).

11. For a comprehensive coverage of the varieties of participatory theory, see G. Parry (1972) and Carole Pateman (1970); for a critical review of the subject, see J. R. Lucas (1976).

12. See M. Sandel (1984) for a rather conservative argument to the effect that communal values should override individual choice.

Bibliography

Ackerman, R. (1980) *Social Justice in the Liberal State* (Yale University Press).

Aiken, H. D. (1948) *Hume's Moral and Political Philosophy* (New York: Hafner).

Alchian, A. A. and Demsetz, H. (1973) 'The property rights paradigm', *Journal of Economic History*, xxxiii.

Arendt. H. (1961) 'What is authority?', in *Between Past and Future* (London: Faber and Faber).

Arrow, K. J. (1963) *Social Choice and Individual Values*, Second edn (New York: Wiley).

Arrow, K. J. (1967a) 'Values and collective decision-making', in P. Laslett and W. G. Runciman (eds), *Philosophy, Politics and Society*, Third Series (Oxford: Blackwell).

Arrow, K. J. (1967b) 'Public and private values', in S. Hook (ed.), *Human Values and Economic Policy* (New York: New York University Press).

Arrow, K. J. (1973) 'Some ordinalist-utilitarian notes on Rawls's theory of justice', *The Journal of Philosophy*, xx.

Austin, J. (1954) *The Province of Jurisprudence Determined*, edited by H. L. A. Hart (London: Weidenfeld & Nicolson).

Axelrod, R. (1984) *The Evolution of Cooperation* (New York: Basic Books).

Bachrach, P. and Baratz, M. (1962) 'The two faces of power', *American Political Science Review*, 56.

Baldwin, D. (1989) *Paradoxes of Power* (Oxford: Blackwell).

Barry, B. (1965) *Political Argument* (London: Routledge & Kegan Paul.

Barry, B. (1967a) 'Justice and the common good', in A. Quinton (ed.), *Political Philosophy* (London: Oxford University Press).

Barry, B. (1967b) 'The public interest' in A. Quinton (ed.), *Political Philosophy* (London: Oxford University Press).

Barry, B. (1973) *The Liberal Theory of Justice* (Oxford: The Clarendon Press).

Barry, B. (1976) 'Power: an economic analysis', in B. Barry (ed.), *Power and Political Theory* (London: Wiley).

Barry, B. (1979) 'Is democracy special?', in P. Laslett and J. Fishkin (eds), *Philosophy, Politics and Society*, Fifth Series (Oxford: Blackwell).

Barry, B. (1990) 'The welfare state versus the relief of poverty', *Ethics*, 101.

Barry, N. P. (1979) *Hayek's Social and Economic Philosophy* (London: Macmillan).

Barry, N. P. (1982) 'The tradition of spontaneous order', *Literature of Liberty*, v.

Barry, N. P. (1984) 'Unanimity, agreement and liberalism', *Political Theory*, 12.

Barry, N. P. (1985) 'The state, pensions and the philosophy of welfare', *Journal of Social Policy*, 14.

314

Barry, N. P. (1986) *On Classical Liberalism and Libertarianism* (London: Macmillan).

Barry, N. P. (1987) *The New Right* (London: Croom Helm).

Barry, N. P. (1988a) *The Invisible Hand in Economics and Politics* (London: Institute of Economic Affairs).

Barry, N. P. (1988b) 'The classical theory of law', *Cornell Law Review*, 73.

Barry, N. P. (1991) *The Morality of Business Enterprise* (Aberdeen: Aberdeen University Press).

Barry, N. P. (1993a) 'The Social Market Economy', *Social Philosophy and Policy*, 10.

Barry, N. P. (1993b) 'The New Right and provision for the elderly', in G. Jordan and Ashford (eds), *Public Policy and the Nature of the New Right* (London: Pinter).

Barry, N. P. (1994a) 'Sovereignty, the rule of recognition and constitutional stability in Britain', *Hume Papers on Public Policy*, 2.

Barry, N. P. (1994b) 'Justice and liberty in marriage and divorce', in C. Quest (ed.), *Liberating Women from Modern Feminism* (London: Institute of Economic Affairs).

Barry, N. P. (1995a) 'Milton Friedman', in V. George and R. Page (eds), *Modern Thinkers on Welfare* (Hemel Hempstead: Harvester).

Barry, N. P. (1995b), 'Hume, Smith and Rousseau on freedom', in R. Wokler (ed.), *Rouseau and Liberty* (Manchester: Manchester University Press).

Barry, N. (1998a) 'Charles Taylor on Multiculturalism and the Politics of Recognition', in G. Carey and B. Frohnen (eds), *Community and Tradition* (Maryland: Rowman & Littlefield).

Barry, N. P. (1998b) *Business Ethics* (London: Macmillan).

Barry, N. P. (1999a) 'Neoclassicism, the New Right and British social welfare', in R. Page and R. Silburn (eds), *British Social Welfare* (London: Macmillan).

Barry, N. P. (1999b) *Welfare*, 2nd edn (Buckingham: Open University Press; First published 1990).

Bastiat, F. (1964) *Selected Essays on Political Economy*, edited by George B. Huzzar (New Jersey: Van Nostrand).

Baumol, W. J. (1965) *Welfare Economics and the Theory of the State*, Second edn (London: Bell).

Becker, G. (1981) *The Economics of the Family* (Chicago: University of Chicago Press).

Beetham, D. (1991) *The Legitimation of Power* (London: Macmillan).

Benn, S. I. (1967) 'Freedom and persuasion', *Australasian Journal of Philosophy*, 45.

Benn, S. I. and Weinstein, W. L. (1971) 'Being free to act, and being a free man', *Mind*, 80.

Bentham, J. (1843) 'Anarchical fallacies', in *Works*, vol. ii edited by J. Bowring (Edinburgh: William Tait).

Bentham, J. (1948) *A Fragment on Government and An Introduction to the Principles of Morals and Legislation*, edited by W. Harrison (Oxford: Blackwell).

Bentham, J. (1970a) *Introduction to the Principles of Morals and Legislation*, edited by J. Burns and H. L. A. Hart (London: Athlone Press).

Bentham, J. (1970b) *Of Laws in General* (London: Athlone Press).
Berlin, Sir I. (1955–6) 'Equality', *Proceedings of the Aristotelian Society*, lvI.
Berlin, Sir I. (1969) *Four Essays on Liberty* (London: Oxford University Press).
Berman, H. (1963) *Justice in the USSR* (Harvard University Press).
Bernstram, W. (1991) *The Wealth of Nations and the Environment* (London: Institute of Economic Affairs).
Bosanquet, B. (1899) *The Philosophical Theory of the State* (London: Macmillan).
Bottomore, T. B. (ed.) (1963) *Karl Marx: Early Writings* (London: Watts).
Bowles, R. (1982) *Law and the Economy* (Oxford: Martin Robertson).
Boyle, J. (1985) 'The Anatomy of a Torts Class', *American University Law Review*, 34.
Brennan, G. and Lomasky, L. (1993) *Democracy and Decision: the Pure Theory of Electoral Preference* (Cambridge: Cambridge University Press).
Brennan, G. and Pettit, P. (1990) 'Unveiling the vote', *British Journal of Political Science*, 20.
Bridge, J. (1987) 'About law and political reality in the post-European-accession British Constitution', *Denning Law Journal*, I.
Brittan, S. (1973) *Capitalism and the Permissive Society* (London: Macmillan).
Brittan, S. (1975) 'The economic contradictions of democracy', *British Journal of Political Science*, 5.
Buchanan, A. (1986) 'The Conceptual Roots of Totalitarian Socialism', in E. Paul, F. Miller, J. Paul, J. Ahrens (eds), *Marxism and Liberalism* (Oxford: Blackwell).
Buchanan, J. (1965) *The Inconsistencies of the National Health Service* (London: Institute of Economic Affairs).
Buchanan, J. (1975) *The Limits of Liberty* (University of Chicago Press).
Buchanan, J. (1978) *The Consequences of Mr. Keynes* (London: Institute of Economic Affairs).
Buchanan, J. and Tullock, G. (1962) *The Calculus of Consent* (Ann Arbor: University of Michigan Press).
Burns, J. (1957) 'J. S. Mill and democracy, 1829–61', *Political Studies*, 5.
Burton, J. (1978) 'Externalities, property rights and public policy', epilogue in S. Cheung, *The Myth of Social Cost* (London: Institute of Economic Affairs).
Campbell, T. (1983) *The Left and Rights* (London: Routledge & Kegan Paul).
Checkland, S. and Checkland, E. (eds) (1974) *The Poor Law Report of 1834* (Harmondsworth: Penguin).
Cheung, S. (1978) *The Myth of Social Cost* (London: Institute of Economic Affairs).
Coase, R. (1960) 'The problem of social cost', *Journal of Law and Economics*, i.
Cohen, G. (1979) 'Capitalism, Freedom and the Proletariat', in A. Ryan, (ed.), *The Idea of Freedom* (London: Oxford University Press).
Connolly, W. (1983) *The Terms of Political Discourse* (Massachusetts: Heath; first published 1974).
Cranston, M. (1953) *Freedom: A New Analysis* (London: Longman).
Cranston, M. (1967) 'Human rights, real and supposed' and 'Human rights: a reply to Professor Raphael', in D. D. Raphael (ed.), *Political Theory and the Rights of Man* (London: Macmillan).

Cranston, M. (1973) *What are Human Rights?* (London: The Bodley Head).
Crenson, M. (1971) *The Un-Politics of Air Pollution* (Baltimore: The Johns Hopkins University Press).
Dahl, R. A. (1956) *A Preface to Democratic Theory* (University of Chicago Press).
Dahl, R. A. (1958) 'A critique of the ruling elite model', *American Political Science Review*, 52.
Dahl, R. A. (1971) *Polyarchy* (Yale University Press).
Dahl, R. A. (1979) 'Procedural democracy', in P. Laslett and J. Fishkin (eds), *Philosophy, Politics and Society*, Fifth Series (Oxford: Blackwell).
Demsetz, H. (1967) 'Toward a theory of property rights', *American Economic Review*, 57 (Supplement).
Devlin, P. (1965) *The Enforcement of Morals* (London: Oxford University Press).
Dowding, K. (1996) *Power* (Buckingham: Open University Press).
Downs, A. (1957) *An Economic Theory of Democracy* (New York: Harper & Row).
Doyall, L. and Gough, I. (1992) *A Theory of Human Need* (London: Macmillan).
Duncan, G. (ed.) (1983) *Democratic Theory and Practice* (Cambridge University Press).
Dworkin, R. (1977) *Taking Rights Seriously* (London: Duckworth).
Dworkin, R. (1981) 'What is equality', Parts I and II, *Philosophy and Public Affairs*, ii.
Dworkin, R. (1986) *Law's Empire* (London: Fontana).
Edgeworth, Y. (1897) 'The pure theory of progressive taxation', *Economic Journal*, vii.
Feinberg, J. (1973) *Social Philosophy* (New Jersey: Prentice-Hall).
Finnis, J. N. (1980) *Natural Law and Natural Rights* (Oxford: Clarendon Press).
Flathman, R. (1976) *The Practice of Rights* (Cambridge University Press).
Flew, A. G. N. (1981) *The Politics of Procrustes* (London: Temple Smith).
Flew, A. G. N. (1985) 'The concept, and conceptions of justice', *Journal of Applied Philosophy*, 2.
Foley, D. K. (1978) 'State expenditure from a Marxist point of view', *Journal of Public Economics*, 9.
Frankena, W. (1962) 'The concept of social justice', in R. Brandt (ed.), *Social Justice* (New Jersey: Prentice-Hall).
Freeden, M. (1991) *Rights* (Milton Keynes: Open University Press).
Freeden, M. (1996) *Ideologies and Political Theory* (Oxford: Clarendon Press).
Frey. B. (1996) 'How intrinsic motivation is crowded out and in', *Rationality and Society*, 6.
Frey, R. G. (1980) *Interests and Rights* (Oxford: Clarendon Press).
Frey, R. G. (1985) 'Act utilitarianism', in R. G. Frey (ed.) *Utility and Rights* (Oxford: Blackwell).
Friedman, D. (1973) *The Machinery of Freedom* (New York: Arlington House).
Friedman, M. (1953) 'The methodology of positive economics', in *Essays in Positive Economics* (University of Chicago Press).

Friedman, M. (1962) *Capitalism and Freedom* (University of Chicago Press).
Friedrich, C. J. (1973) 'Authority, reason and discretion', in R. Flatham (ed.), *Concepts in Social and Political Philosophy* (New York: Macmillan).
Frohlich, N. and Oppenheimer, J. (1978) *Modern Political Economy* (New Jersey: Prentice Hall).
Fuller, L. (1969) *The Morality of Law* (Yale University Press; First published 1964).
Furniss, N. (1978) 'The political implications of the public choice-property rights school', *American Political Science Review*, 72.
Gallie, W. B. (1964) *Philosophy and the Historical Understanding* (London: Chatto & Windus).
Garner, R. (1993) *Politics, Animals and Morality* (Manchester University Press).
Gauthier, A. (1986) *Morals by Agreement* (Oxford: Clarendon Press).
Gewirth, A. (1982) *Human Rights* (University of Chicago Press).
Gewirth, A. (1987) 'Private philanthropy and positive rights', in E. Frankel Paul, F. Miller and J. Paul (eds), *Benificence, Philanthropy and the Public Good* (Oxford: Blackwell).
Gilligan, C. (1982) *In a Different Voice: Psychological Theory and Women's Development* (Cambridge, Mass.: Harvard University Press).
Glazer, N. (1988) *The Limits of Social Policy* (Cambridge, Mass.: Harvard University Press).
Gluckman, M. (1965) *Politics, Law and Ritual in Tribal Society* (Oxford: Blackwell)
Golding, M. (1975) *Philosophy of Law* (New Jersey: Prentice-Hall).
Goodin, R. (1988) *Reasons for Welfare* (Princeton: Princeton University Press).
Goodin, R. and Le Grand, J. (1987) *Not Only The Poor: the Middle Classes and the Welfare State* (London: Allen & Unwin).
Graham, K. (1986) *The Battle for Democracy* (Brighton: Wheatsheaf).
Grasso, K. (1998) 'Contemporary communitarianism, the lure of the state and the modern quest for community', in G. Carey and B. Frohnen (eds), *Community and Tradition* (Lanham: Rowan & Littlefield).
Gray, J. N. (1978) 'On liberty, liberalism and essential contestability', *British Journal of Political Science*, 8.
Gray, J. N. (1983) 'Political power, social theory and essential contestability', in D. Miller and L. Siedentop (eds), *The Nature of Political Theory* (Oxford: Clarendon Press).
Gray, J. N. (1984) 'Indirect utility and fundamental rights', in E. Paul, F. Miller and J. Paul (eds), *Human Rights* (Oxford: Blackwell).
Gray, J. N. (1989) *Liberalisms* (London: Routledge).
Gray, J. N. (1992) *The Moral Foundations of Market Institutions* (London: Institute of Economic Affairs).
Gray, J. N. (1993) *Post-Liberalism* (London: Routledge).
Gray, T. (1987) *Freedom* (London: Macmillan).
Green, D. (1993) *Reinventing Civil Society* (London: Institute of Economic Affairs).
Green, L. (1988) *The Authority of the State* (Oxford: Oxford University Press).

Green, T. H. (1941) *Lectures on the Principles of Political Obligation*, edited by A. D. Lindsay (London: Longman).

Green, T. H. (1888) *Works*, edited by R. Nettleship (London: Oxford University Press).

Hailsham, Lord (1976) *The Dilemma of Democracy* (London: Collins).

Hamlin, A. (1986) *Ethics, Economics and the State* (Brighton; Wheatsheaf).

Hamowy, R. (1961) 'Hayek's concept of freedom', *New Individualist Review*.

Hare, R. M. (1963) *Freedom and Reason* (Oxford: The Clarendon Press).

Harris, D. (1987) *Justifying State Welfare* (Oxford: Blackwell).

Harris, J. (1980) *Legal Philosophies* (London: Butterworth).

Harris, R. and Seldon, A. (1979) *Over-ruled on Welfare* (London: Institute of Economic Affairs).

Harsanyi, J. (1976) *Essays in Ethics, Social Behavior and Scientific Explanation* (Dordrecht: D. Reidel).

Hart, H. L. A. (1958) 'Positivism and the separation of law and morals', *Harvard Law Review*, lxxi.

Hart, H. L. A. (1961) *The Concept of Law* (Oxford: Clarendon Press).

Hart, H. L. A. (1963) *Law, Liberty and Morality* (London: Oxford University Press).

Hart, H. L. A. (1967) 'Are there any natural rights', in A. Quinton (ed.), *Political Philosophy* (London: Oxford University Press).

Hart, H. L. A. (1982) *Essays on Bentham* (Oxford: Oxford University Press).

Harvey, D. (1989) *The Condition of Postmodernity* (Oxford: Basil Blackwell).

Hayek, F. A. von (1944) *The Road to Serfdom* (London: Routledge & Kegan Paul).

Hayek, F. A. von (1952) *The Counter-Revolution of Science* (Glencoe, Ill.: The Free Press).

Hayek, F. A. von (1960) *The Constitution of Liberty* (London: Routledge & Kegan Paul).

Hayek, F. A. von (1967) *Studies in Philosophy, Politics and Economics* (London: Routledge & Kegan Paul).

Hayek, F. A. von (1973) *Law, Legislation and Liberty*, vol. 1, *Rules and Order* (London: Routledge & Kegan Paul).

Hayek, F. A. von (1975) 'The pretence of knowledge', in *Full Employment at Any Price?* (London: Institute of Economic Affairs).

Hayek, F. A. von (1976) *Law, Legislation and Liberty*, vol. 2, *The Mirage of Social Justice* (London: Routledge & Kegan Paul).

Hegel, G. W. F. (1942) *The Philosophy of Right*, trans. T. M. Knox (Oxford: Clarendon Press).

Held, D. (1996) *Models of Democracy* (London: Polity).

Hobbes, T. (1968) *Leviathan*, edited by C. B. Macpherson (Harmondsworth: Penguin).

Hobhouse, L. T. (1918) *The Metaphysical Theory of the State* (London: Allen & Unwin).

Hochschild, J. (1981) *What's Fair: American Beliefs about Distributive Justice* (Cambridge, Mass.: Harvard University Press).

Hohfeld, W. (1919) *Fundamental Legal Conceptions* (Yale University Press).

Holden, B. (1974) *The Nature of Democracy* (London: Nelson).

Holmes, O. W. (1897) 'The path of law', *Harvard Law Review*, 10.
Hume, D. (1972) *A Treatise of Human Nature*, edited by L. Selby-Bigge (Oxford: Clarendon Press).
Husami, Z. (1978), 'Marx on distributive justice', *Philosophy and Public Affairs*, 8.
James, M. H. (1973) 'Bentham on the individuation of laws', in M. H. James, (ed.), *Bentham and Legal Theory* (Northern Ireland Legal Quarterly).
Jasay, A. de (1985) *The State* (London: Oxford University Press).
Kamenka, E. and Erh-Soon Tay, A. (eds) (1978) *Human Rights* (London: Arnold).
Kennedy, D. (1982) 'Legal Education as Training for Hierarchy', in D. Kaireys (ed), *The Politics of Law: A Progressive Critique* (Cambridge, Mass: Harvard).
Kirzner, I. (1973) *Competition and Entrepreneurship* (Chicago: University of Chicago Press).
Kirzner, I. (1989) *Discovery, Capitalism and Distributive Justice* (Oxford: Blackwell).
Krader. L. (1968) *Formation of the State* (New Jersey: Prentice-Hall).
Kristol, I. (1972) 'When virtue loses all her loveliness', in I. Kristol and D. Bell (eds), *Capitalism Today* (New York: Basic Books).
Kymlicka, W. (1990) *Contemporary Political Philosophy* (Oxford: Oxford University Press).
Le Grand, J. (1982) *The Strategy of Equality* (London: Allen & Unwin).
Letwin, W. (1983) *Against Equality* (London: Macmillan).
Littlechild, S. C. (1981) 'Misleading calculations of the social costs of monopoly power', *Economic Journal*, 91.
Lively, J. (1975) *Democracy* (Oxford: Blackwell).
Lloyd, D. (1972) *Introduction to Jurisprudence* (London: Stevens).
Lloyd Thomas, D. (1988) *In Defence of Liberalism* (Oxford: Blackwell).
Locke, J. (1960) *Two Treatises of Government*, edited by P. Laslett (Cambridge University Press).
Lucas, J. R. (1966) *The Principles of Politics* (Oxford: Clarendon Press).
Lucas, J. R. (1971) 'Against equality', in *Justice and Equality*, edited by Hugo A. Bedau (New Jersey: Prentice-Hall).
Lucas, J. R. (1972) 'Justice', *Philosophy*, 47.
Lucas, J. R. (1976) *Democracy and Participation* (Harmondsworth: Penguin).
Lukes, S. (1972) *Individualism* (Oxford: Blackwell).
Lukes, S. (1974) *Power: A Radical View* (London: Macmillan).
Lyons, D. (1965) *Forms and Limits of Utilitarianism* (London: Oxford University Press).
Mabbott, J. D. (1956), 'Interpretations of Mill's "Utilitarianism"', *Philosophical Quarterly*, vi.
MacCallum, G. (1972) 'Negative and positive liberty', in P. Laslett, W. C. Runciman and Q. Skinner (eds), *Philosophy, Politics and Society*, Fourth series (Oxford: Blackwell).
MacIntyre, A. (1981) *After Virtue* (London: Duckworth).
Mackie, J. (1977) *Ethics* (Harmondsworth: Penguin).
Mackinnon, C. (1989) *Toward a Feminist Theory of the State* (Cambridge, Mass.: Harvard University Press).

Macpherson, C. B. (1966) *The Real World of Democracy* (Oxford: Clarendon Press).

Macpherson, C. B. (1973) *Democratic Theory: Essays in Retrieval* (Oxford: Clarendon Press).

Macpherson, C. B. (1977) *The Life and Times of Liberal Democracy* (London: Oxford University Press).

Mandeville, B. (1924) *The Fable of the Bees*, edited by F. B. Kaye (London: Oxford University Press). First published 1705.

Marcuse, H. (1964) *One-dimensional Man* (Boston: Beacon Press).

Marcuse, H. (1967) 'Repressive Tolerance', in R. Wolff and J. Barrington Moore (eds), *A Critique of Pure Tolerance* (Boston: Beacon Press).

Marcuse, H. (1969) *An Essay on Liberation* (Boston: Beacon Press).

Marx, K. and Engels, F. (1968) *Selected Works* (London: Lawrence & Wishart).

Marx, K. (1971) *Early Texts*, edited by D. McLellan (Oxford: Blackwell).

Marx, K. (1977) *Selected Writings*, edited by D. McLellan (London: Oxford University Press).

Maynard, A. K. (1975) *Experiment with Choice in Education* (London: Institute of Economic Affairs).

Mead, L. (1986) *Beyond Entitlement* (New York: Basic Books).

Mead, L. (1992) *The New Politics of Poverty* (New York: Basic Books).

Meisel, J. (ed.) (1965) *Pareto and Mosca* (New Jersey: Prentice-Hall).

Melden, A. I. (1977) *Rights and Persons* (Oxford: Blackwell).

Michels, R. (1958) *Political Parties* (Glencoe, Ill.: Free Press; First published 1911).

Mill, James (1955) *An Essay on Government*, edited by C. V. Shields (New York: The Liberal Arts Press).

Mill, John Stuart (1944) *Utilitarianism, Liberty and Representative Government*, edited by A. D. Lindsay (London: Everyman).

Mill, John Stuart (1974) *On Liberty*, edited by Gertrude Himmelfarb (Harmondsworth: Penguin).

Miller, D. (1976) *Social Justice* (Oxford: Clarendon Press).

Miller, D. (1981) *Philosophy and Ideology in Hume's Political Thought* (Oxford: Clarendon Press).

Miller, D. (1983) 'Linguistic philosophy and political theory', in D. Miller and L. Siedentop (eds), *The Nature of Political Theory* (Oxford: Clarendon Press).

Miller, D. (1984) *Anarchism* (London: Dent).

Miller, D. (1990) 'Equality' in G.K. Hunt (ed.), *Philosophy and Politics* (Cambridge: Cambridge University Press).

Miller, D. (1992) 'Deliberative democracy and social choice', *Political Studies*, XL.

Mills, C. Wright (1959) *The Power Elite* (New York: Galaxy).

Moore, G. E. (1903) *Principia Ethica* (Cambridge University Press).

Mulhall, S. and Swift, A. (1992) *Liberals and Communitarians* (Oxford: Blackwell).

Murray, C. (1984) *Losing Ground* (New York: Basic Books).

Murray, C. (1996) *The Emerging British Underclass* (London: Institute of Ecoomic Affairs).

Narveson, J. (1983) 'On Dworkinian Equality', *Social Philosophy and Policy*, i.
Nelson, W. (1980) *On Justifying Democracy* (London: Routledge & Kegan Paul).
Ng, Y. (1979) *Welfare Economics* (London: Macmillan).
Niskanen, W. A. (1973) *Bureaucracy: Servant or Master?* (London: Institute of Economic Affairs).
Nozick, R. (1974) *Anarchy, State and Utopia* (Oxford: Blackwell).
Nozick, R. (1989) *The Examined Life* (New York: Simon & Schuster).
O'Connor, D. (1967) *Aquinas and Natural Law* (London: Macmillan).
Okin, S. (1989) *Justice, Gender and the Family* (New York: Basic Books).
Okun, A. (1975) *Equality and Efficiency* (Washington DC: The Brookings Institution).
Olson, M. (1965) *The Logic of Collective Action* (Harvard University Press).
Oppenheim, F. (1981) *Political Concepts* (Yale University Press).
Paine, T. (1984) *The Rights of Man* (Harmondsworth: Penguin).
Parent, W. (1974) 'Some recent work on the concept of liberty', *American Philosophical Quarterly*, 11.
Parry, G. (ed.) (1972) *Participation and Politics* (Manchester University Press).
Partridge, P. H. (1963) 'Some notes on the concept of power', *Political Studies*, 11.
Pateman, C. (1970) *Participation and Democratic Theory* (Cambridge University Press).
Pateman, C. (1983) 'Feminist critiques of the public/private dichotomy', in S. I. Benn and G. F. Gaus, (eds), *Public and Private in Social Life* (London: Croom Helm).
Peele, G. (1986) 'The state and civil liberties' in H. Drucker, P. Dunleavy, A. Gamble and G. Peele (eds), *Developments in British Politics 2* (London: Macmillan).
Peffer, R. (1978) 'A defence of rights to well-being', *Philosophy and Public Affairs*, 8.
Pennock, J. R. (1978) *Liberal Democracy* (New York: Greenwood).
Peters, R. (1967) 'Authority', in A. Quinton (ed.), *Political Philosophy* (London: Oxford University Press).
Pettit, P. (1980) *Judging Justice* (London: Routledge & Kegan Paul).
Pettit, P. (1984) 'The prisoners' dilemma and politics', *Politics*, 22.
Phelps Brown, H. (1988) *Egalitarianism and the Generation of Inequality* (Oxford: Clarendon Press).
Pigou, A. (1920) *The Economics of Welfare* (London: Macmillan).
Plamenatz, J. (1973) *Democracy and Illusion* (London: Longman).
Plant, R. (1986) 'Needs, agency and rights', in C. Sampford and D. Galligan (eds), *Law, Rights and the Welfare State* (London: Croom Helm).
Plant, R. (1991) *Modern Political Thought* (Oxford: Blackwell)
Plant, R. (1994) 'Hayek on social justice: a critique', in J. Birner and R. van Zijp (eds), *Hayek, Co-ordination and Evolution* (London: Routledge).
Plant, R., Lesser, H. and Taylor-Gooby P. (1980) *Political Philosophy and Social Welfare* (London: Routledge & Kegan Paul).
Polsby, N. (1963) *Community Power and Political Theory* (Yale University Press).

Popper, Sir K. (1957) *The Poverty of Historicism* (London: Routledge & Kegan Paul).
Popper, Sir K. (1962) *The Open Society and Its Enemies*, Fourth edition, vol. I, *Plato*; vol. II, *Hegel and Marx* (London: Routledge & Kegan Paul).
Popper, Sir K. (1976) *Unended Quest* (London: Fontana/Collins).
Posner, R. A. (1990) *The Problems of Jurisprudence* (Cambridge, Mass.: Harvard University Press).
Radcliffe Richards, J. (1980) *The Sceptical Feminist: A Philosophical Enquiry* (London: Routledge & Kegan Paul.
Raphael, D. D. (1967) 'Human rights, old and new', in D. D. Raphael (ed.), *Political Theory and the Rights of Man* (London: Macmillan).
Rawls, J. (1972) *A Theory of Justice* (London: Oxford University Press).
Rawls, J. (1993) *Political Liberalism* (New York: Simon and Schuster).
Raz, J. (1970) *The Concept of a Legal System* (Oxford: Clarendon Press).
Raz, J. (1977) 'The rule of law and its virtue', *Law Quarterly Review*, 93.
Raz, J. (1986) *The Morality of Freedom* (Oxford: Clarendon Press).
Raz, J. (1990) 'Authority and justification', in Raz, J. (ed.), *Authority* (New York: New York University Press).
Rees, J. (1971) *Equality* (London: Macmillan).
Regan, T. (1984) *The Case for Animal Rights* (New York: Basic Books).
Robinson, R. (1990) *Competition and Health Care* (London: King's Fund Institute).
Rothbard, M. (1970) *Power and Market* (California: Institute for Humane Studies).
Rothbard, M. (1973) *For a New Liberty* (New York: Macmillan).
Rothbard, M. (1977) 'Robert Nozick and the immaculate conception of the state', *Journal of Libertarian Studies*, i.
Rousseau, J.-J. (1913) *The Social Contract and Discourses*, edited by G. D. H. Cole (London: Dent).
Rowley, C. K. (1979) 'Liberalism and collective choice', *National Westminster Bank Review*, October.
Rowley, C. and Peacock, A. (1975) *Welfare Economics: a Liberal Restatement* (Oxford: Martin Robertson).
Russell, B. (1938) *Power: a New Social Analysis* (London: Allen & Unwin).
Sandel, M. (1982) *Liberalism and the Limits of Justice* (Cambridge University Press).
Sandel, M. (1984) 'The procedural republic and the unencumbered self', *Political Theory*, 12.
Sartori, G. (1965) *Democratic Theory* (New York: R. Praeger).
Sartori, G. (1987) *Democratic Theory Revisited* (New Jersey: Chatham House).
Sartorius, R. (1971) 'Hart's concept of Law', in R. Summers, *More Essays in Legal Philosophy* (Oxford: Blackwell).
Scarman, L. (1974) *English Law: the New Dimension* (London: Stevens).
Schumpeter, J. S. (1954) *Capitalism, Socialism and Democracy*, Fourth edition (London: Allen & Unwin).
Scruton, R. (1981) *The Meaning of Conservatism* (Harmondsworth: Penguin).
Sen, A. (1981) *Poverty and Famine: an Essay on Entitlement and Deprivation* (Oxford: Clarendon Press).

Sen, A. (1985), 'The moral standing of the market', in E. Paul, F. Miller and J. Paul (eds), *Ethics and Economics* (Oxford: Blackwell).

Sen, A. (1992) *Inequality Examined* (London: Oxford University Press).

Sen, A. and Williams, B. (1982) *Utilitarianism and Beyond* (Cambridge: Cambridge University Press).

Sidgwick, H. (1874) *The Methods of Ethics* (London: Macmillan).

Siegan, B. (1980) *Economic Liberties and the Constitution* (Chicago: University of Chicago Press).

Simon, R. (1974) 'Preferential hiring', *Philosophy and Public Affairs*, 3.

Singer, P. (1993) *Practical Ethics* (Cambridge: Cambridge University Press).

Smart, J. J. C. and Williams, B. (1973) *Utilitarianism: For and Against* (Cambridge University Press).

Smith, A. (1976) *Theory of Moral Sentiments*, edited by E. West (Indianapolis: Liberty Press).

Sorauf, F. (1973) 'The conceptual muddle', in R. Flathman (ed.), *Concepts in Social and Political Philosophy* (New York: Macmillan).

Steiner, H. (1974) 'Individual liberty', *Proceedings of the Aristotelian Society*, 75.

Steiner, H. (1979) 'The structure of a set of compossible rights', *Journal of Philosophy*, 74.

Stephen, J. F. (1967) *Liberty, Equality, Fraternity*, edited by R. J. Whyte (Cambridge University Press).

Sugden, R. (1984) *Who Cares?* (London: Institute of Economic Affairs).

Sugden, R. (1986) *The Economics of Rights, Co-operation and Welfare* (Oxford: Blackwell).

Szasz. T. (1961) *The Myth of Mental Illness* (New York: Dell).

Tawney, R. H. (1969) *Equality*, Fifth edition (London: Allen and Unwin).

Taylor, C. (1985) *Philosophical Papers* (Cambridge: Cambridge University Press).

Taylor, C. (1992) *Multiculturalism and the Politics of Recognition* (Princeton: Princeton University Press).

Taylor, J. K. (1992) *Reclaiming the Mainstream: Individualist Feminism Rediscovered* (New York: Prometheus).

Taylor, P. (1973) 'Reverse discrimination and compensatory justice', *Analysis*, 33.

Thomson, J. (1973) 'Preferential hiring', *Philosophy and Public Affairs*, 2.

Titmuss, R. (1970) *The Gift Relationship* (London: Allen and Unwin).

Trakman, L. (1983) *The Law Merchant: The Evolution of Commercial Law* (Colorado: Littleton).

Tuck, R. (1979) *Natural Rights Theories* (Cambridge: Cambridge University Press).

Tullock, G. (1976) *The Vote Motive* (London: Institute of Economic Affairs).

Twining, W. and Miers, D. (1976) *How to Do Things with Rules* (London: Weidenfeld & Nicolson).

Ullmann-Margalit, E. (1979) 'Invisible hand explanations', *Synthese*, 30.

Usher, P. (1981) *The Economic Prequisites to Democracy* (Oxford: Blackwell).

Waldron, J. (1984) *Theories of Rights* (Oxford University Press).

Waldron, J. (1987) *Nonsense upon Stilts* (London: Methuen).

Walzer, M. (1983) *Spheres of Justice* (New York: Basic Books).

Wasserstrom, R. (1971) 'Rights, human rights and racial discrimination', in James Rachels (ed.), *Moral Problems* (New York: Harper & Row).

Weale, A. (1983) *Political Theory and Social Policy* (London: Macmillan).

Weber, M. (1947) *Theory of Social and Economic Organisation*, translated by A. M. Henderson and T. Parsons (Glencoe, Ill.: The Free Press).

Weinstein, W. (1965) 'The concept of liberty in nineteenth century political thought', *Political Studies*, xiii.

Weldon, T. D. (1956) 'Political principles', in P. Laslett (ed.), *Philosophy, Politics and Society*, First Series (Oxford: Blackwell).

West, R. (1988) 'Jurisprudence and gender', *University of Chicago Law Review*, 55.

Whynes, D. and Bowles, R. (1981) *The Economic Theory of the State* (Oxford: Martin Robertson).

Williams, B. (1963) 'The ideal of equality', in P. Laslett and W. C. Runciman, *Philosophy, Politics and Society*, Second Series (Oxford: Blackwell).

Wilson, J. (1966) *Equality* (London: Hutchinson).

Winch, P. (1958) *The Idea of a Social Science* (London: Routledge & Kegan Paul).

Winch, P. (1967) 'Authority', in A. Quinton (ed.), *Political Philosophy* (London: Oxford University Press).

Wittman, D. (1973) 'Parties as utility maximizers', *American Political Science Review*, 67.

Wolff, R. P. (1976) *In Defence of Anarchism* (New York: Harper Colophon).

Young, M. (1961) *The Rise of the Meritocracy* (Harmondsworth: Penguin).

Name Index

326

Subject Index

Note: page references given in **bold** indicate a glossary entry.

330